The Importance of Being Monogamous
MARRIAGE AND NATION BUILDING IN WESTERN CANADA TO 1915

SARAH CARTER

The Importance

of Being Monogamous

MARRIAGE AND NATION BUILDING
IN WESTERN CANADA TO 1915

THE UNIVERSITY OF ALBERTA PRESS

AU PRESS
Athabasca University

Published by

The University of Alberta Press
Ring House 2
Edmonton, Alberta, Canada   T6G 2E1

and

AU Press
Athabasca University
1 University Drive
Athabasca, Alberta, Canada   T9S 3A3

Printed and bound in Canada by Houghton Boston
Printers, Saskatoon, Saskatchewan.
First edition, first printing, 2008

A volume in The West Unbound: Social and Cultural
Studies series, edited by Alvin Finkel and Sarah Carter.

LIBRARY AND ARCHIVES CANADA
CATALOGUING IN PUBLICATION

Carter, Sarah, 1954–
     The importance of being monogamous : marriage and
nation building in Western Canada to 1915 / Sarah Carter.

(West unbound : social and cultural studies)
Includes bibliographical references and index.
ISBN 978-0-88864-490-9

     1. Marriage—Canada, Western—History—19th
century. 2. Monogamous relationships—Canada,
Western—History—19th century. 3. Indian women—
Canada, Western—History—19th century.
4. Mormons—Canada, Western—History—19th century.
5. Canada, Western—Social conditions—19th century.
I. Title.

HQ560.15.W4C37 2008   306.84'2209712
C2007-907579-7

The University of Alberta Press is committed to protecting
our natural environment. As part of our efforts, this
book is printed on Enviro Paper: it contains 100% post-
consumer recycled fibres and is acid- and chlorine-free.

The University of Alberta Press and AU Press gratefully
acknowledge the support received for their publishing
programs from The Canada Council for the Arts. They
also gratefully acknowledge the financial support of the
Government of Canada through the Book Publishing
Industry Development Program (BPIDP) and from the
Alberta Foundation for the Arts for their publishing
activities.

Canada Council   Conseil des Arts
for the Arts   du Canada

Canadä

This book has been published with the help of a grant
from the Canadian Federation for the Humanities and
Social Sciences, through the Aid to Scholarly Publications
Program, using the funds provided by the Social Sciences
and Humanities Research Council of Canada.

Titlepage photo: Métis married couple Sarah (née Petit
Couteau) and Joseph Descheneau, Camrose, Alberta,
c. 1905. (GAA NA-3474-8)

For my mother:
Mary Y. Carter

Now the first argument that comes ready to my hand is that the real homestead of the concept "good" is sought and located in the wrong place: the judgment "good" did not originate among those to whom goodness was shown. Much rather has it been the good themselves, that is the aristocratic, the powerful, the high-stationed, the high-minded, who have felt that they themselves were good, and that their actions were good, that is to say of the first order, in contradistinction to all the low, the low-minded, the vulgar and the plebian. It was out of this pathos of distance that they first arrogated the right to create values for their own profit, and to coin the names of such values: what had they to do with utility?

—FRIEDRICH NIETZSCHE
    "Good and Evil, Good and Bad," *The Genealogy of Morals*

Contents

XI   *Acknowledgements*

ONE
1   Creating, Challenging, Imposing, and Defending the
    Marriage "Fortress"

TWO
19 Customs Not in Common
    THE MONOGAMOUS IDEAL AND DIVERSE MARITAL LANDSCAPE
    OF WESTERN CANADA

THREE
63 Making Newcomers to Western Canada Monogamous

FOUR
103 "A Striking Contrast…Where Perpetuity of Union and
     Exclusiveness is Not a Rule, at Least Not a Strict Rule"
     PLAINS ABORIGINAL MARRIAGE

FIVE
147 The 1886 "Traffic in Indian Girls" Panic and the Foundation of
     the Federal Approach to Aboriginal Marriage and Divorce

SIX

193   Creating "Semi-Widows" and "Supernumerary Wives"
PROHIBITING POLYGAMY IN PRAIRIE CANADA'S ABORIGINAL COMMUNITIES

SEVEN

231   "Undigested, Conflicting and Inharmonious"
ADMINISTERING FIRST NATIONS MARRIAGE AND DIVORCE

EIGHT

279   Conclusion

287   *Appendix*
297   *Notes*
343   *Bibliography*
361   *Index*

Acknowledgements

IN 1993 I first wrote an abstract sketching out some dimensions of this study for a conference paper proposal. The paper was not accepted. Undeterred, I've continued to work on this topic ever since although many other projects and responsibilities have intervened. I am grateful to the many people who helped me over many years and I hope I haven't forgotten anyone. I would like to first acknowledge and thank my researchers at the Universities of Calgary, Alberta and elsewhere (some of whom will likely have forgotten that they helped me with this project): Alana Bourque, Kristin Burnett, Peter Fortna, Patricia Gordon, Laurel Halladay, Michel Hogue, Kenneth J. Hughes (of Ottawa, not to be confused with an old friend of the same name in Winnipeg), Pernille Jakobsen, Nadine Kozak, Siri Louie, Melanie Methot, Ted McCoy, Jill St. Germaine, and Char Smith. While I did not have a Social Sciences and Humanities Research Council of Canada standard research grant specifically for this project, some of the research from two others (one on Alberta women and another on Great Plains gender and land distribution history) spilled over and was lapped up by this project and I am very grateful for these grants. The study was also enriched by the assistance, comments, suggestions and leads of many friends, colleagues and archivists including Judith Beattie, Mary Eggermont, Keith Goulet, Alice Kehoe, Maureen Lux, Bryan Palmer, Donald B. Smith, David E. Wilkins, H.C. Wolfart. Thanks to my father Roger Colenso Carter, Saskatoon, for his comments on a final draft. Special thanks to the Calgary Institute for the Humanities of the University of Calgary that provided important intellectual and physical space during the year I spent there as a fellow. I am grateful to Rev. John Pilling for permission to use the Records of the Anglican Diocese of Calgary at the University of Calgary Archives and Special Collections. Thanks to Sean England and Scott Anderson for their careful editorial work, and to Lesley Erickson for compiling the bibliography. Thanks to Erna Dominey and Peter Midgley for their assistance with the many tasks involved in preparing the final version of the manuscript; thanks also to the anonymous readers of the original submission for their comments and to Moira Calder for the index.

I have given papers based on this research on many occasions over the years and have found several to be significant moments in helping me formulate my ideas and engage with audiences. Thanks to Adele Perry and other organizers of the 2002 conference "Manitoba, Canada, Empire: A Day of History in Honor of John Kendle," to Joan Sangster for asking me to give the 2003 W. L. Morton Lecture at Trent University, to Georgina Taylor for asking me to speak at the Saskatoon Campus of First Nations University in the spring of 2007 and to Joanna Dean for the invitation to give the 2007 Shannon Lecture in History at Carleton University.

Earlier versions of some of this material has appeared in two articles: "Creating 'Semi-Widows" and 'Supernumerary Wives': Prohibiting Polygamy in Prairie Canada's Aboriginal Communities to 1900," in *Contact Zones: Aboriginal and Settler Women in Canada's Colonial Past*," ed., Katie Pickles and Myra Rutherdale (Vancouver: University of British Columbia Press, 2005), 131–59; and "'Complicated and Clouded': The Federal Administration of First Nations Marriage and Divorce Among the First Nations of Western Canada, 1887–1906," in *Unsettled Pasts: Reconceiving the West Through Women's History*, ed. Sarah Carter, Lesley Erickson, Patricia Roome and Char Smith (Calgary: University of Calgary Press, 2005): 151–78. I am grateful for permission to reprint this material.

Special thanks as always to my partner, Walter Hildebrandt, for his support and comments during the many years of this project and I hope he hasn't tired of (hearing about) monogamy. The book is dedicated to my mother, Mary Y. Carter, who had a long career as a lawyer, magistrate and judge in Saskatoon and was herself a "pioneer" in family law in Western Canada.

List of Abbreviations

APS   Aborigines Protection Society
CMS   Church Missionary Society (of the Anglican Church)
DIA   Department of Indian Affairs
HBC   Hudson's Bay Company
NWC   North West Company
NWMP   North West Mounted Police
MSRCC   Moral and Social Reform Council of Canada

ONE

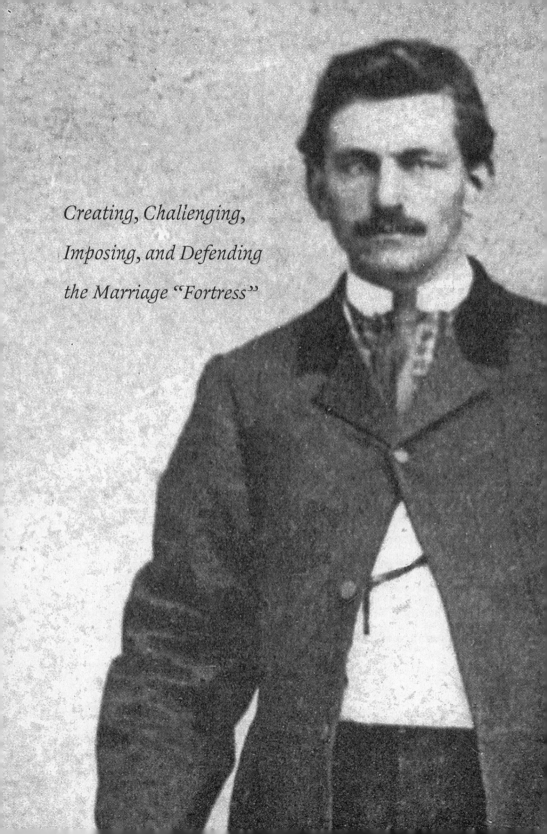

Creating, Chalienging,

Imposing, and Defending

the Marriage "Fortress"

"MARRIAGE 'FORTRESS' GUARDS WAY OF LIFE"; this was the headline of a 3 June 2006 editorial by Ted Byfield in the *Calgary Sunday Sun*. The highlighted quotation read, "A viable society depends on stable families, which depend on stable marriages." The next day marriage was once again on the front page, this time in Toronto's *Globe and Mail*, as Prime Minister Stephen Harper had announced that Members of Parliament would vote in the fall on a motion asking if they wanted to reopen debate on the contentious issue of same-sex marriage. That same month President George W. Bush called for a ban on same-sex marriage in the United States. Conservative authors, politicians, and religious leaders in North America are continually informing us that we are living at a time of profound social and cultural crisis, when the erosion of the institution of marriage is eating away at society's very foundations.[1] They insist on one definition of marriage, the union of one man and one woman (hopefully for life) to the exclusion of all others: a definition represented as ancient, universal, and founded on "common sense."

Behind such notions is a wistful nostalgia for an imaginary simpler time, when gender roles were firmly in place with the husband as family head and provider, and the wife as the dependent partner—obedient, unobtrusive, and submissive. According to Byfield, marriages used to be more stable because nearly every family depended on one income, so that the "rival interests of two competing careers did not constantly work to tear the marriage apart." He also blamed women for the majority of divorces as he found they tended to be the ones to kick out their "astonished and utterly devastated husband[s]" simply because they are "disillusioned" or have "disappointed expectations." Marriage has been a powerful tool for shaping the gender order; those who bemoan the erosion of marriage mainly regret the erosion of the powerful husband/dependent wife model.

A main point of this study is that the "traditional" definition of marriage is not as ancient and universal as conservative thinkers typified by Ted Byfield would have us believe. In *Public Vows: A History of Marriage and the Nation*, a 2000 study that focuses on the United States, Nancy Cott argues that the Christian model of lifelong monogamous marriage was not a dominant worldview until the late nineteenth century, that it took work to make monogamous marriage seem like a foregone conclusion, and that people had to choose to make marriage the foundation for the new nation.[2] Even then, Cott argues, this dominant monogamous vision was contested, demonstrating how legislation, court cases, and community pressure curbed and contained alternative forms of marriage. By the late nineteenth century there was much less flexibility in the meaning of marriage, and far fewer alternatives to monogamy. Relations between a wife and husband were more starkly inequitable than ever before. Gender is at the heart of Cott's analysis; marriage forged meanings of men and women, and the state shaped the gender order through the imposition of a particular model of marriage. Cott writes: "the whole system of attribution and meaning that we call gender relies on and to a great extent derives from the structuring provided by marriage. Turning men and women into husbands and wives, marriage has designated the way both sexes act in the world."[3] Cott also argues that to be interested in American identity is to be interested in marriage. Marriage served as a metaphor for voluntary allegiance and permanent union, the foundation for national morality. This was contrasted with the evils of other models of marriage and governance such as polygamy and despotism.

My study shows that marriage was also part of the national agenda in Canada—the marriage "fortress" was established to guard our way of life. To be interested in Canadian identity is to be interested in marriage. In the late nineteenth century there was widespread anxiety about the state of marriage, family, and home: all perceived to be the cornerstones of the social order. The very foundation of the nation was thought to be under threat. The remedy was to shore up the fortress of marriage, permitting no deviations, no divorce, and no remarriage, thereby ensuring "the maintenance within Canada of the purity of the marriage state," and protecting Canadians from the adoption of the "demoralizing and degrading" marriage and divorce laws of the United States.[4] Indeed, it was considered vital to defend the "fortress" of Canadian marriage in North America against the pernicious, corrupt, and immoral influence of the United States, where it was understood that the marriage tie was loose and lax. Canada would not repeat the American mistake. Canada would protect its marital purity. Politicians, social reformers, and judges widely agreed that marriage was a sacred institution that supported the whole social fabric and was essential to peace, order, and good government in Canada. It would be a "deadly stab upon the constitution of the Dominion" to relax laws of marriage and divorce.[5]

Western Canada presented particular challenges to the national agenda in the late nineteenth century, as the region was home to a diverse population with multiple definitions of marriage, divorce, and sexuality—the Christian, heterosexual, and monogamous ideal had to be made the sole option.[6] Historian Adele Perry has suggested that the term "Christian conjugality—by which I mean lifelong, domestic, heterosexual unions sanctioned by colonial law and the Christian church" best describes the model of marriage that missionaries and others sought to impose on this diversity.[7] Before the late nineteenth century, the predominance of this model was not a foregone conclusion, and many marriages departed from the often-quoted "classic" nineteenth-century definition of marriage presented by the English judge, Sir James O. Wilde (Lord

Penzance). He wrote, "Marriage, as understood in Christendom may...
be defined as the voluntary union for life of one man and one woman,
to the exclusion of all others."⁸ In Western Canada, however, there
existed diverse forms of marriage among Aboriginal people, including
monogamy, polygamy, and same-sex marriage, and no marriage needed
to be for life as divorce was easily obtained and remarriage was accepted
and expected. There were varied types of marriages to be found in
the interracial "fur-trade" society, and many Métis marriages drew on
Aboriginal precedent and reflected the same flexibility, but some also
drew on the informal means of gaining community sanction for divorce
and remarriage that persisted in Europe to the mid-nineteenth century.

New arrivals to the west had marriage laws and domestic units that
departed from the monogamous model. These multiple definitions of
marriage and family formation posed a threat, endangering convictions
about the naturalness of the monogamous and nuclear family model.
Among these newcomers, the Mormons, who practiced polygamy, were
the clearest example of those who challenged the monogamous ideal, but
there were others with alternative views of marriage and divorce. Some
groups wished to alter relations between men and women, providing
more options and freedom for women than were permitted under the
monogamous model. The preponderance of single men among the
immigrants represented yet another threat to the heterosexual monogamous order as the foundation for the nation. Single women, although
present in much smaller numbers, were also a menace to this foundation. Perceived as the most dangerous set of "others," however, were
the large numbers of Americans who poured north into Canada's West,
providing models of alternative approaches to marriage and divorce.

As in other British colonial settings, architects of this new region of
Canada were determined to proclaim that their heritage was the most
"civilized" and advanced. Claiming to have superior marriage laws that
supposedly permitted women freedom and power was (and continues
to be) a common boast of imperial powers. As historian Bettina Bradbury
has shown in her study, "Colonial Comparisons: Rethinking Marriage,
Civilization and Nation in Nineteenth-Century White Settler Societies,"
colonial politicians distinguished the "civilized heritage" of their marriage

laws from that of "ancient barbarians, 'heathens,' and other peoples they characterized as uncivilized. They also took pains to dissociate their own future from what they represented as the dangerous results of marriage regimes in some other Western societies."[9] The United States was an example to be avoided. The politicians and other makers of Western Canada confronted and had to fight off alternative marriage laws on all fronts—from the ancient inhabitants, from the Métis who were the offspring of two hundred years of intermarriage, from newly arriving European immigrants and from the US. "Proper" marriage would help maintain the new settlers' social and sexual distance from the Aboriginal population, and it would forge the new settler identity.[10] Insisting on the superiority of British, Christian and common-law marriage played a critical role in the forging of a British Canadian identity in Western Canada, and it also played a critical role in the consolidation of state power in that region.[11]

A variety of forces combined to contain and undermine alternative logics and to ensure the ascendancy of the monogamous, intra-racial model in Western Canada, seen as vital to the stability and prosperity of the newest region of the Dominion. As Sylvia Van Kirk has shown, hostility and prejudice toward the marriages of Aboriginal women and non-Aboriginal men grew from the mid-nineteenth century.[12] These attitudes were exemplified in colonial discourses that denounced race-mixing, in the courts, and in missionary circles. Advice books and works of fiction, along with journal and newspaper articles, all further promoted the monogamous model as the key institution to ensure the status and happiness that white women enjoyed. Through sermons, missionary work, lay organizations, and publications, the dominant Christian churches also promoted this ideal. Single and divorced women were stigmatized while sympathy was expressed for the lonely, unkempt bachelors of the west who needed wives to transform their lives and farms.

Federal land laws deliberately fostered "family farms," with the monogamous couple at the core of the vision. Single women were excluded

> *The ideal building block for Western Canada: the monogamous couple. Mary and Robert Jamison's wedding portrait, c. 1879, when the new Mrs. Jamison was sixteen. The Jamisons came from Ontario in 1884 and settled in the Pine Creek, Alberta area.* (GAA NA-3571-13)

from qualifying for homestead land as this permitted women an opportunity to be free of marriage. Instead, single white women were imported into the region in large numbers, as domestics, but also as wives and mothers of the "race." Federal legislation was introduced to prohibit alternative marriages, such as Mormon polygamy, while North-West Territories legislators moved to legalize Doukhobor and Quaker marriage in order to draw these groups into the obligations and responsibilities set by the state for married people. The enforcement of bigamy laws, and the near impossibility of divorce in Canada, also ensured the ascendancy of the monogamous model. The Canadian monogamous model of marriage, idealized as an institution that cherished and elevated women, left many people impoverished and alone, often with children to support. They were unable to get a divorce from a spouse who deserted them, or to remarry even after years of desertion or separation. There were many unhappily "attached" yet unattached people throughout the west, and the greater burden fell on deserted wives.

In the more heavily populated areas of Canada, this widespread anxiety about the state of marriage has been attributed to fears of a disintegrating social order in the wake of industrialization, rural depopulation, and urbanization. In Western Canada, however, there were different reasons for anxiety over marriage. It was a region undergoing colonization, and in most areas Aboriginal people outnumbered Euro-Canadian colonizers at the outset of the time period examined in this study. Before that there had been a period of over two hundred years when Aboriginal women had married European and Canadian men, and their offspring had married and mingled, creating a sizeable Métis population. Interracial marriage was deprecated in the post-1870 order, however, and a continual thread running through this study is the persistent calls for legislation that would prohibit and police such unions. The monogamous white husband-and-wife team was to be the basic economic and social building block of the west. They were to help produce not only crops, but also the future "race" of Canadians who would populate the west. The health and wealth of the new region, and that of the entire nation, was seen as dependent on the establishment of the Christian, monogamous, and lifelong model of marriage and family—the "white life for two."[13] Irregular domestic arrangements imperilled progress, prosperity, and the health of the "race." Much work was required to realize the monogamous vision.

These are the themes and arguments of chapters two and three of this book, which then turns to the complicated history of the imposition of the monogamous model on prairie First Nations with particular focus on women. The context provided in the first two chapters is vital to an understanding of this initiative, which was but one component of a much broader program to impose the monogamous model on the diverse people of Western Canada. The same cluster of laws, attitudes, and expectations deposited on First Nations were similarly applied to everyone else. Aboriginal people were compelled to conform to the laws, attitudes, and expectations that governed all married people in the rest of Canada. These expectations included the gender roles encoded in the monogamous model of the submissive, dependent wife and the powerful head-of-household husband. The broader context is important to understanding, for example, that both Aboriginal and non-Aboriginal women who "lost their virtue" before marriage, or who engaged in extramarital relations, were regarded as prostitutes "utterly destitute of moral principle."[14] Marriage was virtually indissoluble in Canada, with divorce nearly impossible for all but a wealthy few, and this rigid attitude was imposed on the First Nations. Similarly the bigamy laws, also applied to the First Nations, meant that deserted wives or husbands, even if they never heard from a spouse again, might never be able to remarry if they knew the spouse to be alive. Under the new legal regime, many Aboriginal women joined the ranks of deserted women with children, who were unable to remarry.

Through the Department of Indian Affairs (DIA) and other associated arms of the federal government, the Canadian state was able to invade the domestic affairs of First Nations societies and impose these laws, attitudes, and expectations to a much greater extent than was possible with other communities. There were destructive consequences to this invasion, but the power of the state was also limited and contested. This study points to the persistence of Aboriginal marriage and divorce law, and to the determined insistence of Aboriginal people that they had the right to live under their own laws. This reflects another present-day issue frequently in the news as I researched and wrote this book—the need to recognize Canada's Aboriginal tradition of law and justice, a "third" legal tradition alongside the British common law and French civil law traditions according to Liberal Minister of Justice Irwin Cotler. Cotler stated in 2004: "We have to start thinking in terms of pluralistic legal traditions of this country. Having a bi-jural, civil law and common law [system] already makes us rather unique in the world. Enlarging that to also have an indigenous legal tradition and maybe being a world leader in mainstreaming that indigenous legal tradition, will mean that we can make a historic contribution—not only domestically, but internationally."[15] Aboriginal marriage law continued to function throughout the period of this study and far into the twentieth century. The government, and to some extent the courts, upheld the validity of Aboriginal marriage law, but did not recognize their divorce law.

The marriage laws of Plains Aboriginal people were complex and flexible, permitting a variety of conjugal unions. There is debate among historians and anthropologists as to whether the various kinds of conjugal unions of Indigenous people can be called "marriage." My position is that they can, and that there is no single definition of marriage, as it changes over time and not all cultures share the same definitions. Aboriginal family law also permitted divorce and remarriage. The ease with which divorce was acquired limited the extent of a husband's power over a wife. The divorce of unhappy people, and their subsequent remarriage, was vital to the well-being of the family and the community. Virtually everyone had a spouse, except those who did not desire to be married. There were no single mothers, and concepts such as "illegitimate" children were unknown. Aboriginal marriage and divorce law was not well understood by non-Aboriginal outsiders, and it was widely presented as an institution that exploited and subordinated women. Polygamy was particularly singled out for criticism, as it allegedly left wives wretched and jealous as they were controlled, abused, and hoarded by a male elite. Because marriage did not appear to be a binding contract in the Euro-Canadian sense, wives were not seen as "true" wives, and they were labelled prostitutes if they had more than one marital or sexual partner.

Saving Aboriginal women from these marriages was one of the main justifications for colonial intervention in their domestic affairs—they too could enjoy the lofty and cherished status of white women. Similar justifications were frequently used for intervention in Afghanistan and Iraq as I wrote this book; as in earlier colonial times, the status of women continues to be manipulated as a political and rhetorical strategy to justify imperial expansion. The women themselves were not consulted, nor was any concern shown for the actual fate of either the women or their children as a result of the upheaval of this intervention.

Despite the colonial critique of Aboriginal marriage, an important 1867 legal decision in the case of *Connolly v. Woolrich* held that Aboriginal marriage law was valid, at least in Aboriginal territory. Using this case as the legal precedent, the DIA adopted the policy in 1887 that Aboriginal marriages would be recognized as valid, while Aboriginal divorces would not be so recognized (even though the decision in *Connolly v. Woolrich* left open the possibility of validating Aboriginal divorce law). The DIA was compelled to articulate a policy at this time in the light of sensational allegations from the west of a "traffic in Indian girls," which was brought to the attention of the Canadian government by the London-based Aborigines Protection Society in England. The allegations were inspired by W.T. Stead's revelations of girls being trafficked in London, a sensational claim that had repercussions throughout the British Empire. Conditions in Western Canada just at that time provided fertile soil in which to sow these hysterical allegations.

In the mid-1880s, new settlers to the west were calling for social and spatial segregation and for measures that would curb the power of the Métis, seen as a dangerous and subversive force. They had fomented two armed resistances, and they were also a drain on the public purse as they received land and money scrip from the government. Fear and anxiety was similarly generated about "Indian depredations," and there were calls for "Indian removal" to more remote northern areas, as well as for the strict enforcement of the pass system to contain people on reserves.

Aboriginal women's alleged promiscuity, their purported luring of white men to depravity, and their presence in the settlements were central components of this hysteria. Authorities at the highest levels of government shared these views, and they were contained in the government position expressed in an 1887 order-in-council that was to become the foundation of Canada's policy on Aboriginal marriage and divorce for decades. John Thompson, then the minister of justice, was instrumental in devising this policy. He had just returned from his first trip to the west in 1887, when the region was rife with alarming reports of "Blackfoot War," defiance, and "lawlessness." Thompson was utterly opposed to divorce under any circumstances. The policy reflected these concerns and attitudes. In recognizing Aboriginal marriage law but not divorce the policy was devised to enhance the control of Aboriginal husbands over their wives. Women had less opportunity to breach rules of conduct under this control. They were no longer able to desert, divorce, and remarry, and they had less freedom to visit towns and settlements. "Legal" divorce through an act of Parliament was out of the question, not only for financial reasons, but also because an application for divorce would not be entertained from those married according to Aboriginal law. Altogether the policy answered calls for greater social and spatial segregation. This policy had parallels in other realms of the British Empire where respect for "customary" law was partly strategic, employed as a means of harnessing male authority while restricting women and binding them to their husbands.

There were other compelling reasons for recognizing the validity of Aboriginal marriage law, including the fact that people were generally unwilling to be married except according to their own laws and ceremonies. Even those who might wish to comply with the new legal order found it impossible in the more remote regions where missionaries seldom visited. It thus became essential to recognize these marriages in order to extend the control of the state over married people. In particular it was vital to regard these as valid marriages in order to enforce the numerous clauses of the Indian Act that referred to marriage. In an 1889 legal decision it was found that the Indian Act constituted a statutory recognition of marriages according to Aboriginal law. Indian women who married white or non-status Indian men lost their "Indian" status under the Indian Act, and for the purposes of administering this clause, marriage according to Aboriginal law was regarded as valid. This greatly expanded the numbers of women whose status was abrogated.

After the arrival of the Mormons in southern Alberta beginning in the late 1880s, attention was drawn to the persistence of polygamy in Aboriginal communities, particularly in that very district. The problem of how to discourage and eradicate polygamy among Indigenous people perplexed and divided missionaries of the British Empire, and their heated debates were reflected in the Western Canadian context. Many missionaries showed deep concern for the fate of abandoned wives and children, and there were those who believed that it was sanctioning divorce to encourage husbands to give up all but one of their wives. The DIA, however, displayed no such concern as it began concerted efforts to abolish polygamy in the early 1890s. The campaign of the DIA to prohibit polygamy in Western Canada clearly illustrates the limited power of the state—for nearly ten years their steps remained tentative and cautious. Officials of the DIA continually threatened prosecution for polygamy, but they were highly reluctant to actually proceed for fear of losing face. There was little assurance that any prosecution for polygamy would hold up in court, as it had to be shown that there was a binding form of contract, and this was difficult in the case of Aboriginal marriage.

Another major reason for the tentative and cautious approach was the resistance of Aboriginal people to interference in their domestic affairs. Men with plural wives included the most influential leaders, and many of them had been the treaty negotiators for their people. In the Treaty 7 communities this resistance was concerted and determined. Young men and women continued to enter into plural marriages even when there were threats of prosecution and withholding annuities. Anger and frustration reached a peak in the mid-1890s when missionaries, working in concert with DIA officials, placed girls in residential schools under new compulsory-attendance legislation to prevent them from being married, while parents betrothed girls at increasingly earlier ages to prevent them from being placed in the schools, where the death rate from tuberculosis soared among students. (A married or betrothed person was not eligible to be a pupil.) One conviction for polygamy, the case of a Kainai man named Bear's Shin Bone, was secured in 1899, but when it had little immediate effect, the authorities turned their attention to undermining the institution of "child marriage" in Treaty 7 communities. As in other localities of the British Empire, concern for child brides was a means of demonstrating the inferiority of Indigenous people, particularly their male leadership. The sensational Alberta charges were challenged and dismissed, as an investigation by Calgary lawyer James Short found no evidence of such marriages.

Aside from battling polygamy, the DIA pursued a vigorous program of extraordinary interference in the ordinary domestic lives of Aboriginal people on reserves, causing widespread instability and upheaval. Rather than upholding the institution of marriage, the program of intervention was actually destructive of it, particularly because people were not permitted their former ability to remarry after separation or divorce. They were informed that second marriages were not legitimate, and they were encouraged to abandon them or face bigamy charges. Agents told people that they were not free to remarry without "legal" divorce, even though they knew such divorces were impossible to acquire. The resident Indian agents wielded a great deal of power as they decided what constituted a family unit for the purposes of annuity payments, adjudicating which wives were "valid," and which children were "legitimate." The agents, often in consultation with their superiors and school principals, arranged marriages, approved of some, and refused to recognize the validity of others. They dispensed marriage counselling, sometimes holding tribunals or hearings, intervened to prevent couples from separating, brought back "runaway" wives, directed the annuities of husbands to deserted wives, and broke up second marriages they regarded as illegitimate. DIA officials decided which widows deserved to inherit from their late husbands—under the Indian Act a widow had to be of "good moral character," and must have resided with her husband at the time of his death.

Despite this invasion of domestic affairs, the DIA had limited and tenuous ability to rigidly impose the monogamous model. Officials were constantly frustrated that Aboriginal family laws persisted, that people protested, that women and men refused to stay in bad marriages, and that some people continued to separate, divorce, and remarry according to these laws. As mentioned above, they also married at an earlier age in order keep young people out of residential schools. Officials continually recommended that the marriage laws of the land be forced on Aboriginal people, but this never happened. To have any measure of control it was necessary to recognize the validity of Aboriginal marriage. Many DIA officials and even missionaries came to see that the refusal to recognize Aboriginal divorce resulted in unhappy couples, with couples living "in sin," and with deserted women with children unable to remarry, and that altogether this destabilized domestic affairs, working directly against the policy of instilling a sense of the sanctity of marriage. There were widespread calls to permit some form of divorce or annulment of marriages, but the DIA consistently refused to permit any such deviation from the policy as outlined in the 1887 order-in-council.

There were consequences, however, for defiant behaviour; these included having children labelled "illegitimate." Other tactics to enforce desirable behaviour included placing children of "immoral" women in residential schools, or threatening to do so. Women were labelled as "immoral" if they left unhappy marriages and formed new relationships that they were instructed to abandon. Another tactic was threatening to prosecute for bigamy, and warning that the penalty for this crime was seven years in the penitentiary. As with the enforcement of anti-polygamy laws, however, there was great hesitation to actually follow through with such threats for fear of losing in court. A case heard in the Supreme Court of British Columbia in 1906 realized these fears. The accused was charged with bigamy for having acquired a second wife according to Aboriginal law. The Canadian Criminal Code could only be applied if the marriage was recognized as valid, and the judge found this not to be the case. This was not marriage, in the judge's opinion, but mere cohabitation. The prisoner was found not guilty and discharged. That the DIA was absolutely powerless to successfully prosecute for bigamy was further illustrated in a 1914 case of a Kainai man who allegedly had several wives, marrying once in a church and three times according to Aboriginal law, all in quick succession. The recommendation from the Department of Justice was that it would be pointless to proceed, that marriage according to Aboriginal law would not be enough to constitute the offence. The wives of this man could not bring any action against him under the Criminal Code, it was further advised, because as wards of the government they were not technically in positions of necessity.

In 1908 the DIA proposed a major overhaul of their policy on Aboriginal marriage and divorce, including special legislation to permit prosecution for bigamy and to permit divorce. Social and moral reform organizations also called for various actions to address the issue of Aboriginal marriage, but no changes were made and the 1908 recommendations were never enacted. Well into the twentieth century the DIA soldiered on with the policy as established in the 1887 order-in-council, and a 1906 circular letter to all DIA employees that outlined the policy declared that people could be prosecuted for bigamy if they defied these directives.

By 1915, when the focus of this study concludes, the monogamous model of marriage had been successfully imposed on most of the diverse newcomers to Western Canada, although there remained individual dissenters. Efforts to impose monogamy on First Nations were damaging to domestic life, but far from entirely successful. Aboriginal family law proved enduring.

In 2003 a statement on marriage, published in the *Globe and Mail* and signed by prominent and eminent Canadians, asked that Canada resist any changes to the monogamous model of marriage, or to the "free consent of one man and one woman to join as husband and wife in a union of life together." To do so would "undermine an institution so essential to the well-being of Canadians, past, present and future." To admit change was "not in continuity with the history, tradition and values of Canadian society. It attempts to redesign an institution older and more fundamental to Canadian society than Parliament itself." Marriage as defined in this statement "predates European colonization and reaches back into Canada's aboriginal traditions."[16]

My hope is that this study establishes that the monogamous model is not ancient and universal. It does not reach back into Canada's Aboriginal traditions, as the 2003 petitioners deposed. It is much more correct to say that the flexible and diverse models of marriage our society now permits, and the relative ease with which divorce can be acquired today, reach back to those traditions. In the late nineteenth to early twentieth centuries it took much work, and even draconian measures, to impose this inflexible and indissoluble form of marriage on Canadians. And contrary to the claims of Ted Byfield and others, the monogamous model did not always enhance the well-being of all Canadians in the past.

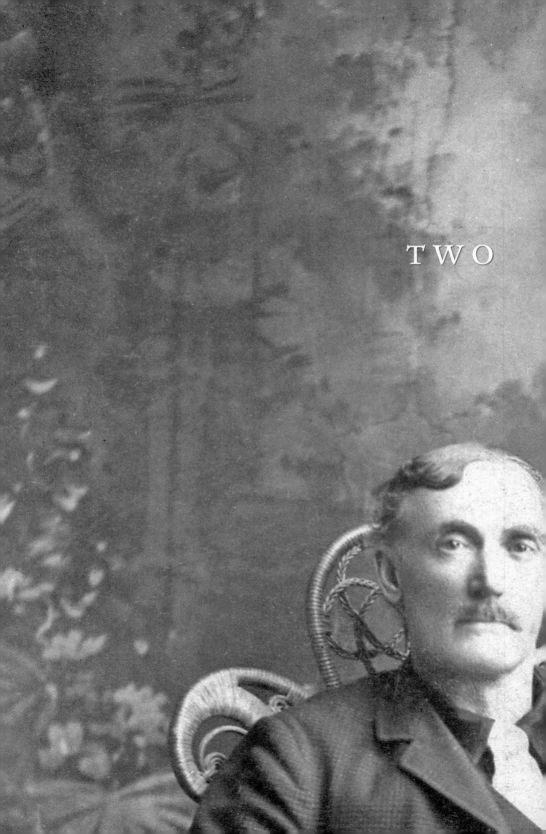

TWO

Customs Not in Common

THE MONOGAMOUS IDEAL AND
DIVERSE MARITAL LANDSCAPE
OF WESTERN CANADA

In John Mackie's fanciful 1899 novel, *The Heart of the Prairie*, a young Englishman named Walter Derringham, along with cowboys and Mounties, helps to tame a wild and violent Western Canada.[1] His adventures include fights, escapes, pursuits, captivities and, in the last chapters "Sioux Indians on the War Path." The Mounties, cowboys, and Walter defeat the Sioux in the final confrontation. Each trooper aimed and "picked off his man as coolly as if practising at the butts," and the cowboys rose together from their cover and "poured their last round into the wavering Indians" who "fell headlong to earth."[2] Those who resisted arrest were promptly killed or disabled, and the remainder were pursued across the border where they warned "their fellows against again venturing into the country of the red-coats." Walter himself was instrumental in bringing about this sharp reprisal against the Sioux, "whose bloody raids had long been a menace to a comparatively unprotected country."[3]

The Sioux had been taught a much-needed lesson, and peace and security were subsequently assured. With turmoil and chaos at an end, Walter could safely purchase an interest in a ranch, and he could also think about marriage—to Muriel, who was waiting back in England. Readers finally learn that it is she who forms the "Heart of the Prairie" of the title, as this is how Walter imagines he sees her as he gazes out over the golden vista: "It was a beautiful face that looked out from amid the wealth of falling hair which, flooded by a shaft of sunlight gleamed like burnished gold." The west was thus made safe for women like Muriel who held the key to the future happiness, stability, and prosperity of the region. White masculine individuals were celebrated throughout the novel, but white female domesticity would be the pervasive theme of the new era dawning in the history of the west.[4]

Similar themes prevailed in the newspapers of the late-nineteenth-century west. The first marriage of a white couple in southern Alberta in 1877 was heralded as the dawn of a new age. As reported in the *Benton River Press*, "Joseph McFarlane and Miss Marcella Sheran were married at Fort Whoop-Up, British North-West Territory, on the 4th of July last. Father Scollan [sic] performed the ceremony, the happy couple receiving a salute of six guns from Fort Whoop-Up, after which they were escorted to the McFarlane mansion [?] by their friends. This is the first marriage of a white couple recorded at Whoop-Up. Such is the progress of civilization."[5] Joseph McFarlane was a rancher/farmer and former member of the North West Mounted Police (NWMP), and he was also credited with introducing another symbol of domesticity to southern Alberta—the first dairy cattle ("a source of wonderment to the men from the neighbouring ranches").[6] Marcella Sheran, known during her lifetime and since as "the first white woman married in the far west," was from New York, having arrived in the Lethbridge area a year before her wedding to keep house for her brother Nicholas, who was the owner of the first commercial coal mine in Alberta."[7] (There will be more on the Sherans later in this book, as the settlement of the estate of Nicholas Sheran resulted in an important decision regarding marriage, inheritance rights and the legitimacy of children in the west.)

In the years following the watershed 1877 nuptials, weddings of Anglo-Celtic couples were given extensive newspaper coverage. "Wedding Bells" were presented as vital indicators of the end of a free, undomesticated, and masculine era, and the establishment of a new regime in which white women and the families they raised were to serve as agents of civilization. There is a well-established tradition in prairie folklore of the fierce competition for the first white women to arrive in the west during the late nineteenth-century era of marriage "fever" or "contagion."[8] Pharmacist John Higginbotham wrote that during the early 1880s in southern Alberta, "I could not count more than four unmarried white women between High River and the international boundary. Every arriving stage was eagerly scanned, sometimes from the housetops, with field glasses, for the sight of parasols, the brighter the better; then the news went quickly round, and a goodly line-up of the male sex watched, with consuming interest, the passengers leaving the coach."[9] In March of 1887 it was reported in the *Lethbridge News* that "the marriage fever is rapidly becoming epidemic. Symptoms of it have broken out in several other quarters."[10] There was more than a hint of nostalgia in the coverage given to the end of the undomesticated era; one-by-one "bachelors" or "old timers" "gave up their liberty," "jumped the broom stick," or finally "went over to the benedict's."

Marriage "fever" was encouraged by the political, legal, and religious leaders of late-nineteenth-century Canada who saw the perpetuation of a particular marriage model as vital to the future stability and prosperity of the new region. There was a determination to impose monogamy, the lifelong unity of one man and one woman until death, and preferably intra-racial monogamy, throughout the territory. The Christian religion and English common law imprinted on this model of marriage the expectation that the wife would be the dependent of the husband, who was the head of family and sole economic provider. Legal historian Constance Backhouse has described the form of marriage that was grounded in

> *A conventional pose of married couples in the second half of the nineteenth century. When there are two people but only one chair, the person with higher rank sits. The bride stands, her hand on her husband's shoulder, demonstrating her submissiveness, obedience and devotion. George Houk and Mrs. Houk, who was Kainai, (name unavailable) at Lethbridge Alberta, n.d.* (GAA NA-2968-1)

English common law as "very rigid, overbearing [and] patriarchal."[11] Husbands were expected to wield all the power, and wives were legally denied any semblance of independence or autonomy. Under the "doctrine of marital unity," the very existence of the wife was legally absorbed by her husband. Husbands had such power over their wives under this model of marriage that they were permitted to "chastise" their wives, and a wife so abused was entitled to leave her husband only if "the chastisement...[was] such as to put her life in jeopardy."[12]

The doctrine of marital unity also functioned to determine the citizenship of married women.[13] A woman marrying a British subject automatically acquired British subject status (Canada did not have its own citizenship until 1947). Immigrant women who married Canadian (British) citizens automatically became British subjects, even though they may not have lived in Canada, while Canadian-born women lost their citizenship if they married foreign nationals. Immigrant women arriving as wives were automatically naturalized with their husbands until 1932.

Married women in Western Canada shared all the features of married life with women in the rest of the country, but there were unique circumstances in the region that penalized them in particular. Under English law, dower rights provided a widow with a life interest in one-third of her husband's land at the time of his death. This meant that if a husband proposed to sell or mortgage the land he had to acquire his wife's signature on a waiver of her interest, known as a "bar" of dower. This form of dower had been received in Canada from England, but married women's dower rights were abolished in Western Canada in 1886. A husband could sell the family home, or mortgage the property, or die, leaving his wife with nothing. In the event of the death of a husband, a widow had no protection against the loss of her home, which in the case of farm women meant the loss of livelihood. A husband had the absolute right to dispose of all or part of "his" property in whatever way he wished, even after death by will. If a husband died without a will a widow could ask for a portion of her husband's property. Combined with the homestead policy that virtually excluded women unless they were heads of families (to be discussed below), the legal regime ensured that property, land, and "therefore wealth, was to be overwhelmingly owned and controlled by men, thus reinforcing a traditional patriarchal social order that dictated a dependent womanhood."[14]

Attached to the idealized monogamous model of marriage were ideas about sexuality and morality, particularly the restriction of sexual intimacy to one man and one woman who were married for life. Women who "lost their virtue" before marriage were regarded as "utterly destitute of moral principle."[15] As one Member of Parliament stated in 1897, any unmarried woman who succumbed to a man became a social outcast.[16] A marriage according to this model was virtually indissoluble. Divorce was rare, as it was troublesome and expensive. In her 1921 book, *Legal Status of Women of Alberta*, Henrietta Muir Edwards estimated that the cost of a divorce was about two thousand dollars.[17] Divorce was particularly difficult to obtain in Canada compared to the United States. Western Canadians (although not in British Columbia, which exercised its own jurisdiction in divorce) had to apply to Parliament for a divorce, and every divorce was granted by a special act of Parliament on each petition.[18] Applicants had to pay the sum of two hundred dollars to the Senate clerk before the petition would be considered. The process required the assistance of a lawyer to advise and prepare the petition, which naturally involved additional fees. The power to grant divorces rested entirely with Parliament and the merits of cases were debated, often even by the prime minister himself, as well as key ministers including the minister of justice. Witnesses were examined before the Senate's Standing Committee on Divorce. It was a very public and often embarrassing procedure, as the names of couples seeking divorces were published for three months in the official *Canada Gazette*, as well as in two newspapers located where the applicants resided. Newspapers reported on the debates about many divorce cases. A husband could obtain a divorce if his wife was proven to have committed adultery; a wife could not divorce a husband found guilty of adultery alone—this had to be combined with desertion, extreme cruelty, or other crimes (sodomy and bestiality). As explained in the British House of Lords by the Lord Chancellor, Lord Cranworth, speaking on the Divorce Bill in 1857, "A wife might, without any loss of caste, and possibly with reference to the interests of her children, or even of her husband, condone an act of adultery on the part of the husband; but a husband could not possibly condone a similar act on the part of the wife...the adultery of the wife might be the means of palming spurious off-spring upon the husband, while the adultery of the husband could have no such effect with regard to the wife."[19] It was not until 1925 that women in Canada could obtain a divorce on the same grounds as men.[20]

Divorces obtained in the United States were not considered legal in Canada (unless the applicants were bona fide US residents or citizens). As the Anglican Lord Bishop of Ontario stated in 1889, "I think the Canadian law is the best in the world, because it makes it so difficult to get a divorce."[21] A social stigma was attached to those who managed to obtain a divorce, particularly divorced women. Divorcing women generally had no property and little capacity to make a living independently. They also risked losing custody of their children. All of these factors secured the ascendancy of marriage as a permanent, indissoluble bond, for better or worse. As a nineteenth-century advice book advised, marriage "resembles a pair of shears, so joined that they cannot be separated, often moving in opposite directions, yet always punishing any one who comes between them."[22]

In the late nineteenth century, this model of marriage was idealized in the popular press, in the pulpit, and in the courts. It was allegedly founded on free consent, personal preference, and on romantic love. It was the path to the greatest joy and contentment for both men and women. "The sublimest moment in a young man's life," according to an advice book, "is when he can take his newly-wed wife by the hand and lead her under his own roof and say to her, 'This is our home.' Married life, with the comfort of children, weaves threads of golden joy into the cares and toils of life."[23] Marriages of eminent persons were given wide coverage in the press, as was the great influence of dedicated wives on notable politicians, clergymen, artists, musicians, authors, and prosperous businessmen. Wives furthered their husbands' work with absolutely selfless devotion, sympathy, guidance, and wise counsel.[24] This model of marriage functioned best if wives were obedient and submissive. There was great consternation in many circles in Canada in 1883 when the

Methodist Conference eliminated the word "obey" from their marriage service. As declared in the Anglican Church journal *Canadian Churchman*, this was "pandering to the least worthy of all classes of women...What sort of wives those are, or are likely to make, who decline to 'obey' their husbands as God bids them most emphatically in His Word, we decline to describe, they are not worthy of the sacred name of 'wife.'"[25] The most effective work of the ideal wife and daughter, according to the *Canadian Churchman*, "depends upon her comparative *inconspicuousness*— her quiet, unobtrusive, modest, retiring work...Not to seek publicity, not to court prominence, not to put themselves forward, not to usurp masculine power and influence, not to displace other and stronger workers."[26]

This model of marriage was also presented as the key to the liberty, happiness, and power that Christian, European, and North American white women allegedly enjoyed. In *Marriage and Home, or Proposal and Espousal: A Christian Treatise on the Most Sacred Relations to Mortals Known: Love, Marriage, Home etc.*, the anonymous clergyman author provided his understanding of marriage among the Chinese, Siberians, North American Indians, and others to show how women were cherished and elevated through marriage according to the Christian religion and English common law.[27] The married woman in these cultures was invariably depicted as little better than a slave or as chattel. There was no love and no consent in these marriages. After lives of hard, degrading labour they were neglected and discarded, reaching the lowest depths of degradation as widows.[28] Articles detailing the horrors of Chinese, East Indian, and African marriages were a regular feature of missionary publications. "Buying a Wife in Africa," was the title of one such article in Canada's *Presbyterian Record* of May 1910.[29] Two gallons of palm wine, thirty large brass bracelets, and twenty long spears was the price of a bride. Marriage in the "East" was invariably presented as "devoid of the romance and sentiment by which it is marked in the west. There is none of the refined feeling, the prolonged and delicate courtship, the romantic glamour."[30] Depictions of "foreign" marriage in which women were regarded as slaves were understood to be in marked contrast to the exalted position that the married woman enjoyed in the Christian and English common law monogamous model of marriage. "Monogamy has done more for the elevation of the female than any other custom of civilization," readers of the 1896 *Ladies Book of Useful Information* were told.[31] "Women's highest sphere is not in the harem or zenana, but in that dignified state in which she is the sole connubial companion of but one man." Monogamy was also in keeping with the natural world, as "The female bird chirps but for her single mate, and she is pugnaciously monogamic, as well as virtuous."

The emerging field of anthropology endorsed monogamy as the highest form of marriage enjoyed by the most "civilized" peoples of the world. In his 1877 book entitled *Ancient Society*, Lewis Henry Morgan, a New York lawyer who had personally visited several Aboriginal nations of North America, concluded that there were three broad stages of human development: savagery, barbarism, and civilization. Domestic life in the first two stages was characterized by promiscuity, no sexual prohibitions, loose or polygamous marriages, and communal property systems. Civilization, however, was characterized by strictly monogamous families, and private ownership of property. As historian John D. Pulsipher has written, "[Morgan] placed the monogamous family at the heart of the success story."[32] "Modern society reposes upon the monogamian family," Morgan wrote. "The whole previous experience and progress of mankind culminated and crystallized in this pre-eminent institution."[33] Morgan's views were very influential; his book became one of the founding texts of the discipline of anthropology, and his theories were the basis for the American policy of the allotment of reservations. These same ideas had an impact on Canadian Indian policy.[34]

Architects of the Canadian nation were determined that the monogamous model of marriage would prevail in the new region of Western Canada. As Nancy Cott argues about the United States in *Public Vows: A History of Marriage and the Nation*, marriage, and control of marriage, is of fundamental concern to a nation as it "designs the architecture of private life," and "facilitates a government's grasp on the populace."[35] Marriage, Cott writes, "is the vehicle through which the apparatus of the state can shape the gender order."[36] Yet as the reaction to the removal of the word "obey" from the Methodist service indicates, there was widespread fear in late-nineteenth-century Canada that the cherished model of marriage, the foundation of the nation and architect of private life, was under siege. The great "Marriage Question" of the day that illuminated some of the anxieties was the propriety of a man marrying his deceased wife's sister, or a deceased brother's wife, or a deceased wife's sister's daughter. To permit these marriages was regarded by many as a "sweeping revolution in the social and marriage customs of the land."[37] There was a lengthy debate in the Senate in 1879 on the question of marriage between a man and his deceased wife's sister. Those opposed argued that tens of thousands of people would be shocked if such a bill passed, that the sister of the wife was equally the sister of the husband because "they twain have become one flesh," and that there would be temptations to "get rid of a wife who stands between the husband and the sister."[38] A sister of a deceased wife could not then remain under the roof of the widower to act as a housekeeper and surrogate mother; no woman of "modesty or delicacy of feeling" could do so. A dying wife would look on her sister with jealousy and suspicion.

Divorce was similarly a "frightful spectacle," with social chaos the predicted result.[39] "No home is assured to remain as permanent; no relationships are sacred; no affections are secure," warned the *Canadian Churchman*. If marriage, an indissoluble sacrament, was to be "degraded to a mere matter of 'leasing' a partner, or assistant, or property, for an undefined length of time," it would mean the "ruin of Christian homes."[40] But an almost greater evil was the remarriage of divorced persons. In 1902 the General Synod of the Anglican Church spent four long sessions discussing the marriage of divorced persons, despite the fact that divorces in Canada were very rare. Such marriages were "repugnant," and few clergymen would remarry, under any circumstances, even the "innocent" party in a divorce.[41]

A concern about the state of marriage pervaded Canada in the late nineteenth century. As historian James Snell has described in his article, "'The White Life for Two': The Defence of Marriage and Sexual Morality in Canada, 1890–1914," there was widespread anxiety that monogamous marriage, the nuclear family, and the home, perceived as cornerstones of the social order, were disintegrating in the wake of industrialization, rural depopulation, and urbanization.[42] Canadian reformers and the clergy called for the state to take a stronger stand in defending and bolstering the nuclear family, and in punishing any deviations from the moral code and social order associated with the monogamous model of marriage. Waves of anxiety about the state of marriage and the family have since appeared with regularity in Canada. As Annalee Gölz has argued, the idea that the nuclear family is "threatened or in a state of crisis has often engendered the idea that the very foundation of the nation was under threat."[43] To Snell's list of causes for anxiety about marriage we could also add concern about the erosion of male privilege and domination, as activist white women of the late nineteenth century in North America and Britain called for changes in matters of marriage and divorce, pointing out the inequities as well as the alternatives to marriage.

Snell's reasons for anxiety about marriage—industrialization, urbanization, and rural depopulation—pertain more to Eastern Canada, and were not present in the same way in Western Canada where there were other challenges to the monogamous model of marriage. The west was a region undergoing intensive colonization in the late nineteenth century, yet this process remained an uncertain and, to some, a dubious enterprise. Potentially there were huge profits to be reaped from the land and resources, but it lacked stability, as was evident in the two "uprisings" of the Aboriginal residents. The establishment of immigrant families, the building block of the economy and society of the region, was a central component of the entire plan embodied in the national policies. In the late nineteenth century there were many areas where Aboriginal people continued to outnumber the immigrants. Here there were people with diverse marriage laws, practices, and ceremonies; all did not share the lifelong monogamous ideal of marriage between one man and one woman, and its predominance was not a foregone conclusion. There were also a variety of approaches to sexuality, divorce, domestic arrangements, and family formation. Among the diverse Aboriginal people of the west there were departures from the cherished monogamous model, although at the same time there were many who did conform. There were marriages of one man and several women, and there were cases of same-sex marriages. Divorce was easily accessible for those who proved incompatible, with no social stigma attached, as was remarriage of divorced persons. (Aboriginal marriage and divorce law, and the critics of these laws, will be explored in chapter four.)

Aside from Aboriginal marriage, there were a host of other dissenters from the monogamous model. In urging us to rethink colonialism as a bourgeois project, Ann Laura Stoler has pointed out that "the regulatory mechanisms of the colonial state were directed not only at the colonized, but as forcefully at 'internal enemies' within the heterogeneous population that comprised the category of Europeans themselves."[44] Dissenters included those white men who married Aboriginal women, transgressing the monogamous and preferably intra-racial ordering of sexuality in the new west. This remained relatively common into the 1870s and early 1880s, and these unions reflected more of the marriage and divorce laws of Aboriginal societies. Transgressors included prominent members of the NWMP, missionaries, and government officials working on reserves.[45] In Western Canada, Aboriginal-newcomer relations rested on an extensive yet varied foundation of intermarriage and kinship ties that first began with the earliest European explorers and fur traders.[46] These unions functioned and ended in many different ways; the term "custom of the country" (or *marriage en façon du pays*) implies, historian Jennifer Brown writes, "a misleading degree of uniformity and consensus."[47] Some were serious lifelong unions of mutual affection, while others were temporary. Some were lengthy but nonetheless temporary, as was the case with fur trader William Connolly, who met his Cree wife Suzanne at Rat River (Manitoba) in 1803. They lived together for twenty-nine years and had six children. Connolly moved with Suzanne and family to Montreal in 1831, but he abandoned them the following year to marry his second cousin, Julia Woolrich. Other fur traders clearly never viewed their relationships as "marriage," although this might not have been the perception of an Aboriginal wife and her extended family. However, we have few sources that shed light on the perceptions of the Aboriginal wives in these relationships. Unions were ended with ease, but this was compatible with Aboriginal definitions of marriage as a relationship that was not necessarily for life. Separation and divorce was quite legal under Cree and Ojibway law, just as it was in many other Aboriginal cultures. Some European fur traders wholeheartedly adopted the diversity of Aboriginal marriage law and had a series of wives, or several at the same time. Many fur traders left a wife behind in England or Scotland and at the same time had a wife in the west. Some had several wives in the west. As historian Sylvia Van Kirk found, many notable chief factors of the Hudson's Bay Company (HBC) in the eighteenth century had more than one wife. While governor at Fort Prince of Wales, Moses Norton allegedly had six wives.[48] Later, when European fur traders tended to marry daughters of mixed ancestry, polygamy was still practiced, although it was not the norm. Two daughters of trader and explorer Matthew Cocking apparently saw nothing amiss in sharing a husband, Chief Factor W. H. Cook.[49] But attitudes in fur trade country began to swing toward the direction of the monogamous model rather than polygamy or serial monogamy. Jane Renton, the wife of Albany HBC officer Thomas Vincent, was deeply wounded when her husband took a second wife in 1817, and she left Vincent, returning to her relatives.[50]

Until the early nineteenth century, and well beyond in many instances, these marriages were without "benefit of clergy." There were virtually no missionaries until that time, and even after that they were very few in number, and they tended to congregate around major settlements such as Red River. The earlier "country" marriages observed Aboriginal ceremony and protocol, but over time there was a gradual move toward European concepts of marriage. A simple exchange of vows in front of witnesses, usually the officer of the post, sufficed in most cases. Marriages were generally celebrated with a dram to all hands, a dance, and a supper. When Charlet Turner married James Harper at Martins Fall in 1841, the bride's father performed the ceremony and left this record of the event: "James [H]arper I this day consent to be your father in law and by the blessings of the ald mite [sic] god join you to my beloved Daughter Charlet Turner hoping that you will consider your self well married to her as if you were joined by a minister."[51] After 1821 the HBC introduced a marriage contract that emphasized the husband's economic responsibilities. In the presence of the chief factor and other witnesses, a couple affixed their signatures or marks to a declaration that provided documentation that the woman had the status of legal wife. Many chief factors were also justices of the peace empowered to perform marriages through a law passed in 1836 in both Canada and England.[52] When Magnus Harper married Peggy La Pierre in 1830 at Oxford House, he promised that "I by this document do hereby bind & promise to cherish and support the said Peggy La Pierre as my lawful married Wife, during the term of her natural life."[53]

Very prominent men in the making of Western Canada had married "without benefit of clergy," and some of them (and their wives) had divorced by mutual consent according to the customs of the country. Donald Smith, later Lord Strathcona, was married to Isabella (Bella) Hardisty in 1859 at North West River, Newfoundland, the headquarters of the HBC's Esquimaux Bay District. As a Justice of the Peace, Donald Smith was the most appropriate person in the district to conduct weddings, and he performed his own ceremony.[54] The law in Newfoundland allowed couples to be married without clergy if none were available, but there was nothing in the colony's legislation that permitted the option of performing your own ceremony. Another feature of this marriage, not an unusual occurrence in "fur trade country," was that the bride and groom had lived together before their wedding, and they had a daughter, Margaret Charlotte, in 1854. The bride, also known as Mrs. Grant, was already married, and although she had left her husband, she had a son from the earlier union. Her father had performed that ceremony in 1851. Smith was concerned about Bella's previous marriage and sought advice from Governor George Simpson. Simpson comforted his friend by writing that "her connexion with Grant was not in form, or any respect, a marriage; it was merely such a union as the peculiar circumstances of the Indian country in former days admitted."[55] Simpson argued that as Newfoundland was not within HBC territory, Hardisty [the bride's father] had no authority to perform the ceremony within the colony of Newfoundland, and that "such an informal proceeding ought to have been legalised by the parties availing themselves of the first opportunity that offered of having the ceremony repeated by a clergyman. So

far from taking that step however, they separated by mutual consent, which was quite sufficient to annul any ties that existed between them as man and wife." The circumstances of the marriage of Donald Smith and Mrs. Grant was the subject of gossip for years, particularly as the couple moved in elite social circles in Canada and Great Britain (although Lady Strathcona was disparagingly referred to as a "squaw" behind her back).[56] For public consumption, and for publications such as the peerage guides, Smith dated his marriage to 1853, legitimising his daughter. To stop "chins wagging" and to ensure the validity of the marriage and the legitimacy of his daughter, they went through a private marriage ceremony in New York in 1896 on their forty-third wedding anniversary when the bride was seventy and the groom seventy-five years of age.[57]

With the arrival of missionaries a clause was added to many of the fur-trade-era marriage contracts indicating that the sanction of the church would be sought by the couple at the earliest possible opportunity. But the more informal marriage custom continued, and there were many in the fur trade world who did not believe that marriage through the clergy was any more valid than the seemingly more informal vows they'd already exchanged. A young HBC clerk who was admonished by a missionary for his marriage by a chief factor provided a learned defence of his marriage saying that "a long tradition of European marriage law... acknowledged that marriage was essentially a civil contract; the religious ceremony was merely a desirable but unnecessary social convention."[58] While there were couples who had their "country" marriages solemnized by clergy, sometimes after decades of marriage, others refused to do so. Marriages by consent continued well into the nineteenth century for a variety of reasons. The clergy, for example, refused to marry individuals who were divorced, separated from, or deserted by their spouses. In his memoirs, English-speaking Métis George W. Sanderson (born on Hudson Bay in 1846) described how he performed a marriage for a Mr. Spence and his (second) bride when the minister refused to do so.[59]

< *Isabella Smith, 1878. The former Isabella Hardisty, born in 1825 in the Rupert River District east of James Bay, was already married to James Grant "according to the custom of the country" and had a son when she took up residence with Donald B. Smith (later Lord Strathcona). A daughter was born to Isabella and Donald in 1854, before their wedding vows were exchanged in a ceremony performed by the groom in 1859.* (Notman Photographic Archives, McCord Museum, Montreal, II-4927.1)

The diversity of marriages in western Canada is illustrated in this painting by Swiss artist Peter Rindisbacher who sketched and painted the Red River settlement in the early 1820s. Rindisbacher's caption was "A Half Breed and His Two Wives." (LAC C-046498)

Spence's first wife had left the marriage and departed for the United States while he remained in Manitoba, where he'd been alone for some years before deciding to marry again. When Sanderson learned of the minister's refusal he said to Spence, "By God, Nechiva [brother], I won't see you stuck, if the minister won't read the church service to you, I will, go and bring your girl friend, and a couple of her friends and I will marry you." Sanderson performed the ceremony, and when the minister found out he demanded to be allowed to remarry the couple. However, this time Spence refused, saying, according to Sanderson, "I asked you once and you would not do it. I consider myself as much married, as if you had performed the ceremony, go your way, I would not love my wife any better if you had married us again, and this is a love match." The couple had no children, Sanderson wrote, which he noted was "just as well, perhaps I would have had to baptize them."

The result of the generations of marriages and families at the Red River Settlement was a population that was overwhelmingly of mixed European and Aboriginal ancestry in the 1860s when Manitoba joined Confederation. Families could be large. One example was Red River resident John F. Grant, born at Fort Edmonton in 1831, although raised by his relatives in Trois-Rivières following the death of his mother (née Marie Ann Breland).[60] He returned to the west at the age of sixteen and before his death in 1907 he had seven wives and at least twenty-one children.[61] His earlier wives were from various Aboriginal nations and his last two were Métis. While living in Montana in the mid-nineteenth century he simultaneously had three or more wives, including (allegedly) "a wife from each surrounding tribe of Indians, and when a war party was sighted, care was taken to ascertain which tribe was to be entertained, and the other three women and their kids were secreted until danger was averted."[62] Grant brought his large family of children, which also included adopted Aboriginal and African-American orphans, to Red River in 1867 following the death of his wife Quarra in Montana.

Mr. A. K. Isbister, an English Métis, wrote in 1861 that at Red River

the half castes or mixed race, not only far outnumber all the other races in the colony put together, but engross nearly all the more important and intellectual offices—furnishing from their number the sheriff, medical officer, the post master, all the teachers but one, a fair proportion of the magistrates and one of the electors and proprietors of the only newspaper in the Hudson's Bay territories… The single fact that every married woman and mother of a family throughout the whole extent of the Hudson's Bay territories, from the ladies of the governors of British Columbia and of the Red River Settlement downwards, is (with the exception of the small Scotch community at Red River, and a few missionaries' wives) of this class, and, with her children, the heir to all the wealth of the country.[63]

The proliferation of single white men in the Canadian West in the later decades of the nineteenth century constituted a challenge to the ideal of monogamous marriage, and of *family* farms as the cornerstones of the new society.[64] Non-Aboriginal Western Canada was overwhelmingly male in the "pioneer" era. There were twice as many males as females listed in the 1891 census for the district of Assiniboia West.[65] Males between the ages of twenty and seventy-four comprised about 65 per cent of the population. Most of these men were unmarried; only 31 per cent of the population of this district were married. Unmarried male settlers were generally young, averaging twenty-nine years at the time of their homestead entry. "Bachelor" homesteaders were perceived to be living in squalor and loneliness, and there was concern about their tendency to become shiftless drifters given to drinking, card playing, engaging the services of prostitutes, and other censured practices associated with rudderless ruffians.[66] The mainly homosocial world of the NWMP was subject to similar criticism—that they drank, brawled, frequented brothels, and suffered from venereal disease.[67] The marriages and more fleeting relationships of these men with Aboriginal women, and the fate of the children of these relationships, increasingly attracted attention and censure by the early 1880s. Missionaries were the most vocal critics of the conduct of the traders, police, Indian agents, and other white males who lived with Aboriginal women, and often a series of women, without being "lawfully married" to them, before deserting them and their children.[68] (This issue too will be dealt with in greater detail in chapters to follow.)

While single non-Aboriginal women were comparatively few in number relative to non-Aboriginal men in Western Canada until well after the turn of the century, there were a number of them who similarly explored alternatives to marriage. Single women immigrants were welcomed and assisted only as domestic labourers, and the other most sizeable group of single women were teachers. But single, sometimes widowed or otherwise, solo women found business opportunities to exploit. In the towns of Fort Macleod and Lethbridge and nearby vicinities in the 1880s and 1890s, solo women were proprietors of hotels, boarding houses, restaurants (such as the Canadian Pacific Railway dining hall), stores, bakeries, ice cream refreshment parlours, and dressmaking and millinery establishments. Some ran their own businesses teaching music, elocution, dancing, and painting. They worked as post-mistresses, book-keepers, midwives, matrons of establishments such as the "Indian Girls' Home" on the Kainai (Blood) Reserve, and as nurses at the Macleod hospital. In 1890, for example, Miss Mary Glendining of Forrest, Ontario, established a successful "Fancy Goods" and millinery business in Lethbridge before her untimely death in 1895. She was "known as a business woman of the strictest integrity, and gained the respect and esteem of her customers," according to her obituary, but it was also stressed that she retained expected feminine traits, as she was "quiet and unassuming, diligent in good works."[69] In 1900, two "Misses McLeay" built a two-storey brick block in downtown Lethbridge for their "fancy goods" store.[70] Mrs. Anne Saunders, an African-Canadian woman on her own who was originally from Nova Scotia, was the proprietor of a number of businesses in Fort Macleod and Pincher Creek, including a restaurant, a laundry, and a boarding house for rural children attending school in Pincher Creek.[71] There were also a large number of brothels in Western Canada where single women were employed, and there were other single women who similarly challenged the conventions of their time, living on the fringes of "respectable" society. Mrs. Caroline Fulham, for example, originally from Ireland, made her living on her own, raising pigs and collecting garbage from Calgary's hotels and restaurants. She often drank alcohol and when intoxicated was known to sing Irish songs from her "throne" on top of her democrat.[72]

Many of the single, "respectable" teachers, businesswomen, and visitors were married before long, but there were other single women in Western Canada who rejected marriage and were determined to remain single. By the turn of the century in North America and Europe, many single women welcomed being single and actively sought to remain that way; they saw advantages to this status and began to develop a pride in it. These included women such as Saskatchewan farmer Georgina Binnie-Clark, a journalist from England who purchased her land in 1905, and was important to the homesteads-for-women campaign in the early twentieth century. Binnie-Clark and other contributors to the journal

The Imperial Colonist (the official publication of the British Women's Emigration Association and South African Colonization Society) presented readers with alternatives to marriage and domestic service for single women. Successful, smart, and plucky solo female farmers were described as owners of grain, poultry, and dairy farms throughout the colonies.[73] This was dangerous and difficult terrain, as negative images of "spinsterhood" abounded in the late nineteenth century.[74] Women were told that they "should consider that a true, pure love is the greatest earthly blessing that the Creator has to bestow on her sex."[75]

Western Canada may also have been seen as a potential haven for escapees from unhappy marriages, and as a place where they might try matrimony again, although not legally divorced, and still avoid charges of bigamy. In 1889 it was discovered that a Pincher Creek man, originally from Montana, misrepresented himself as a bachelor when, at age thirty-eight, he was married to a girl of sixteen. When confronted with the evidence of his first marriage, a certificate from Oregon acquired through enquiries made by Father Albert Lacombe, the man took wife number two and escaped across the border to Montana to avoid charges of bigamy.[76] In 1891 a woman from Ireland arrived in Lethbridge to find the husband who had deserted her and their two children eight years earlier. Her arrival caused a sensation in that town as her husband and wife number two were well known in the community. It was reported that she promised to leave Lethbridge if he agreed to provide for her and their children.[77]

The proximity of the border with the United States permitted a range of options and, sometimes, methods of escape from marital and parental obligations. As historian Catherine Cavanaugh found, "Husbands deserting to the United States was apparently so common that in 1922 the UFA [United Farmers of Alberta] government considered extradition as means of forcing their return but no action was taken."[78] Husbands from elsewhere commonly disappeared into Western Canada. In 1908, very anxious to hear from her husband, one Mrs. Anton Johnson wrote from Minneapolis to the *Moose Jaw Times* as the last letter she had received from him was mailed from Moose Jaw.[79] In 1886 the wife of a Mountie stationed at Regina (Trooper Callendar) placed her three children in the care of family in Balgonie and left for St. Paul, Minnesota, where it was alleged she lived with a former member of the force named Alexander.[80] In 1890 a Montana man, T. Eglington, borrowed horses from outlaw Dutch Henry and headed north to Canada with his wife's sister, but the NWMP were notified to be on the lookout and they located the couple camped on Milk River.[81] Escape from obligations, responsibilities, and the law was not easy, even on the "frontier."

The spouses of convicted bigamists were not able to remarry without expensive and protracted divorce proceedings. In 1917 a Toronto woman wrote to the minister of justice to enquire about "what steps I should take to secure my freedom." Three years earlier her husband was placed in Stony Mountain Penitentiary in Manitoba for bigamy.[82] She had no means of supporting herself and her child and she wanted to remarry. The deputy minister of justice informed her that her case would justify Parliamentary proceedings for the granting of a divorce, and that "there are no other means by which you can be made free."[83]

Many newcomers to Western Canada brought marriage laws and customs that departed from the monogamous model. Among the new-comers it was the followers of the Church of Jesus Christ of Latter Day Saints (LDS), or the Mormons, who constituted the most serious threat to the cherished model of marriage and thereby caused the greatest con-sternation. They believed they were mandated to engage in plural or "spiritual" marriage; this was essential to attaining the highest level of eternal salvation. They claimed to be following the practice of the Old Testament prophets in order to be compliant with God's law. Utah Mormon leader Brigham Young told his followers that monogamists would receive a lesser eternal reward in heaven, and certainly could not attain exaltation.[84] To attain the pinnacle of glory in the next world men needed to marry at least three wives. Women, however, had only one husband that they might share among several wives. Plural marriages were to be between consenting individuals, and a first wife's permission was supposed to be sought before her husband married other wives. Divorces were permitted on a variety of grounds and an individual was free to remarry after divorce. Women were more readily granted divorces than men.[85] A judge could grant a divorce if it was clear that the parties could not live together in peace and harmony, and if he decided that their welfare required a separation.[86] Territorial laws in Utah, through the numerical dominance of Mormons, had initially permitted the Saints sufficient autonomy to develop and practice plural marriage, but the US government launched an aggressive campaign by the late nineteenth century to prohibit their practices of marriage and divorce, which were viewed by authorities as "two sides of the same corrupt coin."[87]

By the mid-1880s there was a wave of anti-polygamy sentiment in the United States directed at the Mormons from clergy, politicians, newspaper editors, novelists, and temperance activists. Polygamy was criticized as a form of slavery for women; it represented tyranny in a land of liberty. Mormon women, it was argued, deserved the same vigorous action that had defeated slavery.[88] The Edmunds Act, passed by Congress in 1882, disenfranchised all who either practiced or believed in polygamy. A subsequent 1887 act took away the right to vote from Mormon women—a right granted to them in Utah Territory in 1870. Heavy fines and terms of imprisonment were given to those convicted of polygamous cohabitation. The children of polygamous marriages were declared illegitimate, no fewer than 1,300 Mormons were sent to jail, and the church was dissolved as a corporate entity.[89] As a result of these measures and, according to one historian, because of the damage to the operation of the free market in Utah, the president of the Mormon Church announced in 1887 that they would end the practice of polygamy. New plural marriages continued to be contracted, but the secrecy surrounding these ceremonies makes it unclear to what extent this was the case.[90] Anti-Mormon and anti-polygamy stories with titles such as "Utah Harems" were published in Canadian newspapers in the 1880s, paving the way for the often hysterical response to Mormon immigration to Canada.[91]

Fleeing anti-polygamy laws, Mormons from Utah under the leadership of Charles Ora Card, founder of the town of Cardston, first began to settle in southern Alberta in 1887. An important community and church leader, Card was married four times, although he was divorced from his first wife. In 1886 Card was arrested in the United States for practicing polygamy, but he escaped custody and, with a small party of colonizers that included his third wife, Zina (daughter of Brigham Young), decided

Elders of the Church of Jesus Christ of Latter Day Saints, or the Mormons, at Cardston, Alberta, early 1900s. Charles Ora Card, founder of Cardston and husband to four wives, is on the right.
(GAA NA-114-11)

to move north to Alberta. They chose land near the Kainai (Blood) Reserve for economic reasons, but also because the Saints intended to pursue missionary work among them.[92] Three Mormon leaders including Card travelled to Ottawa in 1888 and met with Prime Minister John A. Macdonald. Macdonald asked the delegation to provide him with a letter outlining their requests. They wrote that they were "being subjected to sore persecution [in the United States]...for fulfilling their sacred obligations to their wives they have long since married in good faith for time and eternity."[93] They asked permission to bring their wives, including their plural wives, "and not be compelled to cast them off and subject them to the charities of a cold world, thus breaking faith with their tender and devoted wives." The letter continued: "If from the dire sufferings of such people they can find an asylum in the Dominion of Canada, they will bring with them their wealth, their experience, their young men, and their young women who have never entered into plural marriage." The Mormon request for polygamy was not considered in Parliament. The delegation received their answer the next day from the minister of customs: they were welcome in Canada but they would not be allowed to practice polygamy. Macdonald later claimed in the House of Commons, when anti-polygamy legislation was being debated, that he had informed them that they could not bring their plural wives, and that they would be prosecuted and punished with the utmost rigour of the law if they continued to practice polygamy. According to Macdonald, "Her Majesty has a good many British subjects who are Mohammedans, and if they came here we would be obliged to receive them; but whether they are Mohammedans or Mormons, when they come here they must obey the laws of Canada."[94]

Many fears and anxieties emerged as the Mormons arrived in Canada. Polygamy was perceived as a major threat to the fabric of the new nation. Distinguished Liberal parliamentarian Edward Blake said in the House of Commons in 1890 that polygamy was "a serious moral and national ulcer."[95] Blake read a letter in the House from a friend of his in Utah in which it was claimed that the Mormons who had gone to Canada had not taken their wives with them but provided themselves with "fresh young wives." He also read from Brigham Young's will, which said that simple consent to live with him constituted marriage.[96] "This is very bad seed grain," said another Member of Parliament in 1889, "and we do not want to see any corner of the North-West poisoned by it."[97] Another stated that he was afraid that "if they get a settlement in the North-West, they will continue secretly to practice those abominations which they are guilty of in other parts of the world."[98] There were concerns that the Mormons would proselytise, dragging young non-Mormon girls into lives of degradation. In Winnipeg-based Methodist missionary James S. Woodsworth's 1909 book, *Strangers Within Our Gates: Coming Canadians*, a map of North America depicted the "Octopus of Mormonism," with the head in Utah and tentacles reaching in all directions; one stretched across the border into southern Alberta.[99] Readers were warned that

Mormon leaders had hoped as recently as 1880 to have Utah admitted into the Union as a polygamous State, and conspired to have their principles spread throughout the United States. Even worse, the followers of this church were alleged to be completely obedient, acknowledging the absolute authority of their leaders. It was noted that Mormon leader Joseph Smith addressed a 1903 convention at Cardston. There he "told with pride how by his six wives he had forty-eight children, and exhorted his followers to increase and multiply and replenish the earth. His programme was that they were the first to occupy the eastern slope of the Rockies—and their colonies now extend from Mexico to Canada—and they were to inherit the whole of the North American Continent."[100] Woodsworth wrote that Mormons believed that God and Jesus were polygamists, and that polygamy was "sacred and fundamental" to their beliefs. He believed that the "practice of polygamy will subvert our most cherished institutions," and concluded his section on the Mormons by asking this question: "Can we as Canadians remain inactive while this 'politico-ecclesiastical' system is fastening itself upon our Western territory?"[101]

There were also fears that Canadian men might be tempted to join up, and these fears seemed to be realized in 1888 when Anthony Maitland Stenhouse, a member of British Columbia's Legislative Assembly, tendered his resignation, renounced his own faith, and joined the Mormons in southern Alberta.[102] He vigorously defended polygamy in the press (although he himself remained unmarried), arguing that polygamy was a "triumphant success...[that] secures a husband for every woman that wants one...Under a well ordered system of plural families, marriage would no longer be a lottery where ladies draw a blank, a fool or a husband, according to luck...and thus the law of natural selection, now so grossly outraged, would find its due accomplishment in the survival and perpetuation of the fittest family and the fittest race."[103] Stenhouse argued that women had greater freedom than they enjoyed under monogamy, which was "invented for the oppression of women. Some thought polygamy the likeliest instrument of oppression. The more knowing ones, and among them our ancestors, discovered that monogamy was best adapted to their brutal purpose...If then, monogamy trammels a woman...

how are we to enlarge her scope?...In allowing the option of plural marriage under a modern covenant."[104] Stenhouse declared that as a "free
born Briton," he claimed "equal rights with the Indian, Mohammedan,
and other subjects of her Majesty," and intended not to be deterred from
seeking "higher honours in matrimony."[105] There were rumours that the
minister of customs was so impressed during his official tour of Mormon
settlements that he, like Stenhouse, intended to convert.[106]

Mormonism was also suspicious because it was considered a potentially "treasonable" organization that encouraged followers to obey their
church before the state.[107] It was declared in the *Edmonton Bulletin* of 8
October 1887 that Mormons "are an utter abomination which no effort
should be spared to rid the nation of," and that "no country, much less
a young and sparsely peopled country, can afford to allow treason to
flourish and social abominations to spread merely because the iniquities
are performed under the name of religion."

Complicating images of subjugated and submissive Mormon wives
were women such as Zina Card, a former college teacher, acclaimed public
speaker, and advocate of women's suffrage and rights. Utah sanctioned
women's suffrage in 1870, making it only the second territory in the west
to do so. LDS officials who sought to counter accusations that Mormon
women were downtrodden slaves of the male hierarchy supported this
action, but Mormon women themselves actively sought the vote.[108] The
Woman's Exponent was a forum for the political and social views of Mormon
women, and the paper advocated both women's rights and plural marriage. Zina Card was an unwavering supporter of plural marriage. Her
father Brigham Young had some fifty wives (although he was divorced and
separated from several), and at least fifty-seven children. She described
her childhood with deep affection: "How joyous were our lives. There
were so many girls of nearly the same age, and everything was so nice...
No scene is more vivid in my mind than the gathering of our mothers
with their families around them [for evening prayers], our loved and
honoured father sitting by the round table in the center of the room...

> *Zina Young Card was the daughter of Utah Mormon leader Brigham Young, who had over fifty
wives. She was the plural wife of Charles O. Card and with him founded the Alberta Mormon
settlements. She was an outspoken proponent of polygamy.* (Utah State Historical Society, 921–11888)

His presence was commanding and comforting, a peaceful control of his family that brought love and respect for him and each other."[109]

Zina Young Williams (then a widow with two young sons, having been the plural wife of a Thomas Williams, who died six years into their marriage) attended the National Women's Suffrage meetings at Washington, D.C., in 1879. She also addressed the US Senate and House Judiciary Committee, presenting the case that polygamy "seemed far more holy and upright and just to womankind than any other order of marriage."[110] In 1884, at age thirty-four, she married Charles Ora Card, who already had two wives. Six months later he married a nineteen-year-old fourth wife. Zina became a plural wife, and then a mother, within the Mormon "underground," hiding and fleeing persecution and arrest. It was jointly decided among the wives of Charles Card that Zina should accompany their husband to Canada, and there she became the undisputed female leader of Alberta's Mormon colonies. She remained an outspoken proponent of polygamy and, in part because of the curiosity this attracted, she entertained a steady stream of visitors to their Cardston home.[111] Zina Card toured the United States in 1898, visiting with dignitaries and talking about her life as a plural wife.[112]

Colonel S.B. Steele of the NWMP was assigned to keep close surveillance on the Mormons, and he found that "the Mormon women-folk [were] the strongest supporters of polygamy." Speaking specifically of "Aunt Zina," as she was known in the community, Steele noted: "Brilliant lawyers and able financiers who were with me had all they could do to hold their own in arguments with the leading lady of the settlement."[113] Such visits began as early as 1888 when it was noted that a party including Senator Cochrane was entertained by Zina Card, who was described as "a very intelligent woman...said to be one of the 52 children of Brigham Young and is not opposed to polygamy." She gave these visitors a Mormon bible, "[which members of Cochrane's party] have since been studying assiduously, and if they do not become converts to the Mormon faith it will not be Mrs. Carr's [sic] fault."[114] There are many accounts of the intelligence and warm hospitality of Zina Card. Lethbridge pharmacist John Higginbotham recalled her as "a woman of grace and charm [who] exercised a far-reaching influence on the life of Southern Alberta." One evening she spent hours in his library, discussing and debating many issues, "consulting many books of references until tables and chairs were covered with them. We debated many questions, drew our own conclusions and parted the best of friends. Later on I received, with her compliments, and autographed the *Book of Mormon*, also a copy of *A Key to the Science of Theology*."[115]

But not all Mormon women agreed with Zina Card, as plural marriage was for many of them a prison that they would escape given the chance. There were wives who suffered neglect, abandonment, abuse, and loneliness.[116] They were afraid, however, to openly question or object to their conditions. As one plural wife wrote in her memoirs, "I had never dared to question the propriety of the principle or analyze its ethics... We were taught that it was Divine, that we should never say anything against it. If one did not approve the principle, it was the advice of the authorities of the Church that nothing be said about it."[117] A Utah-based "Ladies Anti-Polygamy Society," formed in 1878 and made up of former plural wives and gentile supporters, condemned polygamy for violating the rights and the dignity of women.[118] Their own print forum, the *Anti-Polygamy Standard*, blamed men for plural marriage, and swore to "fight to the death that system which so enslaves and degrades our sex, and which robs them of so much happiness."[119]

The Mormons had strong supporters in Canada, provided the Saints agreed to give up polygamy, as they were seen as experienced and industrious dry-land farmers. After all, the majority of Mormons lived in monogamous relationships; only between 10 and 20 per cent of Mormon marriages before 1890 in Utah were polygamous.[120] In 1890 a correspondent with Regina's *The Leader* wrote, "The Mormons have neither horns nor cloven feet. In short they are but ordinary mortals of extraordinary industry, enterprise, frugality and prosperity."[121] They were also sober, never spending a cent over the bar. The correspondent was told that they "respect our law because we are consistent in our monogamy as compared with the Americans who persecute them, whilst their easy divorce laws and prostitution point out their inconsistency. They say that the latter vice is unknown to Mormonism and claim that conjugal fidelity and domestic felicity are leading characteristics of their religion."

Another supporter pointed out that "there are no half-breed children in their colony, nor in Utah," and that "these Mormons are white people, industrious, thrifty and honest, so that if any class of settlers can make these long neglected plains blossom like the rose they are the men."[122]

While the Mormons constituted the most concerted challenge to the monogamous model of marriage, there were other dissenters among the newcomers to Western Canada. Over seven thousand Doukhobors, Russian pacifists from the Caucasus region, arrived in the North-West Territories in 1899. They believed in communal institutions, including communal landholding and farming, and they hoped to establish these customs in their new home. They had broken away from the Russian Orthodox religion during the seventeenth century and they rejected church organization, hierarchy, and ritual as corrupt and unnecessary to salvation. They refused to take oaths; their allegiance was to God alone. They regarded marriage as a sacred relationship between two individuals and objected to the intervention of any third party, such as religious or civil authorities, and thus did not recognize the role of government in marriage.[123] They felt it was wrong to register births, deaths, and marriages. A 1901 petition to the government of Canada, signed by twenty-two Doukhobor leaders, stated that "we cannot recognize as correct and cannot accept any human laws as to the marriage union, being sure that all pertaining to it is in the province of God's will and human conscience."[124] They considered marriage the free union of two people. Marriages required the consent of the individuals and of the parents, and "an inward oath and vow, before all-seeing God, in the souls of those who are marrying, that they will to the end of their days remain faithful and inseparable."[125] There was little ceremony—just a declaration of love in front of relatives and elders. Doukhobors also practiced divorce; when two people ceased to love each other (even if this applied to only one of the spouses), there was sufficient reason for divorce, which could then be followed by remarriage.[126] Deserted spouses regarded themselves as free to remarry.

Doukhobor marriage and divorce was sharply criticized by outsiders who felt they were "a strange people" with "loose ideas of social life and marriage...steeped in their ancient traditions, still foreign in the ex-

Doukhobor women pulling a plough to break the prairie sod, Thunder Hill Colony, c. 1899. Images of the "downtrodden" Doukhobor woman were used by critics of the settlement of these Russian pacifists in Western Canada. (LAC C–000681)

treme."[127] The editor of the Battleford *Saskatchewan Herald* wrote in 1899 that Doukhobor marriage was "simpler and less ceremonious than even marriage amongst the Indians. The contracting parties simply shake hands and kiss each other and they are man and wife."[128] "There is no romance in the life of a Doukhobor woman," wrote a correspondent to *Collier's Weekly*. "One day young Joseph, finding himself in need of a helpmate— which means a willing worker—takes her to his house. She is his woman. He does not bind himself to cherish and protect, she makes no contract to love and obey. In fact, there is no ceremony in connection with the mating…They are willing to become partners, but as for the glow and gladness, the melting glance and the wild heart-beat, these form no part or parcel of a Doukhobor mating."[129] A British woman, employed by the Canadian Pacific Railway to assist other British women to adapt to settlement on the prairies, reported that "There are very primitive Russian peasants practicing a strict communal life—as far as I could gather there were no marriage laws, and all babies were put in nurseries at a year old."[130] The image of the downtrodden Doukhobor woman as "beast of burden" was solidified in Western Canada when some were observed hitched to the ploughs in teams in the earliest days of their settlements.[131]

The Doukhobors were also censured as bigamists. Their leader Peter Veregin had divorced (according to Doukhobor law) his first wife, and she had remained in the Caucasus. He had remarried, and his second wife was regarded as his wife in his own community, but Veregin and other divorced and remarried Doukhobors were regarded by outsiders as "bigamists."[132] The Doukhobors were also criticized for their communal living and farming, their socialism, pacifism, for their resistance to seeking naturalization and to swearing the oath of allegiance, and even for their vegetarianism. They attracted a great deal of attention and negative reactions when a faction of the Doukhobors known as the Sons of Freedom protested the government's treatment of them by marching in the nude.

Supporters of the Doukhobors disputed the image of the downtrodden Doukhobor woman. Emily Murphy, author and prominent first-wave feminist, was complimentary in her description of Doukhobor women in her book, *Janey Canuck in the West*. She wrote that "unfriendly critics" had made much of them harnessing themselves to the plough. However, as Murphy pointed out, with only a few draught horses available, and with women at first outnumbering the men of the colony, the women "volunteered, with true Spartan fortitude, to break up the land."[133] Doukhobor women, one journalist noted, were eligible to sit in their councils, or peoples' parliaments, which made decisions pertaining to law and order in their community, sitting in judgement of cases, settling disputes, and adjusting wrongs.[134] Peter Veregin was quoted as saying, "Our women work as hard for the community as we do, are equally interested in its welfare and prosperity. Why should they not have a voice in the council?"[135]

As historian Frances Swyripa has written, Ukrainian women settlers to Western Canada were portrayed in missionary reports, travel writing, magazines and newspapers as "uniformly passive, helpless, downtrodden, and lacking a native tradition of self-help for change."[136] Overall, the peasant Ukrainian woman was characterized as lacking in femininity in contrast to the delicate and pure Anglo-Canadian woman. These negative representations were every similar to the descriptions of Aboriginal women—Ukrainian women were also depicted as enslaved, servile, beasts of burden. Critics condemned early and arranged marriages; they impeded progress and assimilation. Ukrainian women too were allegedly sold by their parents, regardless of their age, provided the price of "two cows or four pigs" was met. "The dominant image," Swyripa writes, "was of a child bride arbitrarily married to a man more her father's age than her own in a business transaction where she was as much a commodity as her dowry, and condemned thereafter to bearing fifteen or sixteen children."[137] Activist Nellie McClung wrote of how Ukrainian girls were not educated as they were married so young: "Many a promising pupil had her education cut short when some grizzled old widower thought a good strong red-cheeked young girl would be right handy around the house and it would be cheaper to marry her than to have to pay her wages."[138] Child brides endangered the future health of the nation. An Alberta Methodist missionary warned that the children of these marriages in which the brides were fourteen or fifteen were often "puny and weak."[139] As Swyripa has shown, many of these prejudices and assumptions were unwarranted. There were very few brides of sixteen or younger for example, and the grooms were usually in their early twenties.[140]

Aside from the Mormons, Doukhobors and Ukrainians, there were less numerous groups who deviated from the monogamous model of marriage. There were first wives and second wives among the Chinese and Japanese. The importation of plural or even monogamous marriage was impossible for most as the head tax imposed on all Chinese immigrants beginning in 1885 reduced overall Chinese immigration, women in particular, as men could rarely afford to bring their wives or prospective wives. Questions and assumptions about first wives and second wives were important during the hearings of the 1885 Royal Commission on Chinese Immigration. One informant told the commission, "As regards public morality, they are not the same as we are. They do not respect the Sabbath or wives. Their wives here, as I understand, are their second wives, and chiefly prostitutes."[141] These rules prevented many Chinese men from marrying and establishing families in Canada, and the non-Asian community censured marriages between Chinese men and white women. As late as 1930, legislation was proposed in British Columbia that would prohibit marriages between white people and Chinese or Japanese people.[142] Headlines such as "Scottish Girl and Chinaman" and "Jap Weds a White Girl" suggest the rarity of these events, and the undisguised disapproval of much of the community.[143] Yet Chinese men were criticized because they did not marry, at the same time as their ability to do so was rendered nearly impossible; they were "damned" whether they did or did not marry, as pointed out in an 1884 edition of the *Edmonton Bulletin*: "One great objection urged against the Chinese is that they do not marry and settle down in the land to which they emigrate...To most minds this would be a redeeming feature in the case. For as long as they make it a point to regard China and China only as their home, there is but little probability of their absolutely over-running this continent; but were they to settle down and raise families then truly there would be a danger of North America becoming a Chinese colony."[144]

When Chinese fiancées or wives were admitted to Canada they were subjected to particular scrutiny and interrogation as well as the head tax. In 1920, Wat Shee, arriving to marry Vancouver jeweller Wong Wai, was cross-examined in the matter of her application for admission upon payment of the five-hundred-dollar head tax.[145] Many questions suggested that authorities suspected women like Wat Shee were prostitutes: "Did neither you nor your mother do anything to help support yourself?" Or, "How did you have the nerve to travel un-accompanied on the boat, such a thing is very unusual under Chinese customs?" But there were a select few who could afford to circumvent such obstacles. Yip Sang, a wealthy merchant who settled in Vancouver in 1888, lived with three of his four wives and their large family in the building that housed his Wing Sang Company.[146]

The Quakers, or Society of Friends, like the Doukhobors, married without the assistance of a minister, and without a license. There were settlements of Quakers, mainly from Ontario, in the west, near Kenlis and Borden, Saskatchewan.[147] They did not believe in priesthoods, hierarchy, ritual, or ceremonies. Men and women always had an equal standing in their governance and ministry. As noted in *The Colonist* (Winnipeg) in 1891, "among the Friends at Kenlis a woman is the equal of a man and enjoys the same rights and privileges."[148] To marry, the consent of parents and notice to a monthly meeting of their governing committee (in which men and women had equal standing) was required.[149] A visiting committee was then appointed to see if the couple was "clear" upon the subject of marriage. That committee reported to the next monthly meeting, and then vows were exchanged at a regular public worship meeting. Women were not asked to promise to be obedient. A special Quaker certificate of marriage declared that the couple had met all of the requirements.

Marriage in Islam departed from the Christian monogamous model, and there were Islamic settlers in the west. There were pockets of Syrian settlement in Western Canada in the larger cities, and also in rural areas, as many homesteaded in Saskatchewan around Saskatoon and Swift Current.[150] An Arab Muslim community grew in Lac La Biche, Alberta, after 1904. Marriage in Islam was not regarded as a "perpetual union," and a marriage could be terminated if it failed to work. Muslims allowed the practice of having more than one wife at a time. The institution of the arranged marriage among Arab Canadians continued into the twentieth century, and a high priority was given to the marriage of cousins on the father's side.[151] Elsewhere in the imperial world of the late nineteenth century, the supposedly degraded role of women in the Arab household, and their oppression due to Islamic laws and customs, became "the favored rhetorical haunts of male writers, both in official and nonofficial discourse."[152]

There were many experiments in communal and co-operative living in Western Canada, and some challenged, blended, and bent "traditional" gender roles. There were early advocates of "free love" in Western Canada. Some of the Hamona Colony (1895–1900) settlers in the Qu'Appelle Valley of Saskatchewan wished to "abolish family life, and individual homes, and all live in one large apartment building with a public dining room under the management of the married ladies," and "an extreme left wing even advocated free love as part of their plans."[153] These families began a community kitchen where all of the colony's women were supposed to take their turns working. Some of the Finnish settlers of the Sojntula Colony, or "Harmony Experiment," in British Columbia at the turn of the century were believers in "free love."[154]

But there was another major set of dangerous "others" lurking at the boundaries, infiltrating the young region of the new nation, heightening anxiety and bolstering Canadian resolve to maintain a firm grasp on the populace through control of marriage. The dreaded Americans were among the largest contingent of newcomers to Western Canada; there were concerns that they would bring their loose ideas about the marriage bond with them and influence Canadians to change their marriage laws. There was also the temptation for Canadians to acquire divorces in the United States, although these divorces were considered illegal in Canada unless the parties were legal US residents or citizens. Within Canada the United States was widely perceived as a land of loose and lax marriage and divorce laws, contributing to the perceived immorality and degradation of that nation. Not only was divorce permissible, but divorced persons could even remarry there. "It is possible for a man to have three or four wives in the United States without violating any statute," declared an 1891 issue of *Canadian Churchman*.[155] As Justice Gwynne wrote in an 1884 judgement in a case involving Canadian marriage law: "Bordering as Canada does on several foreign States, in many of which laws relating to marriage and divorce are loose, demoralizing and degrading to the marriage state [such legislation] seems to be absolutely essential to the peace, order and good government of Canada, and in particular to the maintenance within Canada of the purity of the marriage state...if the courts should hold otherwise they would, in my opinion inflict a deadly stab upon the constitution of the Dominion."[156]

These views of an immoral, corrupting American influence on pristine Canadian marriage were widely disseminated in the press. Canadian editorialists were overwhelmingly in favour of the refusal to recognize the legality of US divorce laws, and were against any similar relaxation of divorce laws in Canada. In 1889, an editorial in the *Edmonton Bulletin* lectured that marriage laws "support the whole social fabric of the country," and any system of easy divorce corrupted the fabric of society "by the degradation of the marriage relation to a matter of mere animal choice as it is surely being degraded in the United States." An advice book for women, published in Toronto in 1871, warned against the "American plan of granting absolute divorces" as "dangerous, and destructive to what is best in life. It leads to hasty, ill-assorted matches, to an unwillingness to yield to each other's peculiarities, to a weakening of family ties, to a lax morality. Carry it a trifle farther than it now is in some States, and marriage will lose all its sacredness, and degenerate into a physical union not nobler than crossing of flies in the air."[157]

A focus for concerns about increasingly lax morals in Canada was an 1889 scandal of epic proportions involving Minister of Finance George Eulas Foster's marriage to Mrs. Chisholm, who had obtained a divorce in Chicago from her previous husband. Many Canadians regarded the couple as "living in sin."[158] "We are necessarily placed in daily and hourly peril of social contamination," readers of an 1892 editorial in *Canadian Churchman* were told, because of close contact with the people of the United States, "who have earned too well a world-wide notoriety for carelessness in regard to the marriage contract." It concluded: "There are worse poisonings than blood poisoning: poisonings of the mind and heart! The question of erecting a quarantine barrier against the importation of cholera is a small one as compared with the protection from the deadly disease of family immorality." "Civilization itself hangs in the balance," readers were told.[159] A *Calgary Herald* editorial of 21 May 1904 warned readers that the "easy throwing on and off of marital relations which obtains across the border, is an evil so vitiating in its effect on the moral tone of a nation and so destructive of the only foundation on which a nation can be supported that it is to be hoped Canada will always as now, be immune." The laws of a nation should foster "permanent homes" and "family circles." One article on divorce in Canada contributed to a Regina newspaper by a "Candid American" observed that "Canadians look upon matrimony as a sacred institution, and justly consider it a cornerstone of society, frowning down all attempts to make its dissolution an easy matter."[160] "Marriage in Canada," he wrote, "like fire, is not to be played with. Fire if kept in the stove is a very useful, cheerful and necessary thing in a house, but if you begin to throw it around for fun it is very apt to set the house on fire. So it is with marriage." However, he was somewhat critical, noting that a Canadian husband could get as drunk as often as he liked, "eject his wife, like an Irish tenant," and "she can have no redress except in a decree of separation and alimony; but through it all she has to remain his wife 'until death do them part,'" as habitual drunkenness was not a sufficient cause for divorce in Canada.

It is true that there was a dramatically different divorce terrain just across the forty-ninth parallel—differences that were not imagined, although they certainly were embellished and twisted in Canada. Historian Paula Petrik described the rate of divorce in Montana, 1865–1907, as "extraordinarily high."[161] In one of the Montana counties examined in her study, there was one divorce for every three marriages, and divorces even exceeded marriages in 1867.[162] Divorce cases were heard and granted by local county courts, in contrast to the situation in Western Canada where divorces were heard and granted only in distant Ottawa. Women had much greater leeway to precipitate divorce action, as just causes and grounds included "impotency, bigamy, abandonment for the space of one year, wilfull [sic] desertion, habitual drunkenness, extreme cruelty, or conviction of a felony or infamous crime."[163] While husbands tended to simply disappear, women petitioned for divorce. Desertion was the most common reason for precipitating divorce action, followed by adultery, cruelty, and drunkenness. Montana's women, through their petitions for divorce for reasons including intemperance, extreme cruelty, and mental suffering, played a critical role in advancing the divorce laws, thereby forcing the courts to recognize and respond to the social and economic conditions they faced. When Montana's domestic laws were compiled following statehood in the Code of 1895, the "threat of bodily injury" was added to consideration in extreme cruelty cases.[164] There were many divorce cases that were dismissed for lack of prosecution by the female petitioners. Petrik argued that "women appear to have used the threat of divorce to pry their wayward mates away from improper behavior of all kinds...spouses, especially husbands, had to treat the other kindly or risk divorce."[165]

There was clearly much to fear if the "contagion" or "disease" or "poison" of American marital relations were to seep across the border, if single women were permitted freedoms such as homestead rights allowing them alternatives to marriage, as they were in the US, or if Aboriginal and migrant groups persisted in their alternative marriages, and easy divorces. "Civilization itself hangs in the balance," were the words of the May 21, 1904 *Calgary Herald* editorial quoted earlier. Intraracial, indissoluble, monogamous, heterosexual, sanctified Christian marriage was to be the cornerstone, foundation and building block of Western Canada, the key to future stability and prosperity. The arrival of white women and of Christian, British common law, monogamous marriage heralded the end of an undomesticated, masculine era when white men experienced freedom, derring-do and fun, but also social turmoil, chaos, even violence. This model of marriage was to be the architect of private life, shaping men and women into submissive, obedient wives, and commanding, providing husbands. Yet the supremacy of this model was not a foregone conclusion. Western Canada posed particular challenges to the monogamous model in the late nineteenth century, with its diverse Aboriginal population, lengthy tradition of "fur trade" marriages, preponderance of single white males, single white women exploring alternatives to marriage, and with the arrival of newcomers like the Mormons, Doukhobors and Quakers. Altogether this was "very bad seed grain" in the newly acquired region of the young nation where there was much profit to be made from the land and resources. As the new region was cultivated and developed, dissenters had to be weeded out. Social stability, at the heart of which were the gender roles that were key to this model of marriage, was critical to economic development. As historian Kathleen Wilson has written, "Historians of British America are in substantial agreement on this point: 'patriarchy,' in the form of the supreme authority of the white, predominantly property-holding male heads of household, was the building block and organizing principle of British-American societies."[166] A region like Western Canada, with diverse gender roles and various definitions of marriage, lacked stability. Most blatantly, a region with two instances of organized resistance by Aboriginal people, the children and descendants of mixed marriages, lacked stability. There were no funds available in Canada for a military force to occupy this territory, to discourage Aboriginal resistance and to keep the territory in Canadian rather than American hands—instead an army of homesteaders, not individual male farmers but families, was a direct substitute. These family farm households were to be the main unit of social order. There was much work to be done to impose and safeguard the monogamous ideal north of the border. Diverse strategies were required to fundamentally reshape the marital terrain of the west and to ensure that the gender order encoded in that model prevailed.

THREE

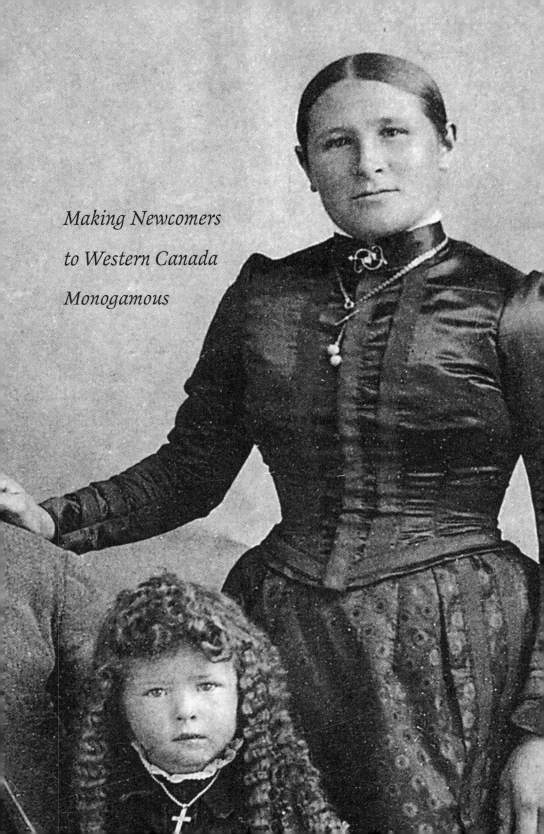

Making Newcomers

to Western Canada

Monogamous

ALTERNATIVE NONCONFORMIST MARRIAGES posed a threat to monogamous marriage, endangering convictions about the superiority, naturalness, and common sense of this institution and its encoded gender roles. Such threats had to be policed and prohibited. The monogamous model was not ancient, enduring, entrenched, or even widely accepted as the only option. It had to be methodically *made* the sole option. As Ann Laura Stoler has argued, "Colonialism was not a secure bourgeois project. It was not only about the importation of middle-class sensibilities to the colonies, but about the *making* of them."[1] While the norm was clearly not invented in Western Canada, it was developed, substantiated, and affirmed there in contrast to the diverse alternatives perceived as threats to bourgeois respectability.

It was not until well into the nineteenth century that the monogamous model of marriage became the most accepted version of marriage in other parts of North America and in Western Europe. Legal historians have pointed out that the monogamous model of marriage was a fairly recent phenomenon that reached ascendancy in Europe in the nineteenth century, and that it was never as fixed, stable, or enduring as presented in the late nineteenth century (and beyond); rather, it was contested and in a state of constant flux. "Things had not always been so starkly inequitable," writes historian Joan Perkin, who notes that in Anglo-Saxon England women had rights to property, could divorce or legally separate, and could depart with the children and half the marital property.[2] Although she shows that this changed dramatically from Anglo-Saxon times, Perkin demonstrates that the working classes of the eighteenth century could live beyond the reach of marriage laws. Many married "without benefit of clergy," and they also found ways to get divorced. In England, the United States, and Canada, marriage and divorce were "relatively informal affairs" with the sanction of the community being a vital consideration before the nineteenth century.[3] In the United States, poor and "backcountry whites," especially in the south and in the sparsely populated west, were married well into the nineteenth century by making reciprocal promises.[4] Courts declared that "reputation, cohabitation and the declaration and conduct of the parties" would serve as adequate evidence of marriage.[5]

Local customs of marriage and divorce in England that persisted into the nineteenth century, and which resembled the "fur trade" marriages described in the last chapter, did not necessarily reflect either legal or religious decrees; there were ways of gaining community consent to marriage, divorce, and remarriage. Among the working class and the poor of England the ritual "sale of wives" was a way of acquiring community consent to divorce and remarriage. In *Customs in Common: Studies in Traditional Popular Culture*, historian E. P. Thompson writes about this ritual, which had disappeared by the 1850s.[6] It was also all but forgotten, dismissed as very rare and "utterly offensive to morality,"[7] but it was a custom that gave people a way out of unhappy marriages. Thomas Hardy's *The Mayor of Casterbridge* offers one powerful reminder of this custom. In the novel,

Michael Henchard sells his wife Susan in a public auction to a passing sailor—a stranger—who bids on impulse. Thompson is critical of Hardy's portrayal of this event, arguing that it perpetuates a stereotype common to contemporary newspaper accounts of such "sales." Thompson writes, "Once this stereotype has become established, it is only too easy to read the evidence through it. It can then be assumed that the wife was auctioned like a beast or chattel, perhaps against her will, either because the husband wished to be rid of her or for merely mercenary motives... It could be taken as a melancholy example of abject feminine oppression, or an illustration of the levity with which marriage was regarded among the male poor."[8]

While the idea of women as property is inescapable, there was more to this ritual, as Thompson demonstrates. He argues that wife sales were "occasioned by the breakdown of marriages, and were a device to enable a public divorce and re-marriage by the exchange of a wife (not any woman) between two men."[9] Hardy, according to Thompson, based his description on opaque newspaper accounts that were abbreviated and sensationalist. Thompson identified certain key rituals common to the "true" wife sale, which he argued was not brutal chattel purchase, but rather a prearranged means of publicly declaring and gaining the consent of the community to a divorce and remarriage. There was a semblance of an open auction, but the women were "purchased" not by strangers, but by their lovers. The "wife sale" was a public demonstration that the husband was a "willing (or resigned) party" to the divorce and remarriage. The delivery of the wife in the halter symbolized the surrender of the wife to another man. When the rope of the halter was transferred from one man to another there was an exchange of pledges analogous to a marriage wherein the wife gave her consent. In one case of the 1830s, the wife in question was angry when her husband tried to get out of the arrangement; she made him continue, saying: "Let be, yer rogue, I wull [sic] be sold. I wants a change."[10] This ceremony was sometimes followed by adjournment of all three with witnesses to the nearest inn where the sale would be "ratified" through the signing of papers. There were many variations. A wife could also be "sold" to her own relatives, a brother or mother, suggesting that it was a device by which a woman could annul or be "bought out" of her existing marriage. The publicity of these rituals ensured general popular endorsement of the legitimacy of these divorces and remarriages.

"Jumping the broom" was another popular informal method of marriage and divorce. This was a ceremony that persisted in England to the mid-nineteenth century. A couple was regarded as married by their community when they jumped over a broomstick in the company of witnesses, and the transaction could be undone by jumping back over the broom. A "broomstick marriage" in Wales could be "sundered by the exact reversal of the form used for marriage. If divorce was desired and twelve months had not elapsed, a broom was again placed in the doorway in the presence of witnesses. The dissatisfied person then jumped backwards over the besom [broom made of twigs] into the open air, making sure neither broom nor door jamb was touched in the process."[11]

The classic definition of marriage as "the voluntary union for life of one man and one woman, to the exclusion of all others," articulated in 1866 by Sir James O. Wilde (Lord Penzance) in the famous *Hyde v. Hyde and Woodmansee* case (involving Mormon marriage, which the judge found did not constitute a marriage in English matrimonial law, even if monogamous), and repeated in many judgements thereafter, was not ancient, universal, immutable, or "commonsensical" at the time of the intensive settlement of Western Canada.[12] A variety of methods were employed to promote the monogamous model, all designed to reform, police, or undermine marital nonconformists. After the formation of the North-West Territories, steps were quickly taken to legislate on marriage through the 1878 Ordinance Respecting Marriage.[13] As Nancy Cott writes, "Typically founders of new political societies in the Western tradition have inaugurated their regimes with marriage regulations, to foster households conducive to their aims and to symbolize a new era."[14] The 1878 ordinance authorized the lieutenant governor to license ministers, clergymen, or Justices of the Peace to solemnize marriages, and it established the system of marriage licenses and certificates. The two persons were to proclaim their intention to marry through the publication of banns, "proclaimed at least once openly and in an audible voice on a Sunday in some public religious assembly." There was provision, however, that if the minister or clergyman was remote from the issuer of marriage licenses, or finding that it was not possible to publish such banns, he could celebrate the marriage anyway if satisfied that there were no legal impediments. All marriages were to be solemnized in the presence of two or more credible witnesses. A fee was attached as the marriage license cost three dollars, and the registrar of deeds charged another fifty cents. Officers in command of the NWMP posts were appointed Justices of the Peace, as well as issuers of marriage licenses and notary publics.[15]

A variety of methods, formal and informal, were used to prohibit or discourage nonconformist marriages, and to censure or make life difficult for those who rejected marriage altogether. Acceptable marriages were heartily endorsed, while others were not. Intra-racial marriage became an index of respectability. Aboriginal women were often labelled immoral prostitutes who posed a serious danger to public health.[16] The movement of Aboriginal women off their reserves was restricted and monitored through a pass system.[17] They were not welcome in the places and spaces newly defined as white. It was noted in the *Regina Leader* of April 12, 1887 for example, that there were complaints about the "squaw nuisance" in that town and it was proposed that if they were "to be tolerated at all off their reserves, why not prohibit them from appearing in town after dark?" The white men who married Aboriginal women were derisively labelled "squaw men."[18] Prominent and not-so prominent white men in the west divorced (according to Aboriginal law), separated, or otherwise abandoned their Aboriginal wives and families, and they often remarried.

Mixed-race marriage was censured in medical and other advice literature of the late nineteenth century. Alexander Reid, a McGill-trained doctor who lived in the Red River settlement in the late 1850s believed that scientific principles of classification could be applied to human society.[19] In an 1875 paper published by the *Journal of the Anthropological Institute of Great Britain and Ireland*, Reid identified nine categories of mixed-race people at Red River.[20] Reid found that his first class, the

> Marie Rose Delorme, who was Métis, married Norwegian Charles Smith in 1877 and they ranched at Pincher Creek Alberta. In this photograph from 1896, they are with their daughter Mary Anne, fifth of their seventeen children. "Mixed" marriages were increasingly censured in late 19th century Western Canada. (GAA NA-2539-1)

"Anglo-Saxon father and Indian mother," and second class "the French 'halfbreeds' or 'natives'" were "honest, industrious, and very energetic" but they resembled the "pure Indian" because "exposure to the open air and the customs of the country give them a swarthier look and different manners than would otherwise be theirs."[21] Reid's scientific conclusion was that "the more distant from the first and second classes the nearer approach to the races of the primitive mother."[22] The mothers' blood could impart "restlessness, slovenliness, impatience of control, wild liberty, superstition, and, when aroused, [a] fiendish hatred and temper."[23] Readers of advice literature also warned of the consequences of inter-racial marriage. "A negress who has borne her first child to a white man, will ever after have children of a lighter color than her own," according to an 1871 book entitled *The Physical Life of Woman*.[24] It was further noted that "Count Strzelewski in his travels in Australia, narrates this curious circumstance: a native woman who has once had offspring by a white man, can never more have children by a male of her own race."

In the emerging non-Aboriginal communities of the west there was unease over marriages that criss-crossed cultural and colonizing bound-aries. White men deserted their Aboriginal spouses, or perhaps divorced according to Aboriginal law. In 1887 for example, one of Fort Macleod's "most honoured citizens" married one of its "fairest daughters." The bride was Lily Grier, a newly arrived teacher from Ontario, and the groom was D.W. Davis, former whiskey trader of Fort Whoop-Up fame. He was soon to be the district's first Member of Parliament. In tendering the happy couples' best wishes for the future, the writer of a column in the *Macleod Gazette* "[felt] sure that it will meet with the hearty endorse-ment of the whole community in so doing."[25] Not mentioned at all was the fact that Davis was already married to a prominent Kainai woman, a sister of Chief Red Crow, and they had four children together. Lily Grier's brother, D.J. Grier of the NWMP, was married to Molly Tailfeathers of the Piikani (Peigan) Nation, and they had three children, but Grier was remarried to a white woman by 1887. Just how these men secured divorces from their first wives is not clear. Davis may have assumed he was never "legally" married to Revenge Walker, or he may have felt himself to have been divorced according to Aboriginal law. Grier had been "legally" married to Molly Tailfeathers, and how he acquired a divorce from her is unknown. In any case it appears that these divorces and subsequent marriages were heartily endorsed in the non-Aboriginal community, although there were those, particularly missionaries, who protested when the children of the earlier interracial marriages were often "abandoned" to lives on the reserves. (Davis and Grier did, however, provide for their children from their first marriages.) A completely different standard was applied to divorces and remarriages among Aboriginal people subject to government administration. They were not permitted to divorce, except through an act of Parliament, which was not a feasible option for them.

A number of proposals were floated in the 1880s and 1890s to discourage intermarriage as well as more temporary relationships, and to simultaneously insist that fathers provide support for the children from these relationships. Legislation to this effect was proposed, although never enacted, including an 1886 ordinance of the North-West Territories Council compelling men in relationships with Aboriginal women to support their "illegitimate" offspring.[26] In 1889 Indian Commissioner Hayter Reed expressed his concern to the deputy superintendent general that, especially in the Macleod district, white men were deserting Aboriginal women after cohabiting and having children with them. He proposed to make an example of one such case by bringing an action in civil court for alimony for both mother and children. He noted they would need to make a careful selection of the case for procedure, as unless there was "some sort of estate, we would have incurred costs to very little purpose." He wrote: "In any case however, if whites see that we are on the alert to protect the rights of the women and their children the effect is likely to be good."[27] In 1894, as Deputy Superintendent Reed remained concerned with the issue; he wished to amend the Indian Act to "meet the case of the whiteman who takes an Indian girl or woman to live with him without undergoing any marriage ceremony and without the idea of any matrimonial obligation."[28] He wanted the law to "prohibit such immoral practices," and to prohibit men from living with Aboriginal women unless married to them. Missionaries and their supporters also advocated such measures, and did so well into the twentieth century. An 1895 Methodist Church petition to the British Columbia Legislature asked for legislation "prohibiting white men from cohabiting with Indian women, and compelling those who have children to marry, or abandon the woman and maintain the children in some educational institution."[29] Despite similar pressure over many years, no such action was ever taken. As Hayter Reed wrote in 1896, "There can be no question as to the desirability of taking measures to prohibit if possible the cohabiting of white men and Indian women, but the subject is one replete with difficulties. It is, in the first place, difficult to frame a law which would be operative; and even if we succeed in that, there would be great difficulty enforcing it."[30] There were jurisdictional problems as well; such legislation, either under the Indian Act or Criminal Code, was under the jurisdiction of the federal government alone. Continuing efforts to introduce such legislation will be discussed in a subsequent chapter.

There were single men who could be, and were, "ordered" to get married. Following the Resistance of 1885, there was criticism in the House of Commons of Indian agents and farm instructors on the reserves who, it was alleged, had "immoral" relations with Aboriginal women and abused their positions of authority. In response to these criticisms, the Department of Indian Affairs drew up a list of the married and single employees, and the single men were ordered to get married or be replaced by married men. In the "remarks" column of an 1886 list it was noted that the remaining single men would be "replaced by married men as soon as suitable men can be obtained."[31] Their wives were required to live on the reserves. One single instructor, J. H. Gooderham, it was noted, "says he will marry when a house is erected for him to live in," and another was "in the east on leave to get married." According to an early Saskatchewan history, the efforts of the agents and instructors to quickly find wives was the source of much amusement: "Most of them [instructors and agents] were single men, and to turn young men, clothed with authority, loose as it were, among a lot of Indian women, was found to have disadvantages which missionary effort was powerless to counteract. And so the word went forth that the single farm instructors were to get married within a certain period or lose their jobs...One doesn't need to be told that while these young fellows were industriously hunting wives, in a country where women were decidedly scarce, their laudable efforts were watched with a good deal of amusement by those who were in the know."[32] This policy too was criticized as some competent instructors lost their jobs, and married farm instructors had to devote a great deal of their attention to their families; they required larger and better-built houses, and more rations were required to feed the extra family members.[33]

When, in 1888, NWMP Commissioner Lawrence Herchmer refused to grant permission to marry to some members of the force, there was sharp community criticism and censure. The *Regina Leader* threatened "dire revenge."[34] In a series of editorials it was claimed that Herchmer pursued a general policy of refusing permission to marry, and of reassigning men, or reducing them in rank, to prevent them from marrying. It was alleged that Herchmer did not allow a Regina-stationed constable to marry, and ordered him off to Maple Creek, telling him "not to put a millstone round his neck."[35] The same thing had allegedly happened to a constable engaged to a young woman at Moosomin; when he asked for permission to marry he was "shipped off to Fort Macleod."[36] This, according to the *Leader*, promoted immorality; "if the moment a policeman hints at marriage he will be removed, all a bad man has to do is to make love to a girl, promise her marriage, perhaps receive her entire confidence, then go and say to the Commissioner, 'I want to marry.' Without appearing wilfully to treat the girl badly, he will be shipped off three or four hundred miles and if the girl follows him shipped off again."[37] The *Leader*'s correspondent at Calgary reported a distressing case of a member of the NWMP who "betrayed" a young woman, took fifty dollars from her, and then had himself transferred to Regina. Upon hearing that the woman had followed him to Regina, he had himself transferred to Battleford. Readers were asked, was Herchmer the "aider of the seducer and thief"? "[W]e know if this man told him he wanted to marry he would reply to him with his favourite weapon—a threat."[38] In the midst of the controversy the *Leader* reported on the lavish Regina wedding of Emma Blanche Royal, a daughter of the lieutenant governor of the

North-West Territories, to the dashing Captain Gagnon of the NWMP.[39] The message was clear—the young policemen should be encouraged rather than discouraged to marry.

Herchmer's policy on marriage did, however, have some support in the west. It was argued in the *Edmonton Bulletin* that for reasons of efficiency, and because of expense to the federal government, the hiring of married non-commissioned officers and constables should be avoided, and their subsequent marriages not permitted. In a 5 January 1889 editorial it was pointed out that "if a constable's marriage adds to the responsibilities and expenses of the government in connection with that man certainly the government should have something to say as to whether these responsibilities should be forced on them or not." Criticism was levelled at the lack of attention to the wives and families of members of the force. An article in the *Leader* calling for an end to the canteen at the Regina NWMP barracks where beer was served reinforced the idea that the wives and families of the force needed more attention.[40] At the end of January 1889 it was reported that Corporal T. B. Wright had spent the entire month since New Year's at the canteen. After that he deserted the force, his wife, and their children who lived at the police barracks.

The challenges posed by an excess of single white men compared to the few adventuresome single white women in the region were in part addressed through the federal government's land distribution policy for the west, which was administered through the Department of the Interior. The monogamous model was deeply embedded in the Dominion Lands Act (DLA) and the homestead system—the economic and social foundation of prairie Canada after 1870. It was adopted from US land policy, which was based on Thomas Jefferson's view of an agricultural society composed of small family farms. The central figure in this social system was the yeoman farmer, and the male-female couple and their family was at the core.[41] In Jefferson's view it was imperative that women be locked up on the land under the control of men. As historian Peter Boag has noted, "the land itself, then, played a role in the preservation of the 'natural' gender system."[42] Women gained access to land only through their relationship with men. The grid survey system and associated land legislation was based not on ideas of how best the land might be farmed, but on cherished cultural, social, religious, and gender ideals. The DLA provided that the patriarchal nuclear family with male heads of households and dependent wives would be the foundation of society. The homesteads were designed as small-scale units of production—family farms. Married men were encouraged to come ahead of their families to get established, and to send for them as soon as possible. The Department of the Interior's strategy for single men was that they should soon "settle down."[43]

The DLA was a powerful tool for imposing the nuclear family model that isolated families and scattered them across the prairies. Many groups such as the Mennonites and Doukhobors, who hoped to establish alternative communal societies, found that they too were eventually compelled to conform to this model.[44] When many of the Doukhobors refused, they were dispossessed of their land.[45] Groups that *purchased* land, such as the Hutterites, were independent of the social constraints imposed by the DLA on homesteaders, and could therefore pursue their communal lifestyle.[46]

Officials of the Department of the Interior went to extraordinary lengths to ensure that very few solo women were permitted to homestead, and thus they were denied access to the main source of income in the west at that time—land—unless they were wealthy enough to purchase directly. In Canada a woman could not homestead unless she had a dependent child or children of her own, and could thus qualify as a "sole" head of household. The word "sole" in the Canadian legislation was used to disqualify a great variety of women whose husbands were alive, but might have deserted, or be ill or incapacitated. In 1895 Catherine Godkin sought permission to homestead. She was the mother of four young children and her husband had been confined in an asylum for seven years with little hope for recovery. The decision was that the circumstances did not constitute Mrs. Godkin as the sole head of her family within the meaning of the statute, as her husband was still alive, even though confined to an asylum.[47] A widowed, separated or divorced woman having no minor children was not a sole head of a family. The majority who qualified were widows with children. Each widowed applicant had to sign a statutory declaration stating she was a widow and including the names and ages of the children who depended on her. If the children were not her own, she was disqualified. In an 1895 case, a single woman named Eliza McFadden applied for a homestead as a head of a family as she had two adopted children. She had a letter from the children's father in which he agreed to relinquish all his legal claims to the children as their parent. McFadden was found not eligible as she could not be considered the sole head of a family as "a father cannot divest himself of his authority over or responsibility for his children by such an agreement."[48] In 1916 cancellation proceedings on the grounds of fraud were instituted against a widow who had filed on a homestead claiming she had a minor child dependent on her for support. This child was later shown to have been her daughter's child.[49] A woman with an "illegitimate" child was not eligible to homestead. In 1919 a woman wrote from Spokane, Washington asking whether a woman who was not married but had a child could take up a homestead in Canada.[50] The reply was "the regulations do not permit of a homestead entry being made in a case of this kind."[51]

A divorced or separated woman had to have legal proof of the divorce or legal separation. Further, the woman had to have been given complete and sole custody of the children through a binding agreement. Even such documentary proof was not always sufficient. In January 1895 Mrs. Maria Heath applied for a homestead near Leduc, Alberta, believing she was entitled to do so as a head of family. She was from Ridgetown, Ontario, and had an adult son and a younger daughter. She had a deed of separation from her husband which was attached to her file, which was referred all the way to the deputy minister of justice in Ottawa.[52] E. L. Newcombe's opinion was that deed of separation did *not* make Mrs. Heath a "sole head of a family within the meaning of the Dominion Lands Act so as to qualify her to obtain a homestead entry. Her husband by this deed does not purport to divest himself of his control over his children, and under the laws in force in Ontario or Manitoba or the North West Territories he could not effectively so divest himself or escape from his duties and responsibilities by any such deed."[53] In a less than magnanimous gesture later that summer, it was decided that Mrs. Heath could purchase the land at $1.00 per acre or for $160.00—land available to any male for a $10.00 filing fee.[54] It is remarkable that Maria Heath remained on her land in the summer of 1895 during the months of indecision about her rights. Snow fell in July and again in August of 1895 in the Leduc district, and many settlers abandoned, leaving their crops unharvested. Those who remained were very hard up that winter, with rabbits being a mainstay in almost every home. It would have been a tremendous strain on her resources to pay for this land.[55]

A main concern about permitting separated women to homestead, as expressed in the House of Commons in 1907 by future Prime Minister R.L. Borden, was that this would provide an inducement to separation, as each spouse would be entitled to a homestead.[56] Rulings with regard to deserted and separated wives were eventually relaxed, but in all cases they had to have minor children. At first women who could prove desertion for five years were permitted homestead entry, and in 1920 this was changed to two years, although permission was not automatically granted—each case was individually scrutinized.[57] Among the duties of homestead inspectors were reports on whether women were actually who they said they were, whether they were indeed widows or deserted. Was a woman truly deserted, or was her husband still in the vicinity? What did the neighbours say?

The Department of the Interior received regular enquiries from women, single, married, widowed, divorced or deserted, asking if they were eligible to homestead, and the answer was invariably "no," or no answer at all. They also wrote to protest the restrictions on women's rights to homestead. In 1913 Mrs. Thomas McNeil, a deserted woman from Dungloe, Saskatchewan, wrote that she had arrived from Ontario with her husband and eleven children seven years earlier. As soon as her husband got his patent to their homestead he sold it and left, claiming he was going to use the proceeds to purchase another homestead, but she had found out that "he has drank the most of it by this time and has not took a purchased homestead yet and about all the satisfaction I can get is that a man in the Saskatchewan can do as he likes with his own property but if he ever does take a purchased homestead I would never go to live on it I got hunger enough on this one. I would often have starved only for what my children had sent me…Let women have a share in property in the west the same as they have in the east it would be alright. I suppose you will think I am crazy for writing such letter and I don't suppose you would be far mistaken."[58] She asked that the minister of the interior do whatever was in his power to allow women to get homesteads.

The policy of making it nearly impossible for women to homestead in Canada was not an oversight of policymakers; it was deliberate and in contrast to the United States, where single women were permitted to homestead, and did so in the thousands.[59] The US legislation permitted a much wider diversity of women to homestead and there was greater flexibility in the interpretations of the regulations. Widows, deserted and divorced women did not need to have minor children dependent on them for support. "Unwed" mothers were permitted to make entry, even if they were not yet twenty-one years of age.[60] A wife whose husband was a "confirmed drunkard" was considered the head of a family. A married woman could make homestead entry if her husband was in the penitentiary, or "incapacitated by disease or otherwise from earning a support for his family."[61]

The restrictions on women's homestead rights in Canada were protested. A "homesteads-for-women" campaign took shape in Western Canada from 1908–1914. When the issue was considered by the federal government, however, the reaction of administrators was to narrow the existing categories of eligible women. In 1910, Minister of the Interior Frank Oliver was asked in the House of Commons why single women could not homestead in Canada as they could in the US West.[62] His response clearly demonstrates how the monogamous model with its embedded gender roles was deeply rooted in the land policy for Western Canada. Oliver said, "our experience is entirely against the idea of women homesteading." In order to make a homestead productive there must be "not a single woman upon it, nor even a single man, but there should be both the man and the woman in order that the homestead may be made fully advantageous to the country. The idea of giving homesteads to single women would tend directly against that idea." Women were to be on the land and working hard, but only under the control of men. Georgina Binnie-Clark was told by the deputy minister of the Department of the Interior that "the object of granting the land-gift to men is to induce them to make a home on the prairie...He held the first requirement of the genuine home-maker to be a wife: he married, he has a family, etc. etc. Women, he assumed, are already averse to marriage, and he considered that to admit them to the opportunities of the land-grant would be to make them more independent of marriage than ever."[63]

There were a variety of ways in which single women were discouraged from remaining single, not all of which were unique to Western Canada. Single women were discouraged from immigrating to Canada unless they were in the category of domestic servant, in which case they were generally assessed as to their suitability, chaperoned during the trip, and placed in a supervised hotel while awaiting placement. Women coming to Canada had to be accompanied by a husband, parent, or other approved relatives. Otherwise, "unaccompanied" women had to obtain an emigration permit from a Canadian government emigration agent. To obtain the permit a woman had to show that she had a job awaiting her, or sufficient money to provide for her needs while she found employment, or that she had relatives or friends willing to support her.[64]

Disparaging comments about "old maids" were frequent in advice literature, novels, and in the press. An 1880s marriage manual advised, "For a woman to live through life unmarried is to be worse than dead... If she, indeed, escape a part of the snares that best the path of the man unmarried, she encounters others of even a more deadly tendency. Some fall, others save themselves—to a prolongation of misery. The career of the old bachelor is bad enough in the name of all that is sensible, but his case is a paradise compared to the ancient maiden."[65] Single women could be criticized and marginalized, becoming local characters in many communities where the stories that circulated about them served to reinforce conventional behaviour for women. Caroline Fulham, a woman who made her own living in Calgary mentioned in the previous chapter, was frequently arrested and prosecuted for her disorderly and unsteady habits. In one courtroom exchange in 1891, lawyer and senator James Lougheed called her a "moral leper," and he regretted the "liberty or rather the licenses granted to such a woman who made herself a notorious nuisance."[66] Her behaviour, which was in contrast to and in conflict with the norms of respectable femininity, functioned to confirm these norms, attesting to the value of "traditional" domestic arrangements that implied little freedom or independence for women. Mrs. Fleming was "A Woman Who Made It Alone," ranching and farming near Brooks, Alberta, and there were numerous stories of her efforts to "show the world that anything a man could do she could do better."[67] She put on men's clothing, and did farm work including irrigating her fields and raising hogs. But her behaviour was cast as decidedly peculiar, and the stories surrounding her emphasized the difficulties of a women on her own, such as when she was once stranded on her roof when she was hammering shingles and the ladder blew down.

The problem of excess "bachelors" in Western Canada was in part addressed through schemes to attract white women as domestic labourers, as it was widely acknowledged that their home-making skills would soon be put to good use in the homes of their new husbands. Scottish correspondent Jessie Saxby reported from the North-West Territories in 1888 that the region was a true "woman's paradise," and she quoted a Canadian gentleman of "influence and education" who said that what was needed most there was a "cargo of home-loving girls."[68] "The want of home life is keenly felt as a very great calamity by those western settlers," wrote Saxby. "[T]here seems about one woman to every fifty men, and I believe the old country could confer no greater boon upon this fine young country than by sending in thousands of our 'rosebud girls' to soften and sweeten life in the Wild West." These women, who would "get the men," in the words of Interior Minister Oliver, were thought essential to the stability, prosperity, and growth of the region. The labour of the women on the family farms was vital, as was their reproductive work, and in turn the work that the resulting children would contribute. Great Britain was the main source of women domestic labourers until the mid-1920s.[69] The process was fuelled by the myth that emerged in the mid-nineteenth century of the "redundant" or "surplus" women of Britain.[70] They were popularly referred to as "stock," essential to the objective of reaching a heterosexual balance, and they were vital to the reproduction of the "race."[71] Single women were not encouraged or assisted to immigrate to Canada in any role other than as domestic labourers.

The plethora of single males was also addressed through farm journal depictions of the lonely, unkempt bachelor who required "a broad-

An excess of single males among the newcomer population was seen as a potential source of danger and subversion of the monogamous foundation for Western Canada. The "bachelor" problem was addressed through various schemes and incentives. These young men in Saskatoon took their own initiative, likely preparing this postcard for their friends and relatives back home.

(Saskatoon Public Library Local History Room LH 3348)

shouldered, stirring wife, who will keep the house in order, as well as the husband who owns it."[72] "The want of feminine influence," wrote Jessie Saxby, "tends to make men (so they acknowledge to me) restless, dissatisfied, reckless and godless."[73] Through marriage the bachelor would be transformed into "one of the lords of creation." Bachelors' balls were held in many centres in the west. At Rosser, Manitoba, according to the local history, the bachelors "seemed to organize themselves into bands for the purpose of competing each with the other as to which could put on the most successful or elaborate 'Ball.' These separate tribes were known as the Bachelors of East Rosser, Bachelors of South Rosser, and Bachelors of West Rosser and their invitation cards so designated them."[74]

At one 1884 Edmonton district "Bach Ball," a transparency was displayed "bearing the legend most suggestive at a bachelor's ball, '1884–Leap Year.'"[75] (February 29th of a leap year was the traditional time when women in British society could propose marriage, a custom sometimes referred to more recently in the United States and Canada as "Sadie Hawkins Day.") Dancing (the quadrille, waltz, polka, cotillion, lancers, schottische, varsovienne, gallop, reel of eight, Sicilian circle, Virginia reel, etc.) began at eight-thirty and continued until morning with but a midnight intermission for supper.

Various ideas were proposed to address the marriage needs of the bachelors of the North-West Territories, including the 1887 "Jubilee Marriage Scheme" of C. F. Lewis, the Canadian Pacific Railway (CPR) agent at Indian Head, published in a brochure entitled *A Revolution: The Worlds' Return Rebate Marriage Certificate or the Want of the West.*[76] The problem, as Lewis saw it, was that the single men of the west could not afford a trip to the east or overseas to find wives, let alone the expense of a return trip for two. He proposed that single males be offered tickets with a return rebate that would allow men returning with wives on the CPR free of charge. Tickets would be issued to eastern destinations, and on the reverse side of each ticket would be a marriage certificate, to be properly filled in and signed by the bride and groom, officiating clergyman, and two witnesses. When these documents were presented, the ticket agent would issue two free tickets to the newlyweds. The plan received widespread and favourable press coverage, although it does not appear that the CPR ever adopted the plan. The proposed scheme is "becoming famous," it was reported in the Regina *Leader*; it was a "Boon to Bachelors."[77] It was also noted in the *Leader* that the St. John *Telegraph* had thrown "cold water on the proposal. It remarks that 'It is a very ingenious scheme, but it will not work. All the Bluenose girls would be shy of a man who came 3,000 miles with a blank marriage certificate in his pocket.'"[78] But the *Leader* advised the hopeful groom to keep the marriage certificate/ticket rebate in his pocket "until he has gone through the 'monkey business' and popped the momentous question. Then he can produce his ticket, go to the minister and return to the North-West with triumph and a wife. Nothing easier."

By the 1890s there was agitation for a tax on unmarried males in Western Canada, and such a tax was introduced in Montana in 1922. A three-dollar "bachelor tax" applied to every unmarried male in the state over the age of twenty-one but the measure was short-lived; it was declared unconstitutional a year later.[79] In Canada the extent to which homesteads were taken up by bachelors was criticized. According to one critic, there was one bachelor shack after another with no "clothes hanging out to dry on the line, or other evidences of progress, family life and civilization"; there were fake homesteads and gopher farms without "horses and cows and women and babies."[80] Bachelor homesteaders were "merely sitting in idleness and dirt on their claims. As a rule, they have but little inducement to work. Some go to town and get drunk and gamble, etc."[81] Bachelor "hired hands" were increasingly censured after the turn of the century as undesirable elements in rural communities. By the early twentieth century, the harvest excursions from Eastern Canada, made up of mainly young single men, were cast as an undesirable force of mischief, mayhem, and (even worse) a threat to respectable women. In August 1908 it was reported that harvesters on their way west at Port Arthur were charged with "stripping and photographing a young woman."[82] That same summer a married woman travelling from Halifax to Edmonton to meet her husband "went insane," according to newspaper reports, "as a result of the lawlessness displayed on the harvest excursion trains from the Maritime provinces."[83] As historian Lyle Dick has argued, there were also deep-seated concerns about the potential threat that bachelors posed to the heterosexual order.[84]

The polygamous challenge to the monogamous west, that became particularly threatening with the arrival of the Latter Day Saints, was fought on a number of fronts. Polygamy was condemned in the press, as mentioned in chapter two. Polygamy was also discussed with disgust in advice literature for Canadian women, indicating that it was perceived as a very real threat. In *The Physical Life of Woman: Advice to the Maiden, Wife and Mother* readers were informed that "such practices lead to physical degradation. The woman who acknowledges more than one husband is generally sterile; the man who has several wives has usually a weakly offspring, principally males...The Mormons of Utah would soon sink into a state of Asiatic effeminacy were they left to themselves."[85] The idea that Mormon polygamy led to a "degenerate," "feeble" and "ill-looking race of children" abounded in the anti-polygamy US press. Some "experts" claimed the Mormons had principally male children, others that they had mainly female offspring. A surgeon for the US army who visited Salt Lake City wrote in 1863 in an article published in *Canada Lancet* that "Under the Polygamic system, the feeble virility of the male, and the precocity of the female, become notorious. The natural equilibrium of the sexes being disturbed, mischief of this kind must ensue; as a consequence, more than two-thirds of the births are females, while the offspring, though numerous, are not long lived, the mortality in infantine life being very much greater than in monogamous society."[86]

Despite the widespread censure of polygamy in Canada, parliamentarians and legal officials learned not long after the arrival of the Mormons that Canadian law had to be amended in order to criminalize polygamy. When this came to light, and when suspicions were aroused that Mormons continued to practice polygamy, steps were taken to amend the Criminal Code. As mentioned in chapter two, Mormon leaders were told at the time of their meeting with Prime Minister John A. Macdonald that they could not continue to practice polygamy, and they could not bring their present plural wives with them to Canada. There were suspicions, however, that plural marriages continued. "Representations" reached the Department of the Interior early in 1890 that the Mormons were engaging in "polygamy and unlawful cohabitation."[87] In a letter to Mormon leader Charles O. Card, Deputy Interior Minister A. M. Burgess warned, "There is likely to be a strong public feeling against your people unless it can be clearly established at once that these statements are absolutely untrue." Burgess reminded Card that while in Ottawa he had given Sir John A. Macdonald and the minister of the interior assurances that the Mormons understood that they were coming to country where the law did not permit polygamy. Card's reply was carefully worded, and did not likely provide the degree of reassurance sought by Burgess.[88] He wrote, "It can be clearly established that the alleged crimes to which you refer of polygamy and cohabitation are not practiced either in or out of Cardston in Canada. About one third of our people live out upon their ranches and all are scattered for several miles around. I am confident our people could not practice either polygamy or cohabitation without the North West Police knowing it." Card further wrote that his people "understood too well the laws of the Dominion of Canada to infringe upon them."

The Mormons understood the laws of Canada well, as Card maintained, and were aware that there was no statute that specifically prohibited polygamy, despite the confident assertions of Macdonald, Burgess, and one parliamentarian who declared, "Polygamy is forbidden by our laws, and whoever practices it infringes them."[89] It was the enterprising Anthony Maitland Stenhouse who publicly pointed out that while there was a law forbidding bigamy (and Stenhouse agreed with this, as bigamy meant criminal deception), polygamy according to the Mormon faith could be practiced "only with the consent of the women interested and is therefore sinless." Stenhouse believed Canadian law could not prevent a man from marrying two women at the same moment, so long as neither of the wives preceded the other, and he declared that "as an undergraduate in matrimony, I propose to test the law as soon as I have found the ladies."[90]

At that time the Criminal Code stated that "everyone who being married, marries any other person during the life of the former husband or wife, whether the second marriage takes place in Canada or elsewhere, is guilty of a felony, and is liable to seven years' imprisonment." The law did not cover Stenhouse's proposal, which was to marry two women "at the same moment." He would not be already married, and therefore would not be marrying another person "during the life of the former... wife."[91] Legislation designed to address Mormon polygamy was introduced in the House of Commons on 7 February 1890. It was initially proposed that "this section shall not apply to any Indian belonging to a tribe or band among whom polygamy is not contrary to law, nor to any person not a subject of Her Majesty, and not resident in Canada," but this was struck out.[92] As one senator explained in the senate debate on the issue: "I think that is a very dangerous exception to make, because it may have the effect of excepting the very class to whom the Bill is intended to apply." It is ironic that, as discussed in chapter six, the only person convicted under this amendment to the Criminal Code, designed to prohibit Mormon polygamy, was a Kainai man, Bear's Shin Bone.

The Act passed on 16 April 1890 was designed to address the situation proposed by Stenhouse, that of marrying two women at the same moment. Minister of Justice Sir John Thompson explained, "Section 8 [that became Section 10] is intended to extend the prohibition of bigamy. It is to make a second marriage punishable...whether the marriage took place in Canada or elsewhere, or whether the marriages takes [sic] place simultaneously or on the same day. In [the latter case]...the parties were not punishable under the present law."[93] Every person found guilty was liable to seven years' imprisonment. Section 11 dealt with polygamy and it was specifically directed at the Mormons. Canadian lawmakers examined the US legislation (Edmunds-Tucker Act), where it had proven difficult to get convictions, and aimed at convicting on the basis of cohabitation, attacking the Mormons' private ceremonies.[94] The amendments to the Canadian Criminal Code stipulated that "Everyone who practices, or by rites, ceremonies, forms, rules or customs of any denomination, sect or society, religious or secular, or by any form of contract, or by mere mutual consent, or by any other method whatsoever, and whether in a manner recognized by law as a binding form of marriage or not, agrees or consents to practice or enter into a) any form of polygamy: or—b) Any kind of conjugal union with more than one person at the same time: or—c) What is known among the persons called Mormons as spiritual or plural marriage...is guilty of a misdemeanour and liable to imprisonment for five years and to a fine of five hundred dollars."[95] The clause "recognized by law as a binding form of marriage or not" was perhaps intended to address Lord Penzance's finding in the Hyde case, in which he decided that Mormon marriage, even if monogamous, was not marriage according to English law. The Hyde marriage might have been binding by *lex loci*—the place where it was contracted—but English law did not acknowledge it as marriage.[96]

It is interesting to note that D.W. Davis was then the Member of Parliament for southern Alberta, where the Mormons were settling at the time of the debate about Mormon polygamy. He might have been somewhat uncomfortable with the condemnation of plural wives as discussed earlier in the previous chapter, as he had recently abandoned or divorced according to Aboriginal law his first wife, and married a white woman. He did not contribute to the debate. Indeed, his most notable contribution to the House was an evening in April 1888 when, according to the *Calgary Herald*, he danced a "Blackfoot war dance... [jumping] along the table on which he was performing, uttering blood curdling yells. Sir John, who came in to witness the dance, enjoyed it immensely."[97]

To ensure that the Mormons had abandoned polygamy, the NWMP kept close surveillance on their communities, gathering information from their gentile neighbours. S. B. Steele of the NWMP reported in 1889 that almost everyone in the district believed the Mormons continued to practice polygamy in secret, and "there are many reasons for believing such to be the case, the number of women of the same age, or nearly so, in several of the houses, the fact that several of them have pretended to be married to certain parties who were away and although the men have been absent for more than a year, children being born in the interval, as many as fourteen months after the departure of the so-called husband... Constables and others have reported that they have seen members of the Mormon Church using the same room and bed as the women whose supposed husbands were away from the district."[98] In 1890, following the amendments to the Canadian Criminal Code prohibiting polygamy, the Mormon Church announced that no further plural marriages would be solemnized. Yet suspicions continued, as did surveillance. A priest who worked with the Blackfoot was sceptical of government efforts to ensure that the Mormons were conforming to the law, reporting that government agents took great care to announce the day they would officially visit, permitting the Mormon men to disappear for a while with their "surplus" wives.[99] It was well known by the police that some Mormon men had one wife in Canada, and others in the United States, but most were thought to be abiding by Canadian law. But the police suspected and gathered evidence to the effect that a few continued to marry and to have more than one wife resident in Alberta. Richard B. Deane of the NWMP reported in 1899 that Charles McCarty, a prominent man among the Mormons, "lived in one room last winter with two women, sisters apparently, one of whom was known as Mrs. McCarty and the other as Mrs. Maude Mercer."[100] The previous summer the corporal who reported to Deane was introduced to the latter as "Mrs. McCarty," which mistake, the corporal wrote, "'appeared to cause some consternation' and was explained away." Also provided as evidence was an extract from the *Salt Lake Herald*, republished in the *Cardston Record*, which announced from the town of American Fork, Utah, that in January 1899 "Charles and Maude McCarty from Cardston, Alberta, Canada, are visiting here at present." Evidence was also taken from a Cardston resident that McCarty had two wives. It appears no action was taken, however, as Deane noted that they needed to obtain evidence of the marriage ceremony to which Charles and Maude were parties, and that allegedly being sisters, the two women had a "reasonable excuse for living in one house, and further, no Mormon would give evidence in a case of this kind unless cornered very tightly." Deane wrote, "These people are up to all kinds of dodges to shield polygamy, which necessity taught them in the U.S.A."[101] There is evidence that a few continued to enter into plural marriages, particularly church leaders who circumvented the law by keeping a family in Canada, one in the United States, and one in Mexico, thereby "remaining…monogamist in the eyes of each country."[102] In her memoirs, the plural but abandoned wife of a leading Mormon educator who farmed in Alberta wrote that, around 1910, one of the younger wives of her husband "had been induced to leave the educational field where she was an eminent success, and move to the Canadian ranch where her work changed to supervising a kitchen and cooking for hired men."[103] Yet no Mormons were ever prosecuted in Canada for polygamy.

In the Alberta Mormon colonies, information about plural wives was kept from the following generations. According to historian Dan Erickson, "They limited public discussion; the church's new policy was to suppress the memory of its polygamous past and to assimilate into pluralistic western society."[104] In the 1900 publication, *Picturesque Cardston and Environments: A Story of Colonization and Progress in Southern Alberta*, there is a great deal of discussion about how the Mormons, a "patriotic community," battled against "bigotry and deviltry, for the rights of

Matriarchs of the Cardston, Alberta Mormon settlement, ca. 1900. Zina Young Card is in the back row in the middle. (GAA NA-147-4)

conscience and against oppression," but nothing at all about polygamy.[105] Although polygamy may no longer have been officially sanctioned, however, the concept was still defended by prominent Mormons in Alberta into the twentieth century. In 1904 Mormon David H. Elton, editor of a weekly paper called the *Alberta Star*, spoke to a journalist for the *Toronto World* and said, "I believe in polygamy. I believe it is authorized by the Bible and by the revelations of the church," but he insisted that "at no time has any Mormon lived, associated, or cohabited with more than one wife in Canada."[106] Elton denied that there were "More women around our homes than around the homes of Gentiles," and declared that this was "another fallacy born of malice and hearsay."

Through a 1901 amendment to the marriage ordinance of the North-West Territories, Doukhobors as well as Quakers were permitted to marry "according to the rites and ceremonies of their own religion or creed."[107] No less than eight days notice of the marriage had to be given in writing by the parties to a marriage commissioner, and after the ceremony they had to sign a declaration of their marriage in the presence of two witnesses; within eight days this declaration had to be delivered to the marriage commissioner. The notice of intention and declaration would then be transmitted to the registrar of births, marriages, and deaths.[108] As Nancy Cott explains of the tolerance of consent or self-marriages in the United States, this did not represent a retreat of the authority of the state. Rather, recognition of its validity drew the couples in question into the obligations set by the law for married people.[109] There was debate, however, about the amendment in the assembly of the North-West Territories. The Attorney General explained that the object was to meet the aversion of the Doukhobors to the present law by allowing them to carry out their ceremonies in their own way. This would result in the enforcement of the marriage law; the Doukhobors would not have to disobey their own convictions, and would have no excuse for not obeying the laws of the country.[110] R.B. Bennett (later prime minister), Calgary Member of the Legislative Assembly, was "opposed to making the marriage law too lax in order to conform to the views of different peoples; he held that we should rather make them conform to our laws."[111] Bennett understood from magazine articles that the Doukhobors left Russia "largely because of the marriage law," and "he thought they ought to proceed carefully as it would be a dangerous thing to encourage indiscriminate marrying." Doukhobors, "or any other kind of 'boers,'" Bennett said, "should know that this country has institutions which must be respected."[112]

The amendment passed, however, despite Bennett's objections. A similar measure was passed in the legislature of British Columbia, but not until 1959. Until that date, BC Doukhobor couples there were not regarded as married outside of their own community, and their children were technically "illegitimate."[113] Doukhobor divorce was not as easy to deal with, and they continued to practice their own laws of divorce. As with the Mormons, the Mounties were used to patrol the Doukhobor settlements in order to gather evidence. To discourage their divorce laws, three Doukhobor "bigamists" were charged and convicted in Yorkton, Saskatchewan, in 1911. In one case the marriage of the accused and his first wife was celebrated through an event at her parent's home.[114] The groom lived with his first wife for two years and they had two children. When the first wife refused to leave their settlement and move to a farm with her husband, he subsequently remarried, although without ceremony, and he had a child with his second wife. The first wife gave evidence that as her husband left her she considered herself divorced and free to remarry. The second wife stated that she considered herself married to the accused. The Doukhobor women called to the witness box "call themselves by the name of their last male associate and regard the union as valid beyond dispute."[115] The interpreter called to the stand by the defence said that the agreement of the parties to live together, even without witnesses or other ceremonies, was enough to constitute marriage to the Doukhobors. Although the accused was found guilty, it was reported that "the general viewpoint seems to be that...bigamous Doukhobors should not be severely dealt with." The trials and convictions were to serve as a warning that this would not be tolerated. There were calls for a commission to investigate Doukhobor marriage and separation.

Missionaries and Anglo-Canadian women's organizations proposed a number of remedies for the alleged evils of Ukrainian marriage. Suggested measures included prohibiting the marriage of Ukrainian girls before the age of seventeen, as requested by a 1913 petition to the Alberta government from the Women's Canadian Club of Calgary.[116] They also asked for residential schools for Ukrainian girls where they could be taught domestic science. The Women's Christian Temperance Union distributed leaflets in the Ukrainian language outlining the evils of child marriage. At one Methodist mission to Ukrainians in Alberta, suitable marriages were arranged by the missionaries. In 1915 a Methodist worker described how a husband was selected for their maid: "Last winter we had the experience of deciding the delicate question of a marriage proposal for our maid. After several suitors had come, a young Methodist Ruthenian came along and asked for Pokeetza in the presence of Miss Yarwood and myself. Being assured that Pokeetza would make a good wife for the right man, Kepha promised to love her and treat her well. The conclusion was that in about two weeks they were married at her home by Rev. C.H. Lawford, M.D. Miss Yarwood and myself having the honor of being bridesmaids." [117]

The west appears to have been a prime destination for those who wanted to start afresh and escape the confines and restrictions of marital rules and laws, but this freedom did not materialize. Government, churches, community pressure, and the law all reached out to ensure conformity. Rules regarding "mixed" religious marriages were not relaxed. This was behind a terrible 1899 tragedy in Edmonton when a young couple committed suicide together, poisoning themselves with strychnine in a swampy willow bluff northeast of the town. Lottie Brunette, twenty-one, was a Catholic, and W.P. Rowland, twenty-two, was a Protestant, and strong objections were made to their marriage. It was reported that in their last letters "they refer to these objections and state that if they cannot live together they will die together."[118]

For all of the newcomers, as well as the Aboriginal people of the North-West Territories, the Canadian Criminal Code, particularly the bigamy laws, and the near impossibility of obtaining divorces in Canada, as well as the refusal to recognize the validity of divorces obtained in the United States, combined to ensure the primacy of monogamy. As historian Cynthia Comacchio has written, "The inflexible divorce law was another available means to enforce standards of morality, domestic life, and sexual conduct, strengthening 'norms' and actively establishing the hegemony of the middle-class family model."[119] Deserted spouses could not remarry unless "on reasonable grounds [he or she] believes his wife or her husband to be dead," or if the "wife or husband has been continually absent for seven years...and he or she is not proved to have known that his wife or her husband was alive at any time during those seven years."[120] Even if a spouse, deserted for seven years, had no evidence at the time of a second marriage that her first husband was alive, she could be convicted if she "had the means of acquiring knowledge of that fact had she chosen to make use of such means."[121] Anyone committing bigamy was liable to seven years' imprisonment.

Deserted spouses were in an unfortunate limbo, and for women this could be particularly difficult, as they often had children and had few options for employment or support. Desertion was not considered grounds for divorce as Canadian legislators were determined to permit no grounds for divorce other than adultery. The 1890 case of Emily Herald Walker of Hamilton illustrates the indeterminate state a woman could find herself in. Reporting the case in the *Macleod Gazette* was a headline reading "Poor Emily Herald: She is Married and Yet Not Married, But Cannot Marry Again."[122] In 1884 Emily Herald and Alfred Percy Walker took the train from Hamilton to Dundas, Ontario, where they were married, and immediately after returned by train where they parted at the door of her family home. The marriage took place without the consent or knowledge of her mother, and her father had died two weeks earlier. She was some months under the age of twenty-one at the time of the marriage. Although Alfred visited Emily several times at her family home, the marriage was never consummated or—as delicately reported in the press—there were no "accompaniments of matrimony" beyond the ceremony.[123] Walker left for Texas shortly after the marriage and Emily received one or two letters, but no indication that he "intended to claim her or treat her as his wife."[124] The case was debated at great length in the Senate and to a lesser extent in the House of Commons. The Senate Committee recommended that Emily Walker be granted a divorce. Those in favour argued that she was a minor, that there was no consent of the parents, that the marriage lacked consummation, and that the husband had deserted the wife. Senator James Lougheed (Calgary) argued that Alfred Walker had not done his husbandly duties, as he had "never provided for her a house; he never made any preparation to give her a home; he never intimated that he would support her; he never spoke to her about future intentions." He had only casually visited and then deserted her altogether.[125] Lougheed used the case to urge that Canadian divorce laws be relaxed. Supporters also argued that "this girl, driven to despair, might commit adultery, to get a legal divorce."[126] The case for the other side rested almost entirely on the argument that there were no grounds for divorce in Canada other than adultery, and that deciding otherwise would create a dangerous precedent.[127] This side also attacked the character and integrity of Emily Walker, contending that she was disappointed with Alfred's low income. Senator Kaulbach, who opposed granting a divorce, argued that Emily Walker was "the transgressor." She was not entitled to any sympathy, as "she has not shown that she has done her part to live with this man and to observe the solemn vows that she took on herself." She had not performed her wifely duties: "It is a strange thing if, after being married, and he coming to the house some weeks or months afterwards, that there was no cohabitation. It seems to be contrary to the husband's rights and duties, and contrary to the obligations imposed upon him and her by the marriage ceremony that there was no cohabitation. This is a matter which does not tend in her favor, but rather condemns her."

In the House of Commons, Minister of Justice Sir John Thompson opposed the divorce, stating that he objected to divorce on general principles, and in this case he argued that the divorce was requested "simply because she found that she was married to a person not able to support her as well as she hoped he would be."[128] Prime Minister John A. Macdonald also opposed any relaxation of the rule that divorces could be granted only with proof of adultery, and in this case maintained that there was no such proof. Macdonald declared, "I think it would be a great misfortune for this country, it would redound to its discredit, it would promote demoralisation to an enormous extent, it would bring on the evils we see on the other side of the line, if we did not adhere to the law of the land, and the law of Scriptures as well, that marriage can only be dissolved for the cause of adultery."[129] The divorce was refused, the application being defeated by a two-to-one majority in the House of Commons.[130]

Letters from across the west from deserted spouses, asking if they were free to remarry, were frequently sent to the Department of Justice in Ottawa, and although responses were generally prefaced with "it would not be proper for the Minister of Justice to advise private citizens upon legal questions," such advice was usually given.[131] In 1921 Mrs. Hazel Cooke wrote from Drumheller, Alberta, asking if she could get a divorce as her husband deserted her and their child seven years earlier. She had not taken "one cent" from her husband, and pointed out that "I have not even known any thing of him or where he is or has been."[132] The reply from E.L. Newcombe, deputy minister of justice, was that she could not, under the laws of the Dominion, obtain a divorce on the ground of desertion, "even if you have not heard from him for seven years."[133] In 1912, Calgarian Florence Fraser sought advice from the minister of justice as her husband had deserted her and she had learned that he had married her under an assumed name.[134] She asked, "Am I legally married? If so, could I procure a divorce for desertion and non-support?" In 1910, at Fort Macleod, she had married a member of the NWMP who claimed his name was A.S. Fraser. They lived very happily together until May 1911, when he was sent to the Royal Coronation in London, England, and deserted the force shortly after landing. Florence Fraser wrote, "He did not write for about 4 months, and then only said how sorry he was etc. Since then I had about 2 letters, one admitting he married me under a false name, and the other asking me for some money. His correct name is Fred Jenkins. I can prove this. He has never sent me support since he left for the Coronation." The reply was that while the minister of justice did not advise private citizens upon legal questions, "I do not think the fact that your husband married you under an assumed name would of itself render the marriage void."[135]

In 1913, Jeanne Josephine Ida Baussart, a Catholic, married Carl Schlosser in a Protestant ceremony at Medicine Hat. Schlosser deserted her one year later, and she knew only that he was living somewhere in the United States. In 1917, J.A. Therien, an Oblate priest from St. Paul des Métis, wrote to the minister of justice on behalf of Jeanne to say that her family had concluded that the husband had left her for good, and she had two children to support. He wanted to know if it was possible to annul the marriage, as "according to the law of the Catholic Church this marriage is not valid." The priest stressed that the young woman was poor and could not afford any legal costs. The reply from the deputy minister was that Baussart/Schlosser could not be released from the marriage bond except by a divorce, which would be "more expensive and troublesome than this young woman or her friends would be able to undertake. Lawyer's fees would have to be incurred and formal proceedings instituted, witnesses examined before the Senate Committee, etc., and I am afraid, and you yourself suggest, that such proceedings would be out of the question for these poor people."[136] The deputy minister did not believe that a petition of divorce would be granted in this case.

Matilda Manderfield, originally from Sweden, arrived with her husband Peter from Minnesota in 1913, and they homesteaded together at St. Victor, Saskatchewan.[137] In 1915 he deserted her and their three-year-old daughter. She remained on the land, carrying out the homestead requirements to gain patent to the land, but was ultimately refused. To receive a patent she had to be naturalized as a British subject, and she was notified in 1920 by the office of the secretary of state for Canada that "being a married woman you are in a state 'of disability' under the terms...of the Naturalization Act for 1919, and are therefore ineligible for naturalization." Peter Manderfield was born in Wisconsin and was thus a citizen of the United States. If she could prove that he was naturalized, then she would automatically also be naturalized, but she had not heard from him since he left. The injustice of the case deeply disturbed Judge C.E.D. Wood of the District Court of Weyburn, Saskatchewan, and he wrote in 1921 to the undersecretary of state for Canada to explain Matilda Manderfield's predicament. He was aware, however, that little could be done beyond changing the legislation, or presuming her husband's death after an absence of seven years in order that she could be deemed a widow, and the disability as a married woman could subsequently be removed.[138] Both took time, and "she would probably have lost all rights to the land under the Dominion Lands Act, and her work on the land would be thrown away." Yet this special plea must have helped Matilda Manderfield, as she did receive title to this land.

A husband or wife could decamp to the United States and acquire a divorce there, but the deserted spouse in Canada was not free to remarry. Such a case was cited in *Crankshaw's Criminal Code of Canada*. A woman obtained a divorce in Michigan, and shortly thereafter her first husband in Ontario received the divorce decree.[139] Believing himself divorced, he married another woman, and was found guilty of bigamy as the American divorce obtained by his first wife was ruled invalid. Even if an accused "honestly believed the divorce was valid and that he was free to marry again, it was recognized that this was no defence in law, the divorce in fact being invalid according to English law."[140]

This was the same situation that Regina resident Harry Miller Ingram described in his 1916 letter to the minister of justice.[141] In 1907 he had married Hope Jessie Hall in Toronto. In 1908 the couple moved to Regina and that year she deserted Ingram, securing a divorce in Fargo, North Dakota, in 1910. Although Ingram received a summons from his wife's attorney to appear at the hearing, he did not attend, although he wrote for and received a letter indicating that the divorce had been granted. He wrote to ask if he "was compelled by the laws of Canada to remain unmarried the rest of my life," or could an annulment be granted after seven years of separation. He wanted advice as to the "proper procedure for clearing myself of this unnatural and unfair handicap which my own country has placed upon me. I am a loyal Canadian but loyalty demands protection in return for protection." The Department of Justice declined to advise Ingram, suggesting only that he consult a solicitor.

The churches did not accept American divorces or subsequent remarriages. No divorces were permitted or recognized in the Catholic faith. American divorce and remarriage would be considered by this faith to be "living in adultery," and Catholics who attempted such a course of action faced another level of public humiliation—excommunication. A Kingston, Ontario, woman was excommunicated from her church in 1889 because she had been "notoriously defying the laws of God and the church by living in adultery with a man not her husband."[142] In her defence the woman had produced a bill of divorce procured from a court in the United States, and she also produced a marriage certificate from the ceremony undergone by herself and partner by a Protestant minister in a neighbouring town. However, "this but added religious insult to her immorality for there is no such thing as divorce under the Christian law." The effect of the woman's public admonishment was "visible upon the congregation in various forms of emotion and has caused great consternation to marriage under similar circumstances amongst persons of high social standing."

Wives did not always wish to accompany their homesteading husbands and undertake years of arduous labour, and these men were, of course, not free to remarry. B. Switzer, a farmer at Court, Saskatchewan, who was originally from New York, was in just such a situation.[143] He wrote to the Department of Justice in 1916 to say that he had sent for his wife from time to time, but she refused to accompany him. Four of their children lived in Saskatchewan, in "different boarding houses," and two remained with her in New York. He claimed his wife was living an "immoral" life, and he wanted to remarry in Canada and settle down with his children on the farm. Switzer was afraid, however, that his wife would lay a charge of bigamy against him. "P. S.," he concluded in his letter, "On account that I have not any money is the reason I cannot go to the U. S. A. to apply for a divorce in the proper legal manner." Once again the reply was simply that Switzer should seek a reliable solicitor, but there was likely very little that could be done for him, as he would have been guilty of bigamy under Canadian law should he have remarried.

While the monogamous model of marriage was successfully imposed on the diverse peoples of Western Canada through the Criminal Code, legislation, the churches, print media, community censure, and other means, there were organized, vocal critics of the inequities and the injustices who achieved a measure of success. Early twentieth-century reformers across the prairie provinces advocated the reinstatement of dower to ensure that women were not economically dependent on their husbands. They were not objecting to the institution of monogamous marriage; rather, they wanted men to live up to the vows they made. As one dower rights supporter wrote, "how can a man say or think he is doing right by his wife (the one he has pledged himself to do right by with the most sacred ties) and has also solemnly said 'with all my worldly goods I thee endow,' when he sells the home over her head and that of his children, thinking they have no right to one dollar of it, after she has worked with him through years of poverty and helped him get what he now calls his?"[144] Significant reforms were achieved across the west in the years of the First World War and immediately thereafter, although the legislation was not satisfactory or far-reaching enough to satisfy many reformers.

The homesteads-for-women campaign, which materialized around 1907 and all but disappeared by 1914 was completely unsuccessful. The leaders of this campaign had decided on the strategy of asking that the privilege of homesteading be granted to "all women of British birth who have resided in Canada for one year," and not to "foreign born" women. This may have narrowed the appeal of their cause, but the responses of the legislators and politicians they had to approach for redress indicate that women were not to be permitted to deviate from the ideal of proper femininity embodied in the idealized monogamous model of marriage in Western Canada.

Monogamous marriage was not ancient, universal, and immutable in the west when that region joined Confederation, and it was only becoming entrenched elsewhere in North America and Europe at that time. Until the mid-nineteenth century informal, consent marriages persisted, particularly among the non-elites, and there were also means of community recognition of divorce and remarriage. The work of banishing informal marriage and divorce, and imposing monogamous, heterosexual, exclusive and intra-racial marriage on the diverse peoples of the west called for a wide variety of strategies, and there was no single force behind this initiative. Rather, a combined cluster of laws, religious institutions, print media, and community pressure spurred it on. Powerful social mores stigmatized Aboriginal women and their non-Aboriginal partners. The land policy that unified the arable west exemplified and was intended to replicate the gender roles encoded in the monogamous model, of patriarchal heads of family and dependent wives. This was cast as the "natural" gender system that had to be preserved. A variety of pressures and inducements to marry, including bachelor balls and a "rebate" scheme, were placed on single white men, and some, such as government farm instructors, were compelled to marry. Single women who had ambitions other than marriage were discouraged as immigrants to the west, although large numbers were imported as domestics on the understanding that they would not remain single for long.

It took a great deal of time and effort to deal with the challenge of Mormon polygamy. An amendment to the federal Criminal Code was required, and when that did not satisfy suspicions, the NWMP kept close watch on their communities. Legislation was required for the Doukhobors and Quakers, permitting them to marry according to their own customs while drawing them into the obligations set by the state for married people. For all Canadians the divorce and bigamy laws and other associated legislation ensured the ascendancy of the monogamous model. Deserted spouses were in an unfortunate limbo, unable to divorce or to remarry. The highest officials in the land, including prime minister John A. Macdonald, opposed any relaxation of the rules of divorce, as it would "bring on the evils we see on the other side of the line," as quoted earlier. Aboriginal marriages and divorces presented the most substantial body of dissenters from the monogamous model, and their marital terrain appeared the most chaotic. As will be seen, efforts to alter this conjugal landscape and impose the monogamous model were the most concerted and insidious.

FOUR

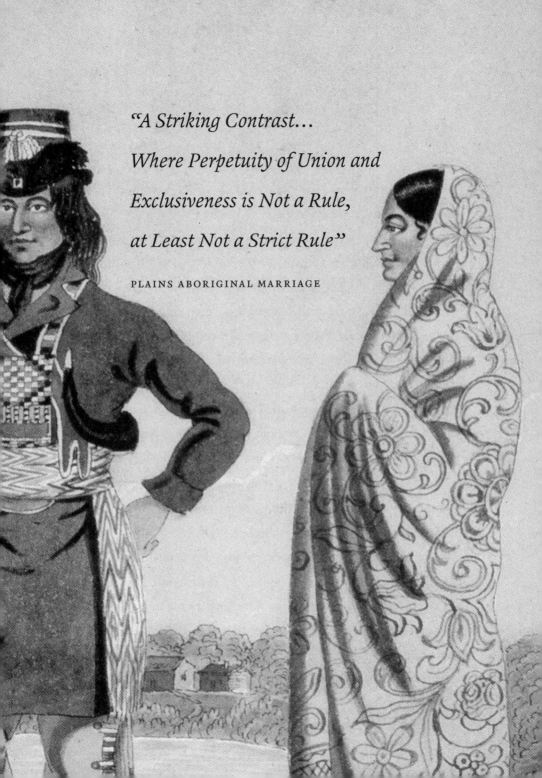

"A Striking Contrast…
Where Perpetuity of Union and
Exclusiveness is Not a Rule,
at Least Not a Strict Rule"

PLAINS ABORIGINAL MARRIAGE

IN HIS DECISION IN THE 1884 CASE *Fraser v. Pouliot,* heard before
the Quebec Superior Court, Judge Alexander Cross found "the relations of male and female in savage life" to form "a striking contrast"
to his own idealized version of marriage in a "civilized" or Christian
country.[1] The contrasts were so marked, that Cross found he could not
regard this as marriage at all, but rather as "concubinage." Aboriginal
laws of marriage and divorce did indeed form a striking contrast, but I
will argue in this chapter that the term "marriage" can apply, although
in legal decisions and in the work of scholars to the present day this
is disputed. Aboriginal people of Western Canada had marriage laws
that were complex, diverse, flexible, and adaptable.[2] They were not
static and immutable but evolved and changed. Plains societies experienced a period of rapid and extreme change during the nineteenth
century, and it is widely theorized that their marriage laws changed
as well.[3] Marriage was deeply embedded in the complex kinship
systems that characterized Aboriginal societies, and which established
patterns of co-operation and respect, as well as standards of conduct.
Kin terms classified relatives, but more importantly they specified
patterns of rights, obligations, proper conduct, and attitudes. In
Aboriginal communities there was a consensus about proper behaviour
and shared responsibilities of wives and husbands, daughters, sons,

sons-in-law, daughters-in-law, and other relatives.[4] There were fundamental differences between the characteristics of the kinship systems
of Euro-North Americans and those of Aboriginal North Americans.

A first step in understanding this, as anthropologist Raymond DeMallie
has pointed out, is to think about biological categories and kin categories independently of one another.[5] While the biological relationship
between parents and children is universally recognized in Aboriginal
America, an individual could have several people that he or she called
"father," "mother," "son," or "daughter." The terms "mother" and "father"
included a mother or father's same-sex siblings and parallel cousins.
"Thus in most American Indian societies," DeMallie writes, "an individual has many mothers and fathers. This does not mean, for example,
that mother's sisters are *like* mothers; they *are* mothers. In other words
the status of the mother is defined in terms of patterns of relations surrounding, but not limited to, the act of giving birth. The biological mother
is no more or less a mother to her children than are all those women she
calls sister."[6] Kin relationships that appeared "fictive" from a European
perspective were considered genuine and permanent in Aboriginal
societies.

Marriage was central to the kinship systems of Aboriginal societies,
as relatives were divided into two basic categories: those related by marriage and those related by birth. The nuclear family of a wife, husband,
and children was a fundamental unit, but extended families were also
important social and residential units, and there were also polygamous
families. Oral traditions along with foundational and teaching texts orig-
inated kinship and instituted marriage. The story of the White Buffalo
Woman, for example, "presents a charter for the Lakota way of life."[7]
The sacred woman of the story names the kin relationships and explains
obligations among kin. Sexual intimacy between husband and wife,
rather than promiscuity, is sanctioned in the story. For the Blackfoot
and other Plains people there are similar foundational texts that institute marriage and teach kinship obligations and codes of behaviour.[8] In
the Piikani story of the origin of the sacred Worm Pipe, a devoted
husband mourns for his deceased wife and the mother of their little

son.[9] He goes a great distance and sees fearful sights in order to persuade the spirits to let her return to him. The husband stays four nights in the ghost world before his ghost father-in-law agrees to give him back his wife. The couple is also given the Worm Pipe that the wife carries back to their people. However, the husband is warned to "Take care, now, that you do as I tell you. Do not whip your wife, nor strike her with a knife, nor hit her with fire; for if you do, she will vanish before your eyes and return to the Sand Hills." Shortly after their return the husband told his wife to do something, and when she did not immediately respond, he "picked up a brand from the fire, not that he intended to strike her with it, but he made as if he would hit her, when at once she vanished, and was never seen again."

The Blackfoot's story of the first marriage taught how men needed women's skills, and that men should not make their choice of spouse on the basis of outward appearance and fine clothing.[10] It begins during the time when men and women lived in separate camps—women on one side of Little Bow River and men on the other. The women lived in good lodges, had fine clothing, and possessed plenty of dried meat and berries. The men had no lodges, proper clothing, or moccasins because they could not tan skins and could not sew. The women invited the men to their camp in order to pick out husbands. The chief of the women had very dirty clothes on, and none of the men knew who she was. She picked Old Man (Napi) because he had fine clothes on. But Old Man thought she looked very common; he pulled back and broke away when she took his hand. The chief of the women went to her lodge and instructed the other women not to choose Old Man. When she returned she was in her best costume. Old Man did not recognize her and thought to himself, "Oh! There is the chief of the women. I wish to be her husband." Although Old Man kept stepping in front of her, she picked out another for her husband. Old Man was very angry when all the men were picked except him. The story concluded with the chief of the women saying to him, "'After this you are to be a tree, and stand just where you are now.' Then he became a tree, and he is mad yet, because he is always caving down the bank."[11]

Any brief description of marriage law greatly simplifies a complex arrangement that involved far more than just the spouses. Among the Blackfoot marriages were extended family affairs, both sets of relatives had to give their consent as the families were from then on joined together in a web of kinship that had an influence on how all family members interacted in other social, political, economic, and religious roles. Marriages were generally arranged among the Elders—the parents, relatives, or close friends of the couple to be married. As Chief Red Crow of the Kainai informed Indian Agent R. N. Wilson, the usual custom was for the parents of a girl to choose a young man they thought suitable, and then a friend of the girl's family interviewed the parents of the young man.[12] The girl's relatives first had to discuss the question of blood relationship—cousins of the first degree were ineligible.[13] Age of marriage, according to HBC explorer David Thompson (who was familiar with the Plains people from the mid-1780s to 1812), was about twenty-two for men and, for women, sixteen to eighteen.[14] A daughter might be pledged or betrothed at a young age although the marriage would not take place until she was older, generally in her later teens.[15] An elderly Blackfoot widow, Elk-Hollering-in-the-Water, told anthropologist John Ewers in the 1940s that she was betrothed to a prominent war chief, Bear Chief, when she was seven, but she did not actually join him as a wife until she was seventeen.[16] As will be discussed in detail later, it appears that marriages were contracted at a younger age for both women and men after the onset of the reserve era.

The marriage was validated and the reciprocal obligations of both parties and their extended families established through the exchange of gifts. Plains men did not "purchase" brides as outsiders commonly assumed. The elderly Blackfoot informants to Ewers took great care to remind him that wives were not purchased; rather, they stressed the importance of the *exchange* of gifts in the marriage ceremony.[17] As Plains ethnologist Robert Lowie explained, "There was generally rather an appearance of purchase than the reality. The girl's kin often gave back as much property as they received. The significant thing was an exchange of gifts between the two families. That exchange marked their sanctioning the new bond and cementing a relationship between two groups rather than two persons."[18] The nature of the gift exchange varied considerably depending on the wealth of the families involved. By the mid-nineteenth century the acquisition of horses, and involvement in the buffalo robe trade, had created social stratification in Blackfoot society. The wealthy had the most and the best horses, and they enjoyed greater access to the other good things in life, including the largest lodges and finest clothing. The poor had fewer or inferior horses and were not able to lavish gifts on prospective in-laws. Between persons of importance and wealth, the gift exchange was an elaborate affair, and it was a very simple matter among those of more humble rank. As Red Crow explained, when people were well-to-do, the daughter was sent away with a complete lodge, furniture, horses, saddles, travois, robes, and fine garments— the best their family could produce.[19] Parents of a favourite (*minipoka*) or only daughter would impoverish themselves to send her off in such a style. The next day there was a return of gifts from the family of the son; in particular they strove to give better horses, and in greater numbers.

When it was first decided a couple would marry, it was customary for the parents of the woman to give a pair of moccasins to each member of her intended husband's family. The man gave to his prospective wife many presents for her to distribute among her relatives.[20] It became a matter of pride for the family receiving the first gifts to return gifts of greater value than those received. According to one of anthropologist Esther Goldfrank's Kainai informants in the 1930s, the bride "gets gifts from her parents and other relatives, even friends if they like her and carries them to the boy's parents. They then distribute gifts to their relatives and receive gifts in exchange from [the] boy's relatives. These are given to girl's parents who distribute them. The boy's father tried to outdo the girl's parents...gifts show how much you care for your son or daughter—so then you are a good parent." Horses were the most prized gift of the pre-reserve nineteenth century. Goldfrank was told about the gift exchange of two *minipokas*, or favourite children, Wakes at Night, the daughter of White Buffalo Robe, and her informant, the son of Yellow Wolf: "She brought blankets and about fifteen pair of moccasins, enough for all the members of my family. She brought a pair for me.

She also brought two broken and six unbroken horses. When this gift was sent to White Buffalo Robe, my father-in-law, Wakes at Night, rode in front on a fine saddle horse. She wore a weasel-tail suit and a head-dress. A wagon was loaded with blankets and goods. They were all taken over to White Buffalo Robe."[21] In another example of the wedding of a *minipoka*, the daughter of Big Wolf, thirty head of horses and the Ancient Pipe [a sacred religious pipe] were given to the family of the groom, Parts His Hair, who gave in exchange fifty head of horses and another pipe.[22] Such obligations were ongoing. A son-in-law was expected to share the proceeds from a hunt with his father-in-law and his family. On returning from a successful horse raid or war a husband would give the best horse to his father-in-law, and the second best to his wife's brother. According to Goldfrank, second marriages (following the breakdown or divorce of first marriages) did not involve an exchange of gifts.[23]

An informant to anthropologists Lucien and Jane Hanks, who worked with the Siksika in the 1930s, gave a detailed description of the marriage between a young man and the daughter of a chief. Her father selected the suitable son-in-law, "some good warrior who gets meat, gets up *early*," and then the chief sent an "old man" to take the proposal for union to the chosen man's father. Sometimes such offers were refused, but if the father of the young man said, "That chief is good and wealthy; you'll have a good wife," then another old man would be chosen to take this answer back. "They then set a date. When girl is ready, they fix her up in beautiful clothes, give her a medicine, *half of all her* [father's] *horses*, moccasins and buffalo hides…She goes over. Three days later, the man's kin gives dresses (no moccasins) and horses back to her kin. Every one of the boy's kin who gets a horse gives one back. They try to give *more* horses than they received to beat them."[24]

When a Blackfoot couple first married they stayed for the first months (until the fall generally, as marriages took place at the summer Sun Dance encampments) near the husband's family but then lived close to her family. According to informants to the Hanks, this was done "so *her* family can do things for the bride."[25] "If a man has lots of [daughters]," an informant stated, "it is better because all the [sons-in-law] come to live with you, but if you have 6 sons they scatter and so you only have visiting sons etc."[26] In a family of many sons, one or two might "stay with the old man," but the others went to live with their fathers-in-law; thus it was rare for a group of brothers to live together.[27] It could take longer for residence to become matrilocal, as "you don't know what kind of a man your [father-in-law] is. If he is not so good, boy won't change to [father-in-law's] band, will stay. But a person can usually count on being in woman's band eventually."[28] A husband became a member of his wife's clan (referred to in the Hanks' notes as the wife's "band"), although this was flexible; if residence remained patrilocal, she became a member of his clan. A chief's daughter might marry a poor man with no relatives, but only if he is a worker, a hunter, and "a great help." The chief would "bring him over to his band," and the son-in-law never left that band, even if the marriage broke up, as he had no other family to go to.[29]

Young men and women were not complete pawns at the hands of family matchmakers. There were "free" marriages, which were the result of personal inclination, and there were elopements, although these were frowned on.[30] A daughter or son could request that their Elders initiate the necessary inquiries that were preliminary to a marriage. A young "virtuous" girl whose Elders had not acted on a marriage for her could "just go over to a man she's in love with and sit there for him to take her."[31] Because of the ease with which divorce was acquired it was difficult to force a couple to marry. According to Red Crow, if a woman refused a match she would be allowed to remain with her parents and another match would be found.[32] If the husband-elect did not like the woman he was to marry he sent her home. A degree of sexual freedom before marriage was tolerated, particularly for men, although it was regarded as a disgrace for unmarried women to become pregnant.[33] The sexual escapades of young men were tolerated to a much greater extent, as these enhanced their masculinity and reputation, while virginity for girls was held in high esteem. There was a high premium placed on the "virtue" of married women. Women were reminded of the grave severity of infidelity to husbands in their teaching texts, in instructions from their parents, and through ceremonies such as the Sun Dance.

In the legend of the Woman Who Married the Morning Star, the Crane Woman had powers only because she has remained true to her husband.[34] Because of this she was able to help the woman of the legend to bring the prairie turnip, the digging stick, and the songs that accompanied these things to the Blackfoot people. All of these were central to the Sun Dance ceremony. This was the major religious ceremony of the Blackfoot, and a woman was selected each year to lead it. But she had to have lived a virtuous life and be an upstanding example to others in order to qualify. Beverly Hungry Wolf called the Sun Dance the "tribal truth test for the virtuousness of women," although she was careful to point out that the ceremony was about much more than that.[35] Husbands could ask their wives to make the vow to hold the Sun Dance. If they refused it would be concluded that they were not chaste. If she lied when making the vow it could bring death and suffering. If a woman made the vow to hold the Sun Dance and for some reason things went wrong before, during, or after the ceremony, she would be suspected of being unchaste, and of having made a false vow. Such was the case with Good Hunter, the wife of a prominent Blackfoot named Big Swan, who was struck and killed by lightning in the midst of the ceremony when a violent storm from the Rockies moved over their camp. There were those who believed that this happened because she had falsely declared in her prayer that she was a pure woman.[36] A false vow was thought to bring sickness and death to the people. Among the Blackfoot the adulterous wife risked very harsh treatment as her nose could be cut off. But it was also regarded as a masculine virtue to forgive an unfaithful wife. The husband could seek redress from the woman's new partner, dispossessing him of his horses and other property.[37]

Unsatisfactory marriages were dissolved fairly easily. Either a husband or wife could terminate a marriage. Red Crow stated that people separated through the fault or wishes of one party or another.[38] Reasons included incompatibility, physical abuse, laziness, or failure to provide. However, divorce was not frequent after the birth of a child.[39] The process was straightforward—the aggrieved party simply left their spouse. Abuse or misconduct by a husband could lead to the wife deserting and returning to her father or brother's lodge, or her people might rescue her from a bad situation. According to Red Crow, if a wife was dissatisfied she merely went back to her parents or some relatives and refused to return to her husband.[40] The children could go with either parent after a permanent divorce or separation. According to a woman informant to the Hanks, they usually went with the mother, but if the father wished it they went with him.[41] Laziness or adultery on the part of the wife were reasons for divorce from the husband's perspective. A divorced woman took her property with her, which included her own horses, the tipi, and the household furnishings.[42] There could be property negotiations and settlements following divorce and remarriage among the Blackfoot— some gifts might be returned to the parents, and a new husband of a woman might compensate her former husband.[43]

Divorced persons were free to marry again. David Thompson wrote, "When contrariety of disposition prevails, so that [a married couple] cannot live peaceably together, they separate with as little ceremony as they came together, and both parties are free to attach themselves to whom they will, without any stain on their characters. But if they have lived so long together so as to have children, one, or both, are severely blamed."[44] As one non-Aboriginal observer of the nineteenth-century Blackfoot wrote, "Divorce was common and rested only upon mutual agreement. The wife, if dissatisfied, might return at will to her father's lodge, or the husband might for a similar reason send her back. The parents also or the brother-in-law might reclaim their daughter and the husband had no redress. This was frequently done temporarily as a check to brutal treatment or an incentive to a lazy husband to better provide for his wife…The ease with which a wife might leave her husband greatly abridged his power over her."[45]

According to David Thompson, the greatest praise that could be given an Aboriginal man was that "he is a man of steady humane disposition and a fortunate hunter," and he also wrote that "they seldom fail of being good husbands."[46] Wife beating was censured in the community. A wife-beater could not be a chief.[47] Teaching texts and legends cautioned against such domestic violence. The Women's Society or Ma'toki of the Kainai and another powerful society, the Horns, were said to have been founded by a married couple consisting of a human male and a female buffalo in human form. She was a perfect wife but one day her husband struck her because she did not quickly prepare food for guests. When this happened the wife and their little son returned to their buffalo form and joined her herd. After a series of trials the chastened husband was reunited with his wife and child and the couple began these two societies.[48] An informant to the Hanks was certain that the old way was better when the father picked out the son-in-law and made sure that he would not be mean to his daughter, saying that in more recent times husbands are inclined to be cruel to their wives.[49] Formerly husbands and their relatives were not mean to wives, and if they were, according to this informant, the father would take his daughter right back. The husband's "kin wouldn't say anything because they knew the [father] was good and had chosen the [son-in-law]...[they] knew their man...had been unworthy, and wouldn't say anything." The husband's friends and relatives might intervene and make several trips to attempt reconciliation and a father might relent and let his daughter return. Some husbands from then on were kind to their wives, fearing that they might leave again for good. According to Piikani Elder Three Calf, if a man was repeatedly mean to his wife, her brothers would go and take her back. "In this way, when the brothers think too much of their sister, she may have many husbands in turn, because her brothers are not satisfied with any of them and keep taking her away."[50]

Among the Plains Cree, "mean" husbands were reformed through gifts that brought social pressure to bear: "The husband might be mean and the girl would return to her parents. The father of the girl would send her back with clothing and horses to shame her husband into being kind to her. By that means many young men were stopped from being cruel to their wives."[51] A lazy husband might find himself the object of censure in the hope that he might reform his ways. One such man was chased about the camp by his wife's grandmother because he was lazy and refused even to do odd jobs. Annie Sioux of the Manitoba Dakota said that women "won't stand beating."[52] According to her a wife could leave and go to her sister, brother, or to her parents, and all of these, including her husband's father, could try to straighten out the husband.

Plains Cree marriage was similar to that of the Blackfoot in many respects but with some variations. There appears to have been more tolerance of women's sexual freedom before marriage, and less censure of adultery. Premarital pregnancy was accepted and no stigma was attached to the mother or child. Nor does there appear to have been the same high premium on wives' fidelity to husbands. An adulterous wife could be "given" to her lover by her husband, who actually earned prestige by doing this rather than punishing his wife. Ethnologist David Mandelbaum wrote, "A brave man, upon discovering his wife's infidelity, gave her to the lover. The lover, in turn, was obligated to reciprocate with a gift of a horse. Thereafter the woman was the other man's wife and the two men formed a special relationship involving the exchange of gifts." Cree elder Fine Day related this incident to Mandelbaum: "My mother's brother once caught a man with his wife. He gave her to the other man. Later, he told us, 'That was the only way I could get over it. It was a hard thing to do. I didn't sleep for four nights; but if I hadn't done it, I might have decided to kill that fellow. I loved my wife. She didn't love me or she wouldn't have done such a thing. Afterward I got over it and I never think about it any more.'"[53]

The Plains Cree also practiced what Mandelbaum termed the "wife exchange." If a young man was attracted to a married woman he could propose an exchange of wives to the woman's husband. If the husband thought the man worthy he could give his consent, and such exchanges would happen from time to time. The two men became companions, exchanged gifts, and had a particular term for each other that meant "co-husband," or "fellow husband." Linguist H.C. Wolfart has a somewhat different interpretation of the term translated as "co-husband," which he writes was "used reciprocally by men married to the same wife: where the wife of one has chosen to live with the other, and the first has demonstrated his [countenance] by accepting the arrangement."[54] Such husbands also had a term for each other: "nita-yim." According to Mandelbaum, "This relationship reflected considerable honour upon the participants, for only the most stout-hearted of men could become intimate companions of their wives' paramours."

Among the Aboriginal people of the Canadian plains there were a variety of ideal types of conjugal union, not just one as in Euro-Canadian society. Lifelong monogamous unions were common, but there were other kinds of conjugal arrangements. Women did not have plural husbands, but they might serially have several husbands, and no stigma was attached to divorce and remarriage. Many of the leading men in Plains societies had more than one spouse. The term "polygamy" does not have a parallel in the Cree or Blackfoot languages, suggesting that it was seen not as a separate, distinct departure from "normalcy," but as one of several possible forms of marriage resulting in desirable family units. Often sisters were married to the same man. A man might also marry his deceased brother's widow, adopting the children and preserving the relationship with the grandparents and extended family. Only hard-working men of wealth and prestige could maintain these large households, so parents sought these marriages for their daughters. It was expected that wealthy men would have more than one wife and share the bounty. A second or more wives were brought into a family generally after consultation with the first wife, and with her approval. These domestic arrangements provided economic assistance, companionship, and enhanced status for the senior wife. Red Crow said that the first wives seldom objected to the presence of other wives, and it was very often they who proposed that sisters or other relatives become second or third wives.[55]

Cree Chief Fine Day provided a detailed description of marriage practices in 1934.[56] Fine Day's father had two wives, his mother being the second wife, and he said that the two got along well. Fine Day stressed that permission was required from the first wife and that the acquisition of a second wife was a joint decision in recognition of the needs of the first wife. If a wife found that she required assistance the husband would ask, "'How would you like to have a helper?' If she said yes, they then both would pick out some likely girl. He would ask her again, 'Would you be kind to her?' She would say, 'Yes, that's why I want her.' Then he would go and get the other woman. But the first wife was always the boss."[57] Fine Day stressed the authority of the wives to determine the size and nature of the family unit:

It was not a man's abilities as a hunter that determined the number of wives he had, but upon the arrangements he made with his wife. Both a man and his wife paid for the second wife. Young girls would not want to be married to a man that was of no account. They wanted to marry a Worthy Man because they know that there would be no quarrelling—he would stop it. If a man wanted to take a third wife, his first would usually agree but his second would often say no. That usually would settle it.[58]

If the permission of the wives had not been obtained there were consequences. Fine Day noted that if a man married a third wife without the permission of his first two they would never be friendly towards her. According to Red Crow, if a husband brought home a second wife to the disgust of the first she would "keep up a continual row until the newcomer was sent away."[59] A second (or third) wife could join a family because of kinship or friendship obligations. David Thompson wrote that "This is seldom a matter of choice; it is frequently from the death of a friend who has left his wife, sister, or daughter to him, for every woman must have a husband."[60]

David Thompson wrote:

Polygamy is allowed and practised [among the Piikani], and the Wife more frequently than the husband [is] the cause of it, for when a family comes a single wife can no longer do the duties and labor required unless she, or her husband, have two widowed relations in their tent, and which frequently is not the case; and a second Wife is necessary, for they have to cook, take care of the meat, split and dry it; procure all the wood for fuel, dress the skins into soft leather for robes and clothing...Some of the chiefs have from three to six wives, for until a woman is near fifty years of age she is sure to find a husband.[61]

< Blackfoot women and their husband, 1870s. (GAA NA-1376-6)

There were diverse circumstances under which second or third wives joined a family. One man of Thompson's acquaintance wanted to remain monogamous but acquired three more wives. The man told Thompson that a close friend of his, who died of wounds inflicted in warfare, "when dying requested his parents to send his two wives to me, where he was sure they would be kindly treated...what could I do but grant the claim of my friend, and make them my wives."[62] A dying cousin similarly bequeathed his third new wife to him. In his life history told in 1938, South Piikani Elder Three Calf said that if a man's wife's sister's husband dies, he asks the widow to marry him, and that a man would often marry his older brother's widow. The widow would "rather marry him than a stranger, because she is already used to that family. If the brother-in-law is a great deal younger, he may not want to marry the widow, but his mother tells him he had better do it for the sake of the children."[63]

Polygamy ensured that there were very few unmarried women. A Siksika woman informant to the Hanks in the 1930s had this to say about one such woman:

She was crippled; her legs were paralysed and she had great big hands. She would pull herself around with her hands. The [men] would tease her about not having a husband and she would say to go look for one for her. She took the teasing well and she would tease back. She did good bead work and good skin work. But she would say she would not get married because she couldn't do enough work, as carrying wood, putting up tents.[64]

According to Kainai historian Beverly Hungry Wolf, women did a tremendous amount of work, and it was thought to be desirable for a young woman to marry a prominent man with several wives as this eased the burden of work.[65] A single wife found it difficult to cope with all of the work in the home of a successful hunter, and so she welcomed the division of such work among new wives. A seventy-three-year-old Blackfoot woman, Middle Woman No Coat, who was interviewed in 1939, recalled the division of labour in her father's household with five wives. "[The first two wives] are older and do all the tanning. Younger wives do the cooking. In winter, all take turns getting wood; someone always present to take care of the fire."[66] There were two wives, one her mother, in the family of Dakota Annie Sioux. The wives were half sisters. "All lived in one house and as far as a child noticed, got along well. She says her feelings were same for half as for whole siblings. It was a good arrangement. When one wife went to Brandon, the other stayed home with the children." When her father died, Annie Sioux's mother remarried and the two wives continued to live together. One woman did housework while the other got meals, and they took turns doing these things.[67] Other advantages for the co-wives were that women in polygamous marriages tended to have less children, and that the mothers of the sister co-wives were often part of the household.[68] In their older age widowed wives continued to live together, assisting each other. A Manitoba Dakota man interviewed in the 1950s said that his father had two wives, and "both lived together as old women. They did quillwork and ribbon work on black broadcloth shirts, and made woven sashes. For a middle part of her married life one of these wives went away and lived alone with her son."[69]

Maxidiwiac (born circa 1839), also known as Buffalo Bird Woman of the Hidatsa, an agricultural Plains nation of present-day North Dakota, explained that sisters married to the same husband might not be sisters in the way Europeans used this term. Rather, they were relatives, sometimes adopted, who were regarded each other as sisters.[70] Maxidiwiac grew up in a household where her mother, her mother's sisters, and a cousin regarded as a sister were all married to her father. When she was six her own mother and one of the other wives died of smallpox, and she regarded and addressed the two surviving wives as her mothers. The mothers of the surviving wives, who had been raised together although not related by blood, also lived in the household, and she addressed both of these as grandmother.

The children of these plural marriages regarded themselves in every way as brothers and sisters regardless of the fact that they had different mothers. The prominent Plains Cree leader Poundmaker was the son of the Cree wife of an Assiniboine (Nakoda) man who also had three Assiniboine wives. When Poundmaker's father died the wives each moved back to their own people but the eleven children of all four women considered themselves brothers and sisters and they kept in touch with one another. One of the wives returned to her home band near Poplar Point, Montana, for example, and her sons continued to visit their brothers and sisters in Saskatchewan into the twentieth century.[71]

Women who could not have children of their own were able to enjoy motherhood in polygamous marriages. A Siksika informant to the Hanks was the first wife of a man who later married her three younger sisters.[72] She did not have children of her own but regarded all of her husband and sisters' children as her children. The mothers fed the children, but she "did all the work of sewing, washing for the babies." This informant was the "sits-beside-him" wife of her husband, and "she was the one who brought her sisters in, 1 by 1." Eventually her brother and mother joined them as well. Among the Blackfoot the first and generally the oldest wife was known as the "sits-beside-him" wife, and this was a position of honour. She was the woman head of household and she had an important role in ceremonies such as those involving sacred bundles. She accompanied her husband to feasts and ceremonies, and she directed the other wives in their work. The other wives did not have as high a standing in the community as the "sits-beside-him" wife, but they also had fewer community or public responsibilities.

These plural marriages were not always successful. A Manitoba Dakota man had two wives (into the twentieth century) who were not related, and the second left him with two children "out of jealousy" although her husband still visited her, and she did not marry again until those children were grown.[73] Non-Aboriginal observers usually assumed jealousy among wives. On 15 May 1889, Battleford's *Saskatchewan Herald* reported the following incident: "One day about a week ago a squaw who occupies the position of wife No. 2 to a hard case of an Indian known as The Carrot was paying a visit to a friend on Little Pine's reserve. She left her horse and cart standing at the door of her friend, and while she went in and having a social time wife No. 1 thrust a knife into her rival's horse, causing him to die in his tracks. No. 2 will probably prosecute No. 1 for maliciously killing her horse."

Discord seems to have been the exception however, in an environment in which co-operation and sharing was vital, and in a society where women did almost all of their work communally. Esther Goldfrank was told of a family in which the three wives were always quarrelling.[74] The family was once out on the prairie and were short of water. One wife had water but refused to share with the others, and they stopped speaking at all to each other. One of the wives died, presumably as a result of the unwillingness to share water. This story was related almost as a cautionary tale, and in such a way as to suggest that it represented a departure from the behaviour that had to normally prevail in a family of several wives. According to Beverly Hungry Wolf there were occasions when a younger wife with a much older husband in a large household suffered from loneliness and a desire to be loved. Some older husbands sanctioned outside relationships as long as they were discreet and brought no public disgrace.[75]

Anthropologist John H. Moore offered this conclusion in his study of the Cheyenne:

> From an American Indian standpoint, the institution of polygyny was seen to benefit both husbands and wives. For men, a larger household meant that they would have more children and more relatives, with concomitant increase in wealth and status in the community. For women, polygyny usually meant that they could maintain co-residence with their sisters as co-wives, could get daily help with child care and other household chores, and have an increased probability of keeping their mother in the household. [76]

But how common was polygamy in Aboriginal Western Canada? Most of the documentary sources generated by Europeans are dubious and slanted on this issue. As discussed below, polygamy was condemned and its extent exaggerated by many outside observers, particularly in the nineteenth century. An 1838 HBC "Indian census" indicates that it was not particularly prevalent at that time, and that it was perhaps slightly more widespread among the people of the plains than the people of the more northerly regions.[77] At Fort Resolution in the Athabasca district, for example, eight of eighty-two men had two wives. One man (François Beaulieu, described as a "half breed") had five wives. At Fort Chipewyan, fifteen of 129 had two wives, two had three wives, and one had four wives. At Île à la Crosse, twenty-four of 109 had two wives, two had three wives, and one had four wives. The more southerly locations, which would have included the Plains Cree and Ojibway (Saulteaux), were Fort Pelly, where fourteen of eighty-three had two wives, and two had three wives; Fort Ellice, where sixty of 308 had two wives, twenty had three wives, and one had five wives; at Lower Fort Garry none of fifty-eight had more than one wife. The census does not include any statistics on the Blackfoot, who had limited contact with the HBC at that time. David Thompson wrote with regard to the Cree, "each man may have as many wives as he can maintain, but few indulge themselves in this liberty, yet some have even three."[78]

Alexander Hunter Murray, founder of the HBC's Fort Yukon, wrote in his journal of the Yukon in 1848 that the men of that district "treat their wives generally with kindness, but are very jealous of them. The principal men of the nation have two and three wives each, one old leader here has five, while others who have few beads (and beads are their riches) to decorate the women, remain bachelors, but a good fighter though a poor man can always have a wife."[79] As discussed below, one of the main explanations for the prevalence of polygamy among Plains people is that there were more women than men. An 1805–1806 census taken by Alexander Henry the Younger of the North West Company (NWC), which covered all of the "Departments" in which his company operated, listed a total of 16,995 Indian women, compared to 7,502 men, and the greatest imbalances were on the plains, particularly in the upper Saskatchewan region where there were 13,632 women to 4,823 men.[80] Also to be discussed below, there is widespread agreement among social scientists that polygamy increased among the Plains people in the nineteenth century with very negative consequences for the multiple wives.

Aboriginal people of the plains also permitted marriages of people of the same sex. One of the spouses might be a "two-spirit" who took on the activities, occupations, and dress of the opposite sex, in whole or in part, temporarily or permanently.[81] There was no insistence on conformity to binaries of masculinity and femininity. Indian agents were frustrated by their inability to tell men and women apart, and they made mistakes, or were misled, when describing certain individuals. Oftentimes they did note the flexibility of gender roles when they described individuals to which annuities were paid, as is evident in terms such as "wife shown as boy last year," "boy paid as girl last year," and "boy now a man formerly ran as a girl."[82] Clothing, hair, footwear, and personal décor did not differentiate men from women in the way that Euro-Canadians were accustomed to. Qu'Appelle storekeeper Edward J. Brooks wrote in an 1882 letter to his wife-to-be that "I saw a couple of pure blooded Indians down at the station a couple of days ago and could not tell whether both were Squaws or not but finally made up my mind that they were man and wife. They were both dressed as nearly alike as possible, had long braided hair, wore lots of jewellery and had their faced painted with Vermillion paint."[83] An English visitor to Western Canada named Edward Roper wrote in his 1891 book that "most of us found it almost impossible to tell the young men and women apart; they were exactly alike in face [the men had no 'beards or whiskers'], and being generally enveloped in blankets the difficulty increased."[84] All wore similar beautifully decorated moccasins, bangles, and earrings, Roper wrote.

In Plains societies there were women who did not marry and pursued activities mostly associated with men. They hunted buffalo and went to war. An informant to Goldfrank described a woman warrior who was treated as a true leader. She was renowned for acts of bravery such as going into an enemy's tipi and taking headdresses from behind the bed. "She used to leave her legging at the enemy camp and they would say 'that woman has been here again.' She always slept alone, while the men remained in camp. She would sleep on top of the hill and she sang a song. The next day she would know where to lead the party."[85] This may have been the warrior another informant identified as "Trim Woman," saying that "that kind of woman is always respected and everyone depends on them. They are admired for their bravery. They are 'lucky' on raids and so the men respect them."[86] Another Kainai woman, Empty Coulee, had a story similar to Trim Woman's, but she had more courage, killing enemies and capturing guns, while Trim Woman only captured horses. After she became expert in raiding she changed her name to Running Eagle, a man's name. She wore women's clothing, but she "got respect as a 'real man.'" She never married.[87]

Some of the women who took on "manly" roles were married. In the book *Five Indian Tribes of the Upper Missouri*, Edwin Thompson Denig, a fur trader during the years 1833 and 1856, described a Gros Ventre woman who was a respected warrior, negotiator and hunter, and who was regarded as the third-ranked chief of her band. She had a wife. Denig wrote, "Strange country this, where males assume the dress and perform the duties of females, while women turn men and mate with their own sex."[88] There were also married women who participated in "manly" activities with their husbands. A Kainai woman named Elk-Yells-in-the-Water went on several war raids with her husband. She gave her adopted mother a horse she captured when she accompanied her husband on a war raid.[89]

The "manly-hearted women" of the Blackfoot excelled at feminine occupations, had the finest (women's) clothing, and were always married, often several times, and had children. But they also displayed characteristics classified as "masculine"; they were aggressive, independent, bold, and sexually forward.[90] As Esther Goldfrank wrote, "the essential pattern of their lives always remains safely within the framework set for woman as a sex," but a manly-hearted woman would "make advances in affairs of the heart; she may refuse to marry the man of her father's choice; she will marry in her own time, and she will not hesitate to beat off an irate husband. She is usually an excellent worker. This as well as her passionate response to love make her a desirable mate despite her wilfulness and domineering ways."[91]

There were also biological males who lived as women, many of whom married men. One Kainai named Pigeon Woman, who was biologically male, "from babyhood until death…lived a female life—like a widow—no husband—used female expressions," according to Goldfrank's notes.[92] Informants to the Hanks described two men who acted like women, had husbands, and did women's work. One of these "really acts like a woman. Dresses like a woman, has bracelets up to his elbows, rings on fingers and had a husband…He made clothes and tanned hides like other women."[93]

Another dressed and acted as a woman "from the start," and he played with girls. His father and mother "were not shy about the way he was acting; all family knew he was a boy." He "looked like a good looking woman" and was married several times. One man who dressed and acted as a woman was a renowned warrior who "sewed moccasins better than any woman, made buckskin suits and beaded blankets better than any woman."[94] He went on highly successful expeditions against the enemy Cree and Crow dressed as a woman. He had a devoted husband and was described as the only wife of the man. In his narrative of his many years spent among the Plains Saulteaux of southern Manitoba, John Tanner wrote about the son of a celebrated chief who was "one of those who make themselves women, and are called women by the Indians."[95] She (Tanner's pronoun) had several husbands in the past and wanted to marry Tanner. When he refused, another man with two wives married her. When asked how they got married "if everyone knew they were not women," a Hanks informant said, "No one said anything. Husbands knew and got them for wives. They knew but didn't care if he was not a woman. Why have a woman like this? These husbands knew they were good at tipi and bead work. That is how they made up their mind. In every way they treated these men just like other women."[96]

"Two Spirits" were believed to have special gifts among Plains societies. Manitoba Dakota Elder Eva McKay explained, "They were special in the way that they seemed to have more skills than a single man or a single woman...He is two persons, this is when people would say they have more power than a single person. They were treated with respect."[97]

Marriage among Plains people then did not always conform to the monogamous model; it was not always one man and one woman, and it was not always for life. Some scholars puzzling over all of this have wondered about applying the term "marriage" at all to the variety of conjugal unions, suggesting that "marriage" is not a universally applicable concept, that it denotes a particularly Western concept, and only some relationships in any Aboriginal society might approximate this.[98] Are concepts such as "marriage," "wife," "husband," and "divorce" categories of colonial control not commensurable with the practices of Aboriginal people? Have these concepts been imposed by colonial administrators, the courts, anthropologists, and historians to create order and clarity and to eliminate flexibility and diversity?

Certainly many Euro-Canadian observers did not see these as "true" marriages because they did not all conform to their most widely accepted definition of marriage as the voluntary union of one man and one woman for life to the exclusion of all others. They simplified and dismissed marriage among Plains peoples as a form of purchase, as an exchange of property in which fathers, husbands, and brothers struck bargains according to the market value of a woman. In 1877, James F. Macleod of the NWMP reported from Fort Macleod: "The marriage ceremony is very simple. Anyone can buy a wife for a number of horses or robes. The bargain being completed with the parents, the transfer is made with the girl's consent, and she goes and lives with the purchaser, no further ceremony being necessary."[99] There was an insistence that Aboriginal marriage enslaved women. There was no love, courtship, or ceremony; a commodity simply changed hands. As a *Toronto Mail* reporter wrote in 1886, women of the Piikani nation were very poorly treated since they were "sold like so many cattle to suitors, and whether willing or not, became the wives of those able to pay the price asked of them."[100] And if women had the ability to switch husbands with relative ease, were they truly "wives"? Many nineteenth-century observers concluded that they were not, and instead asserted that they were prostitutes. Unsympathetic observers saw the availability of divorce, and the rate of marital dissolution, not as a means through which the supposedly enslaved women could gain freedom, but rather as a sign of moral deficiency and dangerous autonomy. Non-Aboriginal observers did not see what they regarded as "true" marriage because marriage was not binding for life on either the husband or the wife. Marriages could be of short duration with frequent changing of spouses. Both were free to separate at any time, and thus marriage did not appear to be a binding contract in the European sense.

But as we know well in our own times, and as established in the earlier chapters of this book, there are diverse definitions of marriage, and these change over time. Marriage in Plains societies was not the same as marriage in Christian practice and English common law, but I think the term, no matter how imperfect, can be used if it is understood that there were diverse definitions of marriage. Like the term "family," there is no fixed or homogenous definition. According to historian and Cree-language scholar Keith Goulet, "there are words for grandparents, parents, in-laws, uncles, aunts, brothers, sisters, cousins, nephews, nieces, grandchildren and great-grandchildren but no family!"[101] In an 1865 Cree dictionary, revised in 1938, it is noted beside the English word "family" that "there is no clear Cree word for this."[102] As presented in any undergraduate class today on the sociology of the family, marriage and family are "social constructs whose meanings have changed over time and from place to place."[103]

In an essay published in 1900 entitled "Indian Women of the Western Provinces," Henriette Forget expressed many of the misunderstandings of marriage that were shared by non-Aboriginal people of this era, stressing the purchase of multiple wives who spent lives of ceaseless toil. "Their lot was indeed hard," wrote Madame Forget. "Polygamy was the general practice. The richer an Indian was (his wealth being horses), the more wives he sought, or rather bought, for the maidens were sold by their paternal relatives to become the wives of those who proffered the greatest number of horses in exchange."[104] Indian men, according to Madame Forget, "often preferred quantity to quality: "Wives were chosen as we chose old plate, Not for their beauty, but their weight." This author had a particularly close acquaintance with the issue of Aboriginal marriage (although not unique insight by virtue of this acquaintance), as she was married to Indian Commissioner Amedée Forget who led the 1890s campaign to eliminate polygamy in Western Canadian First Nations communities.

In one succinct paragraph botanist John Macoun bundled together many of the prevailing misrepresentations of Aboriginal marriage in his 1882 book, *Manitoba and the Great North-West*, in which he praised the agricultural potential of the southern plains. Aboriginal marriage meant patriarchal tyranny for the unfortunate wives, in Macoun's view. He wrote, "Marriage amongst the Indians has never been looked upon by them in the same light as it has been by us. All Indian women are slaves, and they know it and act accordingly. The will of the man is supreme, and no woman ever thinks of opposing him in the slightest. Men, as a rule, take as many wives as they can feed, and too often, when they are tired of them, 'throw them off.' This is the universal custom, and is practised from Lake Superior to the Pacific."[105]

These views were widely shared, disseminated, and often wildly embellished. In 1916, Oblate missionary Father Joseph Hugonnard gave a talk to the Regina Canadian Club on "Indians of the West," and spoke about the lowly position of women, concluding that "Among pagan Indians, woman is considered as an inferior being; the name of 'isquao' which has been corrupted into 'squaw' means the lowest or last being. A woman had no choice in marriage; she simply belonged to the man who bought her and kept her during his pleasure. I know an Indian who is still alive who bought two sisters; he killed one and kept the other, who had to stay with him."[106]

Those with the deepest investments in the creation of the new capitalist and agricultural order in the Canadian West were the most critical of the position of women and of marriage in Aboriginal societies. Earlier non-Aboriginal observers, and a few others into the twentieth century, were not as condemning, and they often admired the power that Aboriginal women exercised. David Thompson described the wife of York Factory fur trader William Budge who was cooking one evening when a polar bear was attracted by the smell of the food. Budge climbed the tent poles leaving his wife and trader John Mellam to deal with the bear. The woman struck the bear with her axe with "an incessant storm of blows," and the bear took off and was eventually shot. According to Thompson: "Budge now wanted to descend from the smoky top of the Tent, but the woman with her axe in her hand (2 ½ lbs) heaped wood on the fire and threatened to brain him if he came down. He begged hard for his life, she was determined, fortunately Mellam snatched the axe from her, but she never forgave him, for the Indian woman pardons Man for everything but want of course, this is her sole support and protection, there are no laws to defend her."[107]

Traveller Anna Brownell Jameson similarly described the power of the Anishinabe wife in her 1837 book, *Winter Studies and Summer Rambles in Canada.* Jameson wrote: "I should doubt, from all I see and hear that the

Indian squaw is that absolute slave, and nonentity in the community, which she has been described. She is despotic in her lodge, and everything it contains is hers; even of the game her husband kills, she has the uncontrolled disposal. If her husband does not please her, she scolds and even cuffs him; and it is in the highest degree unmanly to answer or to strike her. I have seen a woman scolding and quarrelling with her husband, seize him by the hair, in a style that might have become civilized Billingsgate, or Christian St. Giles's, and the next day I have beheld the same couple sit lovingly on the sunny side of the wigwam.[108]

In her 1909 book, *The People of the Plains*, author Amelia McLean Paget, who was of Métis ancestry, challenged dominant representations of the "squaw drudge." She presented polygamy in a sympathetic light, noting that the wives "called each other 'sister' and might, indeed, have been sisters in so far as their fondness for one another was concerned. They divided their labours equally, and tried in every way to cultivate mutual forbearance."[109]

Missionary, government, political, and legal authorities however, were particularly shrill in their condemnation of polygamy in Aboriginal societies. It was seen as deviant and morally depraved. Polygamy became a towering example of the shortcomings of Aboriginal societies that were understood to subordinate women, in contrast to the ideal of monogamous marriage, which was cherished as an institution that elevated women. Polygamy was viewed as a system that exploited and degraded women, depriving them of respect and influence. It was thought that jealousy and friction among the wives was inevitable. The husbands in polygamous marriages were seen as idle, debauched, and tyrannical. The sexual desires of the husband were seen as a main motivation for polygamy. As John Moore has noted, this notion probably tells us more about the sexual fantasies of European male observers than about the culture and values of Aboriginal people.[110] The extent of polygamy was, I would argue, widely exaggerated to evoke indignant condemnation. It was not the "general practice" as described by Henriette Forget or the "universal custom" described by John Macoun. The HBC census clearly suggests otherwise. James F. Macleod did not have full knowledge of the facts, or exaggerated them, when he reported in 1877 from Fort Macleod that "Polygamy is universally practiced among them; every man has at least three wives and…[he]…knew one old fellow who rejoiced in the possession of eleven dusky helpmates."[111]

Missionaries were among the most outspoken critics of Aboriginal marriages. They were deeply concerned about the propriety of a host of customs involving sexuality, marriage, and divorce.[112] But polygamy topped the list of forces that allegedly degraded women. As Methodist missionary John Semmens wrote in his 1884 memoirs, multiple wives were "general slaves, subject to the behests of the most thoughtless and relentless of taskmasters."[113] Many of the stories included in Methodist missionary John Maclean's collection entitled *The Warden of the Plains* dealt with the cruelties and indignities Aboriginal women suffered through their "sale or marriage" and by becoming plural wives.[114] In one story a chief arranged for his young and beautiful fourteen-year-old daughter Asokoa to become the fourth wife of an old man named Running Deer. She was not informed or consulted but was suddenly told "she was now his wife and must dwell with him for the future."[115] The other wives were jealous of her and saw her as an intruder, but Asokoa did not stoop to their level, and did not engage in "family brawls." She kept herself clean and neat unlike other "women in the camps [who] after marriage generally become careless and untidy, and in some instances filthy."[116] Asokoa ran away with a lover, and fortunately escaped the cruel "cut nose" penalty for women adulterers, but her lover died in battle. She married once again but soon learned what it was like to suddenly find, with no warning, a new wife in her home. "Greater sorrow had never fallen upon Asokoa. Her love and pride were hurt by the knowledge that she had been superseded by another…the days which followed the arrival of the new wife were a dull round of drudgery and sorrow." The story concludes with her death soon afterwards.

It is important to note that there were dissenting views among the missionaries. Maclean and Semmens' Methodist missionary contemporary John McDougall, who was much more deeply acquainted with Aboriginal Western Canada, did not condemn polygamy and Aboriginal marriage in the same way as his colleagues, although he could not have condoned the perpetuation of the practice. Describing domestic life in a 1914 article entitled "The Red Men of Canada's West Yesterday and Today," McDougall wrote:

> These people were both monogamous and polygamous. This was altogether optional with both men and women. There were no marriage customs or rights. Quietly and without any fuss men and women went together and became man and wife. Sometimes this was arranged by their friends and again it was the parties [sic] mutual choice and arrangement. Monogamy was more common among the mountain and wood Indians and on the other hand polygamy was frequent among the plains people. War decimated the male population of the plains tribes more than that of the mountain and wood people. The remarkable quiet and concord of a family of from two to ten women and one man living together in a big buffalo skin lodge was the regular condition and anywhere to be met with among these people 30, 40 or 50 years ago and doubtless for many ages previously.[117]

But condemnations of polygamy and Aboriginal marriage laws were much more common throughout the imperial world in the late nineteenth century than the sympathetic views expressed by such as McDougall. In a book entitled *Women of the Orient*, author Rev. R.C. Houghton described his thoughts on polygamy:

> Deceit, bickerings, strife, jealousies, intrigues, murder and licentiousness have followed in its train; true love has, in its presence, given place to sensual passion, and woman has become the slave, rather than the companion of man. The word home, as symbolical of confidence, sympathy, rest, happiness and true affection, is not found in the vocabulary of polygamous lands. Polygamy is subversive of God's order; and, beginning by poisoning the very sources of domestic and social prosperity, its blighting influences are felt and seen in every department of national life.[118]

In a chapter entitled "Women and Missions: Female Degradation in Heathen Lands," in the book *Woman, Her Character, Culture and Calling*, readers learned that "Girl-life among more than half the population of the globe seems the cheapest thing in the dust-bin of human possessions." Polygamy was one of the "devices of the devil which intensify the misery of heathen women…How very much like the Mormon ideas, which are copied from heathendom, and devised originally by the devil!"[119] By favourable contrast to the supposed domestic despotism under polygamy, the monogamous model of lifelong marriage was held up as an institution that elevated rather than enslaved women, placing them on a pedestal while allowing them a high degree of liberty. As Inderpal Grewal has written about India, the discourse of the "caged" woman became the "necessary 'Other' for the construction of the English woman presumably free and happy in the home."[120] All of this served as significant indicators that the colonizers were introducing a superior civilization at the core of which was the "proper" gender identities embedded in the cherished marriage model.

Anthropologists and ethnologists of the twentieth century have suggested several reasons for polygamy among Plains people, and most have tended to continue in the tradition of condemnation, particularly with regard to the status and treatment of women in these marriages. These social scientists appear to harbour the assumption that monogamy and the nuclear family is the universal norm, or the "traditional" unit of domestic production, and polygamy is perceived as a departure from this norm. Anthropologist John Ewers explained polygamy as a custom that offered protection and a home to "surplus" single women.[121] He estimated that among the early nineteenth-century Blackfoot, adult women exceeded the number of men by a ratio of about five to three. Ewers wrote that polygamy was "a practical means of caring for the excess of women created by heavy war losses."[122] Other scholars have taken a dimmer view of polygamy, describing it as a practice that diminished rather than protected women. Alan Klein and David Nugent have concluded that multiple wives became a necessity to Blackfoot males in the nineteenth century when they became heavily involved in the market economy based on the buffalo robe and hide trade, and as an emphasis on the accumulation of individual wealth became more entrenched.[123] These scholars perceived growth in the frequency of polygamy from the early nineteenth century when women were increasingly required as processors of buffalo products. A male hunter could amass great wealth and acquire the guns and other European products necessary to sustain wealth by providing unprocessed hides to more than one woman worker. Polygamy therefore increased, and women declined into a subordinate position in a previously more egalitarian society. David Nugent found that with a rise in polygamy, "the formerly homogenous social category of 'married woman' became clearly differentiated into 'first or favourite wife,' and 'subsidiary wife.'"[124] The subsidiary wife had a much lower position within the household, according to Nugent. Anthropologist Oscar Lewis similarly condemned polygamy in his scholarship on the northern Piikani, writing that there was a sharp contrast in status between upper and lower wives, with the lower wives being treated little better than slaves. He maintained, "If a poor, lower wife became troublesome and bossy, she would be beaten unmercifully until cowed or sent away."[125]

An emphasis on the wretchedness and misery of Plains women in plural marriages has been taken to new heights in Pekka Hämäläinen's article, "The Rise and Fall of Plains Indian Horse Cultures," in which he stresses the "bleak undercurrent" of harmful effects that horses had on the socio-economic systems of Plains people and the environment. Horses led to the concentration of wealth and power in the hands of a few:

[This] had a particularly strong impact on the lives of women who married into large polygynous households; Blackfeet used the term "slave wife" to refer to any additional wife beyond a man's first three. Such women worked hard feeding and watering horses, scraping and tanning hides, and cutting and drying meat, and yet, unlike women in general, often had subordinate positions in the households. They had few personal possessions, wore inferior clothes, and were frequently abused by their husbands, who relied on violence to control their growing labor pool. Many of them also married very young, bore children while still in puberty, and consequently ran a high risk of losing their lives while giving birth. Exploited, controlled, and hoarded by the male elite, the extra wives were considered less companions than instruments of production.[126]

While Hämäläinen noted in a footnote that contemporary non-Aboriginal accounts of the workload and status of Aboriginal women of the plains must be used with extreme caution, as they were often "distorted by the male observers' cultural premise that women should be sequestered and protected," he nevertheless asserts that "it seems clear that the 'extra wives' in large polygynous households suffered widespread abuse."[127]

Despite all of the critics, the validity and legality of Aboriginal marriage law (when marriage was found to be monogamous) was upheld in the courts until the late nineteenth century when this began to erode. But curiously, as we will see in subsequent chapters, Canada's Department of Indian Affairs became a staunch supporter of the validity of Aboriginal marriage law, or Aboriginal marriage ceremonies (if these marriages conformed to the monogamous and lifelong model), well into the twentieth century despite the change in legal climate. Of particular importance to their position was the case of *Connolly v. Woolrich and Johnson et al.* of 1867. At the age of seventeen in 1803, William Connolly, an employee of the NWC, married Suzanne "Pas-de-Nom," a Cree woman, "in the manner of the country" at Rivière-aux-Rats in Athabasca Country. They were married for twenty-eight years, "without violation or infidelity on either side," had six children together, and lived in dozens of locations together across the west and north.[128] William Connolly retired from the fur trade in 1831 and took his family to settle in his birthplace of Lachine, Quebec. There Suzanne was introduced by William as "Mrs. Connolly," and was generally known as such, but then Connolly suddenly married his cousin Julia Woolrich. They had two children together and lived in Montreal, while Connolly continued to support Suzanne, who by then lived in a convent in Winnipeg. When Connolly died, he left his entire estate to Julia and their two children. Julia died in 1864 and the lawsuit involved Connolly's children by Suzanne and his children by Julia. The estate was large—one of the largest ever probated in Quebec up to that time.[129]

The lawsuit, according to legal historian Sidney L. Harring, was "carefully framed and brilliantly argued by what was probably the best legal talent then available in Montreal." The decision was authored by Justice Samuel C. Monk, originally of Halifax, whose father had been Indian commissioner of Nova Scotia for some twenty years. The lawyer for Suzanne's children argued that their parents were legally married under Cree law, as well as under existing English and French law, and that the second marriage was null and void. Lawyer Alexander Cross argued the opposing side, representing Julia's children. He cast Suzanne as a concubine, and her children as illegitimate, and argued that these fur-trade unions were not binding or valid without consecration. The Cree were presented as "barbarians" with "infidel laws," and it was further argued that a Cree marriage could never be valid in Canada because it was potentially polygamous and therefore barbaric. A version of this same argument was used with respect to Mormon marriage in the Hyde case, and accepted by Lord Penzance in his 1866 decision, which decided that Hyde's Mormon marriage, although monogamous (and Hyde was himself opposed to polygamy), was invalid as "Mormon monogamous marriages always had the potential of becoming polygamous ones."[130]

In the Connolly case many witnesses were called and contradictory evidence given as to the binding nature of marriages according to the custom of the country, and precisely what ceremony, if any, was involved. Englishman and HBC trader John Edward Harriott described his marriage to the daughter of Chief Trader John Pruden as an agreement between father-in-law and son-in-law, which he regarded as valid and binding: "We lived as married people when married this way...I was married after the custom of the country myself...when I took a wife as above mentioned, I made a solemn promise to her father to live with her and treat her as my wife as long as we both lived."[131] By contrast former NWC employee Joseph Laroque gave evidence that marriage according to the custom of the country was not regarded as legally binding. He claimed that "according to reputation," Susanne was not married to Connolly;

"*that is, he was married according to the custom of the country there*—that is taking a woman and sending her off when he pleased. When I say the custom of the country, I mean that the people did that as a common practice in those days. There was not a legal binding marriage."[132]

In his decision, described recently as "the boldest and most creative common law decision on Indian rights in nineteenth-century Canada," in which he "gave as much recognition to Cree law as he possibly could have," Justice Monk quoted ethnographers on the topic of Indian marriages, and he also quoted at length from US Chief Justice John Marshall's opinion in *Worcester v. Georgia*, describing the Indians as "a distinct people, divided into separate nations, independent of each other and of the rest of the world, having institutions of their own, and governing themselves by their own laws."[133] Justice Monk "recognized not only the marriage but the Cree law that governed it." He argued that there was nothing to be found in either the 1670 HBC Charter or the Royal Proclamation of 1763, "abolishing or changing the customs of the Indians...nothing which introduced the English common law into these territories. When Connolly went to Athabaska, in 1803, he found the Indian usages as they had existed for ages, unchanged by European power of Christian legislation. He did not take English law with him."[134] Monk found that English law was not in force at Rivière-aux-Rats in 1803. In his verbal remarks reported in the Montreal press, Monk stated, "it was only in modern civilization that it was necessary to register the marriage. In this Indian territory there were no registers and no priests. It was quite preposterous to call this a pagan marriage...it would be different if it were only intended to be a fugitive connection for the purpose of concubinage." In his written judgement Monk wrote, "[marriage] between a Cree Squaw, without any religious or civil ceremony, but according to the custom of the Cree Indians, and followed by constant co-habitation and repute and bringing up of a numerous family, during a series of years is valid...if the right of divorce or repudiation be not exercised whilst the parties reside in the territory in question."[135] Nor could Connolly "invoke the Cree law of divorce at will" in Quebec. Justice Monk wrote that Connolly could not "carry with him this common law of England to Rat River in his knapsack, and much less could he bring back to Lower Canada the law of repudiation in a bark canoe." Justice Monk mocked the notion that English common law "followed the flag," and he recognized the legitimacy of Cree law in Cree territory, just as English common law functioned in British territories.

Monk dismissed the argument that the marriage was invalid because it was potentially polygamous. It was proven to his satisfaction that polygamy was not a necessary accompaniment of marriage.[136] Although it was found that some of the chiefs took three or four wives, the evidence provided no evidence of any "European taking two Indian wives; but, on the contrary, it was established that Europeans when they took an Indian to wife, restricted themselves to one wife." Monk concluded that the case had nothing to do with polygamy.

According to Harring, Monk also "made fun of the legal opportunism of Connolly's Quebec heirs: on the one hand, they wanted to apply the English common law of marriage to Rat River, but they also wanted to apply the Cree law of divorce in Quebec to end Connolly's twenty-eight-year-old marriage without formal legal action."[137] The case therefore also dealt in part with Cree law of divorce, which was recognized as a law of divorce with the clear suggestion that it was valid in Cree country.

Justice Monk declared that Suzanne's children had the right to inherit, and he went further, holding that the second Roman Catholic marriage was bigamous and void, making Julia's children—members of elite Montreal society—illegitimate. A dissenting judge provided a sense of the indignation this decision was greeted with in Montreal circles, as Julia had "contracted with him [Connolly] a marriage ratified by religious and civil authority and under the protection of public law. How could she be removed from her place, deprived of her station and see her children disgraced as bastards and replaced by those who had always been considered illegitimate, and see her own place occupied by the Indian woman, it is this that appears unjustifiable to me."[138]

Yet Justice Monk did not recognize the validity of the diverse forms of Cree law and it was not an unqualified vindication of marriage according to Cree law. As historian Jennifer S.H. Brown has written, Monk's decision was "a recognition of Indian custom as *ius gentium* (law of the people), that is as customary law valid in a region where more formal legal structures were absent."[139] He found the Connollys to have had a valid marriage because it conformed to the monogamous model. It was determined that the marriage of Suzanne and William exhibited voluntariness, exclusivity, and permanence.

Connolly v. Woolrich and Johnson et al. is interpreted today as the leading case respecting recognition of Aboriginal marriage law, as a recognition of a nation-to-nation relationship, as an early recognition of Aboriginal self-government, as evidence that our laws are written and unwritten, and that sources of law are diverse and include Aboriginal law.[140] As legal scholar Douglas Saunders has observed, however, the case is meaningless as a precedent, and "could not govern the legality of later custom marriages."[141] The William and Suzanne Connolly marriage preceded the first British Imperial or Canadian legislation for the introduction of English law to the Northwest. Later cases denied the legality of Aboriginal marriage law. In 1884 the Quebec Superior Court came to the opposite decision in the case *Fraser v. Pouliot* in which two sets of children contested the considerable fortune of their fur-trader father, Alexander Fraser.

In 1788 Fraser had married Angelique Meadows in the Northwest "in the manner of the country." Their children together took Fraser's name, and several were taken to Quebec for baptism. Fraser retired to Quebec in 1806 and built a small house near his manor home for Angelique and children. Meanwhile, he fathered seven more children with two house servants, whom he never married. He had six children with one of these, Pauline Michaud. Angelique's children won in the trial court, but the case was appealed to the Quebec Court of Queen's Bench. Alexander Cross, the losing attorney in the Connolly case, wrote the majority decision in the case, and he completely denied the validity of Aboriginal marriage law, even among Aboriginal people, finding that marriage had to be contracted "in a Christian sense."[142] He understood there to be no contract and no marital obligations; in his view the union was nothing more than an arrangement made by "savages in a state of nature."[143] Cross was concerned that Angelique had admitted to having another husband before Fraser, he was not satisfied that this man was dead, and he believed that "It is a well known fact that polygamy prevails among pagan Indians."[144] A key consideration in this case, and those that followed which denied the validity of Aboriginal marriage law, was the assumed intention and understanding of the white male involved; the intentions or understandings of the women were not considered to be important. In Cross's opinion Fraser could not have wished legality for the marriage. If he had, "then he should have made a voyage to civilization, imported an ordained clergyman, or at the very least, solemnized the marriage upon returning to a 'civilized' country. Otherwise the relationship would be more properly characterized as concubinage than marriage."[145] Cross pronounced upon the legality of Aboriginal marriage laws, casting them in an unfavourable light compared to his idealized view of marriage in his own society: "Civilization introduces obligatory duties, for the protection of women and children. In Christian countries, the relation of husband and wife is distinguished by an amplification of reciprocal, obligatory duties and consequences, as affecting property… forming a striking contrast to the relations of male and female in savage life, where perpetuity of union and exclusiveness is not a rule, at least not a strict rule."[146]

An 1889 case heard before the Supreme Court of the North-West Territories, however, upheld the legality of Aboriginal marriage when the man and the woman were both of that ancestry. In the case of *Regina v. Nan-e-quis-a-ka*, a man was tried on a charge of having committed an assault and inflicting bodily harm.[147] The man had two wives, and the question arose as to whether the first wife of the accused was a wife in law, and therefore neither compellable nor competent to testify against her husband. The first wife (identified only as "Maggie") was dismissed as a witness because Justice Edward L. Wetmore accepted that she was the man's wife, as there was found to be sufficient evidence of a legally binding marriage. Her husband had promised to keep her for all her life, and she had promised to stay with him. Wetmore decided that "marriage between Indians and by mutual consent and according to Indian custom since 15 July 1870 [when the laws of England came into effect] is a valid marriage, providing neither party had a husband or wife as the case may be, living at the time." It was further found that it would be monstrous to hold that the laws of England relating forms and ceremonies of marriage were applicable in the North-West Territories, "*quoad* the Indian population and probably in any case." As discussed in the next chapter, Wetmore also interpreted the Indian Act, with its numerous references to marriage, wives, husbands, and widows, as recognizing Aboriginal marriages.[148] He wrote, "I cannot conceive that these references were intended only to Indians married according to Christian rites. No doubt there are many such Indians, especially in the East, but I think these expressions were intended to apply to all Indians, Pagan and Christians alike. If so they amount to a statutory recognition of these marriages according to Indian custom in the Territories." Respect for Aboriginal marriage law only went so far, however. The evidence of the second wife, Keewaseens, *was* admitted, as she was not regarded as a legally valid wife.

A case that assisted to diminish the legal rights of an Aboriginal woman married to a non-Aboriginal man, involved Nicholas Sheran and a Piikani woman, Awatoyakew, or White-Tailed Deer Woman, also known as Mary Brown. The Sheran family name, which set such a sterling example of the "progress of civilization" through Marcella's 1877 marriage (mentioned in chapter two), was forever to be associated more publicly with another marriage, or as the court found, an invalid marriage. Marcella's brother Nicholas operated the first commercial coal mine in Lethbridge and he had amassed a considerable fortune. Before that he had served in the US Civil War, and then as a whiskey trader, trapper, and prospector in the Fort Whoop-Up region.[149] Very shortly after Marcella Sheran married Joseph McFarland, Nicholas Sheran began to court Awatoyakew, who was then living at Fort Macleod with her sister, who was married to a white man. They began to live together in 1878. According to Awatoyakew's testimony at the trial, "When we went to live together it was agreed between us, that I was to have no other husband during his life, and that he was to have no other wife during my life."[150] When a visiting Protestant minister christened their eldest son Charles, Sheran promised her that they would get married "in the white man's way," but Sheran drowned in 1882 as he attempted to cross the Old Man River. Six months later their second son, William, was born.

Marcella McFarland was appointed administrator of her brother's estate. She listed as heirs herself, a brother, and a sister, indicating that Nicholas had died a bachelor. At some point Awatoyakew gave up the care of her sons to Marcella McFarland who placed them in the Sisters of Charity Orphanage in St. Albert. Nicholas Sheran died intestate, and in the 1899 court case, heard in the North-West Territories Supreme Court, his two sons claimed entitlement to the estate as next of kin. Marcella died in 1896, and the only surviving Sheran claimant aside from the two sons was a sister named Ellen. Mary Brown, as Awatoyakew was referred to in the court documents, did not make claim to any portion of the estate for herself. J.R. Costigan, lawyer for the Sheran sons, argued that the marriage was a voluntary union of one man and one woman for life to the exclusion of all others, and that such a union constituted a binding marriage according to the laws of England. Mary Brown testified that she never saw a Roman Catholic priest in all the years they lived together. One Father Lebret stated that if they were married by clergy of another denomination this would infringe on the rules of the church. (According to historian Alex Johnston, Father Constantine Scollen, who had married Joseph and Marcella McFarland, was not permitted to perform the sacrament of marriage in later years.[151]) Joseph McFarland testified that it was generally known that they were cohabiting as man and wife, although he said that she was referred to as "Mary" and not as "Mrs. Sheran." He further stated, "Nicholas Sheran told me on several occasions that he intended to marry her whenever a clergyman came along." McFarland said that while there was no resident Catholic clergyman in the neighbourhood, Sheran could have made an effort and obtained the services of a clergyman.

As in the Fraser case it was decided that Nicholas Sheran and Awatoyakew did not have a legally valid marriage. Justice Scott ruled that if it had been intended to be a legally valid marriage, the services of a clergyman would have been obtained. Scott found that the North-West Territories was not "strictly barbarous" in 1878 when the couple formed their union; there was a form of government from the 1875 North-West Territories Act, and provision made for the administration of civil and criminal justice, as well as the August 1878 "Ordinance Respecting Marriage." There was a police force and stipendiary magistrates had been appointed. It was held that the Connolly case did not apply, as at that time there were no priest or clergymen in the North-West Territories, and the only form of marriage that was possible was marriage *per verba de presenti*. The judge found that no ceremony of any kind took place—the evidence of Agent R. N. Wilson on Kainai marriage was found not material, as there was no evidence of any marriage according to Aboriginal law. Ellen Sheran was awarded the mine and all other assets of the estate. Sheran's sons were given no consideration at all in the judgement, even though no one disputed that they were his children. The Sheran sons never received any direct returns from their father's estate, nor did Awatoyakew. The last record of Charles and William Sheran was their applications for Métis scrip in 1900. Awatoyakew was married again in the 1890s to a Kainai man, and they had three sons who became respected Elders in that community.

It is interesting to compare the decision in the Sheran case with a similar case heard in 1894 in the circuit court in Seattle.[152] Thirty-three year old Rebecca Lena Graham, whose mother was from the Duwamish First Nation, claimed that her father was Franklin Matthias, a wealthy white settler who died in 1891 leaving a substantial fortune. Although the evidence of witnesses differed as to whether Graham's parents were married or just living together, her lawyers argued she was Matthias's "legitimate child, by virtue of a good and valid marriage between the parents, contracted at a time when this was Indian country and Indian customs prevailed here," and that she was the child of a common-law marriage when these were recognized in Washington territory.[153] Graham testified that from what her mother and others told her, she had always regarded herself as the daughter of Frank Matthias. As in the Sheran case, the deceased's relatives claimed that he had never married and had no children. The decision however, was very different from the Sheran judgement. The judge found that though the couple were never legally married, they had lived together as man and wife for a time, and that Frank Matthias was the father of Rebecca Graham, and she was his legitimate heir. The judge stated that "The law does simple justice to the innocent offspring of men and women who live together as if they were married."[154] The decision in the Connolly case was closer to the "simple justice" of the Matthias case, but in Canada by the late nineteenth century unions of Aboriginal women and non-Aboriginal men did not produce legitimate heirs, as the Sheran case demonstrated.

Plains Aboriginal marriages were far removed from the narrow definition described in English common law—they were not necessarily one man and one woman, nor were they necessarily for life. A man might have several wives at the same time, and women, as well as men, could have a sequence of spouses. Marriages were generally arranged by Elders, but people could not be forced to marry. People could be either monogamous or polygamous, and the choice was theirs. The ease with which divorce was acquired precluded coercion. Both parties could refuse to marry. Once married either party could terminate a marriage. Parents and siblings intervened if they thought a daughter or sister was not happy in a marriage, or was not well-treated. Gifts were exchanged between the families of the bride and groom but women were not "sold" into marriage. Polygamous marriages were seen as desirable arrangements, to both the men and women involved, and their parents. Polygamy ensured that there were marital options for women who were divorced or widowed, and in such military societies, widowed women were common. Men added to their households by marrying a deceased brother's widow, for example, and the children remained within that family. Women who could not or did not have biological children of their own could enjoy motherhood in polygamous families as they too were mothers of the children of the household. Same-sex marriage was permitted, and altogether there was not the same pressure to conform to binaries of masculine and feminine in behaviour or appearance.

While I argue in this chapter that the term "marriage" can apply to this variety of conjugal unions, scholars do not agree on this point, and in the nineteenth century, Euro-Canadian observers did not see "true" marriages in Aboriginal societies, as they did not conform to the definition of the voluntary union of one man and one woman for life to the exclusion of all others. The Aboriginal wife was perceived as a slave, a commodity that was bought, sold, and forced into these arrangements.

Critics were particularly strident in their condemnation of polygamy, a tradition which has continued in academic studies to the present day, with an emphasis on the wretchedness and misery of plural wives in Plains societies. Despite these criticisms, however, the validity and legality of Aboriginal marriage (when it closely matched the definition of marriage acceptable to jurists) was upheld in the courts in mid-nineteenth-century Canada. The decision in the 1867 Connolly case is critical to understanding the approach of the DIA to Aboriginal marriage and divorce well into the twentieth century. An 1889 case heard before the Supreme Court of the North-West Territories (*Regina v. Nan-e-quis-a-ka*) upheld the legality of Aboriginal marriage when the man and woman were both of that ancestry. The judge in this case also interpreted the Indian Act, with its numerous references to marriage, as recognizing the validity of Aboriginal marriage. By the late nineteenth century however, as demonstrated in *Fraser v. Pouliot* and to some extent in the Sheran estate, Aboriginal marriage law was not regarded as valid, and the children of these marriages were not legitimate heirs. As demonstrated in the next chapter, however, the DIA relied on the Connolly decision (ignoring subsequent decisions) in devising their policy, and they were galvanized into articulating a policy on Aboriginal marriage because of sensational allegations that emerged in 1886 of a "traffic in Indian girls" in southern Alberta.

FIVE

The 1886 "Traffic in
Indian Girls" Panic
and the Foundation of
the Federal Approach to
Aboriginal Marriage
and Divorce

"A VERY DISASTROUS STATE OF AFFAIRS." These were the words
of one Indian agent who urged in 1912 that "the marriage laws of
the land should be forced on these people."[1] Many others in Western
Canada shared this sentiment. What this agent and others found
"disastrous" about the state of marriage was the freedom in Aboriginal
communities to not necessarily regard marriage as monogamous. They
could separate, divorce, and remarry. Agents requested with regularity
that legislation be adopted that would prohibit and abolish Aboriginal
marriage law, and that the "laws of the land" be imposed instead in
the hope that this would instil an appreciation for the permanence of
the marriage bond. But no such legal steps were ever taken. Aboriginal
marriage law was recognized as valid well into the twentieth century,
although there were concerted efforts to graft the monogamous
Christian model onto Aboriginal marriage.

The government of Canada's official stand on Aboriginal marriage was contained in an extraordinary 1887 Report of a Committee of the Privy Council respecting "the alleged sale of Indian girls to white men in the Canadian North West."[2] It was drawn up in response to the concerns of the Aborigines Protection Society (APS) of England about relations between white men and Aboriginal women in this far corner of the empire, southern Alberta in particular, and who should be held responsible for their children. Members of the APS had learned of an alarming letter published in *The Toronto Mail* of 2 July 1886 entitled, "A Foul Traffic: A Missionary's Protest Against A Hideous System," by Reverend H.T. Bourne of the Anglican Church Missionary Society, and resident on the Piikani Reserve near Fort Macleod. Bourne protested against the "state of immorality" in the district, including over "twenty cases of bargain and sale of young Indian girls to white men within the last three years." In most of these cases, Bourne claimed, the man or woman proved unfaithful within six months, and either the woman returned to her parents "to be sold again at the first opportunity, or she becomes a common prostitute." He asked that there be a law, "such as exists in the State of Montana...compelling a man to marry the woman with whom he cohabits, or whom he has purchased, and that under the severest penalty." Bourne claimed that the white men of the Canadian West refused to marry their Aboriginal companions, saying the "Indian custom of marriage is quite good enough." But to Bourne the "Indian custom is nothing more than a right of possession by purchasing—as a man would buy a horse or a slave." It was rumoured, Bourne wrote, that if he and other missionaries did not cease to agitate, a league would be formed against them, and already the church at Fort Macleod had been destroyed by arson. Bourne concluded his letter with a call for legislation asking: "Is ours a land where such a thing can be done with impunity? Let the Government of Canada and the North-West answer by legislating on this serious question, and setting it at rest forever."

As his letter indicated, Bourne was part of a much broader agitation over "immorality" in the Northwest, spearheaded by missionaries, widely publicized in Canadian newspapers, and debated in Parliament. White male government officials too were implicated, including the NWMP and the agents and farm instructors on reserves. In April of 1886, Canadian Member of Parliament Malcolm Cameron stated in the House of Commons that he knew of a young Indian agent from England who was unfit to do anything there who was living on a reserve in "open adultery with two young squaws...revelling in the sensual enjoyments of a western harem, plentifully supplied with select cullings from the western prairie flowers."[3] Samuel Trivett, Church of England missionary to the Kainai, was also an outspoken critic of what he perceived as the vices of the district. Like Bourne, Trivett called for "a stop to white men living with Indian women unless they are lawfully married to them. Where are the young girls of 13 to 16 that have been partly taught in our schools and others before them? Sold to white men for from $10.00 to $20! Where are their children? Running around the reserves wearing rags! Where are the women themselves? They are prostitutes hanging around the towns. Stop the sale of Indian girls to white men and another great step is taken." (These missionaries were active in the agitation to have only married Christian men employed on the reserves—the men who hastened to marry or lose their jobs, as presented in chapter three.) Trivett was always careful to say that he did not take issue with those "upright" men who showed "their manly action by keeping the Indian women by whom they had children." His concern was with those who, after a few months or years, "rejected" their Aboriginal wives, who were then "thrown upon the mercy of the camp."[4] These women were not recognized as government wards, because they had married white men.

Helping to inspire the "traffic in Indian girls" scandal in Western Canada, and thereby assisting to generate indignant outrage, were the 1885 W.T. Stead revelations, published in instalments in London's *Pall Mall Gazette*. Stead, the editor of the *Pall Mall Gazette*, and others spent four weeks investigating the traffic in girls in London, and his findings were published in a series entitled, "The Maiden Tribute of Modern Babylon," described by historian Judith R. Walkowitz as "one of the most successful pieces of scandal journalism of the nineteenth century," which had "repercussions...throughout the Empire in the form of age-of-consent (marriage) laws, efforts to abolish state-regulated prostitution, and eventually, official prohibitions against liaisons with 'native' women."[5]

"The Maiden Tribute" told the lurid story of how young girls were being snared and outraged by vicious aristocrats, and it included Stead's account of his own purchase of a young girl for five pounds. Stead's account drew on melodrama, fantasy, the Gothic fairy tale, and late-Victorian pornography to produce his narrative, which was exaggerated and distorted, but nevertheless compelling to a wide variety of social constituencies who took it up and reworked it. It generated great excitement and grassroots political activity dedicated to eradicating vice, and to imposing a single standard of chastity. Social purity groups, vigilance committees, and feminists combined in a loose but zealous network, constituting what Walkowitz described as a "massive political initiative against non-marital, non-reproductive sexuality."[6] In covering the allegations of immorality in the Canadian Northwest, Canadian papers made comparisons to the scandalous situation uncovered by Stead. In *The Globe* (Toronto) it was declared, "Let anyone read the worst part of the Stead revelations, and let him then understand that reliable men and Christian missionaries declare that similar things are going forward among the Indians of our North-west."[7] Samuel Trivett may have been directly influenced by the Stead revelations, as he was in England in 1885.[8] He was accused in the *Macleod Gazette* of "seeking the glory of a Stead or a *Pall Mall Gazette*."[9]

The sensational Stead revelations, as translated into and grafted onto the situation in Western Canada, were of assistance to promoters of social and spatial segregation. The accusations of widespread immorality in the Canadian West were made at a critical time in that region's history, and they served to justify policies that established boundaries between Aboriginal people and newcomers. In the spring of 1885, the "rebellion" of the Métis and a Plains Cree political campaign of resistance had been checked and repulsed through a massive military campaign along with the subsequent hangings and imprisonment of Aboriginal leaders, but tensions and uncertainties about the future remained. The authority of the Canadian government, of the NWMP, and the network of agents and inspectors assigned to the reserves, was far from secure in the mid-1880s. The Métis had fomented two rebellions and were seen as a nefarious and threatening influence; steps had to be taken to discredit them and to ensure that a mixed-ancestry population did not increase through further marriages or informal unions. As in many other colonial settings, miscegenation was "Conceived as a dangerous source of subversion, it was seen as a threat to white prestige, as an embodiment of European degeneration and moral decay."[10] Discourses of racial and social purity that warned of the decline and pollution of the "imperial race" characterized English-Canadian constructions of national identity in the 1880s.[11] Race mixing also potentially jeopardized Euro-Canadian efforts to acquire Indigenous land.[12] The Métis had successfully bargained for 1.4 million acres of land in Manitoba in 1870, and the North-West Rebellion Scrip Commissions allotted more land and money scrip. If the Métis became assimilated into the white population, they could potentially claim homesteading and other privileges, and if they assimilated into the Indian population they enhanced the numbers of government "wards" who were seen as a financial burden.

From the mid-1880s there were loud and persistent complaints from non-Aboriginal settlers about "Indian competition" in the marketplace, and calls that they not be permitted to compete with the "true" settlers by selling the hay, potatoes, and grain that they were producing on the reserves. In some localities reserve agriculturalists were beginning to produce marketable surpluses by the mid- and late 1880s, and this was not welcomed. In a *Macleod Gazette* letter to the editor in 1895 a white farmer claimed, "it is altogether unfair to allow these Indians to enter into competition with white men who, even with hard work, find it difficult to make both ends meet and provide for their families."[13]

Evidence of "unfair" competition, and the threat of "Indian depredations," was kept before the public eye in the 1880s, and there was a campaign to have First Nations people removed from their reserves near the settlements and relocated in more remote locations in the north.[14] At this time powerfully negative images of Aboriginal women emerged and became entrenched. They were cast as the complete opposite of idealized white women, as agents of the destruction of the moral health of the new non-Aboriginal community. A pass system, implemented as a temporary measure during the 1885 uprising, persisted and was particularly aimed at keeping Aboriginal women, defined as prostitutes, out of the towns. The idea of a pass system was first raised in 1883 by Deputy Superintendent General of Indian Affairs L. Vankoughnet, who toured the west in 1883 and wrote to Prime Minister Sir John A. Macdonald that tents "pitched by Indians near towns and villages are occupied by women of abandoned character who were there for the worst purposes," and that "all respectable parties in the North West complain of the nuisance."[15] Aboriginal men were cast as a danger to the "honour" of white women during and after 1885 through sensational accounts of white women captives and "kidnapped" girls.[16] Aboriginal people had to be kept on the reserves so that they could not continue, it was alleged, to steal cattle and horses, and destroy the wild fowl and game. Although an original concern of the missionaries in drawing attention to "immorality" was the treatment of Aboriginal women, the result was to entrench the representation of Aboriginal woman as immoral harlots and prostitutes who were a dangerous threat to the emerging settlements. Best to not only keep them on their reserves, as isolated as possible, but to keep them under the control of their husbands, as in the cherished colonial monogamous model of marriage.

The shrillest and most concerted reply to the Trivett and Bourne allegations, and the lasting legacy of the scandal, was the representation of Aboriginal women as prostitutes and as an immoral, corrupting influence. If there was immorality and depravity, these women were to blame, not white men, because, it was claimed, they were prostitutes before they went to live with white men. In nineteenth-century England, and it appears in Canada as well, the term "prostitute" was often used to refer to a woman cohabiting without matrimony. A woman "labelled a 'prostitute' might be guilty of no more than cohabitation."[17] Women who had sexual relations outside of marriage, or who had more than one partner in her lifetime, could also be labelled prostitutes.

What upset the editor of the *Macleod Gazette* was that the honour and character of the white men of the region was besmirched by the Trivett allegations; they were being branded as "little better than beasts." "The character of the men of this country has been assailed," it was bemoaned.[18] The accusations were first of all denied and mockery made of them. In the great majority of cases, the editor wrote on 16 March 1886, it was claimed the "men have honourably clung to their bargain and have provided for their Indian wives." Nevertheless, "According to Trivett's statements one not acquainted with the facts might easily imagine a market for Indian women in full blast at Macleod. One might almost imagine the auctioneer introducing the various victims, dwelling upon their merits and extolling the article he offered for sale for the most grossly immoral purposes. We can imagine their horror struck faces as they listened in fancy to the going, going—third and last time—are you all done?—gone! Another pure minded Indian maiden sacrificed on the altar of human depravity for a small consideration of dollars and cents." And these were not "pure minded" maidens in the opinion of this newspaper. Trivett claimed that the women were taken from the camps by white men, kept for a time, and then abandoned to become prostitutes about the towns, but "Nothing is said about the fact that many of these women were prostitutes before they went to live with the white man, and that in the majority of cases the overtures for this so-called immorality comes from the women or Indians themselves." However, Trivett had his supporters, particularly the Liberal newspapers that wished to find fault with Conservative management of the Northwest, and there was considerable debate in the press over the allegations. It was argued in the Toronto *Globe* that "it shows how low the standard of morality has fallen when in defence of white men the plea is set up that the women with whom they live are more immoral than themselves, or the still more infamous and revolting plea that Indians peddle their women."[19]

The question of "Indian marriage" was critical to the scandal and to the debate in the press. The editor of the *Macleod Gazette* argued that there was no ceremony, just a little "lively bartering" with the bride's "old man," and a wife could be secured for two or three horses.[20] It was pointed out, "According to the law of the Indians—according to the law laid down by the government, this marriage is recognized, and is legal. A white man can 'marry' an Indian woman in the same way, and it has in the Northwest been held to be a legal marriage." However, it was noted that this system of "barter" for a wife was fast becoming a thing of the past. *The Globe* indignantly replied: "Christians are not justified in adopting the customs of Pagans. White men can not excuse wrong-doing by pleading that Indians have set them the example. Whites should always get married in such a manner that there could be no doubt as to the relations they bore to the women with whom they lived." By February of 1886, *The Globe* called for a thorough and impartial investigation into the "abominations," including the claim that government officials "are principals in the nefarious traffic." It was necessary to immediately "crush out the brutal, heartless and ostentatious licentiousness which is making the QUEEN's uniform and a white skin a hissing and a bye-word even among the not very supersensitive natives of our wide North-west."[21]

The Canadian government's response to the brewing controversy over "Indian marriage" and alleged immorality in the Northwest was to order unmarried farm instructors and Indian agents to get married, and missionaries were instructed in May of 1886 not to communicate with the newspapers "even if allegations against public officials were true."[22] In 1886 the DIA issued a pamphlet, *The Facts Respecting Indian Administration in the North-West*, in which all allegations of mismanagement and misconduct were denied, and any blame for the problems was placed on the Aboriginal mode of marriage. Malcolm Cameron's charges of "incompetency and immorality against officials" rested "wholly on his bare assertion."[23] It was denied that a man employed by the DIA revelled in a "western harem," as Cameron had contended, and it was declared that: "Only two officials of the Government live with Indian women to whom they are not married under the Christian rite. These two took their wives as Indians take them, under the pagan rite, and in both cases the men have asked for the performance of the Christian ceremony." It was admitted that some white men in the Northwest had "purchased" Indian wives, but these were not officials of the DIA and, it was emphasized, "that is the Indian mode of acquiring wives. No young Indian ever dreams of letting his daughter leave his wigwam till he has received a valuable consideration for her...And doubtless if the Government should forbid the continuance of that custom the Indians would indulge in louder protests than any their 'chronic habit of grumbling' has yet induced them to raise."

Similar views of Aboriginal marriage were reflected in an 1887 order-in-council. The deputy superintendent general of Indian Affairs, Lawrence

Vankoughnet, forwarded Rev. Bourne's 2 July 1886 letter in *The Mail* to Prime Minister Macdonald (and superintendent general of Indian Affairs) on 7 July, writing that in his opinion the legislation Bourne requested was called for, and suggesting the matter be given serious consideration by the government.[24] Little might have come of this but for the intervention of the APS, which brought a new level of international attention to the issue. The APS was founded in 1837 to "promote the interests of native races, especially those under British control, by providing correct information, by appealing to the Government and to Parliament when appeal is needed, and by bringing public opinion to exert its proper influence in advancing the cause of justice."[25] The organization had had a lengthy history of interest in the welfare of Canadian Aboriginal people. Prominent members of the Anglican Church Missionary Society were among the leaders of the APS. Just why Reverend Bourne's letter galvanized the APS into action is not clear. Bourne worked in southern Alberta from at least 1884 when he was stationed on the Kainai Reserve. One of his 1884 letters, published in *The Evangelical Churchman* describing his "work amongst these worse than heathen savages" stressed the unhappy marriages of young girls. Bourne wrote that a girl of fourteen had taken refuge in their mission from her husband, a man old enough to be her father. Her husband demanded she return saying he had paid seven loads of wood for her. When the man threatened violence Bourne pushed him out the door, but "Not long after the man's two other wives, one of whom was the girl's aunt, appeared upon the scene, all of them in turn violently assaulting the poor creature and strapping her on a horse, carried the weeping child away."[26]

F.W. Chesson, the secretary of the APS located in Westminster, London, contacted Charles Tupper, Canada's High Commissioner in London concerning Bourne's 1886 allegations, and the matter was then referred to Canada's Privy Council. The first draft response, dated 5 October 1886, was written to Vankoughnet by Deputy Minister of Justice George W. Burbridge.[27] Burbridge had no acquaintance with the Aboriginal people of the Northwest, and it is not clear where he got his information, but his letter reflected the predominant misrepresentations of Aboriginal marriage as the sale of women, and of Aboriginal women as prostitutes.

The "evil complained of," Burbridge wrote, was their custom of marriage, that permitted the sale of girls to white men "without lawful marriage." He predicted that at an early date society in the territories would "protect itself...by the social ostracism of the offenders." "So far as the Indian girls are themselves concerned it is probably that the evil is not so great as that resulting from their prostitution while yet remaining with the band to which they belong," Burbridge wrote. "They look upon the sale as a marriage and the white man at least for the time being as their husbands. The latter are interested in keeping them free from uncleanliness and disease." He proposed several ways to deal with the difficulty, "no one of which is entirely free from objection." A first proposal was to legalize such marriages in respect of past and in respect of future marriages. A second proposal was to prohibit white men from buying a woman or girl and living with her as his wife without being lawfully married. A third and more "radical" proposal was to "provide that no person not an Indian shall have sexual commerce with an Indian woman or girl without being lawfully married to her." None of these proposals were enacted, although the same ideas were proposed on many other occasions well into the twentieth century.

A lengthier response, the draft of the 1887 Report of the Privy Council, was prepared under the direction of John Thompson, minister of justice (and prime minister from 1892–1894) in October 1887. The draft includes interlineations in Thompson's own writing.[28] Thompson was a Halifax lawyer, alderman, and judge, and John A. Macdonald recruited him in 1885 to bring "new blood" to the Conservative cabinet.[29] According to his biographer P. B. Waite, Thompson had nothing to do with the Riel case or the decision to hang Riel, as his predecessor had already made this recommendation. However, he was not sympathetic to Riel, describing him as "a paltry hero who struggled so long and so hard for the privilege of hanging."[30]

Thompson's views were imprinted on the 1887 document that was to guide the approach to Aboriginal marriage and divorce for decades thereafter. He was a convert to the Roman Catholic faith, and he was utterly opposed to divorce in all circumstances. As minister of justice he was called upon to explain the law, in some cases outlining why a certain

divorce was justified, but like other Catholics voted against it in every case, regardless of the legal merits. In June of 1887, for example, Thompson voted against granting a divorce to Susan Ash Manton of Kingston, whose husband had obtained a divorce in Massachusetts, remarried, and had children with a second wife.[31] This despite the fact that he instructed the House that she was entitled to a divorce, as her husband had contracted a bigamous second marriage. As discussed in chapter three, in 1890 Thompson voted against granting a divorce to Emily Walker, the woman who was married, yet not married, but could never remarry.

In his draft that formed the 1887 report, Thompson drew on Burbridge's letter of a year earlier, but his response was also likely influenced by his recent, first, and only visit to the west in August and September 1887. There are no detailed records of this visit, but it coincided with a time of excitement and alarm over reports of "lawless Indians" in southern Alberta. Headlines on the front pages of newspapers that Thompson likely read during this visit included the *Manitoba Free Press*, which declared on August 26 that "Gleichen Settlers Demand Police Protection—Redskins on the Rampage." A similar headline in the *Macleod Gazette* spoke of "The Blackfoot War."[32] Other lurid allegations included one of a Blackfoot boy attempting to "outrage" a young white girl, the daughter of a CPR employee. The father, it was reported, gave the boy a "thrashing" and then shot at him twice with a revolver.[33] There were reports of the looting of settlers' houses, and of the theft of horses. One of the alleged looters of a home was Deerfoot, the famous runner, who stood off a corporal and five policemen with an axe, was taken into custody, and then escaped. A white settler in High River shot and killed a Blackfoot man he accused of looting his home, and another was badly wounded in the altercation. Agent Magnus Begg of the Blackfoot agency reported that "the whole tribe wanted to go in pursuit and kill the man."[34] Just at the time when Thompson would have been travelling through southern Alberta there

< *John Thompson, minister of justice from 1885–1894, and Canada's fourth prime minister (1892–1894). He was a Roman Catholic and was opposed to divorce in all circumstances. He crafted the 1887 policy on First Nations marriage and divorce that was pursued by the federal government well in the 20th century, and he was also the architect of the 1890 Criminal Code amendment on Mormon polygamy. While at Windsor Castle in 1894 he died of a heart attack at age 49.* (LAC PA-025702)

were renewed calls for measures to forbid Aboriginal people from leaving their reserves. In the *Manitoba Free Press* of 31 August 1887, an article entitled "Depredations of the Bloods" endorsed calls for measures to confine people to their reserves and concluded, "Of late Indian squabbles have become far too frequent in the Territories, and the Government should be willing to receive any hint that may help it to maintain peaceful relations between the settlers and the redskins."

With a few minor changes Thompson's response became the 31 October 1887 Report of the Committee of the Privy Council. Many prominent men of the age were members of the Privy Council and present when the order-in-council was approved, including a future prime minister, Sir Mackenzie Bowell, and Minister of Finance George E. Foster, who was soon to be embroiled in a scandal concerning his marriage to a woman who obtained a divorce in the US from her previous husband.[35] The report stated that, according to Superintendent General of Indian Affairs, Prime Minister John A. Macdonald:

> The evil complained of results from the habits and customs of the Indians themselves, with whom "marriage" requires only consent of the parties and of the father of the female without any rite and without the idea of continuing obligation. The assent of the father is generally procured by a gift, or is at least signified by the acceptance of such. Hence it is that that which is a mere marriage custom has come to be so frequently spoken of as the "sale" of women and girls. The Indian who accepts a gift for his daughter from a white man does not consider that in so doing he is dishonoring the girl. So long as she continues to live with the person by whom she has been chosen, she is to all intents and purposes his wife, and is so regarded by her tribe. When from any cause, she ceases to live with him, the female returns to her father's wigwam, without any stain on her character, and may, and often does, again enter into the same relation with another man, Indian or White.[36]

The document continued with the statement that among "nearly, if not quite all" of the tribes of North America from earliest recorded time, "the practice of marriage by consent, and of divorce at the will of the husband has prevailed," and that these have been held to be valid marriages and divorces in the United States. In Canada, it was noted, the Connolly case had established the validity of marriage according to Indian custom, but "the validity of such a divorce has never been affirmed." This was followed by lengthy extracts from the Connolly decision regarding the existence of marriage law or custom, which included Justice Monk's eloquent summary that "This law or custom of the Indian Nations is not found recorded in the solemn pages of human commentaries but is written in the great volume of nature as one of the social necessities, one of the moral obligations of our race, through all time and under all circumstances, binding, essential and inevitable; and without which neither man, nor even barbarism itself, could exist upon earth," and that "it would be sheer legal pedantry and pretension, for any man, or for any tribunal to disregard this Indian custom of marriage inspired and taught, as it must have been, by the law and religion of nature among barbarians."

It was deplored that "a higher conception of the dignity of marriage," one that did not permit polygamy, divorce, and prostitution, was not held by these people. But the minister of Indian Affairs doubted whether it was "possible by legal means to bring about a better condition of affairs, or whether, if the customs referred to could be altogether prohibited, the object of the Aborigines Protection Society, which is the moral good of the Indians, would be at all advanced." Reflecting Burbridge's view of Aboriginal women as prostitutes, it was feared that to prohibit Aboriginal marriage customs would "convert women, now regarded as reputable, by themselves and the society in which they live, into prostitutes, and thus, by causing them to lose their own self-respect greatly to aggravate the evil which it is desired to cure." The minister's final opinion, to be quoted often in future years by DIA officials to explain or in answer to critics of their policy was as follows:

> That the true remedy of this lax state of things must come from the gradual civilization of the Indians, and more especially by the inculcation into their minds of the views which prevail in civilized communities as regards women's true position in the family, and

of the christian [sic] doctrine respecting the sanctity and indis-
solubility of the marriage tie. When they come to grasp this higher
morality, it will no doubt be easy to bring about the desired change
in their social relations.[37]

The same year as this Privy Council report was issued, the Department
of Justice advised the DIA that Aboriginal marriage was to be regarded as
legally valid, although the wording was cautious and even tormented.
Augustus Power of the Department of Justice wrote, "By direction of
the Minister of Justice, I am to state that he is of opinion that your
Department should not assume that marriages of Indians which have
been contracted in accordance with the customs of the tribe to which
such Indians belong are invalid, the presumption being rather in favour
of their validity."[38] In 1888 the Department of Justice provided an opinion
that was aimed at further clarifying the policy with regard to marriage,
divorce, and the legitimacy of children. The document set out the policy
that the DIA would attempt to pursue for the next several decades:

> Marriages of Pagan Indians which have been contracted in accord-
> ance with tribal customs should be treated by your Department
> as *Prima facie* valid and the issue of such marriage as legitimate. If,
> however, an Indian so married deserts the woman who is recog-
> nized or is entitled to recognition as his wife, and during her life
> time lives with and has children by another woman, the Minister
> does not think that such cohabitation should in any case be recog-
> nized as marriage, unless there has been an actual divorce from
> the first wife. The resulting issue should therefore be treated all
> illegitimate and as having no right to share in the annuities of the
> band.[39]

The DIA sought the end of "tribal customs and pagan views," and
wished to facilitate an understanding of the "true nature and obligations of the marriage tie."[40] It was hoped that missionary work and
"growing contact with civilization" would have an impact, inducing
people to be married by clergy.[41] But in the meantime the policy to be

pursued was that Aboriginal marriages were to be recognized as valid, as long as these marriages conformed to the Euro-North American definition of marriage as the union of one man and one woman for life, to be dissolved only by legal divorce. Divorce according to Aboriginal law was not recognized. DIA official Frank Oliver outlined the policy followed by his department most succinctly in a report of 1907:

> With regard to marital relations, fundamental to the welfare of a people, the position of the aboriginal communities is distinct from that of other classes of communities. The law, with the laudable desire to protect the sanctity of the marriage tie, recognizes, at any rate under certain restrictions...the validity of aboriginal marriage customs, but with the same motive, refuses to recognize their separation or divorces...It would of course, be obviously improper to force upon the Indians either religious or civil ceremonies which might have no real significance to them nor binding force upon their consciences.[42]

The legal position of the DIA as outlined in the 1887 Privy Council Report, along with the opinions of the Justice Department, was strengthened by the 1889 legal decision in the case of *Regina vs. Nan-e-quis-a-ka*. Justice Wetmore decided that it would be "monstrous" to hold that the laws of England relating to forms and ceremonies of marriage were applicable in the North-West Territories, and that the Indian Act, which included numerous references to marriage, wives, husbands, and widows, amounted to a "statutory recognition of these marriages according to Indian custom in the Territories."[43]

There were compelling reasons to devise and maintain this policy despite years of criticisms and doubts, vacillations and prevarications that continually emerged, and legal decisions that contradicted the policy. From the earliest years of settlement on reserves, officials wished to impose what they regarded as legal or Christian marriage, but they found this to be impossible. All of the marriages in existence at the time of the treaties of the 1870s, even those that were regarded as polygamous, were accepted as valid. Indian agents were obliged to recognize the post-treaty marriages of couples according to Aboriginal law because the vast majority of Aboriginal people were indifferent or opposed to marrying in any way other than their own. The insistence that their marriage laws were the valid marriage laws is best described by Aboriginal poet and fiction writer E. Pauline Johnson in her 1893 story "A Red Girl's Reasoning."[44] It is an eloquent, passionate defence of the sanctity of Aboriginal marriage law, expressed through the indignant outrage of her mixed-ancestry character Christie, when her white husband Charlie tells her that her parents were "never married, and that you are the child of—what shall we call it—love? Certainly not legality."[45] She had explained that evening to a group at the lieutenant-governor's dance that her parents were married according to "Indian rite," and later at their home her husband accused her of disgracing and shaming him for informing the "whole city." She left her husband that night and never returned to him, telling him that *they* were not married:

> I tell you we are not married. Why should I recognize the rites of your nation when you do not acknowledge the rites of mine? According to your own words, my parents should have gone through your church ceremony as well as through an Indian contract; according to my words, we should go through an Indian contract as well as through a church marriage. If their union is illegal, so is ours. If you think my father is living in dishonour with my mother, my people will think I am living in dishonour with you. How do I know when another nation will come and conquer you as you white men conquered us?[46]

She hurled her ring at him, saying "That thing is as empty to me as the Indian rites to you." In the story Christie's Aboriginal mother had equally insisted on the validity of their own marriage law and had refused pressure from a priest to be re-married in a church, saying "Never—never—I have never had but this one husband; he has had none but me for wife, and to have you re-marry us would be to say as much to the whole world as that we had never been married before. You go away; *I* do not ask that *your* people be re-married; talk not so to me. I *am* married, and you or the Church cannot do or undo it."[47]

As an indicator of the indifference and opposition of Aboriginal people to Christian marriage, it was not until 1895 that the first marriage of a Blackfoot couple, "conducted through the authorized channel of a marriage certificate," took place in the Fort Macleod district, and the first marriage performed at the Catholic mission on the Siksika Reserve took place two years later, fifty-five years after the first Catholic missionaries arrived on the prairies.[48] In his report for 1896, Reverend F. Swainson of the Diocese of Calgary reported that during the past year he married two couples among the Kainai, the first to be joined together in the Anglican Church, noting that "the majority of these Indians still cling to their old heathen superstitions."[49] In 1894 a frustrated Reverend E. Matheson of the Anglican Church at Onion Lake wrote to his bishop that in several locations he tried to induce Cree couples that professed Christianity to be "lawfully married according to the rites of the Church," but had no luck, although they promised "faithfully to be lawfully married in the near future."[50]

In the aftermath of the 1870s treaties there was limited government interference in the leadership and laws of First Nations within their own reserve communities. The DIA recognized existing chiefs, appointed by their own people before and during treaty negotiations, and many of these leading men had more than one wife. There was a need to preserve consent and not alienate the leading men. These chiefs and other spokesmen insisted on their right to make decisions for their people. They were determined to maintain their own legal system, to resolve disputes according to their own laws, and they insisted on their right to practice their own religious ceremonies. Chief Piapot of Treaty 4 stated in 1885 that the treaty to him meant that he was "not to interfere with the white man and the white man [was] not to interfere with me."[51] The government's attempt to impose a new legal layer focused on the prohibition of inter-band warfare and horse raiding, particularly across the border. Canadian authorities approached the imposition of Canadian criminal law on Aboriginal people very cautiously.[52] To a large degree Aboriginal people continued to rely on their own legal structure, although historians R.C. Macleod and Heather Rollason argue that "eventually the debilitating environment of the reserves and the unrelenting assault on cultural practices by government agents and missionaries would sap the authority of traditional institutions."[53] Canadian authorities also approached the imposition of new marriage and family law with caution.

There was concern about the potential for "serious trouble" if authorities intervened in the domestic affairs of First Nations. In 1885, as Superintendent of Indian Affairs as well as Prime Minister, John A. Macdonald expressed his concern about the potential for trouble as a main reason for not enacting legislation to suppress the "evil of polygamy":

> Were legislation, having for its object the forcible suppression of the evil, to be introduced, I fear that, if it proved operative at all, it would only become so after very serious trouble had ensued, especially with the more populous tribes; and the enforcement of such a law would certainly be attended with difficulties of a most complicated character when it came to individual cases...the enforcement of any law that would interfere with their preconceived ideas as to marital rights would be so strongly resisted by heathen tribes generally as to render it inoperative.[54]

As discussed in the next chapter, this statement was used by the opposition during an 1885 debate in the House of Commons on Indian enfranchisement to argue that "heathenish" practices prevailed and were condoned in the west.[55]

In devising this approach to Aboriginal marriage and divorce, a policy never codified in the Indian Act or any other act of Parliament, government officials may have considered the precedent set in the United States, where "Indian marriage and divorce, offences between Indians, and sales of personal property between Indians are matters over which the state cannot exercise control, so long as the Indians concerned remained within the reservation." The personal and domestic relations of US Indians were thus dealt with "according to their tribal customs and laws."[56] However, Canada deliberately took a different approach in 1887, as detailed in the Report of the Privy Council, which acknowledged that divorces according to Aboriginal law were held to be valid in the United States, but they were not to be regarded as valid in Canada.

Canada's approach to Aboriginal marriage and divorce as embodied in the 1887 report also reflects a response to the outcry over the alleged "immorality" and "depravity" of Aboriginal women, who were widely regarded as prostitutes, even among officials at the highest level of government. The policy was intended to eradicate non-marital, non-reproductive sexuality, particularly among Aboriginal women. Even though Aboriginal marriage was seen to be at the heart of women's alleged promiscuity and their treatment as chattels within their own communities, these laws were to be upheld as valid. It was contended in the 1887 document that to not recognize these as valid marriages would convert all Aboriginal wives into prostitutes. The policy of recognizing these marriages as valid also served to keep women under the control of their husbands, and they were now to have only one husband. The problem of women's numerous partners, perceived to be at the heart of the 1886 "traffic in Indian girls" outcry, was thus solved. As Aboriginal divorce and remarriage was not to be recognized as valid, the control of husbands was enhanced, and the alleged promiscuity of Aboriginal women, their freedom to form new relationships, was significantly diminished. There was less likelihood of large numbers of unattached Aboriginal women in the urban centres of the west. The disease and uncleanliness of these women, as assumed by Burbridge, would be contained. The policy would assist to impose Euro-Canadian gender roles of submissive and subordinate wives under the control of their more powerful husbands. Aboriginal women would have less opportunity to breach rules of conduct and violate the normative framework of gender relations. Altogether the policy enhanced the social and spatial segregation that many in the non-Aboriginal community called for during the 1886 "traffic in Indian girls" panic, and during the 1887 outcry over the supposed "Indian depredations" that allegedly occurred when Thompson visited the west.

As with the legislation permitting Doukhobor and Quaker marriage in the North-West Territories, in recognizing Aboriginal marriage as valid the government enhanced, and did not diminish the power of the state, drawing the couple into the obligations set by the state for married people. In addition, those defined as "Indian" had to comply with all of the rules, regulations, and restrictions that applied to married people under the Indian Act. As Justice Wetmore noted in his 1889 decision, the act was full of references to marriage, although nowhere was there any effort to define marriage or to stipulate that marriage meant Christian, or civil common-law marriage. Until the mid-twentieth century, marriage with regard to the Indian Act was interpreted as including marriage according to Aboriginal law. It would have been impossible to enforce if there was insistence that "marriage" meant Euro-Canadian marriage. This act embodied and attempted to impose gender roles and identities drawn from Euro-Canadian society, and the Indian Act also reflected a range of stereotypes about Aboriginal women, particularly their alleged potential for "immorality." Under the act, "Indian women" were not considered "persons" and they were also not considered "Indians," except by virtue of their relationship to Indian males. The term "Indian" was defined as "*First*. Any male person of Indian blood reputed to belong to a particular band; *Second*. Any child of such person; *Thirdly*. Any woman who is or was lawfully married to such person."[57] According to section 12 of the 1880 Indian Act, "the term 'person' means an individual other than an Indian, unless the context clearly requires another construction."[58]

The effects of certain marriages on women classified as "Indian" under the act were profound; a woman's very identity was subsumed and defined by her husband. To some extent, however, they shared this disability with non-Aboriginal women because the citizenship of non-Aboriginal women was also determined and altered by marriage. Under the Indian Act, if an Indian woman married "any other than an Indian or a non-treaty Indian she shall cease to be an Indian in any respect within the meaning of this Act," and if she married an Indian of another band, or a non-treaty Indian she "shall cease to be a member of the band to which she formerly belonged, and become[s] a member of the band or irregular band of which her husband is a member."[59] Nevertheless, she could continue to collect her annuities and any other band monies (from a land surrender for example), or she could accept a lump sum "commutation" of her annuities, generally a payment of fifty dollars for ten years. If her husband became enfranchised, giving up his Indian status, she was automatically enfranchised as well. If widowed or separated, a woman who had "married out" was not permitted to return to her reserve (and her own family) and could be evicted if she attempted to do so. For the purposes of interpreting this act, the marriages could be according to Aboriginal law or "legal" Christian marriage, and this continued well into the twentieth century. To limit the application of the act to the latter would have greatly reduced the numbers of women who "ceased to be Indian." Inquiries were generally not made into the nature of the marriage ceremony when women "married out," although agents did ask those requesting commutation of annuities whether their husbands earned a living, and if they were able to provide support.[60]

Under the Indian Act a white woman who married an Indian man automatically became an Indian in the eyes of the law, and she could partake of annuities and other benefits. She was an Indian for life, unless she remarried a non-Indian, and could not choose to withdraw from this status. If widowed, separated, or divorced her status did not alter; she could live on a reserve and not be evicted. Similarly, Métis women who married Indian men became Indian in the eyes of the law. In their case this meant forfeiting their right to Métis scrip, if they had not taken advantage of this right before their marriage. The history of Métis scrip is long and complicated but, in brief, both land scrip and money scrip was available to Métis men and women under the terms of the Manitoba Act of 1870, and through the work of the "Half-breed" scrip commissions initiated in the mid-1880s. An 1884 amendment to the Indian Act allowed "Half-breeds" who had taken treaty to withdraw from treaty in order to take scrip. Complicated questions immediately arose. For example, would a "Half-breed woman who ceases to be an Indian because her husband, a half-breed, on withdrawing from the Treaty ceases to be an Indian...[be] entitled to share in the annuities, interest, money and rents of the band or to have the same commuted, and also to have land or scrip as a halfbreed?"[61] If so, the deputy minister of justice wrote in May 1886, "she will be in a better position than an Indian woman married to a half-breed would be under the same circumstances, and that as a matter of fact the Indian title would be twice extinguished."[62] The Department of Justice advised that "A Half breed woman married to an Indian is an Indian within the meaning of the Indian Act, and she cannot as a Half breed withdraw from the Treaty. Therefore she could not forfeit her right as an Indian by any attempted withdrawal."[63] Yet an Indian or Métis wife of a "Half-breed" man who withdrew from treaty to take scrip ceased to be an Indian. The daughter of parents who withdrew from treaty to take scrip would, if a minor, "cease to be an Indian," but if she were of age, the withdrawal of her parents would not affect her status.[64] (If it seems confusing, that's because it was. Correspondence on these questions is full of statements that would have appeared very puzzling to the uninitiated; for example, "a half breed woman married to an Indian is an Indian and not a half breed."[65])

Under an 1884 amendment to the Indian Act, a wife could inherit property from her deceased husband only if she proved to be of good moral character, and if she was living with her husband at the date of his death.[66] And the widow had to continue to be of "good moral character" as the "Superintendent General may, at any time, remove the widow from such administration and charge, and confer the same upon some other person."[67] It was added in 1906 that "The Superintendent General shall be the sole and final judge as to the moral character of the widow of any intestate Indian," and there was no definition provided of what was meant by "moral character," giving white male officials considerable power and discretion to interpret the law. If the widow was "not of good moral character," the whole inheritance devolved upon his children.[68]

The Indian Act contained various clauses that were intended to help enforce the monogamous model of marriage. The payment of annuities and any interest money could be withheld from any Indian "who may be proved...to have been guilty of deserting his or her family and...[may be paid] towards the support of any family, woman or child so deserted." Annuity and interest money payments could also be stopped "of any woman having no children, who deserts her husband and lives immorally with another man."[69] Any parent of an "illegitimate" child could have their annuities directed toward the support of that child.[70]

Officials of the DIA at the highest level found themselves defending the validity of Aboriginal marriage. These marriages were to be regarded as valid, as J. D. McLean wrote in 1911, "even though the ceremony may have been of ever so simple or crude a character."[71] Officials had no ability to compel people to marry otherwise, and they were reluctant in any circumstance to give orders that could not be enforced. They hesitated to take any steps that might allow married people to claim that their marriage was not binding. DIA officials even advised missionaries and school officials to take care in asserting the superiority of Christian marriages, as it was feared that this could raise doubts in the minds of reserve residents as to the validity, and especially the binding nature, of Aboriginal marriage.[72] Officials also argued that efforts to impose Christian and English marriage law might encourage people to disregard all marriage law, preferring to simply cohabit, as it was assumed they would see this as a "loophole" that would free them from all potential legal penalties and constraints.[73] In order to successfully prosecute for bigamy or polygamy, marriages according to Aboriginal law had to be recognized as valid, as it was necessary to prove a valid first marriage, although this was not necessary with the second or bigamous marriage, as a person needed only "to go through a form of marriage" with any other person.[74]

It also became clear that even when couples were married by clergy, there was no guarantee that these would be viewed as more binding than marriage according to their own laws; indeed, it may have had the opposite effect. Cree Elder Glecia Bear stated in an interview that divorce was much less common in earlier times, before the introduction of marrying "in church": "And this business of getting married in church… in the old days there was none of that marrying business; when you found someone, a man for yourself to marry, you straight away married him, you never separated from him…As you had married him, so you remained by virtue of that fact…there was no church marriage and thus they lived together until one of them would depart this world."[75]

The problem of a lack of access to clergy or Justices of the Peace persisted into the twentieth century in some locales. In 1893, Manitoba Superintendent Inspector Ebenezer McColl wrote that in "remote" regions of his superintendency it was very difficult to have marriages "properly solemnized."[76] People did not have the means or opportunity to obtain licenses, and the visiting missionary seldom stayed long enough to enable him to publish the banns the requisite number of times to legalize a marriage. "Hence," McColl wrote, "they have either to postpone indefinitely the regular consummation of their nuptials or live unlawfully together without having any authorized wedding ceremony performed." "Legal" marriage was expensive. The 1878 North-West Territories "Ordinance Respecting Marriages" stipulated that three dollars had to be paid to the issuer of marriage licenses.[77] Considering that each treaty person was paid five dollars per year under terms of the treaties, this was a considerable sum. No license was required and no fee paid when there was a proclamation of three banns, but this was not always possible, as McColl reported that "the Missionary, who occasionally happens to visit their reserves, seldom remains long enough there to enable him to publish the banns the requisite number of times to legalize their union." In 1911 a missionary reported from the Wabasca district that he was unable to visit a couple that might consent to being married by him the previous winter because of the deep snow. He was going to try again the next winter but wrote that the man "is not at all anxious for me to do it. Now if I say to him I can only marry you if you buy a license for three dollars, he is very poor and will say he can not pay, never mind them being married they are all right as they are and I can not fairly read the banns as there will be only his father in law's family there and I shall be only there a day or two at most. This is the sort of thing we [sic] constantly met with."[78]

The appointment of Justices of the Peace with authority to solemnize marriages addressed the problem to some extent. Officers commanding the NWMP posts were appointed Justices of the Peace and Notary Publics, or issuer of marriage licenses. In some localities the Indian agents were appointed Justices of the Peace. Under the Indian Act, Indian agents were, along with the Indian commissioner, assistant Indian commissioner,

Indian superintendents, and Indian inspectors, *ex officio* Justices of the Peace for the purpose of the act.[79] In 1889 fourteen men and women of The Pas Band petitioned to have their Indian agent, Joseph Reader, permitted to solemnize marriages. They stated in their petition that they were "Christians known as Brethren," and had no representatives of their denomination in their district and for that reason wished to nominate Reader to receive this authority.[80]

As Aboriginal marriage law was recognized as valid, a case could well have been made that Aboriginal divorce law was also valid; indeed, the Connolly decision, as mentioned previously, had upheld the possibility of the validity of Cree divorce in Cree territory. There were officials who clearly felt that Aboriginal divorce might well be valid if their marriage law was valid. Indian Commissioner Hayter Reed asked in 1893 correspondence that if a marriage according to Indian custom was valid, could such a marriage then be dissolved according to Indian custom?[81] In 1912 a Vancouver lawyer advised the DIA that Aboriginal divorce was likely legal if such marriages were valid. He further advised that the courts would likely not entertain an application for "legal" divorce from someone married according to Aboriginal law, "in view of the fact that it was possible to get a divorce by Indian custom without coming into the courts of the province."[82] However, the validity of Aboriginal divorce law was never tested, and DIA authorities would have been loath to do so. Officials remained insistent that only "legal" divorces would be regarded as valid, while recognizing that this was an impossibility for Aboriginal people.

There were compelling financial reasons for the government's refusal to recognize the validity of Aboriginal divorce law and insistence that first marriages alone were valid. As a man on the Broken Head Reserve was advised in 1905, he could not collect the annuity payment for the wife of his "second so called marriage," as the marriage was "illegal."[83] New families formed following such divorces would mean adding more children to the pay lists, so these children were to be regarded as "illegitimate." A Department of Justice clerk advised in 1888, as quoted earlier, "the resulting issue should therefore be treated as illegitimate and as having no right to share in the annuities of the band."[84] Even if a couple married subsequent to the birth of children together, these children were still not regarded as "legitimate," according to a Department of Justice ruling in which it was noted that it was only in the Province of Quebec that "children born out of wedlock, other than the issue of incestuous or adulterous connection, are legitimatized [sic] by the subsequent marriage of their father and mother."[85] (Following entry into Confederation in 1871 the provincial legislature of British Columbia had passed a bill legitimising the children of unions between Aboriginal women and non-Aboriginal men whose parents subsequently married, but the bill was disallowed by the federal government.[86])

Although there is no evidence of consultation with colonial officials in England or elsewhere in the British Empire, the policy pursued in Canada with regard to Aboriginal marriage shared consistent themes with the history of colonial administration and lawmaking in other settings, and gender issues were often at the heart of this lawmaking. Similar misunderstandings, obsessions, and perceptions of marital anarchy dominated the occupying community. There were similar conflicting understandings of marriage, divorce, adultery, and sexual identity among the colonized and colonizers. The thinking of colonial officials and missionaries was similar—Indigenous marriages were condemned for their alleged oppression of women and for their perversity, particularly polygamy and the "purchase" and "sale" of brides. Indigenous marriages were regarded as involving no true companionship or affection. The fragility of the marriage bond, especially the ease with which wives could leave husbands, was disturbing. Yet while Indigenous women were cast as the victims they were also perceived as perpetrators of perversity, originators of immoral influence, and as sexual predators. Single women in urban areas were almost everywhere viewed as undesirable. As mentioned earlier, Stead's 1885 scandal-mongering and the moral reform campaign that followed in the United Kingdom reverberated throughout the empire. "Stereotypes from the other side of the world" influenced how Indigenous marriage, prostitution, and sexuality were observed and interpreted in diverse colonial settings.[87] Colonial intervention in the marital, domestic affairs of Indigenous people was often initially non-existent, and then cautious and tentative, performed generally with the professed goal of enhancing the status of women, although these women were seldom consulted. Indeed, they were manipulated as a political and rhetorical strategy, and an enhanced independence for Indigenous women was ultimately seen as undesirable in many colonial locales. Measures were then taken to restrict women's autonomy and to bind them to their husbands, limiting their marriage choices and freedom to enter into new partnerships. Indigenous women could be kept under control through boosting patriarchal power in their own societies.

Drawing on imperial experience in India, British colonial officials from the late eighteenth century onward believed that their task was not to invent or import new laws for those they governed, but to co-opt Indigenous law and subsequently manipulate and administer it for hegemonic advantage.[88] In 1848 Sir Theophilus Shepstone, a diplomatic agent in Natal, South Africa, described the principles of "indirect rule" when he wrote that the colonial state was prepared to accept "any law or custom or usage prevailing among the inhabitants...except so far as the same may be repugnant to the general principles of humanity recognized throughout the whole civilized world."[89] The "Imperial fiction," according to historian Rosalind O'Hanlon, was that the British were the "benevolent guardians of local systems of law and justice and neutral arbiters between their diverse and often fractious subjects."[90] "Change and progress in this picture," O'Hanlon writes, "were to come about less through the deliberate interference of the state, and more through the 'natural' forces of education, commerce, and contact with more advanced societies." But, as O'Hanlon notes, the task of "discovering" law often meant profound innovation: "traditions" were invented with Indigenous laws arranged and rearranged and efforts made to graft Christian principles and British common law onto these laws. Officials intervened to both preserve and refashion Indigenous cultures. In many colonial locations there was an initial reluctance to intervene in marriage and domestic life for fear of provoking large-scale social and economic disruption, although this initial reluctance rarely persisted and interventions as well as changes in the economy led to gender and marital chaos.[91]

But there were many variations on these themes, and localized variations emerged throughout the British Empire. There existed, at least initially, many alternatives to monogamous marriage within Africa because people had diverse and complex marriage systems. The basic pattern among the Anaguta of central Nigeria, for example, was that a woman contracted a primary marriage and up to three or four secondary marriages, a system sometimes called serial polyandry.[92] The mothers or grandmothers typically arranged the first or primary marriage at infancy, but such unions were only solemnized when the girl was pregnant. Women could acquire several secondary husbands and they were free to leave one and live with another. Women had a socially sanctioned variety of sexual partners. There was a lack of concern with identifying the biological father of children, and all children were welcomed. Colonial authorities and missionaries were uniformly hostile to serial polyandry, and this had a profound impact on Anaguta marriage laws. The system of primary and secondary marriage was eroded and has been replaced, since the 1950s, by marriage with "bridewealth."

In Natal the history of African marriage and the colonial state is a lengthy saga. Colonial officials were wracked by divisions and conflicts, and the missionaries and new settlers did not always agree with British policy. There were officials who protested against the continuation of African law, arguing that it would be detrimental to their management, and would give Africans the belief that "Her Majesty intends to acknowledge their entire independence from all our laws."[93] But Diplomatic Agent Shepstone did not believe that a multiracial society was viable, and his policy that Africans should remain separate, in their own communities, and governed by their own laws became the antecedent of apartheid in South Africa. The policy of separate African reserves or locations was pioneered in Natal. Africans could be brought before the colonial courts in Natal only if they had committed crimes "repugnant to the general principles of humanity recognized throughout the whole civilised world."[94] But it was only in Natal and the Transkeian Territories that African marriages were regarded as legal. In the rest of South Africa no legal recognition was given, even if Indigenous marriage was broadly tolerated. In the Cape Colony, African marriage was not recognized on the grounds that it was "contrary to natural justice."[95] In 1869 Shepstone initiated an official compulsory register of Zulu marriages in Natal and declared conditions governing the registration: these were the consent of the bride's father, the presence of an officially approved witness, and the free and public consent of the bride. Shepstone's goal was to permit the state and the courts a role in adjudicating marital, inheritance, and property disputes, and to gradually alter what he considered the tendency within Zulu society to "treat the women as chattel."[96] He sought to establish control, but also to preserve popular consent and not seriously alienate the Zulu chiefs. The system Shepstone created gave him enormous power to administer African law, to appoint chiefs where none existed, and he had direct control over these groups.

The need for Indigenous labour could have a significant influence on the way Indigenous marriage and related domestic institutions were conceptualised by colonizers. In mid-nineteenth-century Natal the white population was a small minority; the colony struggled economically and a shortage of labour was a constant complaint. African domestic institutions along with Shepstone's policies were blamed by colonists for a host of problems that beset the colony. In Natal in the 1860s and 1870s, "rape scares," the alleged threat to white women from African men, gripped the colonial imagination.[97] At a time of economic downturn in the colony, whites resented the relative autonomy and prosperity of African communities that enabled them to compete with colonists. They competed with white farmers instead of being the source of agricultural labour. Whites wanted Africans drawn into the new economy, and they wanted their labour, but they wished to regulate and channel their labour, removing Africans' choices in the kinds of employment they entered. Shepstone's policy of keeping Africans separate on their own land and governed by their own laws did not assist colonists to acquire land and labour. Colonists claimed that granting Africans extensive autonomous locations allowed them to enjoy independence, thus hindering the ambitions of white colonists.[98] African male migrant workers were consistently blamed for "outrages" on white women in urban centres such as Durban and Pietermaritzburg. Colonists asserted that "the barbarous domestic condition of African society produced wandering unmanly idlers who lived off the labour of women, had no respect for women, lacked discipline and who therefore presented a sexual danger to female settlers."[99] As to be discussed at great length in chapter six, the great "social evil" of polygamy was in particular to blame as colonists alleged that only wealthy older men could afford to marry, absorbing all the young women into their large families, thereby leaving young African men sexually frustrated. It was further alleged that polygamy and other African domestic arrangements fostered idle vagabonds. Vagrancy laws were passed in Natal to facilitate the control of independent African men in the settlements.

"The battle for Christian marriage, monogamous and indissoluble, was fought all over Africa," writes historian Martin Charnock.[100] If there is one discernable pattern it is that missionaries and colonial offices intervened first to ostensibly protect and assist women, and these efforts, combined with other changes introduced through the new economies and demands for labour, resulted in strains on African households and marriage systems. Matrimony and family were crucial to the African world, and when missionaries and others intervened they had, as Jean and John Comaroff have written, "scant idea what was at issue…none were aware quite how profoundly they were tampering with the invisible scaffolding of the sociocultural order."[101] As historian Rosalind O'Hanlon writes, "gender could not be remade without unravelling much wider aspects of social organization."[102] As in Natal, colonial officials in Malawi and Zambia enacted legislation that made women's consent necessary for a legally recognizable marriage, and elsewhere there was legislation to prohibit the "forced" marriages of African women.[103] But as O'Hanlon writes, "the same officials came increasingly to dislike the uses to which African women put their new independence."[104] The mobility of African women and their presence in the towns and cities was of particular concern not only to colonial administrators and missionaries, but to traditional male African elders and chiefs as well. There was discomfort with their assertiveness and independence. Women took their complaints to courts and to colonial administrators and used a variety of strategies including divorce and adultery to attain greater autonomy and security.

African men, sometimes in alliance with colonial officials and missionaries, became fierce defenders of "customary ways," as they shared concerns about the increasing loss of control over women. As a result measures were taken in many localities to restrict women's mobility, limit their marriage choices, punish adultery, and bind women to their husbands.[105] Marriage certificates, issued by colonial authorities, became requisite for being in urban areas, and stringent laws against divorce and adultery were introduced. Women faced the concerted action of missionaries, colonial officials, and African men to turn them into dutiful wives and mothers.[106] It was in the interest of the colonial administrators to boost and reha-bilitate patriarchal traditions. In South Africa beginning in the 1920s, politicians and administrators saw the erosion of male authority as a cause of the growing numbers of single African women in the town-ships, and their efforts to address this were "premised, in part, on a declared commitment to rehabilitating patriarchal 'traditions' of male domi-nance as the basis for restoring 'family life.'"[107] Respect for "customary" marriage law was partly strategic, as it was seen as a means of preserving and harnessing existing forms of male authority.[108]

In Southern Rhodesia colonial administrators initially made little effort to interfere in the marriage laws of the local people "so far as that law is not repugnant to natural justice or morality."[109] African marriage law, even polygamy and bridewealth, was officially recognized. It was hoped that the influence of "civilization" would erode these, but as historian Diana Jeater has written, settlers paid little serious attention at first, seeing "their role as raising forced labour rather than reporting on the marriage arrangements of their victims."[110] A Southern Rhodesian order-in-council of 1898 stated, "if in any civil case between natives a question arises as to the effect of a marriage contracted, according to native law or custom, the court may treat such a marriage as valid for all civil purposes, in so far as polygamous marriages are recognised by the said native law or custom."[111] State regulation and monitoring began with the 1901 Native Marriages Ordinance, which was an effort to both preserve and refashion African marriage. Under this ordinance African women had the right to choose their own partners regardless of lineage obligations. Marriages were to be registered, a policy based on the notion that a marriage would carry greater social force if given official sanction, and that Africans would be more likely to respect marriage if it carried a stamp of state approval. [112] The ordinance policy enhanced the independence of women from family and lineage control, and they as well as young men found work in mining compounds, missions, and towns. The new options for women reduced the degree of control family heads had over them, and reduced the severity of the sanctions they could apply. The policy contained in the ordinance also encouraged rather than discouraged more "informal" unions by limiting what would be regarded as a "formal" unions. Very few complied with the requirement to register their marriages as this brought them under new scrutiny and regulation.

Colonial authorities as well as African leaders became concerned about the autonomy of young women who made independent occupational and sexual choices, which was equated with criminality and prostitution. Husbands and fathers sought to curb this behaviour. The 1916 Natives Adultery Punishment Ordinance, premised on the allegedly inherent "immorality" of independent African women, was a response to the lobby from rural African patriarchs.[113] It permitted communities to punish unfaithful wives and pulled women back under the control of husbands and fathers.

An alliance of government officials, missionaries, and Aboriginal male leaders determined to keep women at home, to tame their sexuality, and ensure they married only Aboriginal men also emerged in British Columbia. Historian Jean Barman has argued that this alliance of men combined there to "tame the wild represented by Aboriginal sexuality," and thereby refashion Aboriginal women to ensure they remained dutiful wives and mothers. She argues that Aboriginal men were concerned about a scarcity of wives, and that they "made deals to behave in accord with missionary aspirations for them in exchange for getting wives."[114] Women left their home communities to work in the hop fields and canneries, and sometimes they also made money by prostitution. Petitions to have women returned to their reserves, signed by Aboriginal men, were orchestrated by missionaries. An 1885 petition circulated by the Oblate missionaries contained the marks of 962 Aboriginal men, including eighteen chiefs. The men sought permission to "bring back the erring ones by force if necessary."[115] An even bolder petition, again with Oblate direction, was sent to the governor general in 1890 from the chiefs of fifty-eight bands.

They were "much aggrieved and annoyed at the fact that our wives, sisters and daughters are frequently decoyed away from our Reserves by ill designing persons." The petitioners sought "a law authorising the infliction of corporal punishment by the lash."[116] In the spring of 1892 an Oblate missionary and five Aboriginal men, including a chief at Lillooet, were convicted and given jail sentences for "flogging a young girl...on the report only of a fourth party." The priest who ordered fifteen lashes without investigating the charges pleaded that this was an "ancient custom" of the people and also that it was a necessary punishment in order to suppress immorality. The Indian agent doubted that flogging women was an "ancient custom" among Aboriginal people.

Many ideas to address the mobility and alleged immorality of Aboriginal women in British Columbia were floated by government officials and expressed through petitions. The advisability of "legislation, making it an offence for a white man to have sexual intercourse with an Indian woman or girl without Christian marriage," was referred to the federal Department of Justice. As one Indian agent wrote in 1890, "Every white-man who takes to himself an Indian concubine should either be made to marry her or be severely punished for his profligacy."[117] The reply from the federal government was that such legislation was unnecessary, as "laws relating to the protection of females and for the punishment of persons who seduce or abduct them, apply to Indian women as well as to white women."[118] Other suggestions included the idea of an Indian agent in 1891 that the police be empowered to "return to their Agents all Indian women found *living* in towns. [An act] might also give the Agent power to grant leave of absence, if he was sure the object was a legitimate one, and every woman found off her Agency should be required to produce, under pain of some penalty, her certificate of leave of absence."[119] It was suggested that the provisions of the Vagrant Act be applied to Aboriginal women to "check them from practising open prostitution in the cities, towns and settlements of the whiteman."[120]

Most of the proposals involved legislation that would keep Aboriginal women in their own communities. In 1891 the superintendent general of Indian Affairs provided a comprehensive reply to these calls, and this included the opinions of the Indian superintendent at Victoria. Legislation confining women to their reserves and villages would be "practically inoperative and the cause of much disquietude to all the Indians in the Province, who would make a general grievance were their women deprived of freedom." If such a law were passed it would likely be ignored, and "then the condition of things would be much worse, as not only would the primary object not be attained, but in addition the Indians...would be forced to disregard what they would be given to understand was 'the law of the land.'" Through the passage of time, and through example and teaching, women would be "induced to eschew the barbarous habits and customs which are generally the outcome of a savage condition and are naturally surrounded by an atmosphere pregnant with superstition and ignorance generating in its course creations bordering upon the bestial and lowest order of sensuousness."[121] The federal response to an 1895 petition from central Vancouver asking that legislation be enacted to prevent "our wives and daughters and sisters" from being "carried to Victoria for illegitimate purposes," was that women already had their travel restricted by the Indian agents "when requested by the husband or brother or anyone having proper authority, to stop a woman from going away, and so the men have the prevention of that of which they complain almost entirely in their own hands."[122]

In the United States it became the policy of Congress to "permit the personal and domestic relations of the Indians with each other to be regulated...according to their tribal customs and laws." Thus the state did not exercise control over Indian marriage and divorce "so long as the Indians concerned remained within the reservation."[123] "Indian custom marriage" was recognized by federal statute, and both state and federal courts also recognized "Indian custom divorce." In numerous cases it was held that marriages and divorces according to tribal law were valid, having "exactly the same validity that marriage by state license has among non-Indians."[124] Legal recognition even included cases of polygamy. An example of this was outlined in the decision handed down in the 1889 case of *Kobogum v. Jackson Iron Co.*:

Among these Indians polygamous marriages have always been recognized as valid, and have never been confounded with such promiscuous or informal temporary intercourse as is not reckoned as marriage. While most civilized nations in our day very wisely discard polygamy, and it is not probably lawful anywhere among English speaking nations, yet it is a recognized and valid institution among many nations, and in no way universally unlawful. We must either hold that there can be no valid Indian marriage, or we must hold that all marriages are valid which by Indian usage are so regarded. There is no middle ground which can be taken, so long as our own laws are not binding on the tribes. They did not occupy their territory by our grace and permission, but by a right beyond our control. They were placed by the constitution of the United States beyond our jurisdiction, and we had no more right to control their domestic usages than those of Turkey or India.[125]

A critical test of the doctrine of self-government in domestic relations was a 1916 decision involving two Lakota alleged to have committed adultery on one of the Sioux reservations of South Dakota. In *United States v. Quiver* the prosecution argued that an 1887 act of Congress had terminated tribal control over their own domestic relations and that they were liable under the section providing that adulterers faced up to three years in the penitentiary. However, the Supreme Court held that this statute did not apply to Indians on Indian reservations. The judge emphatically held that "the relations of the Indians, among themselves—the conduct of one toward another—is to be controlled by the customs and laws of the tribe, save when Congress expressly or clearly directs otherwise." The judge found nothing in the relevant statutes that dealt with bigamy, polygamy, incest, or adultery, "these matters always having been left to the tribal customs and laws."[126] This affirmation of self-government in domestic affairs did not diminish in the twentieth century. In 1935 the recognition of the validity of "Indian custom marriage and divorce" was reaffirmed through Law and Order Regulations of the Indian Service.[127] The tribes also had the power to prescribe how property would descend and be distributed, in contrast to Canada's laws under the Indian Act. This is not to suggest that there was no pressure on US Indian reservations to confine sexual activity to permanent, monogamous marriages, and preferably those of a state-sanctioned nature. As Katherine Osburn's study of Southern Ute women confirms, there was just such pressure from the Office of Indian Affairs aimed at containing the independent behaviour of women. Agents employed a wide variety of punitive tactics including the institution of corporal punishment against recalcitrant women, removing women who continued to have "illegitimate" children to insane asylums, and returning "runaway" wives to their husbands.[128]

Marriages between non-Aboriginal males and Aboriginal women in North America were increasingly discouraged, discredited, and even in some cases prohibited by the late nineteenth century. By that time new models of bourgeois morality and respectability, along with calls for a sharpening of racial and spatial boundaries, permeated much of the British Empire. Indeed, there was heightened public scrutiny and censure of these relationships resulting in official prohibitions of marriage and/or "concubinage" in many colonial locations.[129] However, this was not the case everywhere, and tactics and goals of colonizers shifted. Fourteen US states prohibited marriages between Aboriginal and white people.[130] For example, in 1866 Oregon passed legislation that prohibited "any white person, male or female, to intermarry with any Negro, Chinese, or any person having one-fourth or more Negro, Chinese or Kanaka blood, or any person having more than one-half Indian blood." This remained the law for eighty-five years.[131] Some states also prohibited cohabitation. In Nevada an act passed in 1861 prohibited "Marriages and Cohabitation of Whites with Indians, Chinese and persons of African descent."[132]

But legal prohibitions against intermarriage did not prevail everywhere. No such action was ever taken in Canada despite continual requests from missionaries, Indian agents and moral reform organizations, dating from the 1886 allegations of "immorality" that began this chapter. One such request was made to the DIA in 1912, from Rev. T. Albert Moore of the Toronto "Department of Temperance and Moral Reform," who forwarded a copy of Oregon's miscegenation legislation, including the clause "forbidding any white person to marry any person having more than one half Indian blood." The reply from J.D. McLean, assistant deputy and secretary of the DIA, was that the legislation "is very little guide to us in Canada. Here we do not object to such marriages, the trouble with us is how to prevent white men having connection with Indian women without marriage. If they are lawfully married, they can at least be prosecuted for bigamy if they desert their wedded partners and marry again."[133]

There were colonial settings where marriages between Indigenous women and white men were encouraged. In South Australia between 1848 and 1911, sections of Aboriginal reserve land were granted to Aboriginal women who married non-Aboriginal men, and there were similar experiments with such land grants in New South Wales and Western Australia. The land was granted to the woman, who could subsequently occupy the section for the term of her life and bequeath the licence to the land to her children. The intention was to encourage these marriages, and to provide a "dowry" for women while ensuring that the land did not become the property of her husband, and thus deter men whose sole intention of marrying such women might be to acquire land. The policy allowed administrators to encourage "legal" marriage rather than concubinage, and they could control marriages by refusing applications if the man was of "bad character."[134] "Legal" marriage was seen as a basic requirement of "civilisation," and land was seen as an appropriate inducement to marriage. In 1901 in the State of Queensland, however, marriage between Aboriginal women and non-Aboriginal men was restricted, allegedly to "protect" Indigenous women from sexual exploitation and to prevent the birth of "half-castes."[135] Two "Chief Protectors," white men, adjudicated the requests of white men to marry Aboriginal women under Queensland law. Aboriginal marriage law was not recognized as legitimate; the introduction of British law "unilaterally quashed" Indigenous law. The children born of such marriages were "illegitimate." One outcome of this situation was Aboriginal women who had two husbands—one white and one Aboriginal. A state-endorsed marriage to a white man meant women gained freedom from many restrictions of the Aboriginal Act that affected her freedom of movement, employment and wages, but women might already be married to Indigenous men, and they viewed their own marriage laws as more important, as less dispensable. As historian Ann McGrath writes,

"Australian Indigenous People saw their own highly regulated marriage laws as a marker of a truly civil society...marriage was a key ordering principle to a gendered system of law and order."[136]

The validity of marriages according to Indigenous laws, when these marriages involved a white man and an Indigenous woman, was increasingly denied in Canadian courts as in other British colonial settings of the late nineteenth century. The 1888 case of *Bethell v. Hildyard* was particularly important, and those who wanted to alter the approach to Aboriginal marriage outlined in the 1887 report often referred it to in Canada. In *Bethell v. Hildyard* it was decided that an Indigenous African marriage was not marriage in the Christian or English sense. The case involved Christopher Bethell, who went to South Africa in 1878 and died there in 1884, having been killed fighting with the Boers of Bechuanaland. Bethell's younger brother William claimed the right to their father's estate on the grounds that his brother had died "without leaving any issue."[137] But in 1883 Christopher had married Teepoo, a woman of the Barolong tribe, according to the customs of her people, and she gave birth to their daughter about ten days after Christopher's death. The chief of the tribe gave evidence that Bethell "really married Teepoo, and that she was his wife and not his paramour," having observed the customs involved in the marriage, including the slaughter of an ox, and ploughing the mother-in-law's garden. Bethell had stated to the chief that he was a Barolong, and would marry according to their customs. The chief also gave evidence that each male was allowed one principal wife, and several concubines, in the Barolong tribe, and that there were those who had two or three wives.[138] Before his death Bethell signed a document providing for Teepoo and any child they might have in the event of his death. The document stipulated, "In case Teepoo remarried or has any more children or conducts herself in an improper way," she would not be entitled and would have to give up the guardianship of their child.

The lawyer for the infant argued the marriage was valid, that "it is the established principle that every marriage is to be universally recognized, which is valid according to the law of the place where it was had, whatever that law may be."[139] The Connolly case was cited in support of the argument that Bethell intended to, and did, enter into a contract of marriage. The document that he signed was critical evidence for this side, as it had stipulated, "In case Teepoo remarried." It was argued that the fact that polygamy was practiced among the Barolong did not mean this marriage was invalid. "It would be a startling proposition to make that in a country where polygamous marriages are allowed a domiciled Englishman cannot marry without the marriage involving polygamy."[140]

However, Justice Stirling decided that this was not a valid marriage according to the laws of England. It was not a marriage in the Christian sense, but in that of the Barolong, which "is essentially different from that which bears the same name [marriage] in Christendom, for the Baralong [sic] husband is at liberty to take more than one wife."[141] The potential for the marriage to have been polygamous, even though this did not occur, was critical to the decision. (Justice Monk had dismissed the same argument in the Connolly case.) "Marriage," Stirling wrote, "is one and the same thing substantially all the Christian world over. Our whole law of marriage assumes...that we regard it as a wholly different thing, a different status from Turkish or other marriages among infidel nations, because we clearly never should recognize the plurality of wives, and consequent validity of second marriages."[142] Stirling wrote that he would have willingly listened to testimony from Teepoo herself, but no application was made, so there was "nothing to show that Teepoo regarded herself as entering into any other union than such as prevails among the tribe to which she belongs."[143] To convince the judge that is was a marriage in any sense other than the Barolong sense, Teepoo would need to have been "aggrieved if Christopher Bethell had availed himself of the Baralong [sic] custom and introduced a second or third wife into his household."[144]

Other arguments for this successful side included that there was no evidence of consents having been interchanged, and that there had to be mutual consent to the union.[145] Teepoo had agreed to become the wife of Christopher Bethell, but she had not agreed to a Christian marriage, and "there was no contract to be his wife exclusive of every other woman."[146] However, it was argued that Bethell refused to marry in a church, did not intend to remain in the colony, and had no intention of bringing Teepoo back to England as his wife. Evidence was produced that he never wrote to relatives in England about his marriage, and that he did not introduce Teepoo as his wife; rather, he called her "that girl of mine."[147] The Connolly case was dismissed as an authority as in that case there was no minister nearer than three-thousand miles away.[148]

The case of *Bethell vs. Hildyard* was brought to the attention of officials of the DIA on occasion by those who argued that the decision in the Connolly case was overturned, and that marriage according to Indigenous law was no longer valid where there were ministers and Justices of the Peace nearby. But this advice and other Canadian cases such as *Fraser vs. Pouliot* were disregarded. The approach outlined in the 1887 order-in-council of recognizing the legality of Aboriginal marriage but not divorce, and asserting that "the true remedy of this lax state of things must come from the gradual civilization of the Indians," prevailed well into the twentieth century.

This chapter has explored when, how and why a position on Aboriginal marriage was devised in 1887, when it was decided that Aboriginal marriage would be regarded as valid, while Aboriginal divorce would not. This policy, which prevailed well into the twentieth century, was generated as a result of an 1886 moral panic over allegations that young Aboriginal girls were being sold to white men. The clamour drew on the 1885 W.T. Stead scandal journalism in England that had repercussions throughout the British Empire. In Western Canada the sensational reports assisted promoters of social and spatial segregation at a critical point in the region's history. A Métis resistance as well as a major Cree political protest had been checked in 1885 with the arrival of the North West Field Force, the imprisonment of leaders, and hangings of Aboriginal men. Discourses of racial and social purity helped justify measures establishing boundaries between Aboriginal and non-Aboriginal people. Intermarriage was increasingly cast as an abomination. These unions not only produced the menacing Métis, they also jeopardized Euro-Canadian acquisition of wealth as the Métis had claims to land. The most lasting legacy of the 1886 "traffic in Indian girls" panic was the perception of Aboriginal women as prostitutes, accustomed to being bought and sold within their own societies, who were unwelcome in the new towns and settlements. It was the honour and character of white men that was tainted by the scandalous allegations.

The Canadian government response, prepared by minister of justice and later prime minister John Thompson, was contained in an 1887 order-in-council. Thompson was a devout Catholic, completely opposed to divorce. He visited the west in 1887 just before he completed the order-in-council, at a time when there were alarming reports of "lawless Indian" and renewed calls that Aboriginal people be confined to their reserves. He decided that the validity of Aboriginal marriage law was to be recognized, but not their divorce law. This policy was affirmed in later department of justice opinions and legal decisions, including an 1889 ruling that the Indian Act amounted to statutory recognition of marriages according to Aboriginal law.

There were compelling reasons to maintain this policy despite criticisms, uncertainties and frustrations. The vast majority of Aboriginal people refused to be married in any other way, believing firmly in the sanctity of their own laws. Canadian authorities, including prime minister John A. Macdonald, expressed fear that any imposition of Canadian marital law could alienate leading men and cause serious trouble. This approach was intended to create dutiful and obedient wives, and to keep women in their place by enhancing the control of husbands as divorce was not to be recognized. In order to enforce the many clauses of the Indian Act that referred to "marriage," "wives," and "husbands," marriage according to Aboriginal law had to be recognized as legal. The Indian Act was designed to create husbands and wives in accordance with the monogamous model of marriage, a function evident for example in the stipulation that a widow had to be "moral" and to have been living with her husband at the time of his death to inherit his estate. For all of these reasons DIA officials found themselves defending Aboriginal marriage law against critics, including missionaries who were advised not to assert the superiority of Christian marriage as it was feared that couples, married according to Aboriginal law, might not regard themselves as married. The DIA also maintained the 1887 policy on Aboriginal divorce law well into the twentieth century, and from their point of view there were compelling financial reasons to do so. If divorces and remarriages were to be viewed as valid, many more children would have to be added to the annuity pay lists.

Similar approaches were pursued elsewhere in the British Empire and in the United States. Colonizers shared assumptions about the anarchical domestic lives of Indigenous people, especially the supposed "slavery" of Indigenous women. As colonial regimes became more entrenched anxieties emerged about the very opposite—that Indigenous women were becoming too assertive, independent and too visible in the white settlements. Colonial policies were directed toward restricting and refashioning women, to moulding them into dutiful wives, and in some locales this meant securing collaborative male elites. The "outsider" marriages of Indigenous women were discouraged and discredited in some colonial settings including Canada, but no legislative measures were ever enacted in this country, although there were many requests that such action be taken. But the validity of marriage according to Aboriginal law was increasingly denied in Canadian courts toward the end of the nineteenth century, when these marriages involved an Aboriginal woman and a non-Aboriginal man. That this was the case throughout the British Empire is illustrated by the case of *Bethell v. Hildyard*, described here at some length because it is represents a dramatic departure from the 1867 Connolly case, and because the case was cited in Canada by those who were opposed to the 1887 order-in-council policy. They argued that no marriages according to Aboriginal law should be regarded as valid. This advice was disregarded however, and the policy articulated in 1887 prevailed. Aboriginal marriage law was to be respected, but these marriages were to resemble the monogamous model as closely as possible. Divorce, remarriage, plural wives, and serial spouses were not to be tolerated. A concerted effort to intervene in the domestic affairs of Aboriginal reserve residents began in the early 1890s. Just as the sensational allegations of the moral panic of 1886 led to the articulation of a policy, external pressures and factors prompted the DIA to tackle polygamy among Aboriginal communities. In the case of polygamy Aboriginal marriage law was not regarded as valid.

SIX

Creating

"Semi-Widows" and

"Supernumerary Wives"

PROHIBITING POLYGAMY
IN PRAIRIE CANADA'S
ABORIGINAL COMMUNITIES

PROHIBITING POLYGAMY among the Aboriginal people of Western Canada was not an isolated or unique development, and this study points to the concerns Canadian colonizers shared with the broader colonizing world about the "intimacies of empire."[1] Polygamy was similarly condemned in other colonial settings as a system that exploited and degraded women, but the nature, timing, purpose, and outcomes of programs of intervention varied widely. It was the missionaries in Western Canada who made the first efforts to discourage polygamy, but they were very divided on this "complicated and knotty problem," and their divisions reflected intense debates about polygamy in international missionary circles, particularly those of the Anglican Church, during the nineteenth century.[2]

Anglican missionaries of the Church Missionary Society (CMS) were instructed not to baptize any man who had more than one wife, but the wives, perceived as victims, could be baptized. This policy, embodied in Henry Venn's memorandum of 1856, was "that while the wives of a polygamist, if believed to be true converts, might be received to baptism, since they were usually the involuntary victims of the custom, no man could be admitted who retained more than one wife."[3] Although the policy was confirmed at the Lambeth Conference of 1888, it was not without considerable discussion of perplexing conundrums that might arise. While the bishops at the conference unanimously agreed that any baptized Christian taking more than one wife would be excommunicated, there was debate about other issues, with some arguing for greater liberty and tolerance, while others were strongly opposed to any concessions. The Bishop of Exeter put forth the following questions:

> But suppose a Heathen chief converted who has three wives already, all lawful wives according to the custom of the country. And suppose "the first in order of time is old and childless, the second the mother of all his children, the third the last married and best beloved." If he is to put away two of the three before baptism, which is he to keep? And what is the condition of the two put away? Are they to be counted as married or single? Can they marry other men? And what of the children?[4]

John William Colenso, the Anglican bishop of Natal, South Africa, shocked his contemporaries in the 1850s by publicly questioning the wisdom of the policies of his church on polygamy. Colenso believed that polygamous marriages were "uncivilized" and in no way desirable or commendable, but he "could not accept that it was compatible with the Christian message to demand that a man put away his wives and children before joining the Christian Church."[5] Colenso felt that the price of conversion to Christianity could never be the dissolution of families and the destitution of wives and children. He argued, "those who broke up families in the name of Christian abhorrence of polygamy denied the true message of Christianity."[6] Colenso sanctioned the baptism of polygamists without requiring them to divorce their second or subsequent wives. His position was somewhat consistent with the position of the Canadian DIA; marriages according to Indigenous law were legal marriages, although he went further, arguing that polygamous marriages were also lawful marriages.

In asking a man to "put away his wives," Colenso wrote, "we are doing a positive 'wrong' perhaps to the man himself, but certainly to the woman, whom he is compelled to divorce. We do wrong to the man's own moral principle—his sense of right and justice—his feelings as a husband and a man. He knows he is under a solemn obligation, ratified by the laws and customs of his people, to those whom he has taken for wives. He knows that they have lived and laboured for him, it may be, for years—have borne him children—have shared the joys and sorrows of family life."[7] Colenso also asked who would marry the discarded wives, who "have already grown old in his service?"[8] To ask men to put away their wives was to sanction divorce, and the discarded wives would be caused to commit adultery if they remarried. He would not be responsible for recommending this act, not even if a wife could be persuaded to leave her husband as "they are lawfully married."[9] Rather, he felt "bound to tell him [a husband] that it is his DUTY to *keep* her, and to *cherish her as his wife*, until 'death parts them.'"[10] Colenso also asked on what principle the wives were to be put away and also who was to have custody of the children. He cited a case of a woman whose husband and child were taken from her. "Our blessed religion already stinks in the nostrils of these people," Colenso observed. "And these things are done in the name of Christianity?"[11]

Others in the missionary world sharply disagreed, arguing that the souls of polygamists were "stained with adultery." As one anonymous missionary critic of Colenso responded, slavery, the burning of widows, and many other "horrid deeds and many other acts of outrage, on humanity, on right, on justice, are ratified by native laws and customs."[12] He further argued that even first marriages in polygamous societies were not marriages as there was no fixed, permanent, and binding obligation until death, and "the word of God restricts marriage to the union of two—the *twain* shall be one flesh."[13] Young women, he argued, were often forced

to marry old polygamists instead of young single men because polygamists could pay the highest price for wives. He knew of a young woman
who preferred to burn herself to death rather than be married to an old
polygamist.[14]

Colenso was not alone in his doubts about the wisdom of casting off
wives and children. Stationed on the Blood Reserve in 1887, Anglican
missionary Samuel Trivett confided his doubts about the strict policy in
his correspondence to his superiors. He wrote that while he had recently
refused to baptize two men who had polygamous marriages, "I must
confess that I have often thought it would be wrong for these Indians to
put away their wives. They are old and have no homes." Trivett noted
that in former days this was the custom, and "they didn't think it was
wrong or give a thought to the matter." However, Trivett was concerned
that any leniency might encourage young men to feel that they should
be permitted more than one wife.[15] His Methodist missionary colleague,
also on the Blood Reserve, may have shared some of these doubts. As
John Maclean wrote in one of his books, the practice of polygamy ensured
that there were no "old maids" in the community.[16]

Missionaries in Western Canada were not in agreement about how to
proceed when dissolving polygamous marriages. Which wife should be
retained? How should the "semi-widows" or "abandoned" wives and
children be provided for? Methodist missionary E.R. Young regretted
the fate of the abandoned ones, but claimed in his memoirs that he felt
obliged to enforce the Methodist approach that the first wife must take
precedence over a later one, even if the first was childless and the later
wife had a larger family.[17] John Semmens, however, another Methodist,
felt that while the rule favoured the claim of the senior wife, there were
"many instances...in which the right is waived voluntarily in favour of
the younger women."[18] In his view the husband should care for the
younger children, permitting the abandoned wives to earn a living on
their own. The Hudson's Bay Company (HBC), he noted, felt charitable
toward these "semi-widows," allowing them job opportunities where
others were refused. The children of a first wife, Semmens wrote, would
grow up able to support their mother. In his memoirs of missionary life,
Anglican John Hines, who worked among the Plains Cree of south-

central Saskatchewan, wrote that he followed no definite rule in deciding which wife should be retained. However, those with the greatest number of small children had the strongest claim.[19] Hines found that it was generally the eldest wife who left the marriage, oftentimes moving to the homes of grown-up daughters.

Canon H.W. Gibbon Stocken, also of the Anglican Church Missionary Society, was missionary to the Tsuu T'ina (Sarcee) near Calgary, and he described how a prominent man asked just before his baptism if it would be alright if he "put away" the younger of his two wives. The missionary said, "Yes."[20] Stocken also approved of the ex-husband making provision for his "discarded wife," setting her up in a shack where she could live, make moccasins, and cook meals for the young men who looked after his horses and cattle. Later, after the death of his first wife, the ex-husband asked the missionary if he could take back his former wife and marry her by Christian rites. Stocken agreed that this was the proper thing to do.

There were critics of missionary efforts to abolish polygamy. Fur traders and travellers of the generations before the era of intensive settlement tended to disapprove, expressing concerns in particular about the fate of "supernumerary" wives. Edwin Thompson Denig, an American fur trader, wrote three important manuscripts concerning the people of the Upper Missouri. Denig had two wives himself, one older and one younger. As an acquaintance at Fort Union wrote, "for the sake of his [Denig's] feeling toward her [his first wife] and of keeping her here as companion for his younger wife…he will not cast her off. Furthermore, he has a son and a daughter by her."[21] Like other fur traders, some polygamous, Denig retired in 1856 with his younger wife to the Red River Settlement in 1856. In his manuscript on the Assiniboine, Denig was sharply critical of missionary initiatives: "The first thing a missionary does is to abuse the Indian for having a plurality of wives. Would the good missionary be so charitable as to clothe, feed, and shelter the supernumerary woman; should all the Indians follow his advice and have but one wife? Will the Indian consent to separate his children from their mothers, or to turn both adrift to please the whim of any man? The advice is uncharitable, unjust, and can only be excused on the plea of ignorance of their customs and feeling."[22]

In his account of his travels through Hudson's Bay Company territory in 1859 and 1860, the Earl of Southesk criticized missionary work at Fort Edmonton, writing that "It seems to me (and to my informants also) that the clergy of every sect make a great mistake in obliging converted Indians who have several wives to put away all but one. A Blackfoot chief lately spoke good sense on this subject. 'Tell the priest... that if he wishes to do anything with my people he must no longer order them to put away their wives. I have eight, all of whom I love, and who all have children by me—which am I to keep and which put away?'"[23] In Southesk's view it was cruel to deprive so many women and children of their "protectors." He noted that there was no "absolute commandment" against polygamy, and that it was "allowed to the Jews and in certain cases even commanded." He approved of the approach of Stanley Livingstone, who, "in dealing with the African savages, allowed them full liberty with regard to their supernumerary wives, merely recommending separation if practicable, and forbidding polygamy in future."

DIA officials took few concerted steps to abolish polygamous marriages until the early 1890s, and even then no action was taken against those who had entered into treaty in plural marriages. The most prominent men, those who negotiated the treaties, were among those with plural wives. Annuity pay lists indicate that there were households with two, three, or four adult women in the household. The DIA hoped that the practice would disappear under the influence of missionaries and under the new conditions of reserve life. This was the policy outlined in 1885 by John A. Macdonald as Superintendent General of Indian Affairs, quoted in part in the last chapter. He was concerned that any intervention in domestic life would cause "serious trouble" and that any legislation would be attended with difficulties and complications: "For instance, the settlement of the question of priority of right when several women claimed the same man as husband would be most difficult; and then another question, most difficult of solution, would arise, in regard to the legal rights of the children, issue of such marriages...Moreover, the inculcation in the minds of Indians of principles that will lead them, from conscientious convictions, to abandon voluntarily the habit of polygamy, as well as other heathenish practices, is, I submit, the work of those who charge themselves with the responsibility of imparting instruction to them in the tenets of Christianity."[24] In an 1885 debate on Indian enfranchisement in the House of Commons, that took place during the North-West resistance, the opposition seized on this passage in the annual report to raise alarm that the Prime Minister was going to give the vote to "heathen polygamists" by submitting to the House a clause "the effect of which is, within the wall of this great national temple of justice and righteousness, to ask this Christian Parliament to put a clause on the Statute Book of Canada that exalts heathen polygamy, with its practices, above Christian religion, with its virtues."[25] No such clause, however, was submitted.

Officials did take steps to discourage any new polygamous marriages. An 1882 departmental circular established a policy that was intended to achieve this goal. Indian Superintendent J. F. Graham wrote, "there is no valid reason for perpetuating polygamy by encouraging its continuance in admitting any further accessions to the number already existing, and I...instruct you not to recognize any additional transgressions by allowing more husbands to draw annuities for more than their legal wives."[26] In 1882 the category "polygamy" was added to the tabular statements that accompanied the published annual reports of the Department of Indian Affairs.[27] Indian agents were to fill in "No. having two Wives," and "No. having three Wives," alongside other information such as "No. of Hand Rakes," "No. of Axes" and "No. of Grooving Picks." The circular reflects the belief that polygamy was being used as means of drawing more money at treaty time. The acquisition of additional wives (and children) was perceived as a ploy to acquire money, and there was concern that the method of payment (to male heads of households for his family members) encouraged polygamy. As a Toronto *Globe and Mail* reporter wrote in 1881, a chief informed him that he had two wives so that he could show more children and collect more money.[28] The reporter had "heard the objection raised to the existing system of paying the Indians that it discourages Christianity by offering a premium on the pagan practice of polygamy."

In 1894 the wife of an Anglican missionary provided a Montreal meeting of the Anglican Women's Auxiliary with details of what she regarded as "abuse" of the system which "demanded legislative action; but which is of a very delicate and difficult nature."[29] "Polygamy is the rule rather than the exception," she stated, "and when a man tires of one of his wives he either sells her or sends her away. As there are so many wives, so of course there are many children." She cited the example of "one sharp old brave who drew at one time $60 for his numerous wives and children, and when reminded that he had repudiated some of these, and that they were no longer living with him, he smiled at the idea of that fact being permitted to diminish his possible profits."

The new reserve regime may have encouraged men to claim more wives than they actually had. It also created conditions that led to parents promising or betrothing their children in marriage at an early age, sometimes to men with wives already, in order to keep them out of residential and industrial schools. J. S. Tims of the St. John's mission on the Siksika Reserve, about whom more shall be said later in this chapter, wrote in 1894 that he was having "extreme difficulty in obtaining girls from the fact that they are allowed to marry from 10 years of age upwards and to become the second or third wife of grown up and middle aged Indians, a custom which I think it is time the Department should take steps to discourage."[30] That same year agent D. L. Clink of the Hobbema Agency reported that young girls between the ages of ten and thirteen were being "given to men for wives," although he stated that he was generally able to part them with the help of missionaries.[31] In the margins of the report a DIA bureaucrat wrote, "would suggest enforcing new school regulations," meaning the 1894 amendments of the Indian Act on compulsory attendance.

Beyond the 1882 circular letter, no formal or concerted steps were taken to prohibit polygamy until the early 1890s. A similar pattern prevailed with regard to the Métis. In allocating the 1.4 million acres promised to the Métis under the 1870 Manitoba Act, "illegitimate" children (from "pagan," bigamous, or polygamous marriages, or born to single women), were allowed to participate. (In 1873 the federal government declared that only Métis children, not adults, would benefit from the land grant.) The official instructions articulated in 1875 were that "In view of the exceptional condition of the country previous to the 15th day of July 1870 the illegitimate child of a half-breed head of a family shall be allowed to participate."[32] The policy changed, however, with the post-1885 Métis scrip commissions when it became the practice of the Department of the Interior to not recognize the claims of the heirs of "illegitimate Half Breed children," and to recognize "pagan" marriages only if people had one spouse. In 1889 a Department of the Interior official wrote that he had many applications from the descendants of fathers who had two or more wives and who had lived with more than one wife when children were born.[33] Complex questions emerged such as "does the fact of a man's cohabiting with two women simultaneously, or with another woman during the lifetime of the first woman he cohabited with, render his issue by either or both of the women illegitimate?"[34] Scrip Commissioner Roger Goulet (himself a Métis) thought that "cohabitation by a man with a second or third woman renders his issue by all of them illegitimate."[35] Examples of those who were turned down included the claim of the heirs of N'Pastchuk Bacon, as his father was married to two sisters.[36] Bacon's father married the second sister after the first left him, and the mother of N'Pastchuk was the second wife, but the claim was denied. Matters could become quite convoluted. Jacob Chatelaine applied in 1889 for scrip as the sole heir to his two children Marie and Pierre Chatelaine.[37] He had two wives from 1864 to 1874, but claimed that the two children were born before he had two wives and was married only to their mother Apiteheiskouis. Scrip Commissioner Goulet turned down the application because those two children died when he had his two wives, and "he could not very well be heir at law of his said children as he was then not legally married to neither of his two wives, having destroyed the legality of his marriage to his first wife, mother of the above children by marrying his second wife." In 1889 the claim at Prince Albert of Christy Bell Beardy as sole heir to her two daughters, Julia and Anglique Arcand, was also denied as she had an earlier marriage, and her first husband Masseuas was alive when she remarried.[38] Furthermore, the father of the children, Abraham Arcand, had "thrown away" Christy Bell Beardy and had remarried. Goulet wrote, "I do not see how these claims could be allowed as both parents of Julia & Anglique Arcand got married a second time while the first husband of mother and wife of father was still living and besides Christy Bell the applicant got married a third time and perhaps a fourth time before the death of Abraham Arcand whose date of death I could not ascertain."

It was at precisely at the same time that the DIA decided that measures had to be taken to abolish polygamy among First Nations. Why did the DIA decide then that more active intervention was necessary? In other colonial settings programs of intervention were motivated by economic factors and the desire for the labour of Indigenous people. In Natal for example, colonial authorities argued that married men could not be compelled to work while they were permitted to live idly at home with their wives doing all the work for them. Thus polygamy was understood to deprive the settler colony of African male labour, undermining the economic progress of the region. It was reasoned then that such men would have to seek wage labour if they could no longer accumulate many wives.[39]

In the US West, punishing polygamists was a means of undermining the authority of many of the leading Native American men. The Court of Indian Offences, established in 1883, took aim at polygamy through punishments including the deprivation of rations, the imposition of fines, and sentencing offenders to hard labour. Judges were to be selected from among the leading men of the reservations, but polygamists were barred from serving as judges. As historian John D. Pulsipher has written, the Court of Indian Offences was designed to strike at the heart of the power of Native American male leaders: "As with Mormons, polygamists in Native groups were usually the leading men of their tribes. By barring polygamists from judicial service—monogamy being the only qualification for serving on the bench—and actively prosecuting anyone who tried to take multiple wives, the Bureau could hope to subvert the existing tribal power structures and replace them with structures which were properly subsumed under federal authority."[40]

In some localities, including Canada, colonial administrators were reluctant to take any steps to limit or prohibit polygamy. Administrators in Southern Rhodesia did not want to erode the powerbase of African leaders when Native policy depended on maintaining their authority. There polygamy was also seen to have some positive attributes. As the resident commissioner explained in 1904, "No native woman is without a protector...if you did away with polygamy altogether and struck a blow at the root of the native system you would introduce the evils that we feel; you would introduce pauperism and you would introduce prostitution, which their social system has enabled them to avoid up to this time."[41] In an example of British concerns surfacing in a colonial setting, administrators were convinced there was a "surplus" women problem, a demographic imbalance that had given rise to polygamy in Southern Africa. As in North America the theory prevailed that "tribal wars" accounted for the necessity of polygamy. Polygamy provided all women protection and ensured the continuation of patriarchal control.

In Western Canada there was little demand for the labour of Aboriginal males, so this concern can be ruled out as a factor motivating the suppression of polygamy. However, economic concerns may have played a role. From the address given to a Montreal chapter of the Anglican Women's Auxiliary, it is clear that by the 1890s there was pressure for legislative action to end polygamy, not necessarily for reasons of morality, but because of the alleged expense at annuity time. There was also Rev. Tims' concern about the difficulty in obtaining girls for the schools. But the more pressing reason was the arrival of the Mormons in Western Canada; they settled next to a community where polygamy was relatively common, yet they were told that polygamy was not tolerated in Canada. There were those who were acutely aware that Canadian officials were not on strong ground declaring that polygamy was not tolerated in this country. Catholic Bishop Vital Grandin of St. Albert travelled to Ottawa in the summer of 1890 to make representations to the government "regarding the probable bad moral effect which the presence of the Mormons will necessarily have on the Blood Indians whose reserve is close to the Mormon colony."[42] Grandin pointed out that his church had been labouring to convert the Bloods from polygamy, and he feared for this work if "the Mormons are to be allowed to teach contrary doctrine by both precept and example close by." Catholic missionaries regarded the Mormon settlement as a "terrible obstacle" to their work among the Treaty 7 people.[43] One Catholic missionary wrote, "What a pernicious influence is exercised on the infidels through these people, supposedly Christians."

The founder of Cardston (known to the Blackfoot as "Many Wives"), Charles Ora Card, chose land near the Blood Reserve for economic reasons, but also because the Mormons had plans for missionary work among their neighbours. In the Book of Mormon it was prophesised that "large numbers of Indians will embrace Mormonism, unite religiously with believing 'Gentile' Mormons, lose their dark complexion over the course of generations, perhaps through intermarriage, and play pivotal roles in events leading up to the millennial return of Jesus Christ anticipated by many Christians."[44] Mormon missionaries told Aboriginal people that the Book of Mormon was an ancient history of their ancestors, which showed that God had promised, "he would not forget them [Native Americans], and [that] through their acceptance of the Gospel [God] would restore all his blessings unto them."[45] This talk of a restoration of power attracted some, but there was limited interest among the Blackfoot of Montana and Alberta. John Jackson "Jack" Galbreath, a Métis whose mother was Blackfoot and who was a nephew of the celebrated Mountain Chief, was a rancher on the Montana Blackfeet Reservation, and he was introduced to the faith by his wife Susan Hudson, a Mormon from Utah who settled with her parents in southern Alberta.[46] Galbreath divided his time between his ranch and a home in Cardston, and he also worked as a Mormon missionary among his people. Indian agents in the United States located on reservations near Mormon settlements claimed that Native Americans were converting to the Mormon faith, "not because they have any profound religious convictions, but because the polygamy of the Mormons suits their tastes."[47] In the 1870s, before concerted anti-Mormon polygamy campaigns began, US Indian agents reported that Mormon polygamy was an obstacle to their efforts to abolish polygamy. An agent on the Nevada Western Shoshoni Agency reported that one polygamist challenged him by (allegedly) asking, "What for you talk

Indians have no two or three wives, when all same your Big Chief at Washington let Mormon man have plenty squaws to heap work all time?"[48] In Canada there was concern that the Mormons would encourage the Treaty 7 groups to continue to practise polygamy, and there was likely also concern to the opposite effect, that the Mormons would learn that polygamy was in fact permitted in Canada.

Given the public attention to the issue of polygamy, the widespread anxiety about the disintegration of the nuclear family, the proximity of the Mormons to a reserve community where polygamy was practised, the fact that new polygamous marriages were being contracted, and armed, with the 1890 legislation that specifically prohibited polygamy, the time had come for the DIA to act. Since 1885 there was also more coercion and less conciliation in the approach of the DIA. By the 1890s the chiefs were not treated with the tolerance they enjoyed in the more immediate aftermath of the treaties. Instead there were threats, often successful, to "depose" chiefs (for alleged incompetence, immorality, and/or intemperance) if they questioned or opposed state policies.[49] In the initial post-treaty era officials were wary of deposing chiefs who had negotiated treaties, as it was feared this could indicate an abrogation of the treaties.[50] A final factor to be considered is that in the early 1890s in Western Canada, the land on fertile Indian reserves was being subdivided at great expense into forty-acre lots that were to be the small-scale farms and homes of nuclear families.[51] This was a plan inspired in part by the US Dawes Severalty Act as well as the Dominion Lands Act, but it was not precisely the same as either form of legislation. It was similar, however, in that the ideal that served as a rationale for the scheme was self-sufficient independent families in which the male was the breadwinner and the farm wife his helpmate. Although the plan did not materialize on many reserves, the early 1890s was the time when Deputy Superintendent General of Indian Affairs Hayter Reed rigorously pursued the idea. Large extended families of several wives, grandmothers, and many children could simply not survive on these miniature farms. In the US West the allotment scheme became a means of finally abolishing polygamy, as they were not assigned to polygamous families.

Yet measures aimed at eradicating polygamy in Canada remained reluctant and hesitant. In 1892 Indian Commissioner Hayter Reed asked his Ottawa superior for an opinion from the Department of Justice on questions that could guide a possible criminal prosecution "to suppress polygamy among our Indians," as cases still continued to occur, "and the question arises whether some more stringent measures than heretofore resorted to should not now be adopted."[52] Not receiving a reply, Reed wrote in a similar vein the next year, saying that "pernicious practices" were "far from showing sign of the gradual eradication which was expected," and he asked for an opinion on questions including: "Is an Indian liable to criminal prosecution, if, in accordance with the customs of his Band, he lives with more than one wife?"[53]

Reed did not receive an answer to his question, but nonetheless steps were taken to warn transgressors that they could be prosecuted, and the NWMP conveyed these warnings. Inspector J.V. Begin reported from Norway House detachment in 1892 that he had learned of an Oxford House man who had six wives, and he had sent him word that "his conduct was illegal and that the first police visit might bring him trouble if he continued his illegal practice."[54] Begin was later informed by the HBC officer in charge of Oxford House that the threat had worked, as the man "had separated from all but one, evidently fearing the consequences, thus showing the moral effect of the presence of the police, even at a distance."

The DIA took a preliminary step toward eradicating polygamy in a December 1893 circular letter that asked each of the Indian agents in Western Canada to report on the state of polygamy in their agencies by ascertaining the numbers and recording the names of husbands and wives, and the number of years of marriage. Agents were also asked to fully explain the law on the subject to reserve residents. In preparing the lists, Assistant Commissioner Amédée Forget emphasized "the necessity for the utmost carefulness, in order that injustice may not be inadvertently done to anyone named therein."[55] What Forget may have meant was that there was great potential for misunderstanding in drawing up these lists; not all of the households with more than one adult woman were necessarily polygamous. Some of the Indian agents were aware that such distinctions were necessary, but that they could not always be made. The Indian agent on the Siksika Reserve reported that "some of the women reckoned as wives are really female relations; it is difficult to prove if they are living with them as wives or not."[56] Agent Allan McDonald from the Crooked Lake Agency reported that there were four such cases there, but in two of these the parties were elderly, and he would "look on the man more in the light of a protector than a husband."[57] On many agencies no cases were reported, and on others there were very few. Not all agents viewed this as a pressing issue. The Indian agent for the Duck Lake Agency, for example, said that there was one case in his agency, but "I may say that they appear to live happily together and give no trouble, and with regard to other Indians there is no inclination on their part to follow his example and break Department rules."[58]

The initial lists of polygamous families were submitted to Ottawa in September 1894, but any action was delayed as bureaucrats there asked that further information be supplied as to the "ages of the Indians shown to have added to the number of their wives since entering into Treaty."[59] Knowing the ages was necessary, it was explained, "in order to learn whether the individuals concerned had reached an age prior to Treaty at which expectation might justly have been entertained of contact with civilization affecting a change in their sentiments and practice regarding such matters, and whether any of the comparatively younger men have continued the custom of having a plurality of wives, despite the improving influences brought to bear upon them."[60] The results so far gave "satisfaction" that those in Treaty the longest had made progress in the right direction.

The Blackfoot of southern Alberta's Treaty 7 nations stood out from the others in the persistence, continuation, and popularity of polygamy. There were seventy-six polygamous families on the Kainai Reserve, and forty-nine on the Siksika Reserve.[61] The list of polygamous marriages entered into since the treaty were twenty-three Kainai, forty-one Siksika, and forty-nine Piikani.[62] Armed with this evidence, and now occupying the position of deputy superintendent general of Indian affairs, Hayter Reed once again sought the advice of the Department of Justice on the question of prosecution. Deputy Minister of Justice and Solicitor of Indian Affairs E. J. Newcombe delivered the following complicated and cautious opinion in January of 1895:

> If such an Indian is validly married to one of the women with whom he lives and has gone through a form of marriage with the other or others which would make her or them his wife or wives but for the fact that he was already married, there can be no question that he is guilty of bigamy and liable to the Penalties for that crime. (Criminal Code, Sec. 276). Even if there has been no valid marriage, but the Indian intended by complying with the customs of the band relating to marriage to make both or all the women his wives, or if, even without such intention he has complied in the case of two or more of the women with the requirements of the tribal customs, I am inclined to think that he may be successfully prosecuted under Sec. 278 of the Criminal Code, the maximum Penalty under which is imprisonment for five years, and a fine of five hundred dollars. [63]

Newcombe was referring to the 1890 Criminal Code amendment that was intended to address Mormon polygamy.

Resolve to take legal action was strengthened when new cases of polygamous marriages continued in the Kainai Agency despite the fact that the people had been notified in the summer of 1894 that no new plural marriages would be permitted.[64] Indian Agent James Wilson reported that plural marriages were defiantly continuing.[65] Two young men had taken second wives and "upon my ordering them to obey instructions of the Department they refuse." Wilson had warned them they were liable to be sent to prison, and he was refusing the families rations until they obeyed. Wilson wanted to send them up before a judge and felt that "a little coercion" was necessary now to "put a stop to what is probably one of the greatest hindrances to their advancement."[66] Threats of legal action and withholding rations worked in two cases, but a man named Plaited Hair refused to give up his second wife. Wilson sought permission to place the second wife in a residential school and Forget agreed with this course of action.[67] An 1894 amendment to the Indian Act permitted agents to commit students to the school until they reached the age of eighteen. In Forget's view, threats of prosecution had been made for years, regard for the "prestige of the law" would be lessened if they did not proceed, and their wards might be emboldened by what would seem to them to be evidence of weakness if no action was taken.[68]

In all of the correspondence concerning the eradication of polygamy, DIA officials expressed almost no concern about the fate of the "semi-widows" that would be the result of a successful policy of prosecution. There is no indication of the kind of discussion of the conundrums that bedevilled the missionaries who asked: which wife would be regarded as legitimate, and which would have to go? Was this legitimising divorce, and were they able to remarry? The records also contain almost no indication of the thoughts or reactions of the wives. Concerns shared with other colonizers about how Indigenous women were treated within their own society, as chattels to be moved about at will, seem hollow when officials were prepared to remove them from their homes and place them in residential schools without any apparent consultation or permission. A central rationale for eradicating polygamy was that women were to be saved from unhappy lives, yet if the initiatives were successful, the "semi-widows" or "supernumerary wives" and children were to be abandoned.

In 1895, Deputy Superintendent General Hayter Reed remained uncertain about the ability to successfully prosecute. He reasoned that while Section 278 of the Criminal Code appeared broad enough to cover the case, it might be necessary to prove that there was some form of contract of marriage, and this was not clear in the case of the marriages of Plaited Hair. The only case tried under the new anti-polygamy law was not encouraging. In 1891 a Montreal man named Labrie became the first to be charged under the law. Labrie was married, but had cohabited with another woman who was also married.[69] Labrie's lawyer argued that the object of the statute was "to repress Mormonism," and that there had to be some form of ceremony joining the parties to constitute a conjugal union. The law, Labrie's lawyer contended, was modelled on the Edmunds Act in the United States, and was "not intended to prevent mere concubinage, but a union of persons of opposite sex which the parties suppose to be binding on them."[70] Although Labrie was initially found guilty, his conviction was overturned in the Court of Queen's Bench, as the judge found that "The evidence adduced did not justify a verdict of unlawfully living and cohabiting in conjugal union with a person already married to another person."[71]

If Reed was advised of this case, he had further reason to proceed with great caution. They had to prove a form of marriage, and they would also have to counter the argument that the law applied specifically to Mormons. It would be dangerous to lose or have to withdraw a case. "As you know," Reed wrote to Forget, "it would be better not to take action at all than to fail after having taken proceedings. And, moreover, it would be necessary to go very cautiously lest any general feeling should be worked up among the Indians on the subject."[72] Reed left it up to Forget to decide whether "sufficient evidence could be procured to give us a moral certainty of convicting." He also recommended that the second wife of Plaited Hair be removed and placed in a residential school.

Casting about for options and precedent in May of 1896, Reed wrote to the commissioner of Indian Affairs in Washington, D.C., inquiring about what he understood to be an important legal decision given in the United States regarding the case of a Native American tried for polygamy. The answer he received would not have been encouraging. Reed was informed that there was no such judicial decision, that in the summer of 1895 prosecutions were begun in South Dakota against a prominent Lakota Chief named American Horse and some others, but that these prosecutions were stopped by orders of the Department of Justice.[73] The approach of the US Court of Indian Offences to abolishing polygamy, described earlier in this chapter, produced few results. The Dawes Severalty Act of 1887 divided reservation land into individual plots and distributed them to each Native American man, woman, and child, except for plural wives who were not entitled to allotments.[74] This policy was regarded as a means of fostering monogamous unions, and of discouraging alternative marital arrangements.[75] But the policy was clearly not working by the summer of 1895 when American Horse was charged with polygamy under the Edmunds Act. Historian Robert Utley described

American Horse as "a man of great dignity and oratorical distinction, [who] had visited the Great Father and travelled with Buffalo Bill," and as one of the "progressive" leaders at Pine Ridge who believed it was necessary to co-operate with the new regime.[76] Utley clearly overlooked the refusal of American Horse to co-operate with the new regime if it meant giving up his wives.

According to *The Rapid City Daily Journal*, it was proposed to "make an example" of American Horse, who had four wives, "and if possible break up the practice of polygamy among the Indians."[77] American Horse was released on bail pending trial. Several days later some other leading men were brought into custody on the same charge. It was reported that the proceedings against the men were based on a recent federal court decision in which it was held that an Indian could have only one valid wife, and that the "surplus" could testify against their husband.[78] It was further reported that the arrests were causing much dissatisfaction at Pine Ridge as they were regarded as "an unwarranted innovation upon their ancient rights and customs and a violation of their treaty with the government which...expressly states that their tribal and domestic relations shall not be interfered with." Residents of the Pine Ridge Agency had decided to "resist to the last extremity these innovations upon their rights, and trouble is feared if the proceedings are not stopped." The Indian agent at Pine Ridge asked that steps be taken to stop the proceedings, claiming that all the other chiefs had "several wives for forty years and no one has dreamed of interfering before."[79] A stop was soon put to the proceedings. The attorney general indicated that the Edmunds Act had no possible application to Indians living in tribal relations. It was also pointed out that such interference could cause serious trouble.[80] As mentioned in chapter four, legal recognition was given to Aboriginal marriage law in the United States even in cases of polygamy. As was said in the 1889 case *Kobogum v. Jackson Iron Co.*, polygamy "is a recognized and valid institution among many nations, and in no way universally unlawful. We must either hold that there can be no valid Indian marriage, or we must hold that all marriages are valid which by Indian usage are so regarded...We cannot interfere with the validity of such marriages without subjecting them to rules of law which never bound them."[81]

It is unclear if Hayter Reed ever learned any more details about these unsuccessful efforts in South Dakota, but if he had they would have added to a list of concerns about the potential for resistance and turmoil, as well as the possibility of losing the case and losing face. The Edmunds Act was thought to have no application to US Aboriginal nations, and a similar argument could be made in Canada, as the anti-polygamy legislation specifically mentioned Mormons. In criminal court a case must be proven beyond the shadow of a doubt, and there were many potential shadows of doubt. For a conviction it would be necessary to show that there was a form of contract, recognized as binding by all parties. No offence was committed between the parties where there was no form of contract as in the Labrie case. In the 1889 case of *Regina vs. Nan-e-quis-a-ka*, a man who had two wives was charged with assault. The court dismissed the first wife who was found to be a wife-in-law and therefore neither compellable nor competent to testify against her husband. The second wife, however, was admitted as a witness as she was not regarded as a legally valid wife.[82] The case could be interpreted to mean that a man could have only one wife. This case also upheld the validity of Aboriginal customary marriage, when such a marriage was monogamous. The court found that "marriage between Indians and by mutual consent and according to Indian custom since 15 July 1870 is a valid marriage, providing neither party had a husband or wife as the case may be, living at the time."[83]

DIA administrators became ever more determined to take stringent measures as new cases of polygamy arose. It was also reported that young girls were being promised in marriage as a means of preventing them from being sent to residential schools.[84] Before proceeding with the uncertain criminal prosecution, further consideration was given to the tactic of placing girls in residential schools under the compulsory education clauses of the Indian Act. In 1895 Forget was wondering whether this might be more successful, causing "less friction than by proceeding to prosecute for bigamy under the Criminal Code."[85] The linking of the residential school program with the campaign to abolish polygamy further inflamed protests on the reserve communities of southern Alberta. The resentment and anger over the residential and boarding schools was particularly high in the mid-1890s as there were many deaths of pupils from tuberculosis. In 1894 Rev. T. H. Bourne of the St. Cyprian's mission on the Piikani Reserve reported that there were five deaths in the residential school there, and many more students were ill.[86]

On the Siksika Reserve early in 1895, zealous Indian Agent Magnus Begg decided to pursue the repression of polygamy according to his own interpretation of the law and instructions from his superiors. His actions generated controversy, and were protested by both his superiors and the people under his supervision. He reported new cases of polygamy in his agency—two girls that Begg thought were no more than twelve were promised to men who already had wives. At a meeting held on the North Reserve in February, Begg declared that no man could marry a girl under the age of eighteen. He also stated that no man could marry a young woman graduate of an industrial or boarding school unless he had built a house with two rooms and had cows and a stable.[87] Begg further said that all children were to remain in schools unless their dis-charge was sanctioned by the Department, and that all school-age children were to be sent to residential schools, as day schools were to be done away with as much as possible. According to Begg's account of this meeting, White Pup, spokesman for the chiefs, said that Begg "might expect blood" if the regulation concerning the age of marriage for girls was carried out.[88] Begg told them they were "talking foolish" about shedding blood, and insisted that all instructions must be carried out. Begg was severely reprimanded for his statements at that meeting. Forget said that the agent had misinformed people, as a girl was marriageable at the age of twelve.[89] Begg was told to correct this false impression, as nothing would be gained by deceiving them.

Agent Begg did little to defuse the situation. At his next meeting held in March he informed the chiefs and headmen that if the betrothed girls were not sent to a school it would be necessary to take them by force, or to arrest the men who married them.[90] The chiefs replied that they were willing to have new regulations apply to the girls already in the schools,

> *In 1895 on the Siksika Reserve Indian Agent Magnus Begg's zealous efforts to suppress polygamy created a tense situation. White Pup was chosen spokesmen for the chiefs who protested Begg's manoeuvres. (Top [White Pup]* GAA NA 1773-25; *Bottom [Magnus Begg]* GAA NA-3867-1)

but that these should not be applied to other girls of the community. Begg suspected that their tactic was to promise all the young girls in marriage so that "there would be none for the schools." He sought Forget's permission to take the girls to the school with the assistance of the police, and warned that arrests might cause trouble as "all the older Indians are strongly against any interference in the matter." Once again Begg was reprimanded for his actions, for not obtaining the permission of the parents of the girls to place them in school, and for threatening the chiefs about the use of force and arrests.[91] Forget advised that having committed himself to such a course, Begg ought to proceed to enforce the compulsory school regulations in the two cases mentioned, "If the prestige of the Department and its Agent is to be maintained." Begg was to act prudently, cautiously, and with great tact, exhausting every peaceful means before considering a resort to any other. The agent soon reported that the two cases had been hastily resolved as one of the fathers took his daughter home, and the other girl was betrothed to a man with no other wife.[92]

Tensions were high on the Siksika Reserve by the summer of 1895. J.W. Tims of the St. John's mission reported in June, "I am sure that the slightest provocation now would start them on the warpath." On April 3, Francis Skynner, the ration issuer on the reserve and an ex-corporal in the NWMP was shot by a man named Scraping Hide, whose nine-year-old son had just died. Although several stories existed to explain why his son died, historian Hugh Dempsey has concluded that the correct version was that the boy had contracted tuberculosis in school and died after being released.[93] Following the shooting, Scraping Hide went to the cemetery where his son was buried and waited for the police to attack him. For two days he stayed by the grave and refused to surrender until he was shot and killed by a member of the NWMP. It was a "tragic, senseless killing," Dempsey wrote. A month after this event, a girl named Mable Cree died at the Anglican boarding school. Missionary Tims had blocked the efforts of the family to remove her.[94] Six other of the seventeen students there were seriously ill with tuberculosis. Much anger and resentment was directed toward Tims, who had implemented compulsory attendance. Tims fled the reserve, reporting in June of 1895 that "owing to Government regulations re detention of pupils, there has been a bad feeling. The Indians were much excited and talked of shooting me, on whom, as Principal, they laid the blame of the girl's death. They also threatened that unless I was removed there would be bloodshed."[95] Tims also reported that the parents of pupils out on leave refused to allow their children to return, and would not permit the police to make arrests of the absentees. Tims and Begg had clearly aggravated the situation at the Siksika Reserve for years. In tendering his resignation Tims noted that Begg "might expect blood"—"thye [sic] bear special animus against me."[96] Tims himself blamed DIA officials for "the way these Indians have been handled." "They are defying the law and running things their own way on the Reserve," Tims concluded, and he recommended that "a force of 200 or more men [be] located on the border of the reserve as a check to their present behaviour." Tims was reassigned, although promoted, becoming director of missions for southern Alberta. In a missionary publication that noted Tims' departure from the Siksika mission, it was explained that the Blackfoot parents were angry at the new government regulations about the detention of their children, and "having got it into their heads Rev. Tims is the originator of them, made things... unpleasant for him."[97]

The 1897 Charcoal case provided further evidence of defiance on the southern Alberta reserves, and it also drew the public's attention to the persistence of diverse marriages including polygamy. Charcoal was a Kainai man who confessed to the murders of another Kainai man, Medicine Pipe Stem, and Sergeant W. B. Wilde of the NWMP. In the trial evidence emerged that Charcoal found one of his wives, Pretty Wolverine, in an act of infidelity. He shot her seducer in retaliation. Charcoal was first married to a woman who had left him in 1890 before marrying Pretty Wolverine in 1891.[98] In 1896 a second wife, Sleeping Woman, was added to the household. Pretty Wolverine was called to the stand but Judge Scott told her that if she really was Charcoal's wife she did not have to give evidence. She swore she was his wife, "and that he was her fifth husband."[99] It was reported in the *Macleod Gazette* that Pretty Wolverine was "examined as to her several matrimonial adventures, and an amusing dialogue took place between counsel and witness. In the course of this examination it transpired that Charcoal was the fifth lucky man to draw this matrimonial

prize. Of the other four, one was dead, and as remarked by Mr. Costigan, there was only one occasion on which the lady had got in on the ground floor, all the other husbands having had wives varying in number, from one to four at the time they married her. The Crown finally came to the conclusion that, while Mrs. Charcoal had evidently been very much married, she was evidently tied up securely enough to No. 5, and she was excused from giving evidence."[100] Witness R. N. Wilson, who at that time was acting as interpreter for Indian Agent James Wilson, provided a lengthy description of marriage customs, including that "the agreement is to live together permanently, not during pleasure." Agent Wilson, perhaps in an effort to deflect criticism from the DIA, testified that Charcoal had only one wife and that "it used to be the custom among the Indians to have as many wives as they liked, but now under the regulations of the department, only one was allowed."[101]

DIA officials were worried about the determination of the Blackfoot to resist interference in their domestic relations. Chief Red Crow of the Kainai continued to live with his four wives despite the fact that in 1896 he was baptized into the Roman Catholic Church, and was married in a Catholic ceremony to his youngest wife Singing Before. Father Emile Legal performed both the baptism and the marriage.[102] This was a distinct departure from the firm rule of the priests not to perform a marriage ceremony of a polygamous husband until he had cast aside his other wives. Agent James Wilson was astonished at this departure, writing that "the Rev. Father Legal put Red Crow and one of his wives through a form of marriage, but as he has *three* other wives living with him, each of whom has been his wife for a longer period than the married (?) one, I fail to see what good this ceremony has done. The Indians on the other hand say it has been done so that his wife may claim all the old man's property to the exclusion of others."[103] According to historian Hugh Dempsey, these speculations were true. Red Crow was wealthy in cattle and horses, and

< Top: The wedding of Reverend J. W. Tims and Violet Wood, 1890, Siksika Reserve, Alberta. The bride, from England, had arrived in the West only weeks earlier, as the travelling companion of the woman beside her on the right, Frances Kirby, who collected Aboriginal artifacts. Reverend Tims contributed to the mid-1890s tensions on the Siksika Reserve over interference in domestic affairs and compulsory attendance at the Anglican boarding school. (GAA NA–1645–1) Bottom: Wedding group at the Anglican mission on the Siksika Reserve, ca. 1900. Jim Abikoki and family. (GAA NC–5-8)

this marriage ensured that his baptized Catholic son Frank, a student in an industrial school, would gain the inheritance.[104]

As evidence of new cases of polygamy accumulated in 1898, Indian Commissioner Forget wrote James Smart, the new deputy superintendent of Indian Affairs, requesting "a definite and unqualified authorization to take measures of repression. Department's sanction of proceedings in such cases having hitherto been so qualified as to practically nullify same."[105] J. D. McLean, acting secretary, replied that the department was willing to leave the matter in his hands. Newcombe's 1895 opinion was quoted, and Forget was told that if he felt it was in the best interests of the Indians, and of public morality, he could take the necessary measures.[106] Forget was determined to take action as he was convinced that "unless severe measures are taken it will be many years before the evil is eradicated."[107] In 1898 Indian Agent James Wilson reported that not-withstanding all his efforts on the Blood Reserve, six or seven young men had taken second wives, and he felt others would follow this example.[108]

In the Treaty 4 district, Cree Chief Star Blanket was reported in the fall of 1898 to have taken another wife.[109] The File Hills Indian agent informed the chief that more was expected of him as he had only recently been reinstated as chief. According to the agent, Star Blanket said, "He would rather give up the Chiefship [sic] than give the woman up."[110] After several months Star Blanket complied with DIA policy to some extent by giving up his first wife, who appealed to the department for assistance, as she was in a state of destitution.[111] Star Blanket was regarded as "difficult" to handle, as he was opposed to policies on schools. It was recommended that he be deposed.

Forget decided to focus on the Kainai Reserve after first giving the parties reasonable notice that they would be prosecuted unless they abandoned polygamy. He hoped that with firmness and the "hearty co-operation" of the police, that the law would be enforced. Forget instructed Agent Wilson in August of 1898 to collect and submit information regarding all the new cases of polygamy to Crown Prosecutor C. F. Conybeare of Lethbridge.[112] If Conybeare thought that criminal proceedings could be brought against any of these men, the agent was to call a meeting of the chiefs, bring the young men before them, and explain the law on the subject. In August 1898, Forget instructed Wilson to emphasize that the DIA had no desire to be harsh with them, "and that while it would see with pleasure the old men abandoning the practice, yet no prosecution is intended regarding them as they commenced the practice before they knew of the existence of the law."[113] As for the others, the greatest leniency was to be extended, as the desire was to prevent wrongdoing and not to punish. The parties were to be informed that they had one month to abandon polygamy or criminal proceedings would begin.

The Kainai, however, were determined to resist. Their resolve was possibly steeled by the fact that Red Crow had been permitted to marry one of his wives in a Catholic ceremony while retaining the other three. By November of 1898, Agent Wilson could report no changes despite numerous meetings on the subject. Wilson tried another tactic during annuity payments by refusing to pay the wives.[114] Wilson explained to Forget that the Indian Act "gave power to refuse payment to women who deserted their families and lived immorally with another man, and that as these women knew what they were doing they were equally guilty with the men." Wilson told Red Crow that the pay-list books would be kept open for ten days, and that during that time the chief was to hold a meeting with the women to persuade them to give up their marriages. A meeting was held, but it was reported that Red Crow's position was that the new rules about marriage should apply only to the graduates of the schools.[115] Wilson declared that the young people were bound to obey and that Red Crow should insist that they obey. The chief refused to do this. Once again the young men were given one month to withdraw from the position they had taken. Agent Wilson reported, however, that the tactic of holding back annuities worked with a number of the wives, but three still refused to comply or to give up their marriages. Wilson sought permission to continue to withhold annuities. In his view these women were "living immorally" as they had "undoubtedly" left their families to reside with men who were already married. Two of the women were widows with children when they remarried. Forget permitted Wilson to withhold the annuities of the women who "still persist to live immorally."[116]

By December 1898, Agent Wilson was determined that legal proceedings should be taken to "enforce the law as those young men still refuse to obey."[117] In consultation with Conybeare it was decided to proceed against Bear's Shin Bone, the most recent of the men to enter into a polygamous marriage, and a scout for the NWMP. Bear's Shin Bone was brought before Judge C. Rouleau at Fort Macleod on March 10, 1899, on a charge of practising polygamy with two women, an offence under Section 278 of the Criminal Code, which was originally designed to address Mormon polygamy.[118] His wives were "Free Cutter Woman" and "Killed Herself," and there is no evidence that either testified during the trial. To do so would have raised the question of whether they were compellable or competent to testify against their husband, as in the case of Charcoal's wife Pretty Wolverine. If, as in *Regina vs. Nan-e-quis-a-ka*, the second wife was not found to be a valid wife, the case for the prosecution for polygamy could be weakened. Conybeare had to prove that there was a form of contract between the parties that they all regarded as binding upon them. M. McKenzie argued for the defence that this section of the statute was never intended to apply to Indians.[119] But the court held that the law "applied to Indians as well as whites," that the marriage customs of the Kainai came within the provisions of the statute, and were a form of contract, recognized as valid by the case of *Regina vs. Nan-e-quis-a-ka*. Both marriages had to be recognized as valid contracts in order to invalidate the second marriage. This anomaly was recognized in the local newspaper's coverage of the case, in which it was noted, "Bare-Shin-Bone [sic], the Blood Indian charged with polygamy, was convicted and allowed to go on suspended sentence, being instructed to annul his latest marriage (?) and cleave to his first spouse and none other."[120]

Bear's Shin Bone was allowed out on suspended sentence on the understanding that he give up his second wife, and that if he did not he would be brought up at any time for sentencing.[121] The DIA regarded this as a test case, with the goal being not to punish but to make the prisoner and the others obey the law. The DIA agreed to pay for the defence barrister, even though the Kainai had raised a sum of money for that purpose. Wilson also sought and received permission to pay arrears for the 1898 annuities withheld from the women who refused to give up their marriages. Wilson further sought permission to have the children listed as legitimate, allowing them to draw rations and annuities. These measures would, in Wilson's view, "help to allay the feeling of soreness which one or two of them feel at having to give up their second wives."[122] Permission was granted; newly-appointed Indian Commissioner David Laird was advised from Ottawa that the offspring of these marriages would be considered legitimate and not only rationed but placed on the pay list.[123] DIA accountant Duncan Campbell Scott endorsed these measures, writing in a memorandum that:

> The right of the women themselves to payment of annuity is not impugned by the relation referred to, and if we were to consider the offspring of such unions illegitimate it would hardly be possible to advance just grounds for our decision, as a great number of adult Indians and children throughout Manitoba and the North West are the fruit of such marriages. The effect of leniency in these cases will assist in furthering an easy transition to civilized ways of matrimony.[124]

The 1890s campaign aimed at prohibiting polygamy that culminated in the Bear's Shin Bone case did not immediately result in the desired goal. The 1901 census for the Blood Reserve indicated over thirty polygamous families (and there might have been more as many adult women were listed as "boarders" in households).[125] Not all of these were marriages contracted before or at the time of Treaty 7, as some involved younger men and women, and Indian agents continued to report polygamous marriages.[126] In 1904 the agent reported from the Siksika Reserve that "I learned that three members of the band were dissatisfied with one wife each and had taken another. I immediately directed the rations of these families to be withheld until such time as they saw fit to obey the rules in this respect. One family missed one ration and then decided that it was better policy to abide by the rules. The other two families held out for several rations, and then succumbed and put away wife number two."[127] The missionaries similarly continued in their campaign to abolish polygamy. The Anglican register of marriages on the Siksika

Reserve indicates that plural wives, generally identified as the younger wives, were being "surrendered" and remarried. In 1904, for example, the "younger of the two wives of Lone Bull—surrendered" was married, as was "one of two wives of Turning Robes, surrendered."[128]

In 1900 the attention of the DIA shifted to concern about "child marriages" among the Siksika, allegedly polygamous in some cases. These reports were sensationalized but soon challenged and dismissed. In several localities throughout the British Empire, but particularly in Bengal, the British passed age-of-consent legislation. Scholars have argued that this legislation was motivated not by a concern for child brides and the status of women, but as a means of "demonstrating the inferiority of Indian, particularly Bengali, masculinity" in order to "justify their unwillingness to share political power and administrative control."[129] It is possible that there was an element of this at work in southern Alberta, as the will of the DIA had not entirely prevailed in their dispute with Blackfoot leaders over interference in their domestic lives. The incident also demonstrates the inability of authorities once again to prosecute and convict. Echoing aspects of the 1886 "immorality" controversy, in 1900 alarming news was conveyed by Siksika Reserve Indian Agent J. A. Markle that "the Indians of this band have been in the habit of bartering their female children to Indians of all ages, to become the wives of the purchaser," and he cited the example of a man who had recently "traded his daughter under 8 years of age to an Indian for about 20 ponies."[130] Indian Commissioner Laird could find nothing in the Criminal Code forbidding such marriages, if the consent of the parents was obtained, but he referred the matter to the Department of Justice, asking if the father could be prosecuted under any other law in Canada.[131] The reply from Law Clerk Reginald Rimmer was that there was no law under which a parent or husband could be successfully prosecuted.[132] The only section of the code that might have bearing was that a man could be "liable to imprisonment for life and to be whipped who carnally knows any girl under fourteen years *not being his wife*."[133] If these were indeed wives, then the section of the code in question did not apply. It might be possible to argue, Rimmer thought, that any marriage of a girl under the age of twelve was null and void. In such cases the words "not being his wife" could afford no protection to the accused. Consummation would have to be proven for a successful prosecution. Rimmer concluded, "until this is shown it seems to be open to doubt whether such child marriages as are spoken of by Agent Markle are of any more revolting nature than those which take place amongst other nations, where a child is given by the parent but the marriage is not consummated until after she attains the age of puberty. I may point out that it is open to the child to avoid the marriage on attaining the age of twelve years."

The issue emerged again in 1903 when Assistant Indian Commissioner J.A. McKenna visited the Siksika, and both the agent there and Catholic missionary Father Riou drew his attention to the "sale of young girls to male members of the band."[134] McKenna knew of Rimmer's advice, that if these were indeed wives no steps could be taken to prosecute, and stated that he was "convinced that there is nothing in the disposal of these girls which could be considered to constitute a form of marriage." The agent and missionary had assured him that "carnal knowledge" was had as a result of these "sales," and that this could be proven to gain a conviction. McKenna recommended action be taken. Once again the matter was referred to the Department of Justice, and this time a different strategy was adopted. Calgary lawyer James Short, the Department of Justice agent in that city, was asked to investigate the matter and confer with the Indian agent with a view to prosecuting if sufficient evidence could be procured. Short was instructed to lay information against any Blackfoot found marrying a girl under the age of fourteen.[135] In the meantime, Rimmer reviewed the issue.[136] He stressed once again that if charges were brought against a man it would have to be shown that the girl was not his wife, and he believed it would be very difficult to obtain a conviction on the grounds that the girl was not a wife. He stated, although obliquely, that the DIA policy to recognize the validity of Aboriginal marriage worked directly against obtaining a conviction. How could it be proved that a girl was not a wife when the DIA had insisted since 1887 that Aboriginal marriage was valid? The question of the validity of the marriage would arise at the outset of any case and the first witness called would be the girl herself, who "will probably say she is his wife." Rimmer noted that while the "law relating to marriages by Indian custom is in a

very unsatisfactory state it may be said that to some extent…[they]…
have received judicial recognition." To argue that marriage according to
Aboriginal law was not valid defied the approach taken by the DIA since
1887. But Rimmer was personally inclined toward the opinion in the
case of *Bethell vs. Hildyard* that it was "essential to a valid marriage that
the union be that of one man with one woman for life to the exclusion of
all others." He did not think that marriages according to "Indian custom"
complied with these requirements, hinting that a conviction could be
obtained but that women were on the DIA pay lists as wives. He concluded, "I therefore think it does not lie with this Department to obtain
the conviction of an Indian for carnally knowing a girl under 14 years if
his union with her is not polygamous but such as the Department has
heretofore recognized." Once again the view was expressed that failure
to obtain a conviction would be very damaging: "the effect on the Indians
would be worse than no action." Prosecution could only be successful if
they found that a man, already married, had connection with a girl under
the age of fourteen. Rimmer further noted that missionaries advocated
early marriage, citing the advice of Bishop Ridley, who advocated early
marriages "amongst the Indians as a safe-guard against greater evils likely
to occur while they remain single."[137]

James Short's report undermined and concluded efforts to address
"child marriage," as he found no evidence. Indeed, Short challenged
McKenna's sensational allegations. In his August 1903 report, the Calgary
lawyer stated that he had interviewed Agent Markle, and as a result had
decided it would be unwise to lay any charges, as the agent stated that
"there have been no bigamous marriages with young girls since he came
to the reserve." Short reported that the young wives on the reserve were
all fourteen years of age or older. Markle had informed him that there
were several "bigamous" marriages before he was assigned to the reserve,
that no action was taken against them, and that "the Indians would justly
complain if action were brought now, particularly as they have been
accustomed to plural marriages from time immemorial."[138] Markle further
told Short that in 1902 there were three cases in which men took second
wives, but the women were all adults. He cut off their rations and within
a month all had put away their second wives. There was one case in

which a man married a Tsuu T'ina girl who was about nine years old, but Markle reported that the marriage had been dissolved by mutual consent. (In this case Aboriginal divorce was clearly encouraged and accepted as valid.) Short found no other such cases in the settlement.

Upon receiving a copy of Short's report, Rimmer concluded that he could not advise any prosecution.[139] He was asked to give his opinion as to whether cases could be dealt with under the polygamy law (Section 278) of the Criminal Code, and he responded that this "is a matter involving grave consideration of policy," and that "moral suasion will be the most effective means of checking these plural marriages."

The efforts to eradicate the "evils" of polygamy were part of a transnational agenda pursued by missionaries and colonial authorities. In missionary circles throughout the British imperial world there were intense debates about how this eradication ought to be accomplished, dogged by difficult questions such as which wives should be discarded, who should decide which wives should be discarded, would this be condoning divorce, and what of the fate of the "semi-widows." Fur traders, some of whom had their own plural wives, and travellers to Western Canada were among the vocal and sharp critics of missionary efforts to abolish polygamy. Few steps were taken by the DIA until the early 1890s because it was feared that intervention in domestic life would cause serious trouble, particularly with leading men who had been the treaty negotiators. A similar approach was taken to Métis marriages. For the purpose of assigning Métis scrip the children of "pagan," bigamous, or polygamous marriages were regarded as legitimate until the mid-1880s, when the policy was changed and only "legitimate" children were granted scrip.

A determination to abolish polygamy arose with the arrival of the Mormons in southern Alberta in the late 1880s. There was concern about the moral effect of the Mormons on their Aboriginal neighbours, among whom they intended to initiate missionary work, and there was also the fear that the Mormons would find evidence that polygamy in fact was accepted in Western Canada. But DIA measures remained hesitant and reluctant. Transgressors were warned that prosecution was imminent and the NWMP was called in to help convey these warnings. A preliminary step was a census of polygamous households which revealed that the practice was still thriving in parts of the west, particularly southern Alberta. Elsewhere many Indian agents found it an aggravating and potentially damaging exercise, noting that the practice was not harming anyone, that some of the men were more like protectors than husbands, and that it was difficult to prove whether the women of a household were truly wives or not.

Despite warnings that transgressors would be prosecuted, new cases emerged from southern Alberta of young people entering into plural marriages. Officials of the DIA now tried withholding rations and placing second wives in residential schools using the new compulsory attendance legislation. Further advice and information was gathered on the wisdom of prosecution, and the advice was not encouraging. In 1895 the deputy minister of justice was "inclined to think" a man with more than one wife could be prosecuted under the new legislation designed to address Mormon polygamy. It had to be proven, however, that there was a form of contract as no offence was committed if there was no contract. There was also the fear of serious protests if such measures were taken. A volatile situation grew on the Siksika Reserve in the mid-1890s with resentment focused on zealous agent Magnus Begg and the inept Anglican missionary J.W. Tims. The attention of the public was drawn to the persistence of polygamy through the sensational trial of Charcoal, a Kainai man found guilty of killing another Kainai man and a NWMP officer. It was revealed during Charcoal's trial that he had two wives, and that a cause of his rampage was suspicion that one of his wives was having an affair.

By the late 1890s officials of the DIA appeared to have no control over their "wards" and their domestic affairs, despite their tactics of threats of prosecution, withholding rations and annuities. The time had come to act and in 1899 a Kainai man named Bear's Shin Bone was found guilty of polygamy under the legislation devised to address Mormon polygamy. But this did not have the immediate desired effect authorities had hoped for, as polygamy was not abandoned. The attention of the DIA then shifted to "child" marriages, and alarm was raised once again about the "bartering" of young brides. Legal action, however, was not possible if these women were indeed wives, and it had been the policy of the DIA to recognize the legality of marriage according to Aboriginal law. An investigation into the allegations by Calgary lawyer James Short found no evidence of child marriage.

Concerted efforts to abolish polygamy and "child" marriage in Aboriginal communities became less pronounced after 1903, but the goal of imposing the monogamous model of marriage and associated cultural assumptions about proper gender roles did not end. DIA officials, acting with missionaries (although often at odds with them), and sometimes with the NWMP, continued this work well into the twentieth century. Yet the state intervened to both refashion and to preserve aspects of the Aboriginal laws pertaining to marriage. Desired changes were not easily or thoroughly imposed. As we will see in the next chapter, efforts to impose the monogamous model were dramatically disruptive, but far from entirely successful.

SEVEN

"Undigested, Conflicting and Inharmonious"

ADMINISTERING
FIRST NATIONS MARRIAGE
AND DIVORCE

IN 1915, Secretary Frederick H. Abbott of the US Board of Indian Commissioners published *The Administration of Indian Affairs in Canada*, and in it he praised the simplicity, clarity, and efficiency of Canada's policies and procedures. In his section on "Indian Marriages and Divorces," Abbott wrote with admiration, "The whole story of Indian marriages and divorces in Canada is told briefly," and he proceeded to quote a circular of the Canadian Department of Indian Affairs.[1] There were five main points established in the circular: 1) that marriage between Indians or between Indians and others in accordance with provincial or territorial laws was valid; 2) that "the validity of marriage between Indians in accordance with the customs of their tribes had been established by the courts," and "the fact that one or both of the contracting parties may profess adherence to Christianity [did not] affect the matter"; 3) that Indian marriages, "if valid, cannot be dissolved according to the Indian customs," as "the validity of Indian divorces has never been affirmed in Canada"; 4) that if an Indian married to one woman goes through a form of marriage with another woman, "which would make her his wife but for the fact that he was already married," he was guilty of bigamy and could be successfully prosecuted under the Criminal Code, "even if there has been no valid marriage but the Indian intended by complying with the customs of the band relating to marriage to make more than the first married his wife or wives, or if, even without such intention, he has complied in the case of two or more women with the requirements of the tribal customs"; 5) that neither a man or woman could legally contract a "fresh alliance," even after an absence of seven years of a spouse, and even if "in good faith and on reasonable grounds" he or she believed the spouse to be deceased, if "both parties to the first marriage contract were alive at the time of the second purported marriage."

It might well have occurred to a careful reader that the convoluted and tortuous wording of the departmental circular pointed to a more complex situation, and that the "whole story" of Indian marriages and divorces was not as simplistic and harmonious as Abbott wished to convey. If so, this careful reader would have been correct. Abbott wished to see clarity and simplicity in the Canadian system. He believed that there were serious and fundamental defects in the administration of Indian affairs in his own country, and that Canada's policy was "immeasurably superior."[2] He particularly wanted to impress on his readers a sense of the clarity and conciseness of Canada's laws, rules, and regulations relating to Indian administration, all of which he could have brought back to Washington with him, as he wrote, "in my coat pocket."[3] This was in marked contrast to what Abbott described as "the thousands of pages of laws and rules and regulations, many of them undigested, conflicting and inharmonious, which hamper efficiency in the Indian Service of our country."[4]

If he had dug deeper during his eight-week visit to Canada, Abbott would have discovered that "undigested, conflicting and inharmonious" aptly described Canada's efforts to administer Indian marriages and divorces, as this was characterized by voluminous correspondence and consternation, doubt over what constituted a legitimate marriage, and a confusing welter of legal decisions and departmental rules and regulations. Abbott neglected to include the first sentence of the circular letter he admired, which read in part as follows: "There seems to be more or less confusion or uncertainty in the minds of officials and Agents of the

Department with regard to the law as to the recognition of Indian marriages and Indian divorces."[5] While it was the case that government and legal officials recognized the validity of marriage according to Aboriginal laws, these marriages had to be permanent, exclusive, and voluntary, all of which reflected a profound misunderstanding of the complexity and flexibility of Aboriginal marriage law.

This policy resulted in significant upheaval and had some disastrous consequences. Indian agents and higher-up officials of the DIA found themselves embroiled in the most personal affairs of the families they administered. They dispensed advice on marriage, intervened to prevent couples from separating, brought back "runaway" wives, directed the annuities of husbands to deserted wives, broke up second marriages they regarded as illegitimate, and became embroiled in disputes with missionaries as to what were legitimate marriages. DIA officials, along with school principals, gave and denied permission for couples to marry, and they also indulged in "matchmaking." Indian agents wielded considerable power as they determined, at least for the purposes of annuity payments, what did and did not constitute a family unit, which children were legitimate and which were not. (Annuity pay lists were organized around the male head of family whose name appeared, followed by the number of women, and children in "his" household.) They also determined whether a widow was of "good moral character," or whether or not she was indeed a bona fide widow in cases of inheritance. Yet despite this concerted intervention, the agents of the DIA were limited in their ability to impose the monogamous model of marriage. Aboriginal laws persisted, people protested the intervention in their domestic affairs, and they continued to make their own choices for themselves and their children. Some women and men refused to stay in bad marriages; they separated, divorced, and remarried according to their own laws. Much went on without the knowledge of any agent, and agents often had to be content with accepting only the appearance of control. But the domestic landscape changed dramatically nonetheless, as "gender could not be remade without unravelling much wider aspects of social organization."[6] Former freedoms and flexible arrangements were constrained. Altogether the new network of laws and regulations functioned to destabilize domestic affairs, and actually worked against the goal of instilling a sense of the sanctity of marriage. Those who were divorced according to Aboriginal law and had remarried were told that these were not valid legal unions, that they risked prosecution as bigamists, and that their children were illegitimate. People could then feel free to desert or abandon second marriages, and DIA officials encouraged them to do so. By the early twentieth century officials were also concerned that as the people they supervised came to understand the "nature of a legal contract, the disregard of which will subject them to legal penalties," the less likely they were to enter into such legal contract. "The worst offenders in that direction," it was contended, "were young men who perverted the knowledge acquired by them at some of the Industrial schools."[7]

While the overall policy directive was to recognize the Aboriginal marriage ceremony as legal and binding (when it was the first and only spouse for each except in the event of the death of a spouse), Indian agents worked alongside missionaries, school principals, and the NWMP to replace associated practices of matrimony and family life with the monogamous Christian model. By the late nineteenth century efforts were being made to arrange suitable marriages among the first graduates of industrial and residential schools. A DIA circular was issued in 1900 calling for the promotion of marriages among graduates, but school principals and DIA employees had collaborated on marriages well before that date.[8] By the 1890s missionaries were instructed to consult with Indian agents before marrying couples.[9] School principals similarly sought permission from the DIA for graduates to marry. In 1894 the principal of the Rupert's Land Industrial School presented DIA Agency Inspector Ebenezer McColl with the "application" of a male student to marry a female student. Although the prospective groom had a house and farm on the St. Peter's Reserve, the principal thought "she would do far better for herself in remaining where she is," and that "I will be very sorry to lose her." He recommended that she be allowed to visit with her parents first. McColl recommended that the matter be placed before the deputy superintendent general when he next visited Winnipeg, and it is unclear if permission to marry was ever given. That same year a young student from St. Joseph's Industrial School at Dunbow, Alberta, wrote directly

to Deputy Superintendent Hayter Reed asking permission to leave the school, as "the girl I love is gone home and I feel very lonesome for her so I want to go out and work some place in order to make some money."[10] Much correspondence ensued; before sanctioning the marriages of pupils, the department would have to be assured that the young man was sufficiently advanced in the "customs of civilized life," that he had a suitable dwelling, an allotment of land on the reserve, and all the necessary household equipment.[11] The prospective bride had to have the skills to make a good housekeeper. In this case the principal of the school recommended that the young man work for two years on the school farm—his wages would be saved for him and he would not be permitted to spend any during those years. Reed agreed with this advice; the marriage would be sanctioned if a favourable report was received from the principal after two years. Reed also wrote a personal letter to the young man, saying that he was glad to receive his "manly and well written letter," explaining how his future would unfold for the next two years, and how he could "succeed in making a happy home for the girl you love."[12]

Agent Magnus Begg of the Siksika Reserve reported in 1894 that a "large girl" had left boarding school and wanted to get married, but that he "had her returned to the school."[13] New amendments to the Indian Act permitted agents to do this, often with the assistance of the NWMP. The new compulsory attendance regulations allowed DIA officials greater power in prohibiting some marriages while sanctioning others. The amendments permitted "the arrest and conveyance to school, and detention there, of truant children and of children who are prevented by their parents or guardians from attending."[14] The regulations, "which shall have the force of law," also permitted "the committal by justices or Indian agents of children of Indian blood under the age of sixteen years to such industrial school or boarding school, there to be kept, cared for and educated for a period not extending beyond the time at which such children shall reach the age of eighteen years."

< *The wedding of Lizzie Acres and Joe Mountain Horse, ex-pupils of St. Paul's Anglican Mission school on the Kainai Reserve. Marriages of ex-pupils of residential and industrial schools and weddings that conformed to Euro-Canadian customs were encouraged and promoted by the Department of Indian Affairs, school administrators and missionaries.* (University of Calgary Archives. Diocese of Calgary's Report on Indian Missions for 1904)

In 1890 Father Joseph Hugonnard, principal of the Qu'Appelle Industrial School, was not acting in accordance with DIA instructions when he was chastised by Indian Commissioner Hayter Reed for allowing marriages between female pupils of the Qu'Appelle school and males not so-educated without "the sanction of the Department having been first obtained."[15] The marriages, according to Hugonnard, were arranged by the parents who had consulted their children. Reed expressed a "feeling of great regret" that Hugonnard had permitted these marriages, and he vehemently disagreed with Hugonnard's view of the role of parents in arranging marriages. Hugonnard wrote to Reed, "the arrangements were made by the parents alone. I did not consider that I had any right to make them myself, nor could I take upon myself the responsibility of preventing them from carrying out the arrangements that they had already made. Their future happiness or unhappiness may depend upon it and if I had interfered, they would undoubtedly have blamed me for it afterwards and not without reason."[16] Hugonnard claimed he could not have waited for Reed's permission: "[I]t was not in my power to stop them, even by refusing discharges to the four girls. The refusal would not have stopped them." Reed fumed in reply: "The contention that the parents have sole right to decide such matters cannot for one moment be admitted." Parents interfered in many directions to prevent actions that were for their own good. Reed contended that the great expense of educating pupils meant that the DIA had acquired "further right in regard to them, and these amounts would be 'thrown away' if they were to return to sink back to their old condition on the Reserve."

Sometimes concerted action was taken by Indian agents, the NWMP, missionaries, and school principals to break up what they saw as illegal marriages. In 1898 a widowed woman, formerly a pupil of the Qu'Appelle Industrial School, made it known that she intended to marry a man who had been previously married. Father Hugonnard, together with Indian Agent W.M. Graham, went to the reserve of the new prospective husband to take her away and return her to her own community.[17] When they could not be located the police were called in to assist. The couple was eventually found and the woman was returned to her own reserve.

Within a few days of this event Father Hugonnard arranged that she be married to a widower of another reserve.

Following the 1900 DIA circular, concerted efforts were made to marry graduates of industrial and residential schools only to other graduates, and there was the expectation that these marriages would be "legal," and not according to Aboriginal law. That year the agent for the Muscowpetung Reserve in Saskatchewan did not approve of the marriage partners of two young male graduates of the Regina Industrial School. He regarded the women as "very undesirable companions for young men who have received a good common education and a Christian training and of whom we have a right to expect better things."[18] He insisted instead that they marry "respectable" graduates of a school. The agent refused to recognize their marriages, and informed the men at the time of annuity payments that the women would not be recognized as their wives, nor would any children born to them be regarded as legitimate. He would pay their annuities separately "unless the parties become legally married." This agent averred that while the government recognized marriages "in accordance with the hereditary customs of the tribe" in the case of "older Indians," this recognition should not be extended to "the present rising generation who have had the benefit of education and Christian training and who had adopted in a measure the customs and manner of life of the whites, and are regarded as civilized." The reply from the Indian commissioner was carefully worded. While he approved of the action the agent proposed to take to "make the Indians conform to the law respecting marriages," he detected a dangerous deviation from policy. "The Indian form of marriage is binding," the Indian commissioner wrote. One of the men under scrutiny, he noted, was listed on the paysheets as a married man and was therefore ineligible to marry another.[19]

A system of incentives was devised to promote marriages among graduates, with approved wives given domestic articles such as sewing machines or household furniture. Approved husbands were given assistance to purchase farm equipment.[20] Lists were drawn up of who was worthy of such assistance and who was not. Agents were to report on the length of time each graduate had been out of school, whether they were married or single, their occupation since leaving school, and where they resided. The pupils were described as "independent of assistance," "worthy of assistance," or "no good."[21] The progress of married recipients of assistance was carefully tracked. A worthy husband was described as industrious, and a worthy wife was "trustworthy and honest as well as being clean personally and a good housekeeper." Circulars concerned with the future of the graduates, which confirmed the policy of encouraging the marriages of ex-pupils, were issued in 1909 and 1914. In 1914 agents and the principals of residential or boarding schools were instructed by Deputy Superintendent General Duncan Campbell Scott to give careful thought to the future of female pupils: "The special difficulties of their position should be recognized and they should be protected as far as possible from temptations to which they are often exposed."[22] As explained in a 1912 article on industrial schools, "unmarried girls, upon graduation, find it difficult to secure positions which harmonize with their ideals, and frequently discouragement leads to a serious falling away from the methods of living outlined at the school. To overcome this difficulty the school authorities have found it a great advantage to encourage their older students to marry when they leave the college."[23]

Mass weddings were held at the schools. On a summer day in 1909, Father Hugonnard married six couples from the Qu'Appelle Industrial School. H. V. Graham, the wife of an Indian agent in southern Saskatchewan, described the same-day wedding of five couples that took place at a Catholic school run by an order of nuns.[24] Preparations had been made for months as they all made their own wedding dresses, and there were five wedding cakes to be made, as "Sister Bohen always insisted that each bride married at school should have a cake." "I shall never forget that wedding," she wrote. "The five brides in their white dresses, kneeling beside the sturdy young grooms, the altar in the school chapel was decorated with flowers, the impressive ceremony and the high voices of the children joining in the responses, the practical little sermon by the Priest, the Indian parents in their best beadwork and blankets, all formed a picture that will never be erased from my mind." In a 1980s interview, Eleanor Brass, a Cree from File Hills, offered a more critical appraisal of such ceremonies. Brass said the pupils "were matched and mated up and told who they would marry. These couples didn't go together or know each other. They weren't even in love with each other."[25]

Indian agents were instructed to cluster ex-pupils into "separate colonies or settlements removed to some extent from the older Indians." The File Hills Colony in Saskatchewan, established in 1901, was a DIA showcase settlement of such married industrial school graduates, isolated from the "older Indians."[26] Frederick Abbott, who admired the colony, described how each male colonist, once he had sufficient land under cultivation and a house built, "is prepared to get married, the match, in most cases, having already been arranged before the young people left school; and perhaps the young wife has been working with some white family during these first two years and earning enough to buy herself some dishes and furniture to begin housekeeping in a simple way. This sort of match-making is encouraged in all the Canadian boarding schools."[27] The colony was also devised to display how gender roles in this Aboriginal community conformed to an idealized the Euro-Canadian model. Founder W.M. Graham boasted in 1912 about the housekeeping abilities of the women of the colony: "If one would visit this colony on a Monday, one would see clothes hanging out to dry at almost every house. If one should go on Saturday, one would find them scrubbing. The work of the home is carried on with some system, which of course is the result of the training they have received at school. Bread-baking, butter-making, care of fowls and gardening are kinds of work that are usually left to the housewife."[28] Eleanor Brass, one of the first children born in the colony, wrote in 1953 that "One outstanding rule that has been kept for years was a by-law made by the colonists themselves, 'That no couples should live together unless lawfully married by the laws of the country or their respective churches.'"[29]

By the early 1920s, enthusiasm for the "match making" of pupils had waned, and it was no longer government policy. The chairman of the Presbytery of Winnipeg's Committee on Indian Work recommended in 1922 that the department make it unlawful for a pupil or ex-pupil to marry without the permission of the Indian agent.[30] The punishment, it was suggested, could be no annuities and no admission to the schools for the children born of non-sanctioned marriages. The answer from the Department of Justice was that there was much to object to in such a proposal. Would an ex-pupil, even if aged fifty, be considered unable to marry without permission? Only those couples with children would be penalized, and why should innocent children pay the penalty for their parents? In 1923 the principal at the St. Paul's School on the Blood Reserve made a similar request, that "action be taken to provide that no Indian shall marry unless first consulting the Indian agent, who would then inquire into the legitimacy of the request, and authorize the recognized marriage service to be performed in any Church."[31] The curt answer from the DIA was that the request could not be complied with, as "there is nothing in the Indian Act whereby Indians could be compelled to consult an Indian Agent before getting married."[32]

Aside from their matchmaking work, Indian agents had numerous other conundrums to deal with relating to marriage and divorce. The instructions they were issued to recognize the validity of Aboriginal marriages but not divorces, and to insist that marriage was indissoluble except through the death of a spouse or a "legal" divorce, resulted in a host of perplexing domestic issues for which they had no training or expertise. Agents at the local level were often sympathetic to requests for recognition of Aboriginal divorce and remarriage, and they were often ambivalent about the directives they were to enforce. Even missionaries at times felt there should be greater flexibility in allowing people separated for years and living together with new partners for years to remarry. But the new regime made it difficult, and at times impossible, for people to pursue their former range of options for new family formation in the event of desertion, separation, or divorce, or to resolve such problems as cruelty.

Vexing questions emerged when separated or deserted spouses wished to marry again as they had always done. In 1905, for example, the Indian agent at Moose Mountain (Saskatchewan) wrote to the Ottawa DIA office asking whether a woman, married according to Aboriginal law but deserted by her husband, could remarry. The agent carefully detailed that the woman's behaviour was not the primary cause of the marriage breakdown. "In a case of this sort," the agent asked, "would it be legal for the woman to marry again, and if not how long would it be before she could do so provided her husband persists in deserting her and refuses to support her and her family"?[33] The very swift reply to this inquiry, from Frank Pedley, deputy superintendent general of Indian affairs, was typical of the responses to all such inquiries. Pedley replied that because Indian divorce was not recognized as valid, this woman could not legally marry another man until the death of her husband unless she obtained a legal divorce. If she thought her husband was dead for seven years at the time of her second marriage, then she could not be prosecuted for bigamy, but if her husband was alive, and she knew him to be alive, then the second marriage would not be regarded as legal. Similar advice was given to all Canadians who were deserted or separated but Aboriginal law permitted much greater flexibility to divorce and to remarry. The best that could be done for an Aboriginal woman was to apply the husband's annuity money to her and any children through Section 72 of the Indian Act.

Puzzling questions emerged in cases of inheritance when, under the Indian Act, an assessment of the "morality" of a widow, and thus her right to inherit, was at issue. As a non-Aboriginal critic of the DIA regime remarked in 1911, "morality (what sort of morality is not stated), is apparently far more essential for the Indians than it is for us, and especially is more essential to an Indian woman than it is to her white sister. For if a husband dies intestate and the widow is not a woman of 'good moral character' she loses her interest in the estate."[34] In 1904–1905 the distribution of the estate of an intestate Kainai man caused Indian Agent R.N. Wilson great consternation. As mentioned previously, a widow could not inherit the property of her deceased spouse under the Indian Act unless she "was a woman of good moral character," and was living with her husband at the time of his death. Wilson had the "unshaken belief" that a woman named "DC" was the legal widow of the deceased, "HO," having married him after the death of his first wife, but his departmental superiors in Ottawa disagreed, holding that the man had died "without leaving a widow or any issue." The first (and in their view only) wife of HO was the legal wife. Also claiming that DC was not a legal wife was the deceased's next-of-kin, including the mother of the deceased, a sister, and two half-brothers. According to Wilson, these family members had already taken forcible possession of the wagon and some other property of the estate a year earlier. Wilson was angered that the DIA wished to turn DC "out of house and home and utterly dispossess her of what she has every reason to believe is her lawful property."[35] The rival claimants who wished to inherit from the estate of HO and dispossess DC appealed directly to Ottawa over Wilson's head, sending affidavits that HO's first wife was alive. They also claimed that DC was not a wife but a concubine, and that she was a woman of "notoriously loose and immoral character."[36] Based on this evidence, Deputy Superintendent General Frank Pedley consulted the Department of Justice about the case, and the ruling was that DC was never lawfully married to HO.[37]

Wilson had evidence that HO married DC after the death of his first wife. He was also angry that DC had no opportunity to hear the evidence upon which it was proposed to turn her out of her house and no opportunity to disprove the charges; he wanted to secure her the right to produce sworn testimony in support of her claim that she was the legal wife. He wanted copies of the affidavits that were sent to Ottawa relative to the case to facilitate his rebuttal. Wilson requested that he be sent the department's definition of a "legal Indian marriage," as "it is necessary that when in future I speak of an Indian's wife I should be in a position to do so advisedly."[38] This case, Wilson contended, was of vast importance as a precedent. "One of the principal chiefs remarked some days ago," Wilson wrote to Ottawa, "if [DC] was not the wife of [HO] then most of us Blood Indians are single men."[39]

Ultimately it was decided, however, that the Crown would acquire the estate. In trying to discredit the rival family claimants to the estate of HO, Wilson informed Ottawa that the alleged half-brothers were not legally brothers of the deceased, and that there was also a problem with the claim of HO's sister. "Their common father," Wilson wrote, "was a polygamist whose plural wife or concubine [was]...the mother of the two last named, who thus are apparently in the eyes of the law illegitimate, which suggests the query, who besides the mother are the next of kin to an illegitimate child?"[40] Pedley once again sought the advice of the Justice Department on the issue. E.L. Newcombe replied in March of 1905, "Assuming the facts to be as you state them, [HO] was an illegitimate son. That being so, and he having left no lawful issue of his body, and having died intestate, the Crown succeeds to his property, and may, I think, with the consent of the band, if it is thought proper to obtain it, make such distribution thereof as in its opinion the justice of the case requires."[41] The estate amounted to very little. When the Fort Macleod lawyers ("Weed and Campbell") who had helped the next-of-kin to discredit the claim of DC attempted to collect from the estate in January of 1905, Wilson replied that the distribution of the property had yet to be decided, and that the deceased had incurred a large balance of debt on the books in his office. Wilson further wrote that to this "may be added whatever is due to [DC] for her care of the cattle during the last year," and that "no matter how ends the squabble over this dead Indian's affairs a settlement of your account by this office is necessarily a somewhat remote possibility."[42]

Indian agents, sometimes in consultation with other officials, had to decide which marriages were valid for the purposes of treaty annuity payments, and they decided which women were no longer considered "Indians" because they had married out. In the case of an Aboriginal woman marrying a white man, a non-treaty "Indian," or a Métis, marriage according to Aboriginal law was generally regarded as valid for the purposes of applying the Indian Act, and the wife ceased "to be an Indian in any respect within the meaning of this Act."[43] As mentioned earlier in this book, questions about what kind of marriage had taken place were not usually asked. The issue emerged for example in 1889 when a Rev. W. Nicolls wrote to the assistant Indian commissioner in Regina about a man named Graham who married a Lakota woman "according to Indian custom (as far as I can learn from other Indians)."[44] (The Lakota were not treaty people in Canada but they still had Indian status.) His wife was ill with tuberculosis and her husband sought government assistance for her. The answer was that he could not expect any aid from the government for his wife.[45] She was no longer an "Indian," and was therefore no longer a ward of the government. Agents drew up lists of the women married to non-treaty or "half breed" men and who were thus "allowed out of treaty."[46] They reported the cases to the Indian commissioner in Regina. In 1893, for example, Agent R.S. McKenzie of the

Duck Lake Agency recommended that Isabella Pruden, the daughter of Robert Bear of John Smith's band, be permitted to withdraw from treaty, writing that "this woman is married to an English Halfbreed and derives no other assistance from the Department than her annuity, and as her husband is in a position to support her, I would recommend that her discharge be granted."[47] The women had to sign documents declaring that they desired to withdraw from treaty. The fifty-dollar commutation of annuity route must have been an attractive enticement to poor people. (The most expensive item in a 1912 Woodward's Catalogue was "The Colonist," a steel range with a high warming closet at $32.00. Women's shoes were $2.75. An oak extension table was $9.00.[48])

The presence of missionaries on reserves complicated the marriage terrain. Missionaries of all denominations were at odds with the policy of the government to recognize the validity of Aboriginal marriage. As one of the earliest Catholic missionaries wrote to his bishop in 1822 from Pembina (North Dakota), "If these Indian marriages are valid and therefore indissoluble, the missionary will always be faced by almost insurmountable difficulties in converting the Indians to Christianity."[49] Their project of introducing Christian marriage was often directly at odds with the agenda of government administrators, and missionaries frequently clashed with Indian agents, disagreeing about what did or did not constitute a legitimate marriage, and about who made respectable partners in marriage. The Roman Catholics were the least co-operative with the DIA in their policy of recognizing the validity of Aboriginal marriage as they carried out the principal of the supremacy of Canon Law over any other law, including government legislation, as a tenet of their faith. Catholic missionaries were often accused of endorsing bigamous marriages, as in many cases they did not recognize the marriage ceremonies of other denominations.

Yet sometimes DIA officials insisted that a church marriage was valid when religious authorities disagreed. Father Hugonnard married a young Assiniboine couple of the Moose Mountain Agency in a 1902 Roman Catholic ceremony, despite the fact, Hugonnard later claimed, that during the ceremony the bride did not give her consent to the marriage.[50] She would not give her verbal consent and her father had to take her hand

and put it in the hand of the groom. Nevertheless, Father Hugonnard declared the marriage valid as the groom allegedly said at the time, according to Hugonnard, that "she would consent alright after having stayed sometime in the house." Two years later, however, Hugonnard decided that there was no marriage, and that the husband was free to remarry. His reasoning was that there was no marriage because the bride had not given sufficient consent, had only gave her hand at the command of her parents, and she had persistently refused to cohabit with her husband. According to Hugonnard, "I therefore state that for want of her consent then and afterwards there was no marriage and Emile is free to marry again at least as far as eccliastical [sic] marriage is concerned." He wrote to the husband and said that there was no religious marriage and that he did not think the "legal marriage" existed without the religious marriage, and although this letter was produced to the DIA officials, they disagreed, insisting that this was a legal marriage that could not be annulled or dissolved. The Indian agent reported that as the couple had cohabited together for about two months after their marriage, "and to my knowledge occupied the same room and bed, I think that the marriage should be looked upon as binding, and if Emile is permitted to marry again I do not think that his example would be conducive to morality on their reserve."[51] Assistant Indian Commissioner J.A.J. McKenna ruled early in 1905 that this was a legal marriage.[52]

Agents and missionaries disagreed over who constituted suitable spouses. Indian Agent W.E. Jones at Coté, Assiniboia, was opposed to the 1894 marriage of fifteen-year-old girl to a "half breed…a useless & unhealthy man & totally unfit to support a wife."[53] Jones explained his objections to the resident Anglican missionary, telling him "not to marry this Indian girl to a non treaty man, as she was a ward of the Government, her family were not looking after her & I felt I was responsible as to her welfare." But according to Jones the missionary "treated the matter with contempt & married them." Jones asked that missionaries be informed that "no marriage should be performed in which Indians are concerned without first informing the Agent." This was done, as the Anglican Bishop of Qu'Appelle was told of the actions of his missionary, and informed that "such marriages…are most unsuitable as they are the means of keeping worthless men hanging about the Reserves and the Department in the interests of its wards is doing all it can to prevent their taking place and it would be glad to have your co-operation in this work."[54] The bishop replied that his informants told him that the young man was hard working, and that "from all accounts marriage was the best thing that could happen to the girl, as it would appear that her brother was trying to sell her to a Pagan Indian."[55]

In 1907, Indian Agent M. Millar of the Crooked Lake Agency insisted that the first marriage of a man according to Aboriginal law was valid while his second marriage with another woman, performed by a Presbyterian missionary named Hugh McKay, was not valid.[56] The man involved in both of these marriages was a Roman Catholic of long standing. He was also a prominent person who aspired to the office of chief. After his first marriage, performed according to Aboriginal law in 1906, the couple was placed on the DIA books as married, and the husband was consequently paid the wife's share of money that was distributed to the band in 1907 as a result of a land surrender. Shortly after this, however, he "cast the woman off," according to the agent's description. The man then wished to marry another woman, to the great disapproval of the agent and the local priest, who tried to persuade him to marry his first wife in a Catholic ceremony. The man asked instead that the priest marry him to the other woman, but the priest refused as he wished to abide by the directives of the agent. The couple then appealed to the Presbyterian missionary who performed the ceremony. Rev. McKay was convinced that the first wife was not a wife at all but rather a housekeeper. Agent Millar was livid at the turn of events and blamed McKay for not making substantial inquiries into the case before performing the ceremony. The woman was not a housekeeper, he retorted, "She had been pregnant, and claims to have lost her child prematurely by overwork attending to this man's cattle in the winter." Millar insisted that the second marriage should be considered invalid, or treated as bigamous. He wrote, "The marriage if allowed to stand is going to have a very serious influence among the Indians. As I understand it, marriage according to the Indian custom is held to be valid in law, in which case this Indian is a bigamist, and in the interest of Indian morals, with regard to marriage, should be prosecuted and the first woman recognized as his wife." Agent Millar argued that if the second Presbyterian marriage was recognized by the department, it "will have a very injurious influence over the Christian morals of the Indians."[57] In this case Assistant Indian Commissioner J. McKenna requested that the Indian agent provide him with "information as to the nature of what he describes as the Indian custom of marriage and the extent to which it prevails in his Agency." Citing the Sheran and Bethell cases, McKenna wrote that there was "danger in extending the doctrine of marriage by Indian custom among civilised bands." The DIA asserted that the second Presbyterian marriage had to be recognized as the valid marriage.

A protracted case of marital discord on the Assiniboine Reserve in 1903 illustrated the disharmony that could prevail among missionaries and government officials, and it also highlighted the degree of involvement that missionaries and even the highest DIA bureaucrats had in the domestic affairs of reserve residents. Indian Commissioner David Laird, formerly a Prince Edward Island newspaper publisher, politician, and lieutenant governor of the North-West Territories, dispensed advice on marriage from his Winnipeg office to people he had likely never met. This particular case also serves as an example of the disputes over marriages that marked relationships between missionaries and Indian agents, and the diverse strategies departmental officials would employ to try to effect reconciliation. A sort of "family court" or mediation session was held by the agent on this reserve, to the towering displeasure of his bureaucratic superiors. But this session was mainly at the request of the estranged wife, and the case now provides us with evidence of the diverse strategies employed by the people whose married lives were the object of so much scrutiny. In this case, which included the estranged wife seeking the protection and support of the resident missionary and his wife, the wife also requested a hearing into the disputes at the heart of the marriage breakdown. Both husband and wife wrote letters to the Indian commissioner setting forth their side of the story.

"NJ" was a student at the Regina Industrial School in 1902 when she was given an honourable discharge in order to get married, at which time she received the gifts given to all ex-pupils in order to assist them in establishing a home. She was married in July of 1902 to "JJ," the son of a former chief who had not attended industrial school. E. McKenzie, the Presbyterian missionary on the reserve, performed the ceremony. All went well initially and they soon had a daughter, but shortly after her birth the marriage broke down. In a letter to Indian Commissioner Laird, NJ stated that her husband struck her, threatened worse violence, and had sent her away, accusing her of being unfaithful.[58] She alleged that her husband made her leave her baby with his aunt so she could work with him making hay, harvesting, and cutting logs and willow poles. NJ believed her husband was being pressured by a Catholic friend, who wanted him to convert and to marry a Catholic woman instead. NJ wanted custody of her daughter, support, and "a fair trial with us all face to face," and she appealed to Laird for his "help in seeing justice done between us." Her husband had initially retained custody of the child, who was cared for by his mother, with the approval of Indian Agent Thomas Aspdin, but NJ explained to Laird that, accompanied by the missionary's wife, she went to her husband's mother's home and took back her child. NJ took refuge first with the agent and his Lakota wife after parting from her husband, and then with the McKenzies.

On receiving this letter, Laird instructed Agent Aspdin to do all he could to effect a reconciliation, to tell JJ to "take back his wife, and treat her properly."[59] He also advised NJ to give up her child to the custody of the grandmother. The husband then wrote a letter of his own to Laird, claiming that his marriage was "planned and executed by third parties," and "it was without courtship or any preliminary knowledge of each others [sic] character."[60] He wrote that he had been "induced to this hasty marriage" by Mr. and Mrs. McKenzie, "in defiance of the Agent's urgent wish to become engaged first and build a house and get a few things together before I got married." The missionary couple, however, advised him to "make haste and that I would gain nothing by taking the advice of the Agent." JJ claimed that his wife was of a jealous nature, which developed into a "mania," culminating with her public accusations of his unfaithfulness. He accused her of being the unfaithful one, and noted her indifference to household work.

Missionary McKenzie sided with NJ, believing her side of the story, and accused Agent Aspdin of trying to discredit the wife and make her admit to adultery that had never happened. McKenzie criticized the agent's "kind of court in the agency office calling [NJ] as a witness, but virtually with the object of discrediting [NJ's] veracity."[61] He further accused Aspdin of trying to make NJ sign a document without reading it, one that "seemed to be a deed of separation which she was to sign in complete ignorance."[62] Agent Aspdin, McKenzie wrote, accused him of "not co-operating with him for peace, but co-operation evidently would be a losing game for [NJ]." He and his wife "found her a young woman who has wonderfully preserved her chastity, truthfulness, and modesty."

Agent Aspdin was more sympathetic to JJ, although he admitted there were faults on both sides. In a lengthy letter detailing his understanding of the issues, he assigned most of the blame to NJ, who he believed was not as tidy and industrious as she ought to be, was not to be believed, and was morally compromised. He wrote that JJ "admits the beating but not to the extent or severity as his wife alleges and [he] claims extreme provocation on account of her jealous nature."[63] With regard to the outdoor work she performed, Aspdin claimed that this was not regarded as women's work in "settled parts, but in a new country like this it is not uncommon to see women doing this work particularly among those starting on small means," and in his view this did not constitute cruelty. The McKenzies, Aspdin wrote, were taking her side entirely because they had not heard the husband's side, and he wrote that NJ "may be vain enough to think that with Mr. and Mrs. McKenzie on her side she can humiliate her husband and make him take her back on her own terms." Aspdin thought the missionary was the cause of NJ refusing to reconcile and he accused him and his wife of "stirring up strife but it has had no effect as I find they are naturally contentious. Moreover it is more often badly informed they are on all matters which they handle. They have not had an Interpreter for nearly two years."[64] Curiously, the almost exact wording made its way into an 8 January 1904 letter addressed to Laird from Chief Carry the Kettle and Headman Crooked Arm, asking for the missionary to be replaced because he had no interpreter, was causing trouble, and worked against the Indian agent.[65]

Matters became even more complicated and the situation inflamed when another woman on the reserve, "CW," claimed that stories were being told about her by a man named RA that connected CW to estranged husband JJ, and that these stories were being told to NJ. Aspdin dealt with this by charging RA under the vagrancy section of the Criminal Code, giving him a "talking to," and then dismissing the case.[66] Aspdin hoped this would serve "a good lesson by letting those who are inclined to make mischief to beware of themselves." The McKenzies, however, accused CW of perjury and asked Aspdin to take their affidavits on the issue, which he refused to do. The missionary couple then went to the home of the chief. According to Aspdin, it was there where CW was "stopping and seem[ed] to have had a scene." The McKenzies, Aspdin contended, with no understanding of the language, believed NJ, who, he wrote, "is regarded as rather a Moral 'oblique' as far as veracity is concerned." CW, however, was in Aspdin's view, "altogether a different girl" as she was also a graduate of the Regina Industrial School, and had been assistant matron at the Alberni (Presbyterian) School for two years. Indian Commissioner Laird was angry at Aspdin's tactics in dealing with the entire matter.[67] He did not see why NJ should be criticized for staying with the McKenzies, as "she must stop somewhere." He also admonished Aspdin for charging RA with vagrancy: "If he is an Indian belonging to the reserve," asked Laird, "how could he be a vagrant?" Laird questioned Aspdin's authority to hold such a trial: "The authority for which you yourself were not clear about...[which]...seems to have caused more strife than it allayed." Laird concluded, "If a reconciliation is to be accomplished the fewer of such trials the better. It is not by offending the missionaries and their guest [NJ], or her husband, that you can succeed in making peace."

Despite his admonishment of Agent Aspdin, Indian Commissioner Laird agreed with him that the marital discord was mainly due to NJ, and he advised her to return to her husband. "You may be to blame for talking too much against your husband," he wrote to her. "You are married for better or for worse, and it is your duty to promise to be reasonable. Reconciliation is almost the only hope I see for you... I advise you make it up with your husband and go back and live with him."[68] But she must have disregarded this advice. Some months later she had given away or sold the things given to her at her wedding. Agent Aspdin believed there was no chance of the couple reconciling.[69]

When there were two or more denominations present in a community there could be many complications. In seeking converts, missionaries cast doubts about the validity of the marriage ceremonies of their rivals. Rev. I. J. Taylor, an Anglican missionary on the Onion Lake Reserve, had to contend with what was described in his journal as the "Romanists," who were "actively vilifying" the Anglican marriage service through "false and malicious inventions."[70] According to Taylor they were questioning the sanctity of the Anglican marriage ceremony and his own power and authority as a minister. Taylor wrote that the priests made untiring efforts to draw the Anglican converts away and used every opportunity to criticize Protestant marriage. A young man who had converted to the Anglican Church wanted to get married and he worked hard to bring several women over to his church, but without success.[71] He then became engaged to a Roman Catholic woman and worked to persuade her to change faiths but "both her mother and herself had made a vow never to join our Communion or be married in our Church." Taylor also tried without success to convert the woman, and finally offered to marry the couple anyway. She refused and the couple was married in the Catholic Church, although Taylor instructed the young man not to convert. But in performing the marriage ceremony the priest withheld the blessing of the church because the man was a "heretic." Taylor described this as a "master stroke" of policy on the part of the priest, for in the weeks that followed the young woman constantly felt that something was wrong as the marriage had not received the blessing. The result was that within two months the young man was baptized and secured into the Catholic Church. Precisely the same thing had happened to another young Anglican and graduate of an industrial school. Taylor was particularly frustrated because he found that "in all matters of religion the men are led by the women, though in all other matters the women are little better than slaves." The missionary also admonished couples who were "together only in Indian Marriage Fashion, informing one man so-married that 'this is indeed accepted at the Agency, but…it will not be satisfactory until they are married in the church.'"[72]

There were occasions and situations when departmental rules and policies were relaxed. In 1906, for example, a Manitoba woman who had three children with a previously married man (whose first wife was still alive) was ordered to end the relationship and return to her community, the Jack Head Reserve. Although the inspector of the Indian agencies for Lake Manitoba, S. R. Marlatt, acknowledged that it would be a "great hardship" to send the woman back to her reserve with three small children to support on her own, "allowing them to remain together would be encouraging vice."[73] The father of the three children wrote to the inspector to say that he was "very sorry that in my ignorance I have broken the law of the land in taking another wife, while the wife who I am lawfully married to is still living…[but] if I should take back the woman I have now and give her up, how are the children which I have with her now, to live. Have I to support them? If so in which way. I would be very glad to support them only I couldn't take and keep them now as they are too young yet to be taken from their mother…I hope you will do your best for me in this matter as if I get into trouble and am sent to jail who is to support my children."[74] He claimed to have lived apart from his "lawful wife" for eight years, and he further stated, "With regard to my lawful wife's children I would say that they have no claim on me as I am not the father of them." Chief Samuel Marsden of the Lake St. Martin Reserve where the couple resided wrote to Marlatt as well, saying that "I am at a loss what to do with regard to [the situation] as they have three little children and if he takes the woman back to Jack Head Reserve where she belongs and gives her up she will not be able to support her children. If they had no children I would send her right back to where she belongs, but as it is I don't know what to do."[75] The decision of Indian Commissioner Laird in this case was that while "we do not approve of his living with this woman, and cannot recognize her as his lawful wife, or his children as legitimate," action to separate the couple and break up the family would not be taken. In this case it likely helped that the man's first wife was cast in the correspondence as "immoral and unfaithful to him."

Some DIA authorities, missionaries, and members of the NWMP wondered if a means of separation or divorce could be devised, aside from the "legal" route widely acknowledged to be an impossibility. It was recognized by many of those who worked directly in these communities that the policy of not permitting or recognizing Aboriginal divorce was undermining the department's own goal of establishing stable families. Under the pre-reserve regime there was no "immorality" attached to such marriages. Under the new regime couples regarded themselves as legally married but they were stigmatised as "immoral," and their children were viewed as illegitimate.

Authorities recognized that the appeal-to-Parliament divorce route was out of the question. The expense was one issue that ensured that "legal" divorce was out of reach, but there were others. As discussed earlier in this book, and as raised by a Vancouver lawyer in 1912, the courts would likely not entertain an application for a divorce from someone married according to Aboriginal law, "in view of the fact that it was possible to get a divorce by Indian custom without coming into the courts of the province."[76] But there were other issues. The first step in a divorce was to prove a valid marriage, and it was "usual to produce and file with the Committee a certificate of marriage, signed by the officiating Minister or to produce and prove an examined copy of the entry in the marriage register, or to file a certificate signed by the Registrar-General, where the marriage was performed in any of the provinces of Canada having such an officer."[77] Those married according to Aboriginal law might not have made it beyond the first step of a divorce proceeding, as it would have been difficult to prove a valid marriage. For couples in the Aboriginal community who were married by clergy, divorce through application to Parliament was the only means of divorce, and it is possible that this too discouraged people from "legal" marriages.

As "legal" divorce was almost impossible, Indian agents and other community workers cast about for other solutions. A frustrated agent on the Morley Reserve wrote in 1903 that while he could get some unhappy couples to reconcile, there were others he could not do anything about. Many wished to remarry, and he wondered if a form of legal separation and/or divorce might be possible. He felt that "the band would be a great deal better for it morally."[78] Laird's reply indicated that he was aware that marriage according to Aboriginal law might not, if ever tested, be subject to the same law and process that governed divorce for others in Canada. He wrote, "When legally married by a missionary there is no way that they can obtain a divorce except by applying to the Parliament of Canada, which is very expensive and costs more than an Indian can afford."[79] He also gave the standard reply that anyone who is married and marries another could be prosecuted for bigamy, and be sent for seven years to a penitentiary.

A similar response was given to P. C. H. Primrose, the superintendent of the police in the Macleod district who wanted to assist a young Piikani man whose wife had left him for another man.[80] He blamed his wife's mother for the situation. If the young man's statement was correct, Primrose wrote, he could proceed against his wife for bigamy, "but we have not taken notice in the past of Indian men having a number of wives, and I do not think it would be the proper way to settle this case to proceed against the woman, when the men are allowed to do the very same thing." According to Primrose the young man had given a gift of thirteen horses to the bride's family and he wondered whether in this and other instances the parents could be "forced to return the purchase price of the wife." He thought it would satisfy the man to have his horses returned, and this would also end parental interference in marriages of their children. Laird replied that while it would be right for the man to get his horses back he did not know of any legal process that could effect this. "At any rate," he observed, "it would not dissolve the marriage, which is for life horses or no horses, unless there is a regular divorce."[81] Laird further advised that the wife could be prosecuted for bigamy only if she "had been married in full legal form" to the man she now lived with, "but the immorality of merely living with another man without any form of marriage is difficult to reach by law in the case of either Indians or white men." Primrose sharply disagreed with Laird's view and wrote to the commissioner of the NWMP complaining that Laird "says this marriage is for life, when, seeing by actual experience marriage according to Indian rites is dissolved every easily and sometimes very quickly."[82]

In 1910 the General Conference of the Methodist Church of Canada came to the conclusion that the solution to the problem of "Indian marriage" was to permit a form of annulment of these marriages. In a letter to Minister of the Interior Frank Oliver, prominent moral reformer and Methodist leader Rev. Samuel D. Chown set out the resolutions of the General Conference.[83] It was assumed that many marriages "amongst our Indian population" were entered into without the full consent of the contracting parties, that subsequent separations and illicit sexual alliances produced children who needed parental care, and that the parents felt "the evil of their state of life and are oppressed in their conscience and desire relief from a contract immaturely and irresponsibly entered into." The recommendation was that the government appoint a small commission to look into the matter and provide "relief of persons suffering from such immoral conditions and to safeguard the welfare of the children." Chown further explained to Oliver, "To annul marriages which are not honoured in later life, and which have been contracted under the conditions set forth in this resolution, would be the easiest way to arrive at a solution of the question." The answer from Duncan Campbell Scott was that special legislation would be needed to permit Indian divorce, that if divorce was allowed many children would be left in an "unenviable position," and that the DIA hesitated to introduce "special legislation regulating Indian marriage customs from the fear that any law upon the Statute Book would be almost impossible of enforcement."[84] Scott quoted from the 1887 order-in-council including that the "true remedy of this lax state of things must come from the gradual civilization of the Indians."

A Methodist missionary at Wabamun, Alberta, also felt that divorces should be permitted in order to sanction second marriages. In 1912 he wrote a letter to his superiors in the church and these concerns were then forwarded to DIA Secretary J. M. McLean in Ottawa. The missionary described a complicated situation that prevented him from performing marriages for two couples, who he felt ought to be permitted to marry:

[MC] married [MH] some ten years ago. They could not agree and soon separated. He has been living with [MB] all these years and they live agreeably and wished me to marry them, which I could not do. His wife has been living with another man and has quite a family of children. Last winter he died and she came back to Paul's Reserve to live where she first lived, but she has no home and no way of making a living so she took up with [AP], and they have been living together for six or eight months in his father's house much against the will of the old man and also of the other Indians. What can be done? The woman must have a living, and to live thus is very bad. Could there not be a divorce on some ground and then the two couples be married? We are trying to do away with all this looseness and have succeeded in many cases already. If the Government would help us in this case, I would be much obliged.

In forwarding this letter to the DIA, the general secretary of the Methodist Church wrote that he did not agree with the missionary that access to divorce was the answer; rather, he suggested that adultery be made a crime.[85] The answer from J. D. McLean, assistant deputy as well as secretary of the DIA, was that his department had no power to secure divorces, that there was no divorce court in Alberta, and that the only way a divorce could be secured was "a method out of reach of Indians by its expense and cumbersome procedure."[86] McLean added that even if they compelled all Indians to marry under Canadian laws, it would not address the cases the missionary described, and that "we can scarcely hope to make adultery a crime for Indians alone." As will be discussed below, the DIA drafted a proposal in 1908 to permit a special form of divorce, although this never materialized.

Efforts of the DIA and missionaries to enforce the monogamy policy were far from successful in many cases. The power of Indian agents was limited and contested—their authority tenuous. As one frustrated agent complained in 1900, "They do not seem to be learning that their free and easy custom of marrying is improper."[87] Agents preferred not to give orders, as one agent wrote, "that may not be enforced."[88] They frequently reported that they did not always succeed in breaking up "matches" that they did not approve of, and efforts to reconcile estranged couples rarely worked.[89] Methods of enforcing monogamy such as withholding and redirecting annuities had little effect. People continued to marry, divorce, and remarry according to Aboriginal law, insisting on their right to do so. Agreeing to a church ceremony did not always mean that they had "discarded" belief in their own marriage law, or that they had rejected the web of kinship obligations and responsibilities that were involved. As George Faithful wrote for the entry on his family in a history of Frog Lake and district, "The white people seemed to think that Philomena and I weren't married and that our children were illegitimate, but we were married in the way of Indian custom. The woman keeps the name of her father or mother. To please our church and the Government of Canada we were married two years ago by a United Church minister who came to visit us from Saskatoon."[90]

People also manipulated the new regime of Indian agents, missionaries, schools, and police to their own advantage if they could, and many examples of this have already been given, including the claimants in the estate of a Kainai named "HO," and the case of the young Piikani man who complained about his wife to Superintendent Primrose and wanted his horses returned. Parents also asked for police intervention in marital disputes involving their children. In 1891, while on patrol near Battleford, Inspector J. Howe of the NWMP was approached by a couple from the Moosomin Reserve who laid a complaint against a man "for taking their daughter a girl of about seventeen years of age and living with her contrary to their wishes, he being a married man." Howe had the man arrested, but the parents of the girl did not want the man punished, and he was discharged with a caution, promising to give the girl up to her parents.[91]

Another strategy that was adopted, and one which yielded the exact opposite effect to the one desired by DIA officials and missionaries, was to marry young people at an increasingly younger age to keep them out of industrial and residential schools. If a student married, he or she was no longer eligible to be a pupil. Through this tactic people evaded the control of agents and school principals to decide whom their children should marry, but it was also part of a larger protest over the incarceration of their children. Esther Goldfrank's 1930s informants gave examples of children who were married "so they wouldn't have to go to the Indian School."[92] The marriages were not to be consummated until the girl was older. In the case of one ten-year-old girl, the "marriage was arranged so that the girl wouldn't have to go to school."[93] Everyone was surprised that she had a baby before she was eleven, as they thought the husband "should have waited until she grew up."

Agents had a number of tactics that they adopted to attempt to enforce the monogamy policy. One was to redirect annuities to a deserted spouse under the authority of the Indian Act. Another was to punish mothers thought to be living "immorally" by threatening to remove their children and place them in residential schools, or send them to live with relatives or the fathers. As mentioned above, after 1894 officials could force children to attend the schools. In 1897 the Crooked Lake agent asked permission to take a child from a mother classified as "immoral" and place that child in whatever school the father chose.[94] A Moose Mountain woman deserted by her first husband intended to remarry in 1906, but was discouraged from doing so through the threat that her children would be taken from her (with the father's agreement) and placed with a grandmother.[95] In 1904 the Indian agent at Morley reported to the Indian commissioner that a young widow and mother of two boys had formed a new family with a previously married man. He had tried to induce the man to return to his first wife and family, but to no avail. "To punish the mother I wish to take her children away," wrote the agent. "These Indians are opposed to sending their children away and I wish to hold this over them so that in similar cases in the future the children may be taken away and sent to Red Deer school."[96]

Indian agents supported husbands and wives perceived to be justifiably aggrieved, but were quick to judge others, particularly women, as "immoral," if they had left unhappy marriages and formed new relationships. Agents and farm instructors took steps to separate couples that they believed did not have permission to be together, and in other cases they gave permission for such unions. In 1906 farm instructor Thomas Cory wrote for instructions from Indian Commissioner Laird in the case of a woman who had formed a new marriage and had a child with the man. "They were together last winter," he wrote, "but were separated by the Agent and they went together again last night but I parted them this morning and took the woman home." He promised to "keep them apart until I hear your decision."[97] Cory described the woman as "notoriously immoral," and her first husband as "a very decent fellow and a good worker."[98] Confusion abounded in this case, as earlier that year Laird had advised that the woman could not be acknowledged as the legal wife of her second husband, but the farm instructor and others in her own community claimed that another DIA official, William M. Graham, had given them permission to marry.[99]

Agents often helped each other out in enforcing monogamy. In the event of a person involved in a second marriage attempting to relocate to the reserve of a new spouse, agents were instructed to treat them as they would any other trespasser, and to deny them permission to reside on the reserve, a power granted agents under the Indian Act.[100] Agents on reservations across the border in the United States were also called upon to co-operate in projects of reconciliation. In 1904 the agent on the Kainai Reserve wrote to the agent at Browning on the Blackfeet Reservation to say that a woman from his reserve had run away from her husband and was living there, and asked "if you will kindly have the young woman sent home...as I wish to reconcile the couple."[101] In 1910 the superintendent at the Fort Belknap Agency (Montana) informed the agent on the Piapot Reserve (Saskatchewan) that a Cree woman from Piapot was visiting Fort Belknap and wanted to marry an Assiniboine man of that agency. "If you have no objection to the marriage and the woman has no other husband," he wrote, "permit will be given them from this office."[102]

Aboriginal recipients of all of this attention to their marital and domestic affairs were aware of the confusions and uncertainties on the whole marriage question, of the inability of the authorities to entirely enforce their will, and of the advantages to be gained by exploiting denominational rivalries. As is particularly clear from the protests against efforts to abolish polygamy, people defied and protested interference in their domestic affairs. It is also clear that threats to prosecute for bigamy were hollow. As many of the examples already discussed have demonstrated, a major tactic of DIA officials was to threaten prosecution for bigamy, to warn that it was a serious crime, and that a convicted biga-mist could be sentenced to seven years in the penitentiary. But officials were always hesitant to proceed because of concerns that such prose-cutions might fail. As stressed earlier, the DIA would lose authority and their level of control if such a case was lost after persistent threats of prosecution, and authorities feared that such a loss could be interpreted as giving sanction to serial matrimony (plurogamy). To commit bigamy, as explained by a Department of Justice clerk in 1914, "one has to go through a form of marriage recognized as a valid form by the law of the place where it is gone through." The law clerk feared that "marriage according to Indian fashion would not be sufficient to constitute the offence."[103] The first marriage had to be proved to have been a valid one, although for the second, or bigamous marriage it was bigamous "for any person, being married, *to go through a form of marriage* with any other person.[104] Fears of failure to convict were justified in 1906 when an attempt to prosecute an Aboriginal man from British Columbia on a charge of bigamy was unsuccessful.

The case of *Rex v. Kekanus* was heard before Justice Hunter in the BC Supreme Court in May of 1906.[105] The accused, from Alert Bay, had acquired a second wife through Aboriginal law. The testimony from the trial reveals the profound difficulties involved in conveying the intrica-cies of Aboriginal laws of marriage and divorce through an interpreter to an unsympathetic court that could not understand the flexibility of Aboriginal marriage law. For example, there was lengthy questioning of a witness (Thomas Newell, an Aboriginal man from Fort Rupert) on marriage customs that concerned the gifts that were given to the wife's family and how and when they were returned when a marriage was dissolved. This was all discussed through an interpreter who was himself placed from time to time in the witness box and questioned by the Court. While the return of the property/gifts signified the end of a marriage, this did not necessarily have to occur for a marriage to end and another marriage entered into and recognized by the community. Here is an example of one such exchange in which the witness responded to a question concerning whether the return of property was necessary to signify a divorce:

A: Although the property may not be returned and she can get married and he can take another wife.

Court: I didn't get that, and I don't think the jury did either. Just repeat that.

A: Before the property is returned to the husband of the woman, she can leave him if she chooses that is, if she don't like her husband, and he also can take another woman for his wife.

Court: Well, before the property goes back to the husband can the woman legally marry again, at least, marry according to the custom—she may live with another man, but is she regarded as married to him?

A: Yes, she can take another husband, and they don't see anything wrong in it.

Q [H.A. Maclean for the Crown]: And her children will be looked on as legitimate?

A: There is no ill-name given to the children; the children will be quite legitimate.

Mr. McHarg [for the Defendant]: Well there is a great deal of that kind of thing done, isn't there, interchanging?

A: Yes, sir.

Q: It doesn't work any hardship on the women does it, because I understand there are more men up there than there are women?

A: What do you mean by "hardship"?

Q: Well the woman can always get another husband, can't she?

A: Yes she can take another husband as I said before.

Q: But don't you understand what I mean by hardship?—Suppose a woman is put away—what are her chances of getting another husband?

A: Yes, she has every chance.[106]

Other exchanges reflected the deep gulf of understanding because of the Court's insistence that marriage was monogamous and for life. The judge asked Newell: "*Q:* But as a rule when an Indian man marries an Indian woman doesn't he live with that woman for life? *A:* There is no such understanding—no such words pass as they shall live together as long as they live. *Q:* Yes, I know there are no words to that effect, but isn't that what usually happens? *A:* Yes—some of them."[107] The witness was questioned about the number of people who married more than once, and the evidence given was imprecise but suggested that there were quite a few. The flexible attitude toward custody of children also perplexed the court, and the following exchange convinced the judge to not proceed further with the case:

Q: When the wife has young children and the husband leaves her, who supports these young children, the first husband, or the new husband?

A: The next husband.

Q: He takes the children over with the wife?

A: Yes.

Q: And the first husband has nothing more to do with them, is that it?

A: Well he looks after the children as well.

Q: Well who do they live with—him or her?

A: In most cases they generally go with the mother.

Q: On the principle that a foal follows the mare, I suppose. Then there is no ceremony among the Indians by which a man and a woman agree to remain together for life?

A: No, there is no such understanding made.

Q: And the man and woman can't bind themselves to live together for life by any ceremony?

A: No.

Q: So that it is only a ceremony—the meaning of the ceremony is that both parties shall live together as long as they like?

A: Yes

Q: And not longer—and that either can quit?

A: Yes, either party can marry again though they may have lived 30 or 40 years together.

Q: And it doesn't make any difference about whether the property is paid back or not?

A: Yes

Court: Well what is the use of going further Mr. Maclean, in this case?

It was Crown Prosecutor H.A. Maclean, Deputy Attorney General for the province of British Columbia, who had to convince the judge and jury that Aboriginal marriage was valid in order to convict for bigamy, and that "English law with regard to marriage, has no application at all."[108] The Criminal Code could apply only if Aboriginal marriage was recognized as valid. Maclean argued, "the matter is not as plain as it might be," and tried to draw attention to an English case, (not named but likely Connolly) and *Regina v. Nan-e-quis-a-ka*, "where all the law on this subject is very carefully considered." But Justice Hunter did not wish to carefully consider the case law and replied, "No I don't know anything about any English case, but it is common sense—it is no marriage ceremony within the meaning of—the essence of the marriage ceremony is that the parties shall be intending to take each other for life." When Maclean replied, "That is the English law, my Lord," Justice Hunter said, "This is a mere agreement to cohabit." The judge called back the witness Thomas Newell after Maclean submitted that "these Indians from time immemorial, have been living under their own customs with regard to marriage, but it is a species of marriage—it is different from our ideas, no doubt about that." The exchange that concluded this case began with Justice Hunter's question:

Court (with interpreter): What is the Indian word for marry?
A: No such word, only wife—taking a wife.
Q: Well what word do they use?
A: Well they use a certain word which I don't know its equivalent in English—I don't think—well there may be, but I don't know it, we have the word (carthaca?) which has nothing to do with marrying.
Q: Well what does that word mean?
A: It simply means as far as I understand the word, it is the parties going into the house—I take it this way, that is the husband go

in to the father of the woman's house, we have no such word as marriage in our language.

Following this exchange, which weakened his case and confirmed Justice Hunter's opinion, Maclean concluded by stating that English law had no application, and that "the circumstances of those Indians are so peculiar that they are governed by their own local customs with regard to marriage up to a certain point, and not by the English law." Justice Hunter, however, decided that this was not marriage at all; it was mere cohabitation. He disagreed sharply with the Crown prosecutor saying: "I don't see how you can call the ceremony a marriage when it is admitted on the face of the proceedings that it wasn't the intention of the parties to live together for life, and never is the intention—I don't see how you can call that a marriage, it is a mere agreement to cohabit."[109] Justice Hunter further stated that if he were to convict for bigamy, (and thereby invalidate the second marriage), the effect would be "that more than one-half the children in this man's tribe are illegitimate. I am not going to hold that, for the purpose of putting this man behind the bars for a so-called bigamy prosecution." The judge concluded that "the evidence clearly shows that there is no intention on the part of the Indians when they go through this ceremony to take each other for life, and that, in my opinion, is the essence of a marriage, or such marriage as is contemplated by a prosecution for bigamy." The case did not go to the jury; the prisoner was found "Not Guilty" and discharged.

The case caused a surge of anxiety among DIA administrators. The decision undermined their policy of recognizing the validity of Aboriginal marriage law and meant that people could not be required, cajoled, or expected to regard even their first marriages as valid and binding, as Aboriginal marriage was, according to Justice Hunter, not marriage at all but a "mere agreement to co-habit." The decision potentially added hundreds, even thousands, of children and adults declared "illegitimate" to the pay lists. If Aboriginal marriages were invalid, would this mean that *all* children of all marriages according to Aboriginal law were "illegitimate"? Administrators greatly feared the consequences if word got out that all their threats about prosecution and possible incarceration were hollow. As the prosecutor in the Kekanus case wrote to one BC Indian agent who wondered about the implications of the decision, "Under the circumstances it would be idle to send for trial any more of such cases."[110] The agent from Alert Bay wrote with alarm that the decision would cause great trouble; he had heard rumours that in the fall a great number of men intended to leave their wives.[111] A month later the same agent reported that a number of young men had complained to him that their wives had left them for fresh husbands who were older and wealthier.[112] In appealing for guidance this agent wrote, "a great deal of my future usefulness and influence depend on what is done in this matter."[113]

Department officials decided to first of all ignore the decision, to hope that word of the decision would not circulate outside of BC communities and to proceed as usual while casting about for alternate strategies. Very hastily the first version of the circular admired in 1915 by Frederick Abbott was distributed to all Indian superintendents, agents, and farm instructors in the Dominion.[114] Threats of potential prosecution for bigamy continued on prairie reserves. But there was a clear awareness that many aspects of the policy outlined in that circular were in doubt. In the case of the man, mentioned earlier, who first married according to Aboriginal law and who was then wed a second time by a Presbyterian missionary, the Indian agent was advised by Commissioner Laird that it would be in vain to prosecute for bigamy in the light of the recent BC decision.[115] As the BC superintendent of Indian affairs wrote, the Kekanus decision "renders it impossible for the Agent to put such laws as are in force respecting bigamy, &c., into operation."[116]

Other strategies were suggested, including a clause in the Indian Act giving agents the power to deal with and punish cases of bigamy, or a clause in the Indian Act legalising marriages according to Aboriginal law.[117] It was also proposed (once again) to make it compulsory that people be "legally" married, although they could be allowed *in addition* to be married according to their own laws.[118] Another idea was to have compulsory registration at each Indian agency of all marriages.[119] One of the reasons for the decision in the Kekanus case was that there was no marriage if there was no record of a marriage.

By October 1907, assistant Indian Commissioner J.A. McKenna was taking the position that the BC decision was welcome, that it concurred with his view as to what was essential to an Indian marriage. Agents, he argued, "Should have instructions that will enable them to differentiate between a valid Indian contract of marriage and mere concubinage." He proposed that it be imposed as a rule "in cases in which Indian men and women live together in alleged marriage according to Indian custom" to insist that the marriage be performed according to "recognized rights" [sic], and that a formal statement be obtained "from the man that he had taken the woman as his wife, and from the woman that she had taken the man as her husband...in connubial union till death did them part."[120] This, he argued, would constitute grounds for proceeding with bigamy charges in the event of either party breaking the union and entering into another marriage contract. The Kekanus case was also used by the DIA to insist that "Christianized" people—those, for example, educated at the industrial and boarding schools—could not contract marriages "by pagan rites."[121]

This initiative was accompanied by an effort to have the Aboriginal ceremony of marriage described and defined, so that all could know what was essential to making a union valid, and so that agents could differentiate between a valid marriage and "mere concubinage." McKenna chastised Indian agents for being too lax in this regard and demanded to know: "Is any rite or ceremony performed, or anything done to indicate that the parties entering into these so called marriages regard themselves as entering into a union of one man and one woman for life, to the exclusion of all others?"[122] Agent Millar from the Crooked Lake Agency of Plains Cree and Saulteaux people attempted to explain:

> I beg to say that the Pagan Indian custom of marriage referred to at present time is that a man desiring a certain girl in marriage asks the parent or guardian for her, and if he is accepted it is customary, although not always followed, for the man to make a present to the one giving consent. Parties entering into marriage according to this custom are regarded as entering into a union of one man and one woman for life to the exclusion of all others. This is in the

Indian mind, notwithstanding, how far the union may be disregarded afterwards.[123]

It is unlikely that this description satisfied McKenna, as Millar indicated that the protocol might not always be followed, and that while the union was regarded as "for life" at the time of marriage, this might be later disregarded. What the assistant Indian commissioner demanded, and could not obtain, was a description of marriage that matched his own definition of marriage as a monogamous, lifelong, and indissoluble union. No other definition constituted marriage in his view. He was never to receive this description from any of the agents, however, and officials of the DIA were affirmed in their belief that they had to adopt the broadest possible view of what constituted a marriage ceremony and a valid marriage in order to insist that people live up to their mutual obligations. If they cast doubt on the validity of any form of marriage there would be, in their view, a "loophole" that would permit evasion of these obligations.

This casting about for new strategies culminated in a 1908 memorandum drafted in the DIA, outlining proposals for the consideration of the Department of Justice.[124] The memo sought to address the main obstacle in the way of suppressing and punishing such problems as wife desertion, which was "the difficulty experienced in establishing the existence of marriage between the parties within the meaning of the law." Special legislation was recommended that would permit prosecution for bigamy if any conjugal contract or alliance whatsoever had been entered into, "No matter what the nature of conditions of such contract may be or whether expressed, implied or understood, or whether containing provisions for the termination thereof by mutual consent or at the will of either of the contracting or contracted parties, or whether all or any conditions have been fulfilled or completed in whole or in part." It was also proposed to permit a special form of divorce. In the presence of an Indian agent or Justice of the Peace, and in the presence of each other, a couple could give consent in writing to the "termination of such conjugal contract or alliance."[125] A fine of fifty dollars or three months hard labour was recommended for any man or woman who deserted a spouse and contracted another conjugal contract unless the marriage had been ter-minated in the manner proposed. A husband (not a wife) could make a special appeal if he could prove immoral conduct on the part of his wife. It was further recommended that legislation be enacted to severely punish anyone who would induce, threaten, or bribe any Indian woman or girl to terminate any conjugal contract. The father of an illegitimate child could be ordered to pay monthly support, and he could have his property seized to satisfy such an order. It was further recommended in the 1908 memo that districts be established within which Indian people would be required to register all "marriages or marital contracts by any Indian rite, ceremony, custom or usage whatsoever."[126]

These recommendations were never enacted, demonstrating again the tenuous and limited degree of control the DIA had over their "wards."[127] The response of the deputy minister of justice in May of 1908 was that he found it impossible to satisfactorily deal with these issues of "marriages and quasi marriages and sexual offences among the Indians" with the information furnished him. The proposals "present very serious questions of policy and law which will call for careful consideration." He also found some of the "remedies" proposed in the memo to be "inadmissible." All required more deliberate consideration than was possible for him to devote at that time.[128] The only action taken that year (1908) was yet another circular letter urging agents to prevent all separations, to warn that there would be punishment of all transgressors.[129] J. D. McLean wrote in August of 1908 that the department "was greatly disappointed despite the expenditure of much thought and labour" that the recommendations in the 1908 memorandum did not materialize, but he "did not despair of ultimately devising some legislative measures to meet the complications of the situation."[130] "The whole subject," he noted, "is fraught with difficulties of which not the least is the danger of driving the Indians to avoid such contracts as they may now be willing to enter into, and which are doubtless better than none."

The DIA soldiered forward with their policy on marriage and divorce and with their threats to prosecute for bigamy, as if the Kekanus case had never happened. Requests for permission to remarry following separation or divorce were met with the same replies as in the past. There were numerous such requests and replies. In 1908 an Aboriginal catechist at Norway House (Manitoba) wrote to Indian Commissioner David Laird to ask if a woman, separated from her husband for twelve years, and who received no support from her husband, could remarry. She was living with another man "as man and wife," and her first husband was living with someone else. Laird's answer was that she could not remarry, as "to do so would be bigamy."[131] In 1909, R. N. Wilson, the Indian agent on the Kainai Reserve, consulted his Ottawa superiors about a young man of twenty-five whose wife had left him, refusing to return.[132] The man sought permission to remarry, which the agent thought only made sense, as it was unrealistic to expect him to remain single for the rest of his life. Wilson remarked that nineteen horses were "paid" at the time of the marriage. He wrote that there were many such divorced couples on the reserve wishing to remarry. In these cases Wilson first tried "reconciliation by talking to the young couple and their relations here in the office. Only occasionally are such efforts successful." He had "sent for her and in his presence tried to persuade her to return but she expressed great unwillingness to do so, stating that she was afraid of him, hated him and would not live with him under any circumstances. The girl was undoubtedly in earnest as she implored me to let her stay with her mother and not compel her to return." Wilson then spoke to the woman's brother, hoping he could get his sister to return to her husband, "But he stated that while he would gladly see her return he would not force her to do so on account of her abhorrence [of her husband]." The husband had informed Wilson that if her relations kept his wife away, and if the department was powerless to help him have her returned, then he would ask permission to marry again. The reply from Deputy Superintendent Frank Pedley was that the law took a "liberal" view "as to what constitutes a binding marriage among Indians," with the desire to "guard the sacred and permanent nature of the nuptial contract," and refused to recognize their divorces for the same reason.[133] The best hope would be to punish bigamists, "for probably if Indians find that after separation they can not without danger of punishment contract fresh alliances, they will hesitate about leaving each other." Pedley did not advise how bigamists were to be punished. Once again the view was expressed that "only time and advance in the spirit and practice of Christian civilization will affect the necessary reform with regard to these." Pedley wrote that the department could not compel the wife to return to her husband, nor could it permit the husband to marry anyone else.

That same year Moose Mountain Indian Agent Thomas Cory wrote to ask whether a young woman in his agency was at liberty to marry again. A man from Turtle Mountain, North Dakota, had been married to her briefly a year earlier, but he had returned across the border, and the horse given to her family at the time of the marriage had been returned.[134] The man had since remarried. The answer was that she was legally married and therefore was not at liberty to marry again. This agent raised a point that perplexed many, especially new recruits to the DIA bureaucracy— just what constituted a valid marriage according to Aboriginal law? How was marriage to be defined, through what ceremony was it solemnized, and how was marriage distinct from a casual agreement to live together for a time? Cory wanted a definite answer on what constituted a "legal" marriage. He did not get an answer. Ottawa bureaucrats grappled with this question for years, but were perennially unable to come up with a definition of Indian marriage that would distinguish a casual arrangement from a marriage.

Meanwhile pressure mounted from moral reform and church organizations to address the issue of "Indian marriage," but in the face of this the DIA maintained the policy determined in the 1887 order-in-council in the light of the unsuccessful 1908 effort to take a new approach. Of particular concern in 1909–1910 were lurid stories from the west coast that girls were being bartered for blankets. In 1909 the Women's Auxiliary to the Missionary Society of the Church of England wrote to the DIA to express concern about the marriage customs of the people of Vancouver Island.[135] The National Council of Women similarly wrote to the minister of Indian affairs lamenting the "grave immorality which exists among the Indians on the west coast of British Columbia owing to the marriage customs of those people."[136] The Women's Baptist Home Missionary Society and the Canada Congregational Women's Board of Missions also made requests for action on the issue of Indian marriage. Similar answers were given to each organization. The Anglican Women's Auxiliary was informed that compulsory legislation might "drive the Indians to cohabit without any form of marriage at all."[137] In a 1910 letter to the National Council of Women the deputy superintendent-general of the DIA wrote that "existing marriage customs are recognized by law with a view to maintaining as far as possible due regard to the sanctity of the nuptial contract, and…they are probably much more binding on their consciences than any more civilized methods whether Christian or civil."[138]

The Moral and Social Reform Council of Canada (MSRCC) also had "Indian marriage" on its agenda. This organization, founded in 1909, was committed to promoting the "pure" life, and to stamping out "vice."[139] One of the founders, Presbyterian purity activist Rev. John G. Shearer, toured Western Canada for a month in 1910 and wrote sensationalistic articles upon his return to Toronto. There were racial aspects to the moral panic that Shearer created. He claimed that Chinese or Japanese proprietors owned most of the establishments in the red light districts.[140] He also wrote that for the purposes of prostitution "the Indians bring their women to the towns and settlements along the coast everywhere."[141] In September of 1910 the MSRCC submitted a number of recommendations to the DIA.[142] One was that "the law relating to immoral relations between (1) Indian and Indian, and—(2) Indian and White, be more carefully defined within the Indian Act itself so that seduction, adultery and violations of the marriage vow may be severely punished, and if possible prevented." Another recommendation under the heading "Indian Marriage" was presented by a MSRCC delegation in person at the DIA offices in Ottawa on 6 October 1910.[143] They asked that "the defining of Indian marriage; the providing of machinery for recording of Indian marriages; dealing with the temporary marriage of white men with Indian women, be submitted to the Department of Indian Affairs, with request that the Department secure from the Department of Justice a report upon these suggestions, and upon the general subject of Indian Marriage and Divorce; And that the Department of Indian Affairs be asked to appoint a small Commission for the purpose of fully investigating Indian Marriage conditions."

No such commission was appointed, but Minister of the Interior Frank Oliver replied to Rev. Canon Tucker, who headed up the delegation, that he had looked into the matter very carefully and found that the subject of Indian marriages had received a "very large measure of consideration" by his own department, the Department of Justice, and the Governor in Council. Oliver described the origins of the 1887 report to council, and enclosed a copy. He also enclosed the draft amendments of 1908 and the letter from the Department of Justice in reply that pointed out the difficulty of adequately amending the law on the question of Indian marriage. He did not think anything could be gained by resubmitting the question to the Department of Justice. Oliver concluded by once again quoting at length from the 1887 report to council as "stating the present attitude of the Government on this question":

> In the meantime, the laws which establish liability on the part of the Indian or White man for the support of such offspring as he may have by and [sic] Indian woman and for the support of the woman with whom he contracts a marriage according to the Indian custom, will be enforced as far as practicable, and such legislation will be recommended from time to time as may tend to improve the social and moral condition of the Indians and to check as far as it is practicable to do so, the tendency among the Whites in proximity to the Indians to avail themselves of the lax notions of the latter with regard to the relations between the sexes.[144]

In assessing where the issue stood in 1912, one DIA official wrote that "tribal customs had persisted longer than anticipated," and that "the marriage laws of the land cannot yet be forced upon all Indians."[145] Marriages according to "tribal customs" were not in themselves objectionable, the assistant deputy and secretary of the DIA noted; rather, it was the separation and desertion of husbands and wives that was becoming all too common. The department had not recognized second marriages and was of the opinion that they could be found to be bigamous if a "tribal custom or ceremony" was observed in the second union, but "the trouble is that in most cases there is no kind of second marriage—only a going and living together immorally. This kind of offence the criminal law of Canada does not reach unless there is some sort of prostitution connected therewith." In this correspondence he was advising an agent not to recognize as valid a second marriage "according to whiteman's law" when there had been a first marriage according to Aboriginal law, as "it would be considered as setting official seal to the fact that no Indian marriage was legal."

The DIA stuck to the "party line" as detailed in the circular letter, that the Connolly case had decided marriage according to Aboriginal law was valid. In 1916 a BC inspector of Indian agencies unearthed the case of *Bethell v. Hildyard*, and asked whether the case superseded *Connolly v. Woolrich*, and wondered further if agents "might be instructed to inform all their Indians that marriages according to tribal custom would have no standing in the courts after a date to be set by the Department." Someone scrawled in the margin "Why? B vs H was decided on Eng law: C vs W was decided on Quebec civil law." No answer to the letter survives, if an answer was ever given.

The 1914 case of a Kainai man, "TMF," demonstrated once again how the policy outlined in the circular letter could not be enforced, and how powerless officials were to pursue criminal proceedings in order to punish bigamy and enforce monogamy. It was alleged that TMF had been married once "by the church" and three times in "Indian fashion" during the previous three years.[146] He lived a short time with each woman and "then sent her home." The Indian agent had the last deserted wife swear an information under the Criminal Code that she required necessities, but the agent was advised by the provincial Attorney General, as well as the Crown prosecutor that "they were inclined to think a prosecution would fail on the ground that an Indian being a ward of the Government is technically not in a condition of necessity." The law clerk in the Department of Justice did not think this point was well taken, but advised, "a prosecution would certainly fail because she is not a wife."[147] In his memorandum for the deputy minister of justice, the law clerk reviewed the case law, as well as the previous department rulings on Indian marriage, and concluded that TMF could not be convicted of bigamy, that "marriage according to Indian fashion would not be sufficient to constitute the offence." The North-West Territories Marriage Act of 1888, and the marriage acts in force in the provinces of Alberta and Saskatchewan, had to be complied with, in his view, in order to constitute bigamy. This advice clearly contradicted and challenged the policy pursued by the DIA of insisting that the Connolly case recognized Aboriginal marriages as valid. In his draft memorandum, the law clerk explained his reasoning at greater length. He thought that the marriage laws applied to marriage among the Indians, as they were British subjects.[148] The only exceptions, he noted, were in reference to Doukhobors and Quakers (as discussed earlier in this book). In the convoluted language of the legal world he wrote, "If a marriage between subjects other than Indians is not valid unless it complies with these Acts it is not easy to see why a distinction in this respect should be made in respect to the Indians who are British subjects and who live in a country where law, civil and criminal, as well as the facilities for complying with the requirements of those Acts exist." The law clerk cited a Manitoba case in which it was "recognized that Indians are British subjects and entitled to all the rights and privileges of such." The law clerk's only suggestions were that TMF could be punished under the Criminal Code if the women were underage, or under section 98 of the Indian Act concerning "the repression of intemperance and profligacy," or his annuities could be discontinued. Based on this advice the DIA was informed that "no effective action can be taken to adequately punish him for his conduct."[149] The deputy minister of justice was "inclined to think that his marriages according to tribal customs did not constitute bigamy as defined by sections 307 and 240 of the Code."

Efforts to impose the monogamous model of marriage on the First Nations of Western Canada were more deliberate, concerted, and invasive than the examples of non-Aboriginal Canadians and "new" Canadians given earlier in this book. Situated on reserves and isolated from the rest of the population, the First Nations were subject to the administration of a bureaucracy dedicated to the implementation and refinement of policies and laws designed to shape and reconstitute their societies to make them conform and assimilate to idealized white ways. The concerted assault, relative isolation, and the presence of a bureaucracy dedicated to refashioning gender roles, should have ensured the success of these efforts, compared to those directed toward the diverse and scattered population of Canadians and "new" Canadians, but it was quite the reverse. The imposition of the monogamous Christian model met with less success than it had with the non-Aboriginal settlers in Western Canada. Reserve communities were powerfully and profoundly influenced by these measures but the state was not able to impose complete control. Resistance to efforts to restructure the foundation of domestic life compelled authorities to recognize the validity of Aboriginal marriage law. The persistence of Aboriginal marriage ensured that prosecutions for bigamy and related transgressions would not be successful within the Canadian legal system. Ultimately, the state had the capacity to disrupt, but not utterly transform, Aboriginal marriage and domestic life; their technologies of control were limited. As historian Antoinette Burton has stressed, the state and other associated instruments of social, political and cultural power have a "limited capacity...to fully contain or successfully control the domain of sexuality." Modern colonial regimes are "always in process, subject to disruption and contest and never fully or finally accomplished, to such an extent that they must be conceived of as 'unfinished business.'"[150]

EIGHT

Conclusion

A 1913 SPECIAL SOUVENIR ISSUE of the Calgary newspaper *Western Standard Illustrated Weekly*, published by the Calgary Women's Press Club, began with these invigorating words: "The Last Best West is the woman's west. Nowhere else in the world is the evolution worked by the great feminist movement of the last century demonstrated more strikingly. Nowhere else may women find the perfect conditions under which to work out a destiny in accord with modern ideals. It is a land new to their hand; new social systems are evolving under their influence; the whole virgin western world is theirs to conquer and claim, with no obstacles of tradition or convention."[1] But a close reading of the special issue suggests that much work remained to work out this destiny, and that while there was opportunity for freedom from conventional restraint and tradition, this opportunity had not yet been realized—"the wonderful possibilities of the last west are but dimly outlined."[2] The organized white women of the young city of Calgary used the special issue and the rhetorical strategy of the golden opportunities and "free field" of the west to call upon western men to be "fair and generous." The women also displayed their determination to see their vision realized and they presented their counter-narrative of the west as a potential place of disrupted gender relations—where women, married or single, voted, owned and ran their own businesses, and farms. Though few in number there were some "outstanding successes" the authors cited, including three women commercial travellers, an architect and several doctors. There were women real-estate brokers with their own offices and motor cars. It was boasted that four of the best mountain and city hotels were managed by women. But none of these women could vote, except in municipal elections, and this was the major reason for the special issue. The material progress of the west meant even more to women than to men, as it was argued in the introduction, "to cope with the moral and social problems of racial development."[3]

But in 1913 the "last best west" was not a land of freedom from conventional restraint, and it was hardly the "woman's west"; a great deal of work had been done to ensure that it was in fact a white "manly space." To begin with, it had taken much work to define the space of a white settler society. Maps and surveys that demarcated towns and farm lands from reserves, the Aboriginal from the non-Aboriginal spaces, were required to carve out white settler space. A cluster of laws, policies, police activities, community pressures, cultural beliefs and social attitudes induced observance of these separate spaces. Yet these barriers were not entirely rigid, people criss-crossed and challenged the boundaries of the white community, particularly Aboriginal women through their marriages with non-Aboriginal men, but these marriages were markedly fewer by 1913. This was in sharp contrast to the situation described by A. K. Isbister in 1861, quoted earlier in this book, when he wrote that "the half castes or mixed race" people outnumbered all others in the colony, held nearly all the important and intellectual offices, and that "every married woman and mother of a family throughout the whole extent of the Hudson's Bay territories...is of this class, and, with her children, heir to all the wealth of the country."[4]

The 1913 special issue of the *Western Standard Illustrated Weekly* included only one woman who continued to cross divides and categories, Mrs. Isabella (Hardisty) Lougheed, the wife of lawyer and senator James A.

Lougheed. Although her part-Aboriginal ancestry was not mentioned in the article entitled "A Daughter of the West," it would have been understood. It was noted that she was one of the "few western born women," and the daughter of a chief factor of the HBC.[5] She was the niece of Lord Strathcona, it was declared, and many readers at that time would have known about Lady Strathcona's Aboriginal ancestry. (As related earlier in this book, Lady Strathcona was referred to as a "squaw wife" by Governor General Lord Minto.) It was further noted in the *Western Standard Illustrated Weekly* article that Mrs. Lougheed had recently entertained royal visitors including a duke, duchess, and princess. However, the article on the same page and just above, the only other article to mention an Aboriginal woman, made a mockery of that woman's ability to properly host a royal visitor, the Marquis of Lorne, some decades earlier. The unnamed woman was married to John Glenn, who ran a "stopping house" in Calgary. According to this article, all the courses were served on the same plate, and when one of the other guests tried to get a fresh plate for the Marquis' pudding, the royal guest replied "Sit down, my man, if you can stand it, I can."

There were no gender maps, but space can be culturally inscribed, and as historian Catherine Cavanaugh has argued, there were conceptual frameworks, or mental maps upon which Euro-Canadian colonization and settlement took place.[6] There is profoundly gendered space such as the domestic or "separate spheres." Cavanaugh examines how and why the myth of the "manly west" was perpetuated from the mid-nineteenth century—how a particular gender division was established early in settler discourse and came to be seen as the natural and inevitable order. When the HBC monopoly collapsed great fortunes were to be made in the west, and the new imperial and patriarchal goals for the region rested on complimentary assumptions of British superiority and white male dominance. Aboriginal women and their children were not regarded as the proper heirs to the wealth of the country. Prominent Aboriginal women of the Red River settlement were denied elite status, were pro-claimed to be promiscuous and a social danger. Nor were fortunes to be shared or dissipated through opportunities for newly arrived white women to have access to land or other wealth. Agriculture was to be an exclusively male enterprise. Through the exclusion of most women from homestead rights, the abolition of dower rights, and the erosion by judicial interpretation of the dower laws that women fought to have introduced in the prairie provinces, the west was deliberately carved out as "manly space" according to Cavanaugh. A "masculinist cultural context sharply narrowed the possibilities for aboriginal women in the new West [and] it also shaped the contours of the lives of newcomer women."[7] The campaigns of white women reformers for access to land on the same basis as men, and to win legal recognition of their contributions to the family farms, struck at the heart of the manly west: "They challenged men's control of land, and therefore wealth, in the predominantly agricultural West, and men's sole authority as *paterfamilias* or head of the prairie household as Minister of the Interior Oliver envisioned it."[8] As women had no vote however, their demands were readily refused by male legislators as too costly, inconvenient, "as well as generally too disruptive to the economy and therefore bad for business."[9] The vote opened the door to manly space, and initially women eagerly embraced the challenges of elected office, but their numbers remained small, and they were excluded from positions of power—the formal political field remained a manly preserve. As Cavanaugh notes, by the 1930s "women had all but disappeared from the ranks of prairie legislators."[10]

Building on Cavanaugh's work, my study has demonstrated that the imposition of the monogamous model of marriage should be understood as a critical component in the deliberate shaping of the west as white "manly space." "Legal," Christian marriage was to be the foundation of the new region of the nation—this marriage system was critical to the health, wealth, and character of Western Canada. It would forge a national identity that was distinct from the old First Nation and mixed ancestry peoples, it would distinguish Canada from the US, and it would facilitate the grasp of the authorities on all of these people as well as the new arrivals to the region. This model of marriage would forge the gender order of the obedient and submissive wife, and provider, head-of-family husband. It took tremendous efforts to impose this model and to make this gender order appear natural. There was a preponderance of challenges and alternatives, and great potential for disruptive gender relations in a region that was not a blank slate, where there were many First Nations with diverse definitions of marriage, where there had been two hundred years of marriages between Europeans, Canadians, and Aboriginal women, where there was a large Métis population, and where people arrived from many parts of the world, some having alternative views of marriage. There was also the proximity of the United States where a perceived state of dangerous marital chaos provided examples of other approaches to marriage and divorce.

Expectations of Christian-model monogamy were successfully imposed on most of the new arrivals to Western Canada by the early twentieth century, although there remained individual dissenters and transgressors and those who went "underground," but the power of individual transgressors was limited. Legislation, court cases, the churches, print media, and community pressures combined to prohibit, contain, and marginalize nonconformist marital arrangements. Monogamy had become the dominant worldview; it was time-honoured, traditional, and based on "common sense." Much less success attended the considerable efforts of the DIA, the department of justice, missionaries, school principals, and teachers and their allies to impose this model. The government's grasp on the populace was far from complete. In the case of First Nations, marriage became, and continues to be, a site of enduring cultural struggle.

It was critical to the fortunes of the white "manly west" to uphold the power of this sector in an expanding and diversifying nation. The monogamous couple was the best "seed grain" and building block, creating an illusion of a national identity that was rendered natural and innate.

Efforts to ensure the uniformity and ascendancy of the monogamous, lifelong, model of marriage among First Nations were of a different scale and intensity. A bureaucracy in Ottawa and resident on the reserves, was armed with special legislation and policy directives never codified in legislation, including the policy on Aboriginal marriage and divorce. Usually assisted by missionaries, and with the aid of the residential and industrial schools, this bureaucracy was dedicated to a program of crafting dutiful, obedient wives under the control of their husbands. This level of surveillance and interference did not have a parallel in the off-reserve population, but it did have a parallel in other colonial settings where initiatives tended to consolidate husbandly power. While these efforts were not entirely successful, they nonetheless left Plains Aboriginal women uniquely vulnerable and disabled compared to other women in Western Canada. A uniquely rapid transformation was expected of them as their options were suddenly and dramatically narrowed; previous generations could be monogamous, or they could separate, divorce, re-marry, form new families, or join a polygamous household.

Although all Western Canadian women of this era had little recourse under the Canadian legal system in the event of marriage breakdown, First Nations women had even less. Under the new regime divorce was not permitted, except through the Parliamentary route that was out of the question for Aboriginal people. As there was no recognized divorce, or means of legal separation, there was no consideration of matrimonial property issues on reserves. Deserted wives were not to form new relationships or remarry according to Aboriginal or any other law as they were warned that to do so would risk bigamy charges, and the children from these relationships would be labelled illegitimate. They also risked losing rations and annuities and were threatened with the removal of their children to residential schools. Nor could a deserted wife argue that she was legally entitled to obtain the necessities of life from her husband, as legal authorities advised in 1914 that as a ward of the government, a First Nations wife was not technically in a condition of necessity, and that if married according to Aboriginal law, such action would certainly fail as she would not be regarded as a wife. There were also the unique provisions of the Indian Act that meant that a First Nations woman marrying "any other than an Indian or a non-treaty Indian... shall cease to be an Indian in any respect," and that a widow had to be judged of "good moral character" to inherit from her deceased husband.[11] New, unfamiliar categories were created as a result of these interventions, including the single mother, and deserted wife, unable to legitimately re-marry if she knew her husband to be alive, and the illegitimate child. Options for the First Nations single mother, deserted wife or widow left without any inheritance were uniquely limited, and were further constrained by the late nineteenth century colonial representations of Aboriginal women as immoral and depraved that prevailed well into the twentieth century that were an important rationale for the residential school system. A widow with a minor child or children could homestead and become the owner of 160 acres, and hundreds took advantage of this opportunity, but this option was not available to First Nations widows, as under the Indian Act, all "Indians" were excluded from homesteading.

Despite this legacy of disabilities and disruptions, the monogamous model of marriage was far from successfully imposed on First Nations communities. It was an arduous process, a constant struggle, demanding diverse strategies that failed frequently. New tactics were continually proposed to suppress and punish transgressors. But government bureaucrats, missionaries and Canadian legal authorities confronted a well entrenched legal culture that was not easily or quickly supplanted.

Appendix

ADMINISTERING FIRST NATIONS MARRIAGE
AND DIVORCE TO 1951

VIGILANT EFFORTS TO ENSURE THE SUPREMACY of the monogamous model of
marriage continued in the twentieth century in the face of successive waves of
anxiety and disquiet over the state of marriage and family. Wives were constantly
reminded, even through the "humour" found in popular magazines, for example,
that they were to be "'passive, loving and submissive' lest they incur the 'rightful'
wrath of husbands unwilling to share privilege and power."[1] The work of reforming
and redesigning marriage continued into the new century with new agendas and
resolve. In early twentieth-century English Canada, fears emerged anew of threats to
marriage and the family, particularly in the light of the arrival of diverse immigrants.
As James G. Snell and Cynthia Comacchio Abeele have argued, "At the centre of these
English-Canadian anxieties was a fear that traditional values and 'British' ideals were
being subverted by the new peoples and the new social environment developing
around them."[2] Various reforms were enacted that were aimed at restricting and
regulating access to marriage during the early decades of the twentieth century. This
emphasis on restriction began before the First World War and gained impetus during
the war years as anxieties developed about the future of the "race." Marriage was to
become a privilege for those who "demonstrated the features most desired in the
future Canada: genetic quality, emotional and mental stability, good health, maturity."[3]
New regulations reflected evolving concerns that couples often married too young
and without parental con-sent. Further, the diseased and the genetically weak were
to be prevented from marrying or at least procreating. New regulations included
Saskatchewan's 1933 application of eugenic principles to marriage. An amendment
to the Marriage Act required any prospective groom to submit a medical certificate

proving that a qualified doctor had examined him within ten days of the planned marriage. In 1941, prospective brides too had to submit a medical certificate. Alberta had less rigorous legislation, but the couple to be wed had to swear they were not infected with venereal disease or tuberculosis. Through these regulations "improper" marriages were to "find less facility."[4] Heightened concern about behaviour identified as immoral or deviant flourished. In this social climate, suggestions were made once again to legislate against interracial marriage and more informal interracial relationships.[5]

Aboriginal people, the subject of much scrutiny during the period of this study, had little place in this emerging discussion about regulating access to marriage. Aside from the missionaries and Indian agents who worked in these communities, little concern was shown about issues of family stability, healthy offspring, and the future of the "race" in their communities. Their domestic affairs had been dramatically disrupted and undermined through the turbulence and disarray of the many late nineteenth and early twentieth century efforts to alter and redesign marital arrangements. As one indicator of the depth of this disruption, historian Lesley Erickson has offered evidence from the late nineteenth and early twentieth centuries that suicides of both men and women, who were predominantly young to middle-aged and married, were associated with "the moral uncertainty and confusion that accompanied government and missionary efforts to impose monogamous, Christian marriages."[6] Aboriginal witnesses connected suicides to the "confusion in gender roles and marital relationships that accompanied colonialism," and they cited domestic disputes as the precipitating cause in 40 per cent of cases. Both Aboriginal and non-Aboriginal observers felt that the marital relations in reserve communities had become increasingly turbulent and temporary. Many more people lived together in temporary relationships with no marriage whatsoever, whether performed by clergy or according to Aboriginal law.[7] Cree Elder Glecia Bear asked another "little old woman" about the old days, and she was very critical of the temporary nature of marriage in her Saskatchewan community: "'For one month, or sometimes not even for a month, they live with their husbands and then they leave them,' she said, 'that did not use to happen,' she said; 'in the old days one used to have respect for everything,' she said, 'and one used to lead a proper life.'"[8]

Well into the twentieth century the DIA continued to attempt to impose monogamy and its policy on marriage and divorce as decided in 1887 and as articulated in the 1906 circular letter; however, it continued to be the case that their degree of control was limited, and their threats of prosecution hollow. Following the 1914 Department of Justice advice in the case of "TMF," no attempts were made to prosecute bigamists. Hundreds of copies of the circular letter on the recognition of Indian marriage and divorce were distributed to Indian agents, missionaries, and other concerned individuals well into the late 1920s.[9] A typical request was from an Anglican missionary at the Griswold (Manitoba) Agency who wrote, "I am sometimes very much in doubt as to what constitutes a valid marriage in the case of Indians."[10] A copy of the circular was sent to the missionary. Sending along the circular letter in answer to any and all inquiries avoided the thorny task of having to address sundry specific situations.

When new bureaucrats arrived on the scene in the departments of Indian Affairs or Justice, the policy was often questioned, and new approaches suggested. For example, in 1917 law clerk A. S. Williams thought that it would be an easy matter for an agent paying treaty money to ask a woman claiming to be the wife of an Indian if she could prove that she was married. If she did not have a marriage certificate she would have to prove that she was married "according to Tribal Custom." "It would not be sufficient," Williams wrote, "for the couple to say that they were so married, they should prove it to the satisfaction of the Agent by evidence in corroboration of their own Tribal Custom, and that all the formalities of that custom have been complied with. They may find it so difficult to do this that they will get married according to the Christian form of marriage in order to draw annuity."[11] No action was taken on this impractical and naïve suggestion.

A new policy direction was debated in the House of Commons in 1921 when an amendment to the Criminal Code was proposed that would make it an offence for any white man to have "illicit connection with an Indian woman." The legislation was generated by agents in British Columbia who called attention to the numbers of young women from the reserves visiting seaports where they met "large numbers of dissolute men of a very cosmopolitan character."[12] Initially it was proposed that the amendment was to apply only to "unmarried" Indian women, but this was struck from the suggested amendment. The deputy minister of justice explained the situation this way: "I do not see why a man should be in any more favourable position because the woman is married."[13] The debate sheds light on the negative representations of Aboriginal people shared and perpetrated by Canadian parliamentarians. It was first suggested that the wording had to be changed to "illicit connection" with any *unenfranchised* Indian woman, as an enfranchised woman was put "on the footing of the every-day, ordinary citizen."[14] One MP thought that the clause would do more harm than good, as "there is nothing to prevent any Indian female laying a charge against a white man and having her buck Indian coming behind her for the few dollars and holding up the white man...we do not want to give the buck Indian an opportunity, by such legislation, to take money out of white people's pockets." Continuing in this vein he said, "Indian women, particularly out in the West, have their bucks to look after them, and they are pretty jealous of and able to look after their women... we are going to pass a law that is going to expose the white man to be the victim of an Indian woman." Another MP said that "the Indian women are, perhaps, not as alive as women of other races in the country to the importance of maintaining their chastity." The section was dropped.

Missionaries too continued to suggest new approaches such as a 1924 resolution, presented by the Missionaries and Teachers of the Methodist Church, that the Indian Act be amended to make wife- or husband-desertion a crime, and together with seduction, punishable by imprisonment.[15] The reply was no, that the Criminal Code covered desertion and seduction, and that it was "not considered advisable to make a distinction between Indians and other residents of the country with respect to Criminal Law."[16]

Suggestions for change were disregarded and the 1906 circular continued as DIA policy to the early 1930s. People were told, as had been previous generations, that they could not remarry unless legally divorced. In 1925 a Whitehorse man, married according to Aboriginal law, wanted to remarry as his wife had been placed in an asylum for life.[17] She had murdered a woman and was declared insane. He was left with three small children, and he was handicapped in caring for them as he hunted for their living and had his trapline to maintain. He needed to remarry and consulted a clergyman, who consulted his bishop, who in turn consulted with officials of the DIA. The answer, sent by telegram, was that "Indian married by tribal rights legally married (stop) Such Indian cannot marry again so long as his present wife is living unless legally divorced."[18] However, no one was ever prosecuted for bigamy, and there was also a clear recognition that the policy outlined in the circular was being disregarded by many individuals. In 1926, W. R. Haynes, a missionary on the Piikani Reserve, received the circular letter in answer to his inquiry about whether he could marry people in the church who had previously been married according to Aboriginal law and had separated. The missionary reported, "It is useless having rules and regulations, if they are not be carried out, it only makes the dept [sic] look ridiculous in the eyes of their wards." As no action was being taken on a very clear case of bigamy, the Indian agent was the "laughing stock of the reserve," at least according to the missionary.

Although the circular letter was widely distributed to those who requested advice and direction, on at least one occasion it was not sent, and its existence even denied. For example, the Wetaskiwin, Alberta, law firm of Loggie and Manley wrote the Ottawa DIA office in 1928 stating, "We should be glad to know whether there are any regulations with reference to the marital life of the Indians promulgated by the Department under any Statute of the Dominion. If there is would you kindly send us a copy or advise us where we can procure same." Under the British North America Act, the provinces were given the exclusive right to make laws with regard to the solemnization of marriage. The federal DIA was on perilous ground with the policy and advice outlined in the 1906 circular that marriage but not divorce according to Aboriginal law was valid. The reply to the Wetaskiwin lawyers from A. F. MacKenzie, acting assistant deputy and secretary, was that "this Department has no regulations with respect to the marital life of Indians." Even an "acting" and "assistant" bureaucrat would have know that reams of correspondence, contained in numerous files housed in the Ottawa office, contradicted this statement.

There was no particularly obvious wellspring of pressure that led to a new policy, initiated in 1933 through a Department of Justice opinion prepared by R.V. Sinclair, that "no marriage celebrated according to the Indian custom is valid," but it may have been due to the growing awareness, reflected in the request of the Wetaskiwin law firm, that the federal government should not be involved in marriage. Aboriginal marriage was no longer to be regarded as valid unless it was a "marriage by necessity, that is if the contracting parties live so far from a person duly authorized to solemnize a marriage that the law would determine that they could not reasonably be required to travel the distance necessary to reach such authorized person."[19] In those cases the marriage would be valid, and the children legitimate, "provided that such marriage involves the union of one man and one woman for life." In a Department of Justice opinion it was argued that as "natural born British subjects, the Indians of Canada...were subject to and entitled to the benefits flowing from the laws of the Provinces or Territories forming part of the Dominion in which they reside. This applies both to their political, civil and domestic life."[20] Bureaucrats in the department began to carefully word their advice on marriage, and to deny the existence of the policy pursued for the previous several decades, saying for example that "the question of Indians being considered legally married...has never been one upon which the department could rule at any time, although the department has been prepared at times to recognize the aboriginal marriages for certain purposes of administration only."[21]

By the early 1930s Indian agents were informed that everyone on the reserves from then on would have to comply with the provincial marriage acts, "the same as other people."[22] Immediate problems and confusions emerged in Saskatchewan, where every male candidate for marriage had to produce a health certificate. No marriage license could be taken out without such a certificate. A DIA doctor wrote for instructions: "As we have nothing to do with Provincial laws am I obliged to give health certificates to Treaty Indians?"[23] The reply was, "yes"; health certificates would have to be produced in accordance with the provisions of the marriage laws of the province. There were also questions concerning the cost of these medical exams, and of who would pay for them. Missionaries complained that they had difficulty persuading men who wished to be married to undergo the required exam when they had to pay for it. It was reported that men refused to pay the fee saying, "If the white men want the Indians to be married in the white man's way, they (the white men) should pay the fees, and not expect the Indians to do so."[24] As a result, wrote one missionary from Prince Albert, "There are now numbers of Indian couples living together without marriage."[25] On one reserve it was reported that there were nine young couples living together without marriage. Missionaries asked for discretionary power to perform marriages without the medical certificates.

A thorny question that also emerged in the light of the new policy was whether or not couples who had been married according to Aboriginal law, and now wished to be married in a Christian or civil ceremony, had to go through the process of acquiring a license, publishing banns, and providing medical certificates. The Prince Albert missionary gave as an example the case of a chief and his wife, married according to "Indian custom" for forty years, who then consented to be married as an example to younger couples. "In such cases the publishing of banns seems superfluous," the missionary wrote.[26]

The cost of obtaining a provincial marriage license, about five dollars, also deterred people from this route, as many did not have the money and travel was necessary to purchase the license in a town or municipal office. They were then required to stay where the license was issued for three complete days before the ceremony could be performed, and few could afford this. Agents and missionaries wondered if the license fee could be dispensed with where all the parties were treaty Indians.[27] However, the new line from the Ottawa office was that "an Indian cannot be considered legally married unless he is married according to the laws of the land," and while it was regretted that people could not afford to purchase marriage licenses, the department had no authority to waive the license fee for treaty people.[28]

In 1940 the department took the position, in contrast to the sixty-plus previous years, that references to "marriage" in the Indian Act meant marriage according to provincial regulations. A clear answer on the issue was extracted by Battleford Indian Agent J. P. B. Ostrander who asked for the exact interpretation of the section defining an Indian as "Any woman who is or was lawfully married to such a person."[29] The matter was referred to the department solicitor who refused to give a clear answer, stating that this particular point could only be determined by reference to the provincial Attorney General and court in the province in which an alleged marriage took place. Secretary T. R. L. MacInnes informed Ostrander, however, that the interpretation placed on this section of the Indian Act was that marriage must be in accordance with provincial regulations. This change in policy had enormous and immediate ramifications. Treaty and status women not "legally" married according to provincial laws, but living with (or married according to Aboriginal law or by "common law") non-treaty or white men were now entitled to their relief, medical, and other benefits. If married according to provincial laws, these women would not be so entitled. As one Indian agent complained, "It seems unreasonable to give privileges to those people who do not get legally married, and deprive those who obey the regulations and do what is right by getting legally married."[30] This agent noted that this was not the department's policy in the past—that hundreds of women lived with "other than Indians," that these marriages had in the past been regarded as valid, and that they would now be eligible for treaty benefits. In only very few cases were their children admitted to treaty, but they would now all be eligible as well. As he understood it, "If this were done it would throw a great responsibility on the Department and the financial part of it would be very heavy. Many of the children have married and have children of their own. These would apparently be entitled to be classified as Treaty Indians." Secretary MacInnes continued to insist throughout 1940, however, that being a "common law" wife of a non-Indian did not affect a woman's Indian status or membership in a band, and that "under the Indian Act, an Indian woman can lose her Indian status only by marriage or by enfranchisement, and is not affected by being what is known as the 'common law' wife of a non-Indian."[31]

One year later, however, a complete about-face had occurred, and it was back to the policy as established in 1887, and as continually emphasized through the widely distributed circular letter of 1906. Clearly a switch to only recognizing marriages according to provincial law could potentially have added and/or restored thousands of women and children to treaty status, and the policy had to be rethought. Aboriginal marriage had to be accepted as valid by the department. Department officials were also being informed that, as school principal A.E. Caldwell wrote in 1939, "the 'Indian marriage' rite is often undertaken deliberately in preference to legal marriage, it being recognized that this marriage is not legally binding, and that desertion may follow without the consequence of the deserter being held legally responsible for support."[32] He had tried to persuade a young couple, married according to Aboriginal law, to become "legally married," but had met with the opposition of an older relative of one of the parties who "advised them not to be legally married, as 'the only time an Indian has trouble is when he has a Certificate.'" Caldwell urged the department to declare that up to a certain date all persons married according to Aboriginal law, who were not previously married, be considered as legally married, and that after this specified date all those uniting in marriage must do so under the marriage act of whatever province they resided in. He also urged (as had many in the past) that a means of divorce be devised, that a solicitor be appointed by the department to hear cases of legal separation and make settlements where separations are granted, and to grant divorces when necessary. He wrote in brackets that it was "unnecessary to point out that Indians are prohibited from taking advantage of divorce legislation because of the expense." All of this, Caldwell thought, would create respect for social and domestic laws and for law in general and promote the stability of domestic life.

This policy was partially adopted. In August 1941 Secretary MacInnis advised a clerk at the agency office in Cardston, Alberta, that "according to my advice Indian marriages by tribal custom are valid and parties thereto should be recognized as lawfully married."[33] The old opinions from the Department of Justice and the 1887 order-in-council were once again dusted off and reviewed. Department Solicitor W. Cory now wondered whether R.V. Sinclair, in preparing his opinion, had been aware of "an old Order in Council No. 345 G dated the 31st day of August, 1887"? In view of this old order-in-council, Cory was "of the opinion that that policy as laid down therein should be adhered to as closely as possible."[34] Indian agents were instructed, however, that new marriages were to be according to provincial laws. While marriage according to Aboriginal law was to be recognized as valid with regard to "old Indians," "in future no recognition should be taken of Indian marriages unless the parties concerned are married by the proper authority, in accordance with Provincial Regulations."[35]

While no action was taken on divorce and separation, hearings were being held into marital disputes at the offices of Indian agents with the agent presiding, who drew up separation agreements. At the File Hills Reserve in 1938, the agent found that one couple could "not agree in their home life and have agreed to break up their home and live separately."[36] The wife was given the children and the home, and the husband agreed to pay to the agent the sum of fifty dollars per month to be administered by the agent for the keep and care of the wife and children. The wife agreed to have the money handled by the agent.

Confusion must have been rampant in reserve communities due to the conflicting and changing directions on marriage and divorce. The question of the validity of marriage according to Aboriginal law emerged during World War II because of the necessity of determining the eligibility of the widows of First Nations soldiers to veterans' benefits. The 1943 opinion of Deputy Justice Minister F. P. Varcoe was cautious and tentative, concluding that "conceivably some marriages performed according to Indian Tribal customs would, under these sections, be valid, assuming of course that the marriage in each particular case is a marriage according to our understanding of the term, namely a voluntary union for life of one man and one woman to the exclusion of all others."[37]

Testimony given at the 1946 and 1947 Special Joint Committee of the Senate and the House of Commons examining the Indian Act provides insight into the effects of the confusing and contradictory policies. There was concern about how "legal" marriages were being avoided, particularly in the case of treaty and status Indian women marrying non-treaty Indians, non-status Indians, or white men. As one witness explained, "If an Indian woman marries a white man, she forfeits entirely her Indian status and rights and so do her children. Yet, if an Indian woman becomes the common law wife of a white man, she is still recognized as an Indian. If the white man deserts her she can return to the reserve but her children are destitute. This provision should be revised, as at present 'it encourages living in sin and tends to lower the moral standard of the band.'"[38] If an Indian woman "legally" married a white man, and he deserted her or died, she could not legally return to her reserve with her children. The children of these relationships were not able to make sustained contacts with their extended family on reserves, as pointed out in presentations to the Joint Committee: "A child either legitimate or illegitimate of a Treaty Indian woman and a white man is precluded from absorption into the maternal grandparents home, even though socially such a placement is desirable and would thereby establish normal family contacts."[39] There were calls for changes to this situation to permit women and their children to be restored to full treaty rights, or to permit the bands to decide on membership.[40] "We think an Indian Band is like a big Family," submitted the Boyer River Band of Alberta, "and therefore the Chief and Councillors should decide whether anyone is or is not of Indian blood, belonging to the band."[41]

As part of the major Indian Act revisions of 1951 that emerged from the Special Committee, there was a reformulation of band membership lists. An "Indian Register" was introduced with the name of every person belonging to a band. The definition of an "Indian" was changed to mean "a person who pursuant to this Act is registered as an Indian or is entitled to be registered as an Indian."[42] In many ways the 1951 revisions continued and even enhanced discrimination against women, particularly those who "married out." The male line of descent was emphasized as the major criterion for inclusion on a band register. Until 1951 women who "married out" could still remain on the band list, receive annuities, and any other monies, if they had not opted to take commutation of their annuities. They were known in the 1930s and 1940s as "red ticket" women for the special treaty card issued to them. After 1951 all women marrying non-Indians were obliged to take the lump sum payment, and they were automatically enfranchised and deprived of Indian status and band rights from the date of marriage. From then on they were no longer entitled to life on their reserves and they had thirty days to sell any property they owned there. Through various provisions of the 1951 amendments, large numbers of children whose parents were both "Indian," but who were identified as "illegitimate," also lost their status. Marriages according to Aboriginal law were recognized for the purposes of membership up to 1951, but after that date, "legal" marriages only were to be recognized.

Notes

ONE *Creating, Challenging, Imposing, and Defending the Marriage "Fortress"*

1. See for example James Q. Wilson, *The Marriage Problem: How Our Culture Has Weakened Families* (New York: HarperCollins, 2002).

2. Nancy Cott, *Public Vows: A History of Marriage and Nation* (Cambridge: Harvard University Press, 2000). See also Stephanie Coontz, *Marriage, a History: From Obedience to Intimacy, or How Love Conquered Marriage* (New York: Viking, 2005).

3. Cott, *Public Vows*, 3.

4. Quoted in W. E. Raney, "Bigamy and Divorces," *The Canadian Law Journal* 34 (January–December 1898): 548.

5. Ibid.

6. The "Western Canada" of this study is the three prairie provinces with particular focus on the region of southern Alberta. While British Columbia will emerge from time to time, particularly in discussion of the administration of "Indian affairs," the situation there is somewhat distinct and many of the same issues discussed here have been dealt with in Adele Perry's excellent study *On the Edge of Empire: Gender, Race and the Making of British Columbia, 1849–1871* (Toronto: University of Toronto Press, 2001).

7. Adele Perry, "Metropolitan Knowledge, Colonial Practice, and Indigenous Womanhood: Missions in Nineteenth-Century British Columbia," in *Contact Zones: Aboriginal and Settler Women in Canada's Colonial Past*, ed. Katie Pickles and Myra Rutherdale (Vancouver: University of British Columbia Press, 2005), 115.

8. Quoted in Kathryn M. Daynes, *More Wives Than One: Transformation of the Mormon Marriage System, 1840–1910* (Urbana and Chicago: University of Illinois Press, 2001), 83.

9. Bettina Bradbury, "Colonial Comparisons: Rethinking Marriage, Civilization, and Nation in the Nineteenth-Century White Settler Societies," in *Rediscovering the British World*, ed. Philip Buckner and R. Douglas Francis (Calgary: University of Calgary Press, 2005), 150.

10. Ibid., 136.

11. Sarah Carter, "Britishness, 'Foreignness,' Women, and Land in Western Canada, 1890s to 1920s," in "Britishness and Whiteness: Locating Marginal White Identities in the Empire," special issue, *Humanities Research* 13, no. 1 (2006): 43–60.

12. Sylvia Van Kirk, "From 'Marrying-In' to 'Marrying-Out': Changing Patterns of Aboriginal/non-Aboriginal Marriage in Colonial Canada," in *Rethinking Canada: The Promise of Women's History*, 5th ed., ed. Mona Gleason and Adele Perry (Don Mills: Oxford University Press, 2006), 121. See also Sylvia Van Kirk, *"Many Tender Ties": Women and Fur Trade Society, 1670–1870* (Winnipeg: Watson and Dwyer Press, 1980); Adele Perry, *On the Edge of Empire: Gender, Race and the Making of British Columbia, 1849–1871* (Toronto: University of Toronto Press, 2001).

13. James G. Snell, "The 'White Life' For Two: The Defense of Marriage and Sexual Morality in Canada, 1890–1914," in *Canadian Family History: Selected Readings*, ed. Bettina Bradbury (Toronto: Copp Clark Pitman, 1992), 381–400.

14. Quoted in Terry L. Chapman, "Women, Sex, and Marriage in Western Canada, 1890–1920," *Alberta History* 33, no. 4 (Autumn 1985): 2.

15. Elizabeth Thompson, "Natives Need Bigger Role in Justice, Cotler Says," *National Post*, 22 November 2004.

16. *The Globe and Mail* (Toronto), "Don't Kiss Off Marriage," 18 June 2003.

TWO *Customs Not in Common*

1. John Mackie, *The Heart of the Prairie* (London: James Nisbet, 1899).

2. Ibid., 267–68.

3. Ibid., 271.

4. For an exploration of these themes in the history of the American West see William R. Handley, *Marriage, Violence, and the Nation in the American Literary West* (Cambridge: Cambridge University Press, 2002).

5. John D. Higginbotham, *When the West Was Young: Historical Reminiscences of the Early Canadian West* (Toronto: The Ryerson Press, 1933), 188.

6. Ibid., 194.

7. *Lethbridge News*, 18 December 1886.

8. Higginbotham, *When the West Was Young*, 89.

9. Ibid., 88.

10. *Lethbridge News*, 9 March 1887.

11. Constance Backhouse, *Petticoats and Prejudice: Women and Law in Nineteenth-Century Canada* (Toronto: The Osgoode Society, 1991), 176.

12. Ibid., 174.

13. For a description of a similar situation in the United States, see Candice Lewis Bredbenner, *A Nationality of Her Own: Women, Marriage, and the Law of Citizenship* (Berkeley: University of California Press, 1998); see also Linda K. Kerber, *No Constitutional Right to Be Ladies: Women and the Obligations of Citizenship* (New York: Hill and Wang, 1998).

14. Catherine Cavanaugh, "The Limitations of the Pioneering Partnership: The Alberta Campaign for Homestead Dower, 1909–1925," in *Making Western Canada: Essays on European Colonization and Settlement*, ed. Catherine Cavanaugh and Jeremy Mouat (Toronto: Garamond Press, 1996), 191; see also R. E. Hawkins, "Lillian Beynon Thomas, Woman's Suffrage, and the Return of Dower to Manitoba," *Manitoba Law Journal* 27, no. 1 (1999): 45–113.

15. Quoted in Terry L. Chapman, "Women, Sex, and Marriage in Western Canada, 1890–1920," *Alberta History* 33 (Autumn 1985): 2.

16. Ibid.

17. Henrietta Muir Edwards, *Legal Status of Women of Alberta* (Edmonton: Office of the Alberta Attorney-General, 1921), 24.

18. The jurisdiction of the Canadian Parliament in reference to divorce is declared in section 91, sub-section 26 of the British North America Act (BNA). At the time of Confederation in 1867, courts exercising jurisdiction in divorce already existed in Nova Scotia and New Brunswick, and these were permitted to continue under section 129 of the BNA. The courts of Prince Edward Island and British Columbia similarly exercised jurisdiction in divorce at the time of admission to Confederation, and they continued to do so afterward. Applications to Parliament for divorce were then confined to persons domiciled in Quebec, Ontario, Manitoba, Saskatchewan, Alberta, and the Yukon Territory. See Robert V. Sinclair, *The Rules and Practice Before the Parliament of Canada Upon Bills of Divorce* (Toronto: Carswell, 1915), 1–2.

19. Quoted in Henry Finlay, "Victorian Sexual Morality: A Case of Double Standards," *Australian Journal of Law and Society* 14 (1998–99): 49.

20. Alison Prentice et al., *Canadian Women: A History* (Toronto: Harcourt, Brace, Jovanovich, 1988), 147, 254–55.

21. *The Globe* (Toronto), 11 July 1889.

22. Anonymous, *How to Be Happy Though Married: Being a Handbook to Marriage by a Graduate in the University of Matrimony* (London: T. Fisher Unwin, 1896), 5. My copy is inscribed "To Miss Jennie Moffatt, in view of her marriage in the Far West."

23. B.G. Jefferis and J.L. Nichols, *The Household Guide or Domestic Cyclopedia* (Toronto: J.L. Nichols, 1897), 22.

24. "Married Happiness: Loves and Marriages of Eminent Persons," *The Globe* (Toronto), 12 April 1890.

25. *Canadian Churchman* 72 (September 1883): 599. My own grandmother, Nell (Weaver) Carter, when married in 1915 in a Church of England ceremony at Greenhithe, Kent, promised to "nobey" her husband.

26. *Canadian Churchman* (4 May 1893): 276.

27. Anonymous, *Marriage and Home, or Proposal and Espousal: A Christian Treatise on the Most Sacred Relations to Mortals Known: Love, Marriage, Home etc.* (Brantford, ON, Port Adelaide and Melbourne, Australia: Bradley, Garretson, 1888).

28. Rev. Ross C. Houghton, *Women of the Orient: An Account of the Religious, Intellectual and Social Condition of Women in Japan, China, Indian, Egypt, Syria and Turkey* (Cincinnati: Hitchcock and Walden, 1877).

29. *The Presbyterian Record* (May 1910): 231.

30. W.H. Withrow, "Every-day Life in Bible Lands: Marriage and Funeral Customs," *The Methodist Magazine and Review* 43 (January–June 1896): 3.

31. Anonymous, *The Ladies Book of Useful Information: Compiled From Many Sources* (London, Ont.: s.n., 1896): 116.

32. John David Pulsipher, "The Americanization of Monogamy: Mormons, Native Americans, and the Nineteenth-Century Perception that Polygamy was a Threat to Democracy" (PhD diss., University of Minnesota, 1999), 122.

33. Ibid.

34. Sarah Carter, *Lost Harvests: Prairie Indian Reserve Farmers and Government Policy* (Montreal: McGill-Queen's Press, 1990), 212–13.

35. Nancy Cott, *Public Vows: A History of Marriage and the Nation* (Cambridge: Harvard University Press, 2000), 1.

36. Ibid., 3.

37. *Debate in the Senate on the Bill Relating to Marriage with Deceased Wife's Sister* (Ottawa: A. and Geo. C. Holland, Senate Reporters, 1879), 5.

38. Ibid., 4–5.

39. *Canadian Churchman* (14 September 1893): 547.

40. Ibid. (13 October 1892): 612.

41. *The Far West* (1902): 155.

42. James G. Snell, "The 'White Life for Two': The Defence of Marriage and Sexual Morality in Canada, 1890–1914," in *Canadian Family History: Selected Readings*, ed. Bettina Bradbury (Toronto: Copp Clark Pitman, 1992), 381.

43. Annalee Gölz, "Family Matters: The Canadian Family and the State in the Postwar Period," *Left History* 1, no. 2 (Fall 1993): 9.

44. Ann Laura Stoler, "Cultivating Bourgeois Bodies and Racial Selves," in *Cultures of Empire: Colonizers in Britain and the Empire in the Nineteenth and Twentieth Centuries*, ed. Catherine Hall (New York: Routledge, 2000), 87–88.

45. Sarah Carter, *Capturing Women: The Manipulation of Cultural Imagery in Canada's Prairie West* (Montreal: McGill-Queen's University Press, 1997), 166–83.

46. Sylvia Van Kirk, *"Many Tender Ties": Women in Fur-Trade Society, 1670–1870* (Winnipeg: Watson and Dwyer, 1980); Jennifer S. H. Brown, *Strangers in Blood: Fur Trade Company Families in Indian Country* (Vancouver: UBC Press, 1980).

47. Jennifer S. H. Brown, "Partial Truths: A Closer Look at Fur Trade Marriage," in *From Rupert's Land to Canada*, ed. Theodore Binnema et al. (Edmonton: The University of Alberta Press, 2002), 61.

48. Van Kirk, *"Many Tender Ties"* 38.

49. Ibid., 115.

50. Ibid., 116.

51. Quoted in Ibid., 115.

52. Ibid., 119.

53. Quoted in Ibid., 119.

54. Donna McDonald, *Lord Strathcona: A Biography of Donald Alexander Smith* (Toronto: Dundurn Press, 1996), 101.

55. Ibid.

56. Ibid., 448.

57. Ibid., 402.

58. Ibid., 119.

59. Irene Spry, ed., "The 'Memories' of George William Sanderson, 1846–1936," *Canadian Ethnic Studies* 17, no. 2 (1985): 124.

60. Lyndel Meikle, ed., *Very Close to Trouble: The Johnny Grant Memoir* (Pullman: Washington State University Press, 1996), vii.

61. Ibid., 79–80.

62. Quoted in Ibid., 80.

63. Quoted in W. L. Morton, *Manitoba: A History*, 2nd ed. (Toronto: University of Toronto Press, 1967), 91.

64. Adele Perry, *On the Edge of Empire: Gender, Race, and the Making of British Columbia* (Toronto: University of Toronto Press, 2001).

65. Lyle Dick, "Male Homosexuality in Saskatchewan's Settlement Era: The 1895 Case of Regina's 'Oscar Wilde'" (paper presented to the eighty-fifth meeting of the Canadian Historical Association, York University, 30 May 2006), 14.

66. Cecilia Danysk, "'A Bachelor's Paradise': Homesteaders, Hired Hands, and the Construction of Masculinity, 1880–1930," in *Making Western Canada: Essays on European Colonization and Settlement*, ed. Catherine Cavanaugh and Jeremy Mouat (Toronto: Garamond Press, 1996), 154–85.

67. Carter, *Capturing Women*, 166–81.

68. Ibid., 166–67.

69. *Lethbridge News*, 9 October 1895.

70. Ibid., 10 May 1900.

71. *The Gazette* (Fort Macleod), 13 January 1883; 24 January 1883; 5 March 1884; 14 March 1884; 19 September 1884; 3 October 1884; 20 October 1884.

72. Grant MacEwan, *Mighty Women: Stories of Western Canadian Pioneers* (1975; repr., Vancouver: Douglas and McIntyre, 1995), 119–26.

73. *The Imperial Colonist* 8, no. 98 (February 1910): 22–24; *The Imperial Colonist* 8, no. 99 (March, 1910): 39–42; *The Imperial Colonist* 8, no. 100 (1910): 52–57.

74. Lucy Bland, *Banishing the Beast: Feminism, Sex and Morality*, (1995; repr., London and New York: Tauris Parke Paperbacks, 2002), 151, 171.

75. *Canadian Churchman* (17 November 1892): 700.

76. *The Gazette*, 14 March 1889.

77. *Lethbridge News*, 10 February 1891.

78. Cavanaugh, "The Limitations of the Pioneering Partnership," 211.

79. *Moose Jaw Times*, 3 July 1908.

80. *Saskatchewan Herald* (Battleford), 15 January 1887.

81. Edwin Allen to Wm. Allen, 14 October 1890, Records of the Customs Department, v. 432, Coutts Letterbooks, Department of National Revenue (RG 16), Library and Archives Canada (LAC).

82. Mrs. L. McInnis to the Minister of Justice, 15 March 1917, file 465–485 (1917), vol. 210, series A-2, Department of Justice (RG 13), LAC.

83. Deputy Minister of Justice to Mr. L. McInnis, 21 March 1917, file 465–485 (1917), vol. 210, series A-2, RG 13, LAC.

84. Kathryn M. Daynes, *More Wives Than One: Transformation of the Mormon Marriage System, 1840–1910* (Urbana and Chicago: University of Illinois Press, 2001), 73.

85. Ibid., 203–04.

86. Sarah Barringer Gordon, "'The Liberty of Self-Degradation': Polygamy, Woman Suffrage, and Consent in Nineteenth-Century America," *Journal of American History* 83, no. 3 (December 1996): 842.

87. Ibid., 835.

88. Jeffrey Nichols, *Prostitution, Polygamy, and Power: Salt Lake City, 1847–1918* (Urbana and Chicago: University of Illinois Press, 2002), 20.

89. Richard White, *"It's Your Misfortune and None of My Own:" A New History of the American West* (Norman: University of Oklahoma Press, 1991), 174.

90. Daynes, *More Wives Than One*, 209.

91. *Manitoba Free Press*, 7 September 1881.

92. Dan Erickson, "Alberta Polygamists? The Canadian Climate and Response to the Introduction of Mormonism's 'Peculiar Institution,'" *Pacific Northwest Quarterly* 86, no. 4 (Fall 1995): 174.

93. Quoted in John R. Hicken, "Events Leading to the Settlement of the Communities of Cardston, Magrath, Stirling and Raymond, Alberta" (master's thesis, Utah State University, 1968), 31–32.

94. Canada, *House of Commons Debates* (10 April 1890) at 3180.

95. Ibid., p. 3177.

96. *Saskatchewan Herald*, 30 April 1890.

97. Canada, *House of Commons Debates* (3 April 1889) at 980.

98. Ibid. (10 April 1890), p. 3178.

99. James S. Woodsworth, *Strangers Within Our Gates: Coming Canadians* (Toronto: F.C. Stephenson, Methodist Mission Rooms, 1909), facing p. 78.

100. Ibid., 80–81.

101. Ibid., 86.

102. Robert J. McCue, "Anthony Maitland Stenhouse, Bachelor 'Polygamist,'" *American History and Life* 23, no. 1 (1990): 108–25.

103. Quoted in Ibid., 118.

104. Quoted in Ibid., 119.

105. *The Gazette*, 10 January 1889.

106. *Edmonton Bulletin*, 21 December 1889.

107. Ibid.

108. Nichols, *Prostitution, Polygamy and Power*, 17–18.

109. Quoted in Donald G. Godfrey, "Zina Presendia Young Williams Card: Brigham's Daughter, Cardston's First Lady," *Journal of Mormon History* 23, no. 2 (1997): 110–11.

110. Quoted in Ibid., 115.

111. Ibid., 125.

112. Ibid., 116. In 1898 Zina Card joined her sister Susan Gates on a speaking tour through the eastern United States.

113. S.B. Steele, *Forty Years in Canada: Reminiscences of the Great North-West* (Winnipeg: Russell Lang; London: Herbert Jenkins, 1915), 269.

114. *The Calgary Tribune*, 8 August 1888.

115. Higginbotham, *When the West Was Young*, 129–30.

116. Nichols, *Prostitution, Polygamy and Power*, 16–17.

117. Annie Clark Tanner, *A Mormon Mother* (Utah: University of Utah Library Tanner Trust Fund, 1983), 151.

118. Nichols, *Prostitution, Polygamy and Power*, 19.

119. Quoted in Ibid., 21.

120. Ibid., 17.

121. *The Leader* (Regina), "Notes By the Way," 9 September 1890.

122. Ibid., "The Mormons," letter to the editor.

123. Koozma J. Tarasoff, *Traditional Doukhobor Folkways: An Ethnographic and Biographic Record of Prescribed Behaviour*, Paper No. 20 (Ottawa: National Museum of Canada, Canadian Centre for Folk Culture Studies, 1977), 1.

124. George Woodcock and Ivan Avakumovic, *The Doukhobors*, Carleton Library no. 108 (Ottawa: McClelland and Stewart, 1977), 170.

125. Aylmer Maude, *A Peculiar People: The Doukhobors* (London: Grant Richards, 1904), 17.

126. Ibid., 201.

127. Frank Yeigh, *Through the Heart of Canada* (Toronto: Henry Frowde, 1910), 184.

128. *Saskatchewan Herald*, 3 February 1899.

129. Jean Blewett, "The Doukhobor Woman," in *Canada's West and Farther West*, ed. Frank Carrel (Quebec: The Telegraph Printing Co., 1911), 223–24. Previously published in *Collier's Weekly* 9 (n.d.).

130. Mrs. Thomas Lavington, "Reminiscences of Life on the Prairies, 1910–1914," 1954, p. 4, manuscript, LAC.

131. *Saskatchewan Herald*, 3 February 1899.

132. Maude, *A Peculiar People*, 318.

133. Emily Murphy, *Janey Canuck in the West* (1910; repr., Toronto: McClelland and Stewart, 1910), 45–46.

134. Blewett, "The Doukhobor Woman," 223.

135. Ibid.

136. Frances Swyripa, *Wedded to the Cause: Ukrainian-Canadian Women and Ethnic Identity, 1891–1991* (Toronto: University of Toronto Press, 1993), 35.

137. Ibid.

138. Quoted in Swyripa, 78.

139. Ibid., 35.

140. Ibid., 87.

141. Canada, *Report of the Royal Commission on Chinese Immigration: Report and Evidence* (Ottawa: Printed by Order of the Commission, 1885), 45.

142. *The Leader*, 26 February 1930.

143. *Lethbridge Daily Herald*, 8 April 1911 and 14 September 1911.

144. *Edmonton Bulletin*, 1 November 1884.

145. Admission of Wat or Kok Shee or Meo Wong Way, file 2419-2.43, vol. 263, RG 13, LAC.

146. Robert A. J. McDonald, *Making Vancouver: Class, Status and Social Boundaries, 1863–1913* (Vancouver: University of British Columbia Press, 1996), 215.

147. Anonymous, "A Quaker District," *Saskatchewan History* 16, no. 1 (Winter 1963): 36.

148. Quoted in Ibid.

149. *The Daily Free Press* (Winnipeg), 11 May 1877.

150. Baha Abu-Laban, *An Olive Branch on the Family Tree: The Arabs in Canada* (Toronto: McClelland and Stewart, 1980), 61.

151. Ibid., 28–29.

152. Julia Clancy-Smith, "Islam, Gender, and Identities in the Making of French Algeria, 1830–1962," in *Domesticating the Empire: Race, Gender and Family Life in French and Dutch Colonialism*, ed. Julia Clancy-Smith and Frances Gouda (Charlottesville and London: University Press of Virginia, 1998), 167.

153. Alex MacDonald, *Practical Utopians: The Lives and Writings of Saskatchewan Cooperative Pioneers Ed and Will Paynter* (Regina: Canadian Plains Research Center, 2004), 27.

154. Anthony Rasporich, "Utopia, Sect, and Millennium in Western Canada, 1870–1940," *Prairie Forum* 12, no. 2 (Fall 1987): 227.

155. *Canadian Churchman* (15 January 1891), 36.

156. Quoted in W. E. Raney, "Bigamy and Divorces," *The Canada Law Journal* 34 (January–December 1898): 548.

157. George H. Napheys, *The Physical Life of Woman: Advice to the Maiden, Wife and Mother* (Toronto: Maclear and Co., 1871), 55.

158. *The Globe*, 11 July 1889.

159. *Canadian Churchman* (13 October 1892), 612.

160. *The Regina Leader*, 20 May 1890.

161. Paula Petrik, "If She Be Content: The Development of Montana Divorce Law, 1865–1907," *The Western Historical Quarterly* 18, no. 3 (July 1987): 264.

162. Ibid.

163. Ibid., 263.

164. Ibid., 285.

165. Ibid., 283, 285.

166. Kathleen Wilson, "Empire, Gender and Modernity in the Eighteenth Century," in *Gender and Empire* ed. Phillipa Levine (Oxford: Oxford University Press, 2004), 25.

THREE   *Making Newcomers to Western Canada Monogamous*

1. Ann Laura Stoler, "Cultivating Bourgeois Bodies and Racial Selves," in *Cultures of Empire: Colonizers in Britain and the Empire in the Nineteenth and Twentieth Centuries*, ed. Catherine Hall (New York: Routledge, 2000), 90.

2. Joan Perkin, *Women and Marriage in Nineteenth-Century England* (London: Routledge, 1989), 1.

3. Henry H. Foster, "Indian and Common Law Marriages," *American Indian Law Review* 3 (1975): 85–87.

4. Nancy Cott, *Public Vows: A History of Marriage and Nation* (Cambridge: Harvard University Press, 2000), 32.

5. Ibid.

6. E. P. Thompson, *Customs in Common: Studies in Traditional Popular Culture* (New York: The New Press, 1993), 404–66.

7. Ibid., 404.

8. Ibid., 406.

9. Ibid., 443.

10. Quoted in Ibid., 462.

11. Quoted in Henry Finlay, "Victorian Sexual Morality: A Case of Double Standards," *Australian Journal of Law and Society* 14 (1988–99): 59.

12. Quoted in Foster, "Indian and Common Law Marriages," 87.

13. *An Ordinance Respecting Marriage*, North-West Territories, No. 9 of 1878, Canadian Inventory of Historic Microreproductions, no. 52120.

14. Cott, *Public Vows*, 6.

15. Officer in command of Fort Walsh to Lieutenant Governor, North-West Territories, 5 August 1880, vol. 2235, series B-3, Royal Canadian Mounted Police (RG 18), Library and Archives Canada (LAC).

16. Sarah Carter, *Capturing Women: The Manipulation of Cultural Imagery in Canada's Prairie West* (Montreal: McGill-Queen's University Press, 1997), 158–93.

17. Letter, Thomas Mitchell to Lieutenant Governor E. Dewdney, 1 October 1886, file 36528, vol. 3774, Department of Indian Affairs (RG 10), LAC.

18. Sarah Carter, "Categories and Terrains of Exclusion: Constructing the 'Indian Woman' in the Early Settlement Era in Western Canada," *Great Plains Quarterly* 13, no. 3 (Summer 1993): 154.

19. Colin D. Howell, "Arthur Alexander Reid," *Dictionary of Canadian Biography*, Vol. 14 (1911–1920), (Toronto: University of Toronto Press, 1998), 864.

20. A. P. Reid, "The Mixed or 'Halfbreed' Races of North-Western Canada," *Journal of the Anthropological Institute of Great Britain and Ireland* 4 (1875): 45–52. Thanks to Donald B. Smith, Department of History, University of Calgary, for references to the work of Alexander Reid.

21. Ibid., 46.

22. Ibid., 47.

23. Ibid., 46.

24. George H. Napheys, *The Physical Life of Woman: Advice to the Maiden, Wife and Mother* (Toronto: Maclear & Company, 1871), 53.

25. *Fort Macleod Gazette*, 8 February 1887.

26. See contents of file 1590, vol. 3600, RG 10, LAC.

27. Hayter Reed to deputy superintendent general of Indian Affairs, 6 July 1889, file 792-1889, vol. 74, Department of Justice (RG 13), LAC.

28. Hayter Reed to E. L. Newcombe, 9 March 1894, file 32345, vol. 3762, RG 10, LAC.

29. Petition to Hon. Theodore Davie, ca. 1895, file 32345, vol. 3762, RG 10, LAC.

30. Hayter Reed to T. Mayne Daly, superintendent general of Indian Affairs, 8 March 1896, file 32345, vol. 3762, RG 10, LAC.

31. "List of Employees," file 31061, vol. 3755, RG 10, LAC.

32. John Hawkes, *The Story of Saskatchewan and Its People* (Regina: S. J. Clarke Publishing Co., 1924), 2:80.

33. Noted in letter, Mitchell to Dewdney, 1 October 1886, file 36528, vol. 8774, RG 10, LAC.

34. *Edmonton Bulletin*, 5 January 1889.

35. *Regina Leader*, 18 December 1888.

36. Ibid., 1 January 1889.

37. Ibid.

38. *Regina Leader*, 25 December 1888.

39. Ibid., 4 December 1888.

40. Ibid., 29 January 1889.

41. Peter Boag, "Thinking Like Mount Rushmore: Sexuality and Gender in the Republican Landscape," in *Seeing Nature Through Gender*, ed. Virginia J. Scharff (Kansas City: University of Kansas Press, 2003), 44.

42. Ibid., 46.

43. Cecilia Danysk, "'A Bachelor's Paradise': Homesteaders, Hired Hands, and the Construction of Masculinity, 1880–1930," in *Making Western Canada: Essays On European Colonization and Settlement*, ed. Catherine Cavanaugh and Jeremy Mouat (Toronto: Garamond Press, 1996), 157.

44. Ronald Rees, *New and Naked Land: Making the Prairies Home* (Saskatoon: Western Producer Prairie Books, 1988), 68–85.

45. John McLaren, "The Failed Experiments: The Demise of Doukhobor Systems of Communal Property Landholding in Saskatchewan and British Columbia, 1899–1925," in *Despotic Dominion: Property Rights in British Settler Colonies*, ed. John McLaren et al. (Vancouver: University of British Columbia Press, 2005), 222–47.

46. Yosse Katz and John C. Lehr, *The Last Best West: Essays on the Historical Geography of the Canadian Prairies* (Jerusalem: The Magnes Press, The Hebrew University, 1999), 132.

47. File 105/1895, vol. 2377, E. Newcombe to L. Pereria, 31 May 1895, RG 13, LAC.

48. File 1895—242, vol. 2277, deputy minister of justice to the secretary, Department of the Interior, 5 March 1895, Department of the Interior (RG 15), LAC.

49. Memorandum, Dominion land ruling, no. 4369, 10 February 1921, RG 15, LAC.

50. C. Herrman to W.D. Scott, n.d., (1919), file 80212 pt. 6, vol. 198, Department of Immigration (RG 76), LAC.

51. Ibid., W.D. Scott to C. Herrman, 6 March 1919.

52. File 1895–432, vol. 97, RG 13, LAC.

53. Ibid., E.J. Newcombe to secretary, Department of the Interior, 3 May 1895.

54. *Edmonton Bulletin*, 1 August 1895.

55. C.H. Stout, *From Frontier Days in Leduc and District: Sixty-Five Years of Progress, 1891–1956* (Leduc: Representative Publishers, 1956), 121.

56. Canada, *House of Commons Debates* (15 March 1907) at 4813–4.

57. Dominion land ruling, no. 4171, vol. 1971, Department of the Interior circular letter, 21 July 1920, RG 15, LAC.

58. Mrs. Thomas McNeil to W. Roche, 6 March 1913, vol. 1105, file 2816596, pt. 1, RG 15, LAC.

59. H. Elaine Lindgren, *Land in Her Own Name: Women as Homesteaders in North Dakota* (Norman and London: University of Oklahoma Press, 1996).

60. James Muhn, "Women and the Homestead Act: Land Department Administration of a Legal Imbroglio, 1863–1934," *Western Legal History* 7, no. 2 (Summer/Fall 1994): 286.

61. Memorandum, 8 November 1894, file interim 25: 74/ 1896, vol. 2247, RG 13, LAC.

62. Canada, *House of Commons Debates* (30 April 1910) at 8490.

63. Georgina Binnie-Clark, *Wheat and Woman* (1914; repr., Toronto: University of Toronto Press, 1979), 308.

64. Mabel Durham, *Canada's Welcome to Women* (London: Canadian Pacific Railway, n.d.), 5.

65. Quoted in Joyce Litz, *The Montana Frontier: One Woman's West* (Albuquerque: University of New Mexico Press, 2004), 61.

66. Grant MacEwan, *Mighty Women: Stories of Western Canadian Pioneers* (1975; repr., Vancouver: Douglas and McIntyre, 1995), 119–26.

67. Eva Delday, *Brooks Beautiful–Bountiful* (Calgary: D.W. Friesen and Sons, 1975), 197.

68. *The Regina Leader*, 31 July 1888.

69. See Marilyn Barber, *Immigrant Domestic Servants in Canada* (Ottawa: Canadian Historical Association, 1991).

70. Katie Pickles, "Empire Settlement and Single British Women as New Zealand Domestic Servants During the 1920s," *New Zealand Journal of History* 35, no. 1 (2001): 23.

71. Anna Davin, "Imperialism and Motherhood," in *Tensions of Empire: Colonial Cultures in a Bourgeois World*, ed. Frederick Cooper and Ann Laura Stoler (Berkeley and Los Angeles: University of California Press, 1997), 87–151.

72. Quoted in Danysk, "A Bachelor's Paradise," 155.

73. *The Regina Leader*, 31 July 1888.

74. Rural Municipality of Rosser Centennial History Book Committee, *The First Hundred Years, 1893–1993: Rural Municipality of Rosser* (Winnipeg: Herff Jones Canada Inc., 1993), 3.

75. *Edmonton Bulletin*, 26 January 1884.

76. *Manitoba Daily Free Press*, 30 August 1887. See also Carter, *Capturing Women*, 3–4.

77. *The Regina Leader*, 30 August 1887 and 13 September 1887.

78. Ibid., 13 September 1887.

79. Lyle Dick, "Male Homosexuality in Saskatchewan's Settlement Era: The 1895 Case of Regina's 'Oscar Wilde'" (paper presented to the eighty-fifth meeting of the Canadian Historical Association, York University, 30 May 2006), 6; *Square Butte Tribune*, (Montana), 13 May, 1921.

80. Ditlew M. Frederiksen, *The Land Laws of Canada and the Land Experience of the United States* (s.l: s.n, 1907), Peel Collection, microform, no. 1932: 10, 18.

81. Ibid., 11.

82. *Moose Jaw Times*, 25 August 1908.

83. Ibid., 21 August 1908.

84. Dick, " Male Homosexuality," 14.

85. Geo. H. Napheys, *The Physical Life of Woman: Advice to Maiden, Wife and Mother* (Toronto: Maclear and Company, 1871), 56.

86. C.C. Furley, "The Physiology of Mormonism," *Canada Lancet* 1, no. 5 (July 1863): 35.

87. A.M. Burgess to Charles O. Card, 24 January 1890, Order in Council no. 1890–0828, Privy Council Office Series A–1–a, vol. 558, RG 10, LAC.

88. Charles O. Card to A.M. Burgess, 28 February 1890, Order in Council no. 1890–0828, Privy Council Office Series A–1–a, vol. 558, RG 10, LAC.

89. Quoted in Brian Champion, "Mormon Polygamy: Parliamentary Concerns, 1889–90," *Alberta History* 35, no. 1 (Spring 1987): 11.

90. Quoted in Robert J. McCue, "Anthony Maitland Stenhouse, Bachelor 'Polygamist,'" *American History and Life* 23, no. 1 (1990): 120.

91. Ibid.

92. *Debates of the Senate of the Dominion of Canada, 1890* (26 February 1890) at 142.

93. McCue., "Anthony Maitland Stenhouse," 121.

94. Dan Erickson, "Alberta Polygamists? The Canadian Climate and Response to the Introduction of Mormonism's 'Peculiar Institution,'" *Pacific Northwest Quarterly* 86, no. 4 (Fall 1995): 162.

95. Quoted in Champion, "Mormon Polygamy?" 16.

96. Kathryn M. Daynes, *More Wives Than One: Transformation of the Mormon Marriage System, 1840–1910* (Urbana and Chicago: University of Illinois Press, 2001), 83.

97. Quoted in Allen Connery, ed., *As Reported in the Herald* (Calgary: Calgary Herald, 1982), 35. Original story in *Calgary Herald*, 18 April 1888.

98. Letter, S. B. Steele to the Commissioner, NWMP (North-West Mounted Police), 4 December 1889, file 250-90, vol. 41, Royal Canadian Mounted Police (RG 18), LAC. Steele reported, "[T]he Mormons are believed by almost all of the people in the district to be practising polygamy in secret, there are many reasons for believing such to be the case, the number of women of the same age, or nearly so, in several of the houses, the fact that several of them have pretended to be married to certain parties who were away and although the men have been absent for more than a year, children being born in the interval, as many as fourteen months after the departure of the so-called husband... Constables and others have reported that they have seen members of the Mormon Church using the same room and bed as the women whose supposed husbands were away from the district."

99. *Missions de la Congrégation des missionaries Oblats de Marie Immaculée* (Paris: Typographie A. Hennuyer, 1897), 402. Thanks to Melanie Méthot for her translation.

100. William M. Baker, ed., *Pioneer Policing in Southern Alberta: Deane of the Mounties, 1888–1914* (Calgary: Historical Society of Alberta, 1993), 118.

101. Ibid., 120.

102. Quoted in Erickson, "Alberta Polygamists?" 162.

103. Annie Clark Tanner, *A Mormon Mother* (Utah: University of Utah Library Tanner Trust Fund, 1983), 221.

104. Erickson, "Alberta Polygamists?" 162.

105. *Picturesque Cardston and Environments: A Story of Colonization and Progress in Southern Alberta* (Cardston: N.W. Macleod, 1900).

106. "Interesting Facts About Alberta Mormons: G.C. Porter Writes in the *Toronto World* his Ideas on the Mormon Settlement in the Southern Portion of Alberta," *The Daily Herald* (Calgary), 7 June 1904.

107. Henrietta Muir Edwards, *Legal Status of Women of Alberta* (Edmonton: University of Alberta Extension, 1917), 13.

108. *Ordinances of the North-West Territories, Passed in the Third Session of the Fourth Legislative Assembly* (Regina: John A. Reid, Government Printer, 1901), 2–6.

109. Ibid., 40.

110. *Regina Leader Post*, 6 June 1901.

111. Ibid.

112. *Manitoba Morning Free Press* (Winnipeg), 10 June 1901.

113. George Woodcock and Ivan Avakumovic, *The Doukhobors*, Carleton Library no. 108 (Ottawa: McClelland and Stewart, 1977), 210.

114. *The Evening Capital* (Saskatoon), 6 May 1911.

115. Ibid., 10 May 1911.

116. Frances Swyripa, *Wedded to the Cause: Ukrainian-Canadian Women and Ethnic Identity, 1891–1991* (Toronto: University of Toronto Press, 1993), 35.

117. Ibid., 78–79.

118. *Edmonton Bulletin*, 24 April 1899.

119. Cynthia R. Comacchio, *The Infinite Bonds of Family: Domesticity in Canada, 1850–1940* (Toronto: University of Toronto Press, 1999), 61.

120. John E. Crankshaw and Alexandre Chevalier, *Crankshaw's Criminal Code of Canada*, 5th ed. (Toronto: The Carswell Co., 1924), 370.

121. Ibid., 377.

122. *Fort Macleod Gazette*, 1 May 1890.

123. Ibid.

124. Ibid.

125. *Debates of the Senate of the Dominion of Canada* (16 April 1890) at 414.

126. Ibid., 2:412.

127. Ibid., 2:404.

128. *Debates of the House of Commons of the Dominion of Canada* (21 April 1890) at 3695.

129. Ibid., 30: 3698.

130. *The Globe* (Toronto), 22 April 1890.

131. Secretary, Department of Justice, to Florence Fraser, 6 June 1912, file 1912–1914, vol. 173, series A-2, RG 13, LAC.

132. Hazel Cooke to the Minister of Justice, 24 January 1921, file 211–231, 1921, vol. 255, RG 13, LAC.

133. E.L. Newcombe to Hazel Cooke, 1 February 1921, file 211–231, 1921, vol. 255, RG 13, LAC.

134. Florence Fraser to C.F. Doherty, 3 June 1912, file 1912–1914, vol. 173, series A-2, RG 13, LAC.

135. See file 1912–1914, vol. 173, series A-2, RG 13, LAC.

136. Deputy minister of justice to J.A. Therien, 21 March 1917, file 465–485, 1917, vol. 210, RG 13, LAC.

137. See Homestead Files, no. 72379, SW 14-6-30-W2, Saskatchewan Archives Board (SAB).

138. C.E.D. Wood to the undersecretary of state for Canada, 15 January 1921, Homestead Files, no. 72379, SW 14-6-30-W2, SAB.

139. Crankshaw and Chevalier, *Crankshaw's Criminal Code*, 379.

140. Ibid.

141. H.M. Ingram to attorney general, Ottawa, 22 May 1916, file 1916–866, vol. 202, RG 13, LAC.

142. *The Regina Leader*, 1 November 1889.

143. B. Switzer to Attorney General Department, 20 May 1916, file 1916—876, vol. 202, RG 13, LAC.

144. R.E. Hawkins, "Lillian Beynon Thomas, Woman's Suffrage, and the Return of Dower to Manitoba," *Manitoba Law Journal* 27, no. 1 (1999): 67.

FOUR *"A Striking Contrast… Where Perpetuity of Union and Exclusiveness is Not a Rule, at Least Not a Strict Rule"*

1. Quoted in Constance Backhouse, *Petticoats and Prejudice: Women and Law in Nineteenth-Century Canada* (Toronto: The Osgoode Society, 1991), 24.

2. Following Sidney L. Harring's example I will not use the term "customary" when speaking of Aboriginal marriage law. He writes that "to call Indian law 'customary law' sets up a false dichotomy between Indian and English or European law—which is itself rooted in custom." Brad Morse has also commented on the failure of the Canadian judiciary to define family law, and specifically the marriage laws of Aboriginal Canada, as "law." "At best, the courts have referred to 'Indian marriages' or 'custom marriages'…This approach, which is reflected by the wording chosen, is to regard native marriages as being conducted pursuant to customs, traditions, or practices, rather than according to law. This then presents customary marriages as being somehow less important and less durable than Christian marriages that meet modern legal requirements developed in England." See Sidney L. Harring, "Indian Law, Sovereignty and State Law," in *A Companion to American Indian History*, ed. Philip J. Deloria and Neal Salisbury (Malden and Oxford: Blackwell Publishers Inc., 2002), 444. See also Bradford W. Morse, "Indian and Inuit Family Law and the Canadian Legal System," *American Indian Law Review* 8 (1980): 219.

3. See Sarah Carter, "Change and Continuity: The World of the Plains," chap. 5 in *Aboriginal People and Colonizers of Western Canada to 1900* (Toronto: University of Toronto Press, 1999), 83–100.

4. James [Sákéj] Henderson, "First Nations' Legal Inheritances in Canada: The Mikmaq Model," *Manitoba Law Journal* 23 (1996): 1.

5. Raymond J. DeMallie, "Kinship: The Foundation for Native American Society," in *Studying Native America: Problems and Prospects*, ed. Russell Thornton (Madison: The University of Wisconsin Press, 1998), 323.

6. Ibid.

7. Ibid., 342.

8. The term Blackfoot refers to the Siksika (Blackfoot), Kainai (Blood) and Piikani (Peigan) people of southern Alberta.

9. George Bird Grinnell, *Blackfoot Lodge Tales: The Story of a Prairie People* (Lincoln and London: University of Nebraska Press, 1962), 125–31.

10. Many versions of this story have been recorded. See Clark Wissler and D. C. Duvall, *Mythology of the Blackfoot Indians* (Lincoln and London: University of Nebraska Press, 1995), 21–22. See also C. C. Uhlenbeck, *A New Series of Blackfoot Texts From the Southern Peigan Blackfoot Reservation, Teton County, Montana* (Amsterdam: Johannes Muller, 1912), 167.

11. Wissler and Duvall, *Mythology of the Blackfoot Indians*, 22.

12. R. N. Wilson fonds, edited and annotated by Philip Godsell, 2: 116, Glenbow Archives (GA).

13. Kenneth E. Kidd, "Blackfoot Ethnography: Being a Synthesis of the Data of Ethnological Science with the Information Concerning the Blackfoot Indians Contained in the Writing of Explorers, Travellers and Traders From the Time of First Contact to the Year 1821" (master's thesis, University of Toronto, 1937), 46.

14. Cited in Ibid., 44.

15. John Ewers, *The Blackfeet: Raiders on the Northwestern Plains* (Norman: University of Oklahoma Press, 1958), 99.

16. Adolf Hungry Wolf, *Pikunni Biographies*, The Blackfoot Papers, vol. 4 (Skookumchuck: The Good Medicine Cultural Foundation, 2006), 943.

17. Ibid.

18. Robert H. Lowie, "Marriage and Family Life Among the Plains Indians," *Scientific Monthly* 34 (1932): 463.

19. Wilson fonds, 2: 117, GA.

20. Walter McClintock, *The Old North Trail: Life, Legends and Religion of the Blackfeet Indians* (1910; repr., Lincoln and London: University of Nebraska Press, 1992), 186.

21. Esther S. Goldfrank, *Changing Configurations in the Social Organization of a Blackfoot Tribe During the Reserve Period*, Monographs of the American Ethnological Society, ed. A. Irving Hallowell (Seattle and London: University of Washington Press, 1944), 16.

22. Ibid., 341.

23. Ibid., 17.

24. Lucien Hanks and Jane Hanks, Hanks field notes, p. 14, file 10, box 3, Hanks fonds, GA.

25. Ibid., 11.

26. Ibid.

27. Ibid., 10.

28. Ibid., 14–15.

29. Ibid. 15.

30. Kidd, *Blackfoot Ethnography*, 49.

31. Hanks and Hanks, Hanks field notes, p. 12, file 57, box 2, Hanks fonds, GA.

32. Wilson fonds, 2: 115, GA.

33. Kidd, *Blackfoot Ethnography*, 47.

34. Wissler and Duvall, *Mythology of the Blackfoot Indians*, 58–61.

35. Beverly Hungry Wolf, *The Ways of My Grandmothers* (New York: Quill, 1982), 27.

36. McClintock, *The Old North Trail*, 182–83.

37. James H. Bradley, *Lieut. James H. Bradley Manuscript*, vol. 9, *Contributions to the Historical Society of Montana* (Boston: J.S. Canner and Co., 1966), 271.

38. Wilson fonds, 2: 118, GA.

39. Kidd, *Blackfoot Ethnography*, 154.

40. Wilson fonds, 2: 118, GA.

41. Mary White Elk, 21 July (no year given), p. 230, box 61, Hanks fonds, GA.

42. Ewers, *The Blackfeet*, 100.

43. Kidd, *Blackfoot Ethnography*, 154–54.

44. Victor G. Hopwood, ed., *David Thompson: Travels in Western North America, 1784–1812* (Toronto: Macmillan of Canada, 1971), 116.

45. Bradley, *Lieut. James H. Bradley*, 274.

46. Hopwood, *David Thompson*, 116.

47. Hanks and Hanks, Hanks field notes, p. 3, folder 10, Hanks fonds, GA.

48. Alice Kehoe, "The Plains: Blackfoot Persons," in *Women and Power in Native North America*, ed. Laura F. Klein and L.A. Ackerman (Norman: University of Oklahoma Press, 1995), 119–20.

49. Hanks and Hanks, Hanks field notes, p. 15–16, file 10, box 3, Hanks fonds, GA.

50. Hungry Wolf, *Pikunni Biographies*, 1336.

51. David G. Mandelbaum, *The Plains Cree: An Ethnographic, Historical and Comparative Study* (Regina: Canadian Plains Research Center, 1979), 148.

52. W.D. Wallis, "Annie Sioux," folder 6, box 293, W.D. and R.S. Wallis papers, Canadian Museum of Civilization (CMC).

53. Mandelbaum, *The Plains Cree*, 148.

54. E-mail correspondence, H.C. Wolfart to author, 15 November 2003.

55. Wilson fonds, 1: 118, GA.

56. David G. Mandelbaum, "Fine Day # 1B," 6 August 1964, 4–5, field notes, Canadian Plains Research Center (CPRC).

57. Ibid., 4.

58. Ibid., 5.

59. Wilson fonds, 2: 118, GA.

60. Hopwood, *David Thompson*, 116.

61. Quoted in Eugene Y. Arima, *Blackfeet and Palefaces: The Piikani and Rocky Mountain House* (Ottawa: The Golden Dog Press, 1995), 87.

62. Ibid.

63. Hungry Wolf, *Pikunni Biographies*, 1336.

64. Mary White Elk, 23 July (no year given), p. 234, box 61, Hanks fonds, GA.

65. Hungry Wolf, *The Ways of My Grandmothers*, 201.

66. Sue Sommers Dietrich, typescript of 1939 interviews on the Blackfoot Reservation, Montana, p. 4, Marquette University Archives. Thanks to Alice Kehoe for this reference.

67. W. D. Wallis, "Annie Sioux."

68. John H. Moore, "The Developmental Cycle of Cheyenne Polygyny," *American Indian Quarterly* (Summer, 1991): 311.

69. W. D. Wallis and R. S. Wallis, "Plural Marriage," file 12, box 293, W. D. and R. S. Wallis collection, CMC.

70. Jeffery R. Hanson, introduction to *Buffalo Bird Woman's Garden: Agriculture of the Hidatsa Indians*, by Gilbert L. Wilson (St. Paul: Minnesota Historical Society Press, 1987), 9.

71. Jean Goodwill and Norma Sluman, *John Tootoosis* (Ottawa: Golden Dog Press, 1982), 87.

72. Hanks and Hanks, Hanks fieldnotes, p. 14–18, folder 14, box 1, GA.

73. W. D. Wallis and R. S. Wallis, "Plural Marriage."

74. Esther Goldfrank, Goldfrank fieldnotes, p. 172, GA.

75. Hungry Wolf, *The Ways of My Grandmothers*, 27.

76. John H. Moore, "The Developmental Cycle of Cheyenne Polygyny," *American Indian Quarterly* 15, no.3 (Summer 1991): 311.

77. Microfilm reel #1M903, B.239/z/10, Hudson's Bay Company Archives (HBCA), Provincial Archives of Manitoba, (PAM). I am very grateful to Judith H. Beattie, Keeper, HBCA, for this information provided to me by e-mail on 18 November 2002.

78. Hopwood, *David Thompson*, 116.

79. Alexander Hunter Murray, *Journal of the Yukon, 1847–48*, ed. L. J. Burpee (Ottawa: Government Printing Bureau, 1910), 86.

80. Jennifer S. H. Brown, *Strangers in Blood: Fur Trade Company Families in Indian Country* (Vancouver: University of British Columbia Press, 1980), 88.

81. Sabine Lang, *Men as Women, Women as Men: Changing Gender in Native American Cultures* (Austin: University of Texas Press, 1998).

82. Treaty pay lists for Sarcee and Stoney, 1887–1903, October 1891 (Sarcee Reserve), September 1891 (Stoney Reserve), September 1893 (Stoney Reserve), GA; see also Blood Agency Treaty pay list for September 1887. Thanks to researcher Kristin Burnett, PhD candidate, York University (Toronto), for providing this information.

83. "The Edward J. Brooks Letters: Part I," *Saskatchewan History* 10, no. 3 (Autumn 1957): 109–10.

84. Edward Roper, *By Track and Trail: A Journey Through Canada* (London: Whalen and Co., 1891), 120.

85. Goldfrank, "Sorrel Horse," 122, Goldfrank papers, GA.

86. Goldfrank, Goldfrank fieldnotes, p. 412.

87. Ibid. See also Hungry Wolf, "Running Eagle: Woman Warrior of the Blackfeet," in *The Ways of My Grandmothers*, 62–68.

88. Quoted in Peter Boag, "Sexuality, Gender, and Identity in Great Plains History and Myth," *Great Plains Quarterly* 18, no. 4 (Fall 1998): 328.

89. Hungry Wolf, *Pikunni Biographies*, 943.

90. Oscar Lewis, "Manly-Hearted Women Among the Northern Piegan," *American Anthropologist* 43 (1941): 173–87.

91. Goldfrank, *Changing Configurations*, 48.

92. Goldfrank, Goldfrank fieldnotes, p. 345.

93. Hanks and Hanks, Hanks fieldnotes, p. 52, file 45, GA.

94. Ibid., p. 1, folder 27, box 1, GA.

95. John Tanner, *A Narrative of the Captivity and Adventures of John Tanner During Thirty Years Residence Among the Indians in the Interior of North America*, prepared for the press by Edwin James (1830; repr., Minneapolis: Ross and Haines, 1956), 89.

96. Ibid., 4

97. Eva McKay (Dakota Sioux, Dakota Tipi, Manitoba), *In the Words of Elders: Aboriginal Cultures in Transition* (Toronto: University of Toronto Press, 1999), 300.

98. This is Sean Hawkins's argument for example in "'The Woman in Question': Marriage and Identity in the Colonial Courts of Northern Ghana, 1907–1954," in *Women in African Colonial Histories*, ed. Jean Allman et al. (Bloomington and Indianapolis: Indiana University Press, 2002), 116–43.

99. *The Daily Free Press* (Winnipeg), 1 June 1877.

100. *Toronto Daily Mail*, 23 January 1886.

101. Keith Goulet, "The Cumberland Cree Nehinuw Concept of Land" (unpublished paper presented at the conference Indigenous Knowledge Systems: International Symposium, University of Saskatchewan, 10–13 May 2004), 21. Thanks to Keith Goulet for sharing this paper with me and for discussions of Cree terms.

102. Cited in Ibid.

103. Mary Ann Schwartz and B.M. Scott eds., *Marriage and Families: Diversity and Change*, 3rd ed. (Toronto: Prentice-Hall Canada Ltd., 2000), xviii.

104. Henriette Forget, "The Indian Women of the Western Provinces," in *Women of Canada: Their Life and Work* (Ottawa: National Council of Women of Canada, 1900), 435–36.

105. John Macoun, *Manitoba and the Great North-West* (Guelph: The World Publishing Co., 1882), 553.

106. *The Leader* (Regina), 27 May 1916.

107. J. B. Tyrrell, ed., *David Thompson's Narrative of the Explorations in North America, 1784–1812* (Toronto: The Champlain Society, 1916), 42.

108. Anna Brownell Jameson, *Winter Studies and Summer Rambles in Canada* (1837; repr., Toronto: Thomas Nelson and Sons, 1943), 181.

109. Amelia M. Paget, *People of the Plains* (1909; repr., Regina: Canadian Plains Research Centre, 2004), 40.

110. Moore, "The Developmental Cycle of Cheyenne Polygyny," 311.

111. *The Daily Free Press*, 1 June 1877.

112. Non-Aboriginal views of Plains societies marriages are discussed in Sarah Carter, *Capturing Women: The Manipulation of Cultural Imagery in Canada's Prairie West* (Montreal: McGill-Queen's Press, 1997), 163–66. The attitudes of missionaries in British Columbia toward Aboriginal and other undesirable marriages are examined in Adele Perry, "Metropolitan Knowledge, Colonial Practice and Indigenous Womanhood: Missions in Nineteenth-Century British Columbia," in *Contact Zones: Aboriginal and Settler Women in Canada's Colonial Past*, ed. Katie Pickles and Myra Rutherdale (Vancouver: University of British Columbia Press, 2005), 115–22.

113. John Semmens, *The Field and the Work: Sketches of Missionary Work in the Far North* (Toronto: Methodist Mission Rooms, 1884), 163.

114. John Maclean, *The Warden of the Plains: And Other Stories of Life in the Canadian North-West* (Toronto: William Briggs: 1896), 185.

115. Ibid., 57.

116. Ibid., 59.

117. John McDougall, "The Red Men of Canada's West Yesterday and Today," in *The 100,000 Manufacturing, Building and Wholesale Book Editions of the Morning Albertan*, n.p. (Calgary: The Albertan, 1914), 146. Thanks to my colleague Donald B. Smith for bringing this to my attention and providing me with a copy of this article.

118. Rev. Ross C. Houghton, *Women of the Orient: An Account of the Religious, Intellectual and Social Condition of Women* (Cincinnati: Hitchcock and Walden, 1877), 190–91.

119. B. F. Austen, *Woman: Her Character, Culture and Calling* (Brantford: Book and Bible House, 1890), 158, 188.

120. Inderpal Grewal, *Home and Harem: Nation, Gender, Empire and the Cultures of Travel* (Durham and London: Duke University Press, 1996), 54.

121. Ewers, *The Blackfeet*, 37.

122. Ibid., 99.

123. Alan Klein, "The Political Economy of Gender: A 19th-Century Plains Indian Case Study," in *The Hidden Half: Studies of Plains Indian Woman*, ed. P. Albers and B. Medicine (Lanham, MD: University Press of America, 1983), 143–73; David Nugent, "Property Relations, Production Relations, and Inequality: Anthropology, Political Economy and the Blackfeet," *American Anthropologist* 20, no. 2 (May 1993): 336–62.

124. Nugent, "Property Relations," 351.

125. Lewis, "Manly-Hearted Women," 175.

126. Pekka Hämäläinen, "The Rise and Fall of Plains Indian Horse Cultures," *The Journal of American History* (December 2003): 851.

127. Ibid., 851n36.

128. *Montreal Herald and Daily Commercial Gazette*, 10 July 1867.

129. Sidney L. Harring, *White Man's Law: Native People in Nineteenth-Century Jurisprudence* (Toronto: Osgoode Society for Canadian Legal History and University of Toronto Press, 1998), 170.

130. Quoted in Kathryn M. Daynes, *More Wives Than One: Transformation of the Mormon Marriage System, 1840–1910* (Urbana and Chicago: University of Illinois Press, 2001), 83.

131. Quoted in Jennifer S. H. Brown, "Partial Truths: A Closer Look at Fur Trade Marriage," in *From Rupert's Land to Canada: Essays in Honour of John E. Foster*, ed. Theodore Binnema, Gerhard Ens, and R.C. McLeod (Edmonton: The University of Alberta Press, 2002), 74–75.

132. Ibid., 94.

133. Harring, *White Man's Law*, 170.

134. Ibid., 171.

135. Extracts from the case of *Connolly v. Woolrich and Johnson et.al.* can be found at the University of Saskatchewan Library website: *http://library.usask.ca/native/cnlc/vol01/070.html*. Accessed November 7, 2007.

136. *Montreal Herald and Daily Commercial Gazette*, 10 July 1867.

137. Harring, *White Man's Law*, 171.

138. Quoted in Brown, "Partial Truths," 95.

139. Ibid., 74–75

140. See "Customary Marriages," Indian and Northern Affairs Canada website: http://www.ainc-inac.gc.ca/pr/pu/matr/cm_e.html. Accessed November 7, 2007.

141. Douglas Sanders, "Indian Women: A Brief History of Their Roles and Rights," *McGill Law Journal* 21, no. 4 (1975): 661.

142. Harring, *White Man's Law*, 173.

143. Quoted in Constance Backhouse, *Petticoats and Prejudice: Women and Law in Nineteenth-Century Canada* (Toronto: The Osgoode Society, 1991), 24.

144. Ibid., 25.

145. Ibid.

146. Ibid., 24.

147. *Regina v. Nan-E-Quis-A-Ka* (1889), *Territories Law Reports* 1: 211 (North-West Territories Supreme Court). Available online at the University of Saskatchewan Library website: http://library.usask.ca/native/cnlc/vol103/636.html. Accessed 7 October 2003.

148. Norman Zlotkin, "Judicial Recognition of Aboriginal Customary Law in Canada: Selected Marriage and Adoption Cases," *Canadian Native Law Reporter* 4 (1984): 3.

149. Alex Johnston "Nicholas and Marcella Sheran: Lethbridge's First Citizens," *Alberta History* 31, no. 4 (Autumn 1983): 1.

150. *Sheran* (1899), *Territories Law Reports* 4: 83 (North-West Territories Supreme Court).

151. Johnston, "Nicholas and Marcella Sheran," 8.

152. Patricia Hackett Nicola, "Rebecca Lena Graham's Fight For Her Inheritance," *Pacific Northwest Quarterly* 97, no. 3 (Summer, 2006): 139–47.

153. Ibid., 142.

154. Ibid., 145.

FIVE   *The 1886 "Traffic in Indian Girls" Panic and the Foundation of the Federal Approach to Aboriginal Marriage and Divorce*

1.   W. M. Halladay to J. D. McLean, 1 February 1912, file 64.535 (pt. 1), vol. 3832, Department of Indian Affairs (RG 10), Library and Archives Canada (LAC).

2.   1887 Report of a Committee of the Privy Council, file 3245-1, vol. 3762, RG 10, (LAC).

3.   Canada, *House of Commons Debates* (1886) vol. 1 at 720.

4.   *The Macleod Gazette*, 23 June 1886.

5.   Judith Walkowitz, *City of Dreadful Delights: Narratives of Sexual Danger in Late-Victorian London* (Chicago: The University of Chicago Press, 1992), 81, 83.

6.   Ibid., 83.

7.   *The Globe* (Toronto), 1 February 1886.

8.   David J. Carter, *Samuel Trivett: Missionary with the Blood Indians* (Calgary: Kyle Printing and Stationery, 1974), 90–91.

9.   *The Macleod Gazette*, 23 March 1886.

10. Ann Laura Stoler, "Sexual Affronts and Racial Frontiers: European Identities and the Cultural Politics of Exclusion in Colonial Southeast Asia," in *Tensions*

of Empire: Colonial Cultures in a Bourgeois World, ed. Frederick Cooper and Ann Laura Stoler (Berkley and Los Angeles: University of California Press, 1997), 198–237.

11. Mariana Valverde, *The Age of Light, Soap and Water: Moral Reform in English Canada, 1885–1925* (Toronto: McClelland and Stewart, 1991). See also Cicely Devereux, "'And Let Them Wash Me From This Clanging World': Hugh and Ion, the 'Last Best West,' and Purity Discourse in 1885," *Journal of Canadian Studies* 32, no. 2 (Summer 1997): 100–15.

12. Renisa Mawani, "In Between and Out of Place: Racial Hybridity, Liquor, and the Law in Late 19th and Early 20th Century British Columbia," *Canadian Journal of Law and Society* 15, no. 2 (2000): 11.

13. Quoted in Sarah Carter, "'We Must Farm to Enable Us to Live': The Plains Cree and Agriculture to 1900," in *Native Peoples: The Canadian Experience*, 3rd ed., ed. R. Bruce Morrison and C. Roderick Wilson (Don Mills: Oxford University Press, 2004), 333.

14. Sarah Carter, *Capturing Women: The Manipulation of Cultural Imagery in Canada's Prairie West* (Montreal: McGill-Queen's University Press, 1997), 145–48.

15. L. Vankoughnet to J.A. Macdonald, 15 November 1883, file 628, vol. 1009, Royal Canadian Mounted Police (RG 18), LAC.

16. Carter, *Capturing Women*, 136–57.

17. Henry Finlay, "Victorian Sexual Morality: A Case of Double Standards," *Australian Journal of Law and Society* 14 (1998–99): 55.

18. *The Macleod Gazette*, 16 March 1886.

19. *The Globe* (Toronto), 29 March 1886.

20. *The Macleod Gazette*, 16 March 1886.

21. Ibid., 1 February 1886.

22. Letter, Edgar Dewdney to Bishop of Saskatchewan, 31 May 1886, file 30613, vol. 3753, RG 10, LAC.

23. Anonymous, *The Facts Respecting Indian Administration in the North-West* (Ottawa: Department of Indian Affairs, 1886), 9.

24. L. Vankoughnet to Sir John A. Macdonald, 7 July 1886, file 32345, vol. 3762, RG 10, LAC.

25. Michael D. Blackstock, "Trust Us: A Case Study in Colonial Social Relations Based on Documents Prepared by the Aborigines Protection Society, 1836–1912," in *With Good Intentions: Euro-Canadian and Aboriginal Relations in Colonial Canada*, ed. Celia Haig-Brown and David A. Nock (Vancouver: University of British Columbia Press, 2006), 58.

26. *The Evangelical Churchman*, 22 May 1884.

27. Letter, George Burbridge to L. Vankoughnet, 5 October 1886, file 32345, vol. 3762, RG 10, LAC.

28. Letter, D. C. Scott to Frank Oliver, 19 October 1910, file 32345, vol. 3762, RG 10, LAC. Scott writes in this letter "Under the Order in Council on file you will find the draft prepared under the late Sir John Thompson's direction; in which you will see interlineations in his own hand writing. Part of Page 24 and all of page 25 are in his own handwriting."

29. P. B. Waite, *The Man From Halifax: Sir John Thompson Prime Minister* (Toronto: University of Toronto Press, 1985), 128.

30. Ibid., 153.

31. Ibid., 183–84.

32. *The Macleod Gazette*, 6 September 1887; 13 September 1887.

33. *Manitoba Free Press*, 30 August 1887.

34. Ibid.

35. Series A -1-a, vol. 510, order-in-council 1887–0345 G, Privy Council Office (RG 2), LAC.

36. Certified copy of a report of a committee of the Honourable the Privy Council approved by His Excellency the Governor General in Council on the 31 October 1887, p. 1–2, file 32345, vol. 3762, RG 10, LAC.

37. Ibid.

38. Quoted in memorandum for the Deputy Minister of Justice, 15 May 1914, p. 3, file 1299–1914, vol. 2406, int. 163, Department of Justice (RG 13), LAC.

39. Ibid., 3–4.

40. Canada, *Sessional Papers*, 1899, no. 14, vol. 33, no. 12, p. xxv.

41. Memorandum to the deputy superintendent general, 29 February 1908, file 180.636, vol. 3990, RG 10, LAC.

42. Canada, *Sessional Papers*, 1907–8, no. 27, vol. 42, no. 14, p. xxix.

43. Brian Slattery, ed., *Canadian Native Law Cases*, vol. 2, 1870–90 (Saskatoon: University of Saskatchewan Native Law Centre, 1981), 372.

44. E. Pauline Johnson, "A Red Girl's Reasoning," in *E. Pauline Johnson (Tekahionwake): Collected Poems and Selected Prose*, intro. and ed. Carole Gerson and Veronica Strong-Boag (Toronto: University of Toronto Press, 2002), 188–202.

45. Ibid., 195–96.

46. Ibid., 197.

47. Ibid., 196.

48. *The Macleod Gazette*, 25 January 1895; M. B. Venini Byrne, *From the Buffalo to the Cross: A History of the Roman Catholic Diocese of Calgary* (Calgary: Calgary Archives Historical Publishers, 1973), 50.

49. Anglican Diocese of Calgary, *Diocese of Calgary: Report on Indian Missions, 1895–6* (Toronto: Oxford Press, 1896), 7. Copy available in box 67.21.1, Records of the Anglican Diocese of Calgary, Synod Office Records (General Files), University of Calgary Archives (UCA).

50. *The Sower in the West and Church Monthly* 11, no. 4 (April 1894): 5. Copy available in box 27, file 27.1, Records of the Anglican Diocese of Calgary, Diocesan Synod Publications, UCA.

51. Chief Piapot to J.A. Macdonald, 30 April 1885, file 19.550–2, vol. 3709, RG 10, LAC.

52. R.C. Macleod and Heather Rollason, "'Restrain the Lawless Savages': Native Defendants in the Criminal Courts of the North West Territories, 1878–1885," *Journal of Historical Sociology* 10, no. 2 (June 1997): 158.

53. Ibid.

54. Canada. *Sessional Papers.* 1885, no. 3, vol. 3, p. lxi.

55. Canada. *House of Commons Debates* (27 May 1885) at 2162.

56. Felix S. Cohen, *Handbook of Federal Indian Law* (Washington: United States Government Printing Office, 1945), 120.

57. Sharon Helen Venne, ed., *Indian Acts and Amendments 1868–1975: An Indexed Collection* (Saskatoon: University of Saskatchewan Native Law Centre, 1981), 24.

58. Ibid., 57.

59. Ibid., 25.

60. A.E. Forget to Nancy LaVallie, 18 April 1895, file 1239, pt. 7, vol. 3594, RG 10, LAC.

61. Deputy minister of justice to deputy minister of the interior, 19 May 1886, vol. 2247, box INT 93, 71/1885, Department of Justice (RG 13), LAC.

62. Ibid.

63. L. Vankoughnet to A.M. Burgess, 20 January 1886, vol. 187, D-II-3, Department of the Interior (RG 15), LAC.

64. Letter, G. Burbridge to L. Vankoughnet, 7 April 1886, file 23,593, vol. 3721, RG 10, LAC.

65. Memo from G. Burbridge, deputy minister of justice, 22 February 1886, file 23,593, vol. 3721, RG 10, LAC.

66. Venne, *Indian Acts and Amendments,* 94.

67. Ibid.

68. Ibid., 183.

69. Ibid., 139.

70. Ibid.

71. J. McLean to R.D. Howell, 13 July 1911, file 64,535, vol. 3832, RG 10, LAC.

72. J. McLean to the principal, Alberni School, 1900, file 180,636, vol. 3990, RG 10, LAC.

73. Secretary of the department of Indian Affairs to M.R. Bogart, 2 December 1909, pt. 1, file 32345, vol. 3762, RG 10, LAC.

74. John E. Crankshaw and Alexandre Chevalier, *Crankshaw's Criminal Code of Canada,* 5th ed. (Toronto: The Carswell Co., 1924), 374.

75. Freda Ahenakew and H.C. Wolfart, eds. and trans., *Kôhkominawak Otâcimowiniwâwa: Our Grandmothers' Lives as Told in Their Own Words* (Saskatoon: Fifth House, 1992), 79.

76. Canada, *Sessional Papers*, 1894, no. 14, vol. 27, no. 10, p. 45.

77. "An Ordinance Respecting Marriages," North-West Territories Ordinance, no. 9, 1878. Canadian Inventors of Historic Microreproduction, no. 52120.

78. Charles R. Weaver to attorney general, 30 August 1911, file 94,189, vol. 3881, RG 10, LAC.

79. Venne, *Indian Acts and Amendments*, 90.

80. Petition from members of The Pas Band, 1889, file 56,941, vol. 3816, RG 10, LAC.

81. Hayter Reed to deputy superintendent general of Indian Affairs, 25 September 1893, file 94,189, vol. 3881, RG 10, LAC.

82. Unsigned letter to undisclosed recipient, 1 February 1912, file 64,535, vol. 3832, RG 10, LAC.

83. David Laird to Indian agent, Selkirk, Manitoba, 15 March 1905, file 74, pt. 28, vol. 3559, RG 10, LAC.

84. Memorandum for the deputy minister of justice, 15 May 1888, file 1299–1914, p. 4, vol. 2406, int. 163, RG 13, LAC.

85. Deputy minister of justice to Hayter Reed, 22 May 1895, file 494 (1895), vol. 97, Series A-2, RG 13, LAC.

86. Jean Barman, "Taming Aboriginal Sexuality: Gender, Power, and Race in British Columbia, 1850–1900," *B.C. Studies* 115/116 (Autumn/Winter 1997/98): 248.

87. Diane Jeater, *Marriage, Perversion and Power: The Construction of Moral Discourse in Southern Rhodesia, 1894–1930* (Oxford: Clarendon Press, 1993), 55.

88. Rosalind O'Hanlon, "Gender in the British Empire," in *The Oxford History of the British Empire*, vol. IV, *The Twentieth Century*, ed. Judith M. Brown and Wm. R. Louis (Oxford and New York: Oxford University Press, 1999), 383.

89. Quoted in Deborah Posel, "State, Power and Gender: Conflict over the Registration of African Customary Marriage in South Africa, ca. 1910–1970," *Journal of Historical Sociology* 8, no. 3 (September 1995): 227.

90. O'Hanlon, "Gender in the British Empire," 383.

91. Barbara M. Cooper, *Marriage in Maradi: Gender and Culture in a Hausa Society in Niger, 1900–1989* (Portsmouth, NH: Heinemann, 1997), xlv.

92. Elizabeth Isichei, "Does Christianity Empower Women? The Case of the Anaguta of Central Nigeria," in *Women and Missions: Past and Present*, ed. Fiona Bowie et al. (Oxford: Berg Publishers, 1993), 209–26.

93. Benjamin Kline, *Genesis of Apartheid: British African Policy in the Colony of Natal, 1845–1893* (Lanham, MD: University Press of America, 1988), 12.

94. Ibid., 14.

95. Jeater, *Marriage, Perversion and Power*, 64.

96. Posel, "State, Power and Gender," 227.

97. See Norman Etherington, "Natal's Black Rape Scares of the 1870s," *Journal of Southern African Studies* 15, no. 1 (1988): 36–53; see also Jeremy Martens, "Polygamy, Sexual Danger, and the Creation of Vagrancy Legislation in Colonial Natal," *The Journal of Imperial and Commonwealth History* 31, no. 3 (September 2003): 24–25.

98. Kline, *Genesis of Apartheid*, 17.

99. Martens, "Polygamy," 37.

100. Martin Chanock, *Law, Custom and Social Order: The Colonial Experience in Malawi and Zambia* (Cambridge: Cambridge University Press, 1985), 150.

101. Jean Comaroff and John Comaroff, *Of Revelation and Revolution: Christianity, Colonialism and Consciousness in South Africa* (Chicago and London: The University of Chicago Press, 1991), 1:132.

102. O'Hanlon, "Gender in the British Empire," 383.

103. Ibid., 385.

104. Ibid.

105. Chanock, *Law, Custom and Social Order*, 207.

106. Jean Allman and Victoria Tashjian, *"I Will Not Eat Stone": A Women's History of Colonial Asante* (Westport: Greenwood Publishing Group, 2000).

107. Posel, "State, Power and Gender," 240.

108. Ibid., 241.

109. Jeater, *Marriage, Perversion and Power*, 56.

110. Ibid., 65.

111. Ibid., 64.

112. Ibid., 84.

113. Ibid., 138–40.

114. Barman, "Taming Aboriginal Sexuality," 251.

115. Ibid., 253.

116. Quoted in Ibid., 254.

117. J.W. Mackay to A.W. Vowell, 4 July 1890, file 57,045–1, vol. 3816, RG 10, LAC.

118. Barman, "Taming Aboriginal Sexuality," 254.

119. R.H. Pidcock to A.W. Vowell, 4 March 1891, file 57,045–1, vol. 3816, RG 10, LAC.

120. J.W. Mackay, to A.W. Vowell, 4 July 1890, file 57,045–1, vol. 3816, RG 10, LAC.

121. Superintendent General of Indian Affairs to the Honourable The Privy Council of Canada, 13 March 1891, file 57,045–1, vol. 3816, RG 10, LAC.

122. Barman, "Taming Aboriginal Sexuality," 258.

123. Felix S. Cohen, *Handbook of Federal Indian Law* (Washington: United States Government Printing Office: 1945), 120.

124. Ibid., 138.

125. Ibid.

126. Quoted in David E. Wilkins, *American Indian Sovereignty and the United States Supreme Court* (Austin: University of Texas Press, 1997), 128–29.

127. Ibid., 139.

128. Katherine M. B. Osburn, *Southern Ute Women: Autonomy and Assimilation on the Reservation, 1887–1934* (Albuquerque: University of New Mexico Press, 1998), 120.

129. O'Hanlon, "Gender in the British Empire," 392.

130. Victoria Freeman, "Attitudes Toward 'Miscegenation' in Canada, the United States, New Zealand, and Australia, 1860–1914," *Native Studies Review* 16, no. 1 (2005): 52.

131. Peggy Pascoe, "The Architecture of White Supremacy in the Multiracial West: The Case of Miscegenation Law" (paper presented at "Dancing on the Rim: Nations, Borderlands and Identities," 2005 Pacific Coast Branch of the American Historical Association, Corvallis, Oregon, 6 August 2005).

132. Ibid.

133. J. D. McLean to Rev. T. Albert Moore, 18 April 1912, file 57,045–1, vol. 3816, RG 10, LAC.

134. Mandy Paul and Robert Foster, "Married to the Land: Land Grants to Aboriginal Women in South Australia, 1848–1911," *Australian Historical Studies* 34, no. 121 (April 2003): 48–68.

135. Ann McGrath, "Consent, Marriage and Colonialism: Indigenous Australian Women and Colonizer Marriages," *Journal of Colonialism and Colonial History* 6, no. 3 (2005): 11.

136. Ibid., p. 12.

137. The judgement in this case is found in re: *Bethell, Bethell v. Hildyard* (1885), p. 220–37, B. 2119, Law Report 38, Chancery Division, file 64, 535, vol. 3832, RG 10, LAC.

138. Ibid., 4.

139. Ibid., 8.

140. Ibid., 12.

141. Ibid., 21.

142. Ibid., 20.

143. Ibid., 23.

144. Ibid., 25.

145. Ibid., 16.

146. Ibid., 16–17.

147. Ibid., 19.

148. Ibid., 16.

1. For an overview of recent "intimacies of empire" studies in postcolonial and US history see Ann Laura Stoler, "Tense and Tender Ties: The Politics of North American History and (Post) Colonial Studies," *The Journal of American History* 88, no. 3 (December 2001): 829–65. I am grateful to Joan Sangster and Bryan Palmer for providing me with a copy of their commentary on this article, which notes that Canadian history does not fall within the rubric of "North American" history in this article.

2. J.M.S., "Missionary Problems in India," *The Missionary Review of the World*, no.1 (January–December 1888): 18

3. Eugene Stock, *The History of the Church Missionary Society: Its Environment, its Men and its Work*, vol. 2 (London: Church Missionary Society, 1899), 111.

4. Ibid., vol. 3:646.

5. Jeff Guy, *The Heretic: A Study of the Life of John William Colenso, 1814–1883* (Pietermartizburg: The University of Natal Press, 1983), 49.

6. Ibid., 78.

7. J.W. Colenso, *Remarks on the Proper Treatment of Polygamy as Found Already Existing in Converts From Heathenism* (Pietermaritzburg: May and Davis, 1855), 15.

8. Ibid., 17.

9. Ibid., 7.

10. Ibid., 20.

11. Ibid., 17.

12. Anonymous, "Reply to J.W. Colenso," in Colenso, *Remarks on the Proper Treatment of Polygamy*, 40.

13. Ibid., 42.

14. Ibid., 46.

15. Samuel Trivett, 22 March 1887, no. 979, reel A114 (microfilm), Church Missionary Society Collection, Provincial Archives of Manitoba (PAM).

16. John Maclean, *Canadian Savage Folk: The Native Tribes of Canada* (Toronto: William Briggs, 1896), 62.

17. John Webster Grant, *Moon of Wintertime: Missionaries and the Indians of Canada* (Toronto: University of Toronto Press, 1984), 235. See also Peter Jones, *History of the Ojibwa Indians* (London: Q.W. Bennett, 1861), 82.

18. John Semmens, *The Field and the Work: Sketches of Missionary Work in the Far North* (Toronto: Methodist Mission Rooms, 1884), 166.

19. John Hines, *The Red Indians of the Plains: Thirty Years' Missionary Experience in the Saskatchewan* (Toronto: McClelland, Goodchild and Stewart, 1916), 158–59.

20. H.W. Gibbon Stocken, *Among the Blackfoot and Sarcee* (Calgary: Glenbow Alberta Institute: 1976), 50.

21. Rudolph Friedrich Kurz, quoted in David Reed Miller, introduction to *The Assiniboine*, by Edwin Thompson Denig, ed. J.N.B. Hewitt (Regina: Canadian Plains Research Center, 1998), xix n10.

22. Ibid., 74.

23. James Carnegie, Earl of Southesk, *Saskatchewan and Rocky Mountains: A Diary and Narrative of Travel, Sport, and Adventure During a Journey Through the Hudson's Bay Company's Territories in 1859 and 1860* (Toronto: J. Campbell, 1875), 155.

24. Canada. *Sessional Papers*, vol. 3, no. 3 (1885): lxi.

25. Canada. *House of Commons Debates*. 26 May 1885 at 2127.

26. Circular letter of J.F. Graham, 24 July 1882, file 1760, vol. 3602, Department of Indian Affairs (RG 10), Library and Archives Canada (LAC).

27. Canada. *Sessional Papers*, no. 6, vol. 5, 1882: 113.

28. *The Globe and Mail*, 8 August 1881.

29. *Letter Leaflet*, July 1894, 809.

30. Extract, letter from J.W. Tims, 2 August 1894, file 486–2–5, pt. 1, vol. 6816, RG 10, LAC.

31. D.L. Clink to the Indian Commissioner, 10 December 1894, file 486–2–5, pt. 1, vol. 6816, RG 10, LAC.

32. A.M. Burgess to Edgar Dewdney, 23 January 1890, file 223719, vol. 614, D-II-1, Department of the Interior (RG 15), LAC.

33. H.H. Smith to A.M. Burgess, 17 December 1889, file 223719, vol. 614, D-II-1, RG 15, LAC.

34. Ibid.

35. Ibid.

36. Précis of the claim written by Roger Goulet, 28 November 1889, file 223719, vol. 614, D-II-1, RG 15, LAC.

37. Ibid.

38. Ibid.

39. Diana Jeater, *Marriage, Perversion and Power: The Construction of Moral Discourse in Southern Rhodesia, 1894–1930* (Oxford: Clarendon Press, 1993), 78.

40. John David Pulsipher, "The Americanization of Monogamy: Mormons, Native Americans and the Nineteenth-Century Perception that Polygamy was a Threat to Democracy" (PhD diss., University of Minnesota, 1999), 162.

41. Quoted in Jeater, *Marriage, Perversion and Power*, 74.

42. *Edmonton Bulletin*, 23 August 1890.

43. *Missions el la Congrégation des missionaries Oblats de Marie Immaculée* (Paris: Typographie A. Hennuyer, 1897), 402.

44. Brian Q. Cannon, "Mormonism in Montana," *Montana: The Magazine of Western History* 6, no. 1 (Spring 2006): 8.

45. Ibid., 9.

46. Ibid., 10–11.

47. Quoted in Pulsipher, "The Americanization of Monogamy," 137.

48. Quoted in Ibid., 136.

49. Vic Satzewich and Linda Mahood, "Indian Affairs and Band Governance: Deposing Indian Chiefs in Western Canada, 1896-1911," *Canadian Ethnic Studies* 26, no 1 (1994): 40-58.

50. Ibid., 45.

51. Sarah Carter, *Lost Harvests: Prairie Indian Reserve Farmers and Government Policy* (Montreal and Kingston: McGill-Queen's Press, 1990), 193-236.

52. Hayter Reed to Deputy Superintendent General of Indian Affairs (DSGIA), 8 September 1892, file 94-189, vol. 3881, RG 10, LAC.

53. Letter, Hayter Reed to DSGIA, 25 September 1893, file 94-189, vol. 3881, RG 10, LAC.

54. Canada. *Sessional Papers*, no. 15, vol. 10, 1892: 111.

55. Circular letter, Assistant Commissioner Amedée Forget to Indian Agents, 19 December 1893, file 94-189, vol. 3881, RG 10, LAC.

56. "Statement showing ages of Indians who have entered into polygamous relations since taking treaty," p. 5, letter, Amedée Forget to DSGIA, 30 January 1895, file 94-189, vol. 3881, RG 10, LAC.

57. Allen McDonald to Assistant Commissioner Forget (copy, n.d.), file 94-189, vol. 3881, RG 10, LAC.

58. R. S. McKenzie to Assistant Commissioner Forget (copy, n.d.), file 94-189, vol. 3881, RG 10, LAC.

59. M. McGirr to A. Forget, 26 September 1894, file 94-189, vol. 3881, RG 10, LAC.

60. Ibid.

61. Ibid. These figures are from the copies of the 1893 agents' reports prepared by A. Forget. The statements for the Piikani are incomplete and unclear.

62. Ibid. These figures are from the "Statement showing ages of Indians who have entered into polygamous relations since taking treaty." See note 56.

63. E. J. Newcombe to Hayter Reed, 4 January 1895, file 94-189, vol. 3881, RG 10, LAC.

64. J. Wilson to A. Forget, 21 January 1895, file 94-189, vol. 3881, RG 10, LAC.

65. Ibid.

66. Ibid.

67. J. Wilson to A. Forget, 20 February 1895, file 94-189, vol. 3881, RG 10, LAC.

68. Forget memo (n.d.), file 94-189, vol. 3881, RG 10, LAC.

69. "Regina v. Labrie," *The Montreal Law Reports: Court of Queen's Bench*, vol. 7 (Montreal: Gazette Printing Co., 1891), 211.

70. Ibid., 213.

71. Ibid.

72. H. Reed to A. Forget, 4 March 1895, file 94-189, vol. 3881, RG 10, LAC.

73. D. M. Browning to H. Reed, 13 June 1896, file 94-189, vol. 3881, RG 10, LAC.

74. Pulsipher, "The Americanization of Monogamy," 169–70.

75. Ibid., 170.

76. Robert M. Utley, *The Indian Frontier of the American West, 1846–1890* (Albuquerque: University of New Mexico Press, 1984), 234–36.

77. *The Rapid City Daily Journal*, 4 May 1895.

78. Ibid., 16 May 1895.

79. Ibid.

80. Ibid., 26 May 1895.

81. Felix S. Cohen, *Handbook of Federal Indian Law* (Washington: United States Government Printing Office, 1945), 138.

82. Brian Slattery, ed., *Canadian Native Law Cases*, vol. 2, *1870–1890* (Saskatoon: University of Saskatchewan Native Law Centre, 1981), 368–72.

83. Ibid., 372.

84. Magnus Begg to A. Forget, 23 March 1895, file 934,189, vol. 3881, RG 10, LAC.

85. A. Forget to M. Begg, 7 February 1895, file 934,189, vol. 3881, RG 10, LAC.

86. St. Cyprian's Mission Parish Records, 15–4, Records of the Anglican Diocese of Calgary, University of Calgary Archives (UCA).

87. M. Begg to A. Forget, 23 February 1895, file 934,189, vol. 3881, RG 10, LAC.

88. Ibid.

89. The federal government of Canada has not yet established a minimum age for marriage, which has resulted in the adoption of the minimum ages under English common law: fourteen years for males, twelve years for females. Provinces and territories have legislation requiring a higher minimum age. See Dwight L. Gibson et al., *All About the Law: Exploring the Canadian Legal System*, 4th ed. (Toronto: Nelson Canada, 1996), 355.

90. M. Begg to A. Forget, 9 March 1895, file 934,189, vol. 3881, RG 10, LAC.

91. A. Forget to M. Begg, 11 March 1895, file 934,189, vol. 3881, RG 10, LAC.

92. M. Begg to A. Forget, 16 March 1895, file 934,189, vol. 3881, RG 10, LAC.

93. Hugh Dempsey, *Charcoal's World* (Saskatoon: Western Producer Prairie Books: 1978), 36.

94. J. R. Miller, *Shingwauk's Vision: A History of Native Residential Schools* (Toronto: University of Toronto Press, 1996), 130.

95. J.W. Tims to Indian Commissioner, 27 June 1895, file RCMP 1895 Commissioners Office Pt. 1, fol. 2182, RG 18, LAC.

96. Ibid.

97. *The Sower in the West and Church Monthly* 3, no. 6 (June 1895).

98. Dempsey, *Charcoal's World*, 12.

99. *The Weekly Herald* (Calgary), 21 January 1897.

100. *The Macleod Gazette*, 15 January 1897.

101. Ibid.

102. Hugh Dempsey, *Red Crow, Warrior Chief* (Saskatoon: Fifth House, 1995), 197.

103. Quoted in Ibid.

104. Ibid., 217.

105. A. Forget to J. Smart, 15 April 1898, file 94,189, vol. 3881, RG 10, LAC.

106. J.D. McLean to A. Forget, 22 April 1898, file 74, pt. 3, vol. 3559, RG 10, LAC.

107. A. Forget to J.D. McLean, 8 August 1898, file 94,189, vol. 3881, RG 10, LAC.

108. J. Wilson to J.D. McLean, 23 July 1898, file 94,189, vol. 3881, RG 10, LAC.

109. A. Forget to the DIA Secretary, 13 September 1890, file 74, pt. 6, vol. 3559, RG 10, LAC.

110. Ibid.

111. A. Forget to Indian agent, File Hills Agency, 20 January 1899, file 74, pt. 6, vol. 3559, RG 10, LAC.

112. A. Forget to J. Wilson, 18 August 1898, file 74, pt. 3, vol. 3559, RG 10, LAC.

113. Ibid.

114. J. Wilson to A. Forget, 4 November 1898, file 74, pt. 19, vol. 3559, RG 10, LAC.

115. Ibid.

116. A. Forget to J. Wilson, 10 December 1898, file 74, pt. 19, vol. 3559, RG 10, LAC.

117. J. Wilson to A. Forget, 6 December 1898, file 74, pt. 19, vol. 3559, RG 10, LAC.

118. Slattery, *Canadian Native Law Cases*, 513.

119. J. Wilson to A. Forget, 13 March 1899, file 74, pt. 19, vol. 3559, RG 10, LAC.

120. *The Macleod Gazette*, 11 March 1899.

121. J. Wilson to A. Forget, 13 March 1899, file 74, pt. 19, vol. 3559, RG 10, LAC.

122. Ibid.

123. Secretary S. Stewart to Indian Commissioner David Laird, 1 April 1899, file 74, pt. 19, vol. 3559, RG 10, LAC.

124. Memorandum, Duncan Campbell Scott, 29 March 1899, file 74, pt. 19, vol. 3559, RG 10, LAC.

125. 1901 Census Data, Canada Census Records, Glenbow Archives (GA).

126. See file 74, part 3–30, vol. 3559, RG 10, LAC.

127. Canada. *Sessional Papers*, no. 27 (1904): 148.

128. See "Marriages on the Blackfoot Reservation," box 75, file 1, Records of the Anglican Diocese of Calgary, UCA.

129. Mrinalini Sinha, "Gender and Imperialism: Colonial Policy and the Ideology of Moral Imperialism in Late Nineteenth-Century Bengal," in *Changing Men: New Directions in Research on Men and Masculinity*, ed. Michael S. Kimmel (Newbury Park: Sage Publications, 1987), 218. See also Himani Bannerji, "Age of Consent and Hegemonic Social Reform," in *Gender and Imperialism*, ed. Claire Midgley (Manchester and New York: Manchester University Press, 1998), 21–44.

130. J.A. Markle to Indian Commissioner, 11 December 1900, file 486–2–5, pt. 1, vol. 6816, RG 10, LAC.

131. D. Laird to J.D. McLean, 15 December 1900, file 486-2-5, pt. 1, vol. 6816, RG 10, LAC.

132. Reginald Rimmer, "Memorandum, Child Marriage," 28 December 1900, file 486-2-5, pt. 1, vol. 6816, RG 10, LAC.

133. Ibid. Underlined in the original document.

134. J.A. McKenna to the DIA Secretary, 6 June 1903, file 486-2-5, pt. 1, vol. 6816, RG 10, LAC.

135. James Short to E.L. Newcombe, 10 August 1903, file 486-2-5, pt. 1, vol. 6816, RG 10, LAC.

136. Reginald Rimmer, "Memorandum, Criminal Liability of Parties to Child Marriage," 26 June 1903, file 486-2-5, pt. 1, vol. 6816, RG 10, LAC.

137. A.W. Vowell to the DIA Secretary, 1898, file 486-2-5, pt. 1, vol. 6816, RG 10, LAC.

138. James Short to E.L. Newcombe, file 486-2-5 pt. 1, vol. 6816, RG 10, LAC, date obscured.

139. R. Rimmer to the DIA Deputy Superintendent General, 21 August 1903, file 486-2-5, pt. 1, vol. 6816, RG 10, LAC.

SEVEN *"Undigested, Conflicting and Inharmonious"*

1. Frederick H. Abbott, *The Administration of Indian Affairs in Canada* (Washington D.C.: 1915), 43.

2. Ibid., 20.

3. Ibid., 21.

4. Ibid., 20.

5. Duncan Campbell Scott's circular letter to Indian agents, 2 January 1914, file 32345, vol. 3762, Department of Indian Affairs (RG 10), Library and Archives Canada (LAC).

6. Rosalind O'Hanlon, "Gender in the British Empire," in *The Oxford History of the British Empire*, vol. IV, *The Twentieth Century*, ed. Judith M. Brown and Wm. Roger Louis (Oxford and New York: Oxford University Press, 1999), 383.

7. J.D. McLean to the Bishop of St. Albert, 6 August 1908, file 94,189, vol. 3881, RG 10, LAC.

8. J.R. Miller, *Shingwauk's Vision: A History of Native Residential Schools* (Toronto: University of Toronto Press, 1996), 22.

9. Extract, letter by W.E. Jones, 6 February 1895, file 486-2-5, vol. 6816, RG 10, LAC.

10. W.P. Osickyas to Hayter Reed, 26 June 1894, file 486-2-5, pt. 1, vol. 6816, RG 10, LAC.

11. H. Reed to A. Nassens, 14 July 1894, file 486-2-5, pt. 1, vol. 6816, RG 10, LAC.

12. H. Reed to W. P. Osickyas, 16 July 1894, file 486–2-5, pt. 1, vol. 6816, RG 10, LAC.

13. Magnus Begg to A. Forget, 4 August 1894, file 486–2-5, pt. 1, vol. 6816, RG 10, LAC.

14. Sharon Helen Venne, ed., *Indian Acts and Amendments 1868–1975: An Indexed Collection* (Saskatoon: University of Saskatchewan Native Law Centre, 1981), 164.

15. H. Reed to J. Hugonnard, 13 June 1890, file 486–2-5, pt. 1, vol. 6816, RG 10, LAC.

16. J. Hugonnard to H. Reed, 31 May 1890, file 486–2-5, pt. 1, vol. 6816, RG 10, LAC.

17. J. P. Wright to Indian Commissioner, 10 August 1898, file 74, pt. 6, vol. 3559, RG 10, LAC.

18. Muscowpetung Reserve (Saskatchewan) Indian agent to Indian Commissioner, 9 July 1900, file 74, pt. 7, vol. 3559, RG 10, LAC.

19. Indian Commissioner to Muscowpetung Reserve Indian agent, 12 July 1900, file 74, pt. 7, vol. 3559, RG 10, LAC.

20. Abbott, *The Administration of Indian Affairs in Canada*, 43.

21. Report, dated 14 March 1914 and 31 March 1914, file 97, BC. 31/B655, Blood Agency Correspondence, Glenbow Archives (GA).

22. Circular letter from Duncan Campbell Scott, 12 March 1914, vol. 1392, RG 10, LAC.

23. "Canadian Citizens in the Making," *Nor'-West Farmer* 31, no. 13 (5 July 1912): 941.

24. H. V. Graham, "Two Weddings," file 9, W. M. Graham Papers, GA.

25. David Roberts, "Indian Students Forced into Marriage, Farm Life," *The Globe and Mail*, 10 December 1990.

26. Sarah Carter, "Demonstrating Success: The File Hills Farm Colony," *Prairie Forum* 16, no. 2 (1991): 157–83.

27. Abbott, *The Administration of Indian Affairs in Canada*, 54.

28. Canada, *Sessional Papers*, 1912, no. 27, vol. 46, no. 20, p. 520.

29. Eleanor Brass, "Recollections and Reminiscences: The File Hills Ex-Pupil Colony," *Saskatchewan History* 6, no. 2 (1953): 67.

30. R. J. MacPherson to DIA Secretary, 1922, file 486–2-6 pt. 1, vol. 6816, RG 10, LAC.

31. S. Middleton to Rev. Dr. Westgate, 8 February 1923, file 486–2-6, vol. 6816, RG 10, LAC.

32. Memorandum (author unclear), 27 February 1923, file 486–2-6, vol. 6816, RG 10, LAC.

33. Indian agent Moose Mountain to Fr. Pedley, 20 February 1905, file 74 pt. 3, vol. 3559, RG 10, LAC.

34. R.V. Sinclair, *Canadian Indians* (Ottawa: Thorburn and Abbott, n.d., ca. 1911), 30.

35. R.N. Wilson to the DIA Secretary, 1904, Blood Agency letterbook, 1903–5, GA.

36. R.N. Wilson to the DIA Secretary, 22 December 1904, Blood Agency letterbook, 1903–5, p. 410, GA.

37. Deputy Minister of Justice to the Deputy Superintendent General of Indian Affairs, 7 November 1904, file 284/1905, vol. 2324, RG 13, LAC.

38. R.N. Wilson to DIA Secretary, 1904 (exact date obscured), Blood Agency letterbook, 1903–5, p. 465–66, GA.

39. R.N. Wilson to DIA Secretary, 22 December 1904, Blood Agency letterbook, 1903–5, p. 411, GA.

40. Ibid.

41. E.L. Newcombe to Deputy Superintendent General of Indian Affairs, 27 March 1905, file 284/1905, vol. 2324, Department of Justice (RG 13), LAC.

42. R.N. Wilson to Messrs. Weed and Campbell, 2 January 1905, Blood Agency letterbook, 1903–5, GA.

43. Venne, *Indian Acts and Amendments 1868–1975*, 25. There may have been a time, however, when women who "married out" had to produce proof of a "legal" marriage before they could receive their fifty dollars for ten years' annuities. In 1895 Indian Commissioner A.E. Forget informed Nancy LaVallie that she would need to sign papers before a local (Swift Current) Justice of the Peace or Minister of the Gospel and to produce evidence of her legal marriage. See A.E. Forget to Nancy LaVallie, 18 April 1895, file 1239 pt. 7, vol. 3594, RG 10, LAC.

44. Rev. W. Nicolls to Assistant Commissioner of Indian Affairs, 1 April 1889, file 1564 pt. 4, vol. 3559, RG 10, LAC.

45. A. Forget to Rev. Nicolls, 4 April 1889, file 1564 pt. 4, vol. 3559, RG 10, LAC.

46. Report from the Duck Lake Agency, 4 August 1887, file 1239 pt. 8, vol. 3594, RG 10, LAC.

47. R.S. McKenzie to Indian Commissioner, 17 April 1893, file 1239 pt. 8, vol. 3594, RG 10, LAC.

48. Robert D. Watt, introduction to *Woodward's Catalogue 1898–1953: The Shopping Guide of the West* (Vancouver: J.J. Douglas, 1977), 66, 77, 96.

49. Grace Lee Nute, ed., *Documents Relating to Northwest Missions* (Saint Paul: Minnesota Historical Society, 1942), 389.

50. J. Hugonnard, 17 December 1904, file 74 pt. 3, vol. 3559, RG 10, LAC.

51. W. Murison to D. Laird, 11 February 1905, file 74 pt. 3, vol. 3559, RG 10, LAC.

52. J.A.J. McKenna to W. Murison, 25 February 1905, file 74 pt. 3, vol. 3559, RG 10, LAC.

53. Extract, letter by W.E. Jones, 24 January 1890, file 486-2-5, vol. 6816, RG 10, LAC.

54. Deputy Superintendent General of Indian Affairs to the Bishop of Qu'Appelle, 11 February 1895, file 486-2-5, vol. 6816, RG 10, LAC.

55. Deputy Superintendent General to W. E. Jones, 16 May 1895, file 486-2-5, vol. 6816, RG 10, LAC.

56. M. Millar to D. Laird, 18 July 1907, file 74 pt. 4, vol. 3559, RG 10, LAC.

57. M. Millar to D. Laird, 7 August 1907, file 74 pt. 4, vol. 3559, RG 10, LAC.

58. "N. J." to D. Laird, 11 December 1903, file 74 pt. 5, vol. 3559, RG 10, LAC.

59. D. Laird to Thomas Aspdin, 18 December 1903, file 74 pt. 5, vol. 3559, RG 10, LAC.

60. "J. J." to D. Laird, 28 December 1903, file 74 pt. 5, vol. 3559, RG 10, LAC.

61. E. McKenzie, "The case of J. J. and his wife N.," 6 October 1904, file 74 pt. 5, vol. 3559, RG 10, LAC.

62. Ibid.

63. T. Aspdin to D. Laird, 30 December 1903, file 74 pt. 5, vol. 3559, RG 10, LAC.

64. T. Aspdin to D. Laird, 13 January 1904, file 74 pt. 5, vol. 3559, RG 10, LAC.

65. Carry the Kettle and Crooked Arm to D. Laird, 8 January 1904, file 74 pt. 5, vol. 3559, RG 10, LAC.

66. T. Aspdin to D. Laird, 13 January 1904.

67. D. Laird to T. Aspdin, 2 January 1904, file 74 pt. 5, vol. 3559, RG 10, LAC.

68. D. Laird to "N. J.," 29 December 1903, file 74 pt. 5, vol. 3559, RG 10, LAC.

69. T. Aspdin to D. Laird, 21 May 1904, file 74 pt. 5, vol. 3559, RG 10, LAC.

70. Rev. I. J. Taylor, "Extracts from the Journal of the Rev. I. J. Taylor for October, November, and December 1891," p. 2, Saskatchewan Archives Board (SAB).

71. I. J. Taylor to the Bishop of Saskatchewan, 19 April 1892, SAB.

72. Taylor, "Extracts," p. 3.

73. S. R. Marlatt to D. Laird, 28 September 1906, file 74 pt. 30, vol. 3559, RG 10, LAC.

74. Arthur Hall to S. Marlatt, 20 August 1906, file 74 pt. 30, vol. 3559, RG 10, LAC.

75. Samuel Marsden to S. Marlatt, 20 August 1906, file 74 pt. 30, vol. 3559, RG 10, LAC.

76. Unnamed author to undisclosed recipient, 1 February 1912, file 64, 535, vol. 3832, RG 10, LAC.

77. Robert V. Sinclair, *The Rules and Practices Before the Parliament of Canada Upon Bills of Divorce* (Toronto: The Carswell Co., 1915), 36.

78. W. Sibbald to D. Laird, 12 December 1903, file 74, pt. 16, vol. 3559, RG 10, LAC.

79. D. Laird to W. Sibbald, 16 December 1903, file 74, pt. 16, vol. 3559, RG 10, LAC.

80. P. C. H. Primrose to D. Laird, 13 March 1903, file 74, pt. 20, vol. 3559, RG 10, LAC.

81. D. Laird to P. Primrose, 19 March 1903, file 74, pt. 20, vol. 3559, RG 10, LAC.

82. P. C. H. Primrose to the Commissioner, NWMP, 25 March 1903, file 411/03, vol. 256, series A-1, Royal Canadian Mounted Police (RG 18), LAC.

83. Rev. S. D. Chown to Frank Oliver, 6 October 1910, file 57,045-1, vol. 3816, RG 18, LAC.

84. D. Scott to S. Chown, 19 October 1910, file 57,045-1, vol. 3816, RG 18, LAC.

85. T. Albert Moore to J. M. [*sic*] McLean, 27 June 1912, file 57,045-1, vol. 3816, RG 18, LAC.

86. J. D. McLean to T. Moore, 3 July 1912, file 57,045-1, vol. 3816, RG 18, LAC.

87. See file 74, pt. 7, vol. 3559, RG 10, LAC.

88. Indian agent, Birtle (Manitoba), to the DIA Secretary, 7 September 1898, file 94, vol. 3881, RG 10, LAC.

89. W. Sibbald to D. Laird, 22 December 1900, file 74, pt. 12, vol. 3559, RG 10, LAC.

90. Frog Lake Community Club, *Land of Red and White, 1875–1975* (Heinsburg: s.n., 1977), 82.

91. Inspector J. Howe, "Report for the month ending 32 December 1891," 7 January 1892, file RCMP 1892, nos. 43–54, box 58, RG 18, LAC.

92. Esther Goldfrank, Goldfrank fieldnotes, p. 21, GA.

93. Ibid., p. 367.

94. Indian agent Crooked Lake to undisclosed recipient, 26 February 1897, file 94, vol. 3881, RG 10, LAC.

95. Laird to undisclosed recipient, 21 April 1906, file 74, pt. 3, vol. 3559, RG 10, LAC.

96. H. E. Sibbald to David Laird, 22 March 1904, file 74 pt. 16, vol. 3559, RG 10, LAC.

97. T. Cory to D. Laird, 7 August 1906, file 74, pt. 3, vol. 3559, RG 10, LAC.

98. T. Cory to D. Laird, 5 July 1907, file 74, pt. 3, vol. 3559, RG 10, LAC.

99. D. Laird to Indian agent, 21 April l906, file 74, pt. 3, vol. 3559, RG 10, LAC.

100. J. McKenna to George Mann, 5 October 1906, file 74, pt. 4, vol. 3559, RG 10, LAC.

101. Indian agent, Blood Reserve, to Indian agent, Browning, Montana, 23 November 1904, vol. 1722, RG 10, LAC.

102. Horton H. Miller to officer in charge, Piapot Reserve (Saskatchewan), 5 December 1910.

103. "JC," "Memorandum for the Deputy Minister of Justice," 15 May 1914, p. 4, file 1299–1914, vol. 2406, int. 163, RG 13, LAC.

104. John E. Crankshaw and Alexandre Chevalier, *Crankshaw's Criminal Code of Canada*, 5th ed. (Toronto: The Carswell Co., 1924), 374.

105. Transcript, *R. v. Kekanus*, file 94,189, vol. 3881, RG 10, LAC.

106. Ibid., 9–10.

107. Ibid., 12.

108. Ibid., 15.

109. Ibid., 17.

110. A. H. Maclean to A.W. Neill, 7 July 1906, file 94,189, vol. 3881, RG 10, LAC.

111. W. M. Halliday to A.W. Vowell, 7 August 1906, file 94,189, vol. 3881, RG 10, LAC.

112. W. Halliday to A. Vowell, 5 September 1906, file 94,189, vol. 3881, RG 10, LAC.

113. W. Halliday to A. Vowell, 7 August 1906.

114. DIA circular letter, 18 May 1906, file 94,189, vol. 3881, RG 10, LAC.

115. D. Laird to M. Millar, 23 July 1907, file 74, pt. 4, vol. 3559, RG 10, LAC.

116. Vowell to Pedley, 4 September 1906, file 94,189, vol. 3881, RG 10, LAC.

117. A.W. Neil to A.W. Vowell, 9 July 1906, file 94,189, vol. 3881, RG 10, LAC; Vowel to Pedley, 4 September 1906.

118. Halliday to McLean, (exact date obscured) 1907, file 486–2-5 pt 1, vol. 6816, RG 10, LAC.

119. A. McLean to A. Vowell, 19 September 1906, file 486–2-5 pt 1, vol. 6816, RG 10, LAC.

120. J. McKenna to the DIA Secretary, 5 October 1907, file 486–2-5 pt 1, vol. 6816, RG 10, LAC.

121. A. McLean to D. Laird, 9 August 1907, file 486–2-5, pt 1 vol. 6816, RG 10, LAC.

122. A. McKenna to M. Millar, 25 July 1907, file 74 pt. 4, vol. 3559, RG 10, LAC.

123. M. Millar to Indian Commissioner, 2 August 1907, file 74 pt. 4, vol. 3559, RG 10, LAC.

124. Memorandum to the Deputy Superintendent General, 24 February 1908, file 180, 636 pt. 1, vol. 3990, RG 10, LAC.

125. Ibid., pt. 5.

126. Ibid., pt. 6.

127. In 1916 in British Columbia, Indian agents were appointed through the province as registrars of births, marriages, and deaths among Indians. They were authorized to issue licenses for marriages and were also authorized to perform marriages, although they were to "guard against any such exercise of the power to perform marriages between Indians as might impinge upon the rights of clergymen as to the performance of marriages." The purpose was to "provide a ready means of marriage by civil contract for Indians who wish to be so married, and especially for those who, if not provided with such means, would resort to so-called marriage by tribal or Indian custom, or to concubinage." They were to keep a scrapbook in which all the forms were to be pasted. See H.E. Young, "form letter to Indian agents," 12 December 1916, file 64,535, vol. 3832, RG 10, LAC. In British Columbia an amendment to the 1897 Births, Deaths and Marriages Act was stated to apply to all races including Aboriginals, Chinese, and Japanese. The act was amended in 1899 to exclude Aboriginals from provincial registration. The act was amended again in 1916 to include the registration of Aboriginal people, with special forms for "Indian registrations" that were discontinued after 1956. Claire E. Gilbert (British

Columbia Provincial Archives), correspondence with author, 4 February 2004. Confusion continued, however, as agents worked with two sets of instructions regarding "Indian marriages," one from the province and one from the DIA. For this confusion see Chas. Perry to DIA Secretary, 12 December 1932, file 64,535, vol. 3832, RG 10, LAC. Perry refers to a then recent decision of a stipendiary magistrate that upheld the validity of marriage according to Aboriginal law.

128. Deputy Minister of Justice to Deputy Superintendent General of Indian Affairs, 32 May 1908, file 32345, vol. 3762, RG 10, LAC.

129. Joan Sangster, *Regulating Girls and Women: Sexuality, Family, and the Law in Ontario, 1920-1960* (Don Mills: Oxford University Press, 2001), 177.

130. J. McLean to undisclosed recipient, 5 August 1908, file 94,189, vol. 3881, RG 10, LAC.

131. David Laird to Edward Paupanakis, 5 October 1908, file 74 pt. 21, vol. 3559, RG 10, LAC.

132. R. N. Wilson to the DIA Secretary, 4 June 1909, folder 59, Blood Indian Agency Series, GA.

133. Frank Pedley to R. N. Wilson, 12 June 1909, folder 59, Blood Indian Agency Series, GA.

134. DIA Secretary to Thomas Cory, 22 November 1899, file 94,189, vol. 3881, RG 10, LAC.

135. Mary R. Bogart to DIA Secretary, 29 November 1909, file 57,045-1, vol. 3816, RG 10, LAC.

136. Emily Cummings to the DIA, 19 February 1910, file 57,045-1, vol. 3816, RG 10, LAC.

137. DIA Secretary to M. Bogart, 2 December 1909, file 57,045-1, vol. 3816, RG 10, LAC.

138. Pedley to the National Council of Women, 28 February 1910, file 57,045-1, vol. 3816, RG 10, LAC.

139. Mariana Valverde, *The Age of Light, Soap and Water: Moral Reform in English Canada, 1885-1925* (Toronto: McClelland and Stewart, 1991), 54-57.

140. *The News* (Toronto), 12 November 1910.

141. *The Globe* (Toronto), 12 November 1910.

142. "Action taken by the Moral and Social Reform Council of Canada," 23 September 1910, file 32345, vol. 3762, RG 10, LAC.

143. Assistant Deputy Superintendent General of Indian Affairs to the Deputy Minister of Justice, 6 October 1910, file 32345, vol. 3762, RG 10, LAC.

144. Oliver to Rev. Canon Tucker, 25 October 1910, file 32345, vol. 3762, RG 10, LAC.

145. Assistant Deputy and Secretary to W. M. Halliday, 17 February 1912, file 64,535, vol. 3832, RG 10, LAC.

146. "J.C.," "Memorandum."

147. Ibid., p. 1.

148. Memorandum, "Question as to what action, if any should be taken against the Indian 'T. M. F.,'" file 1299–1914, vol. 2406, int. 163, RG 13, LAC

149. Deputy Minister of Justice to Assistant Deputy and DIA Secretary, 20 May 1914, file 1299–1914, vol. 2406, int. 163, RG 13, LAC.

150. Antoinette Burton, *Gender, Sexuality and Colonial Modernities* (London and New York: Routledge, 1999), 1.

EIGHT *Conclusion*

1. *Western Standard Illustrated Weekly* (Calgary), 12 June 1913, n.p. (first article, editorial).

2. Ibid.

3. Ibid.

4. Quoted in W. L. Morton, *Manitoba: A History*, 2nd ed. (Toronto: University of Toronto Press, 1967), 91.

5. Ibid., n.p.

6. Catherine A. Cavanaugh, "'No Place For A Woman': Engendering Western Canadian Settlement," *Western Historical Quarterly* 28 (Winter 1997): 493–518.

7. Ibid., 505.

8. Ibid., 510.

9. Ibid., 509–10.

10. Ibid., 510.

11. Sharon Helen Venne, ed., *Indian Acts and Amendments 1868–1975: An Indexed Collection* (Saskatoon: University of Saskatchewan Native Law Centre, 1981), 25.

APPENDIX

1. Veronica Strong-Boag, *The New Day Recalled: Lives of Girls and Women in English Canada, 1919–1939* (Markham: Penguin Books, 1988), 95.

2. James G. Snell and Cynthia Comacchio Abeele, "Regulating Nuptiality: Restricting Access to Marriage in Early Twentieth-Century English-Speaking Canada," *Canadian Historical Review* 69, no. 4 (1988): 468.

3. Ibid., 470.

4. Ibid., 473.

5. Ibid., 477.

6. Lesley Erickson, "Constructed and Contested Truths: Aboriginal Suicide, Law and Colonialism in the Canadian West(s), 1823–1927," *Canadian Historical Review* 86, no. 4 (December 2005): 614.

7. M. Christianson to the DIA Secretary, 12 November 1941, file 486-2-8, pt. 1, vol. 6816, RG 10, LAC.

8. Freda Ahenakew and H.C. Wolfart, eds. and trans., *Kohkôminawak Otâcimowiniwâwa: Our Grandmothers' Lives as Told in Their Own Words* (Saskatoon: Fifth House Publishers, 1992), 79.

9. Duncan Campbell Scott, "Circular to Indian Agents," 2 January 1914, file 486-2-8, vol. 6816, RG 10, LAC. On one copy of this circular in this file a note to the deputy minister is written saying that "a couple of hundred copies have been obtained."

10. Thomas Dewhirst to the Minister of Indian Affairs, 17 August 1914, file 486–2-8, vol. 6816, RG 10, LAC.

11. A.S. Williams to D. Scott, 20 June 1917, file 486-2-8, vol. 6816, RG 10, LAC.

12. Letter, Charles C. Perry to the DIA Secretary, 20 October 1921, file 1921, 2203, vol. 263, RG 13, LAC.

13. Letter, E.L. Newcombe to D.C. Scott, 10 February 1921, file 1921, 156–175, vol. 255, RG 13, LAC.

14. Canada, *House of Commons Debates* (26 May 1921), vol. 4, p. 3907.

15. Letter, Rev. T. Ferrier to DIA Deputy Superintendent General, 25 January 1924, file 486-2-8, vol. 6816, RG 10, LAC.

16. Letter, DIA Deputy Superintendent General to Rev. T. Ferrier, 25 January 1924, file 486-2-8, vol. 6816, RG 10, LAC.

17. Letter, John Hawksley to J.D. McLean, 3 April 1925, file 486-2-8, vol. 6816, RG 10, LAC.

18. Telegram, J.D. McLean to J. Hawksley, 1 April 1925, file 486–2-8, vol. 6816, RG 10, LAC.

19. Department of Justice, "Opinion of the Department of Justice," ca. 1933, file 486–2-8, vol. 6816, RG 10, LAC.

20. Whether those defined as "Indians" are British subjects or not has been a subject of debate. In their submission to the Special Joint Committee of the Senate and the House of Commons appointed to examine and consider the Indian Act, Session 1946, the Grand Council, North American Indian Brotherhood, argued that as wards of the Crown, Indians were not British subjects. They did not have the powers and privileges of British subjects who, "in the ordinary accepted sense, are those born on British soil, or naturalized, who at the age of 21 are fully competent persons, competent to vote at Federal and Provincial elections, competent to vote on Referenda or Plebiscites; have a voice in Parliament and representation therein; may run for office in Federal and Provincial elections; are competent to manage their own affairs

so that they may buy or sell their real holdings from whom and to whomever they choose without permission of any Governmental body; are fully competent to sue and be sued before any of the Courts of this country, have absolute freedom of testation, etc., etc. But the Indian is in an entirely different category. He has none of the powers mentioned above." See Canada, *Special Joint Committee of the Senate and the House of Commons Appointed to Examine and Consider the Indian Act*, minutes of proceedings and evidence no. 21, Tuesday, 13 August 1946 (Ottawa: Edmond Cloutier, 1946), 837.

21. T.R.L. MacInnes to Frank Edwards, 23 November 1939, file 486-2-8, vol. 6816, RG 10, LAC.

22. DIA Secretary to S.L. Macdonald, Indian agent, Battleford, 3 January 1933, file 486-2-8, vol. 6816, RG 10, LAC.

23. C.P. Schmidt, quoting Dr. Alfred Montreuil, to the DIA Secretary, 15 January 1934, file 486-2-8, vol. 6816, RG 10, LAC.

24. W.E.J. Paul to the Registrar General, Saskatchewan Department of Public Health, 30 October 1941, file 486-2-8, vol. 6816, RG 10, LAC.

25. W. Paul to W. Christianson, 30 October 1941, file 486-2-8, pt. 1, vol. 6816, RG 10, LAC.

26. W. Paul to Registrar General, 30 October 1941.

27. Letters, F. Edwards to T. MacInnes, 6 November and 17 November 1939, file 486-2-8, pt. 1, vol. 6816, RG 10, LAC.

28. T. MacInnes to F. Edwards, 23 November 1939, file 486-2-8, pt. 1, vol. 6816, RG 10, LAC.

29. J.P.B. Ostrander to T. MacInnes, 17 April 1940, file 486-2-8, pt. 1, vol. 6816, RG 10, LAC.

30. F. Edwards to T. MacInnes, 31 July 1940, file 486-2-8, pt. 1, vol. 6816, RG 10, LAC.

31. Letters, T. MacInnes to F. Edwards, 8 August and 27 November 1940, file 486-2-8, pt. 1, vol. 6816, RG 10, LAC.

32. A.E. Caldwell to R.A. Hoey, 12 December 1939, file 44, box 5, H.W. McGill Papers, GA.

33. T. MacInnes to R. MacMillan, 20 August 1941, file 44, box 5, H.W. McGill Papers, GA.

34. W. Cory, memorandum prepared to T. MacInnes, 13 August 1941, file 44, box 5, H.W. McGill Papers, GA.

35. T. MacInnes to J. Ostrander, 23 December 1941, file 44, box 5, H.W. McGill Papers, GA.

36. Office of the Indian Agent, File Hills Agency, January 1938, file P-3, vol. 9139, RG 10, LAC.

37. Quoted in Douglas Sanders, "Indian Women: A Brief History of ther Roles and Rights," *McGill Law Journal* 21, no.4 (1975): 665.

38. Canada, *Special Joint Committee, Minutes of Proceedings and Evidence*, no. 3, Friday, 14 March 1947, p. 85.

39. Ibid., 157.

40. Ibid., 199.

41. Ibid., 202.

42. Sharon Helen Venne, *Indian Acts and Amendments, 1868–1975: An Indexed Collection* (Saskatoon: University of Saskatchewan Native Law Centre, 1981), 315.

Bibliography

ARCHIVAL SOURCES

Canadian Museum of Civilization (CMC)
    W. D. and R. S. Wallis Papers
Canadian Plains Research Center (CPRC)
    David G. Mandelbaum Field Notes
Glenbow Archives (GA)
    Blood Agency Correspondence
    Canadian Census Records
    Esther Goldfrank Papers
    Lucien and Jane Hanks Fonds
    H. W. McGill Papers
    R. N. Wilson Fonds
    W. M. Graham Papers
Hudson's Bay Company Archives (HBCA)
Library and Archives Canada (LAC)
    Lavington, Mrs. Thomas. "Reminiscences of Life on the Prairies, 1910–1914."
        Unpublished manuscript, 1954.
    Department of Indian Affairs, RG 10
    Department of Immigration, RG 76
    Department of the Interior, RG 15
    Department of Justice, RG 13
    Department of National Revenue, RG 16
    Coutts Letterbooks
    Royal Canadian Mounted Police, RG 18
    Privy Council Office, RG 2

Provincial Archives of Manitoba (PAM)
    Church Missionary Society Collection
Saskatchewan Archives Board (SAB)
    Taylor, Rev. I. J. "Extracts from the Journal of the Rev. I. J. Taylor for October, November, and December 1891."
    Homestead Files
University of Calgary Archives (UCA)
    Anglican Diocese of Calgary, Synod Office Records

NEWSPAPERS AND JOURNALS

The Calgary Herald
The Calgary Tribune
Canada Lancet
Canadian Churchman
Edmonton Bulletin
The Evening Capital (Saskatoon)
The Far West
The Gazette (Fort Macleod)
The Globe and Mail
The Imperial Colonist
The Leader (Regina)
Lethbridge Daily Herald
Lethbridge News
The Methodist Magazine and Review
The Missionary Review of the World
Montreal Herald and Daily Commercial Gazette
Moose Jaw Times
Nor'-West Farmer
The Presbyterian Record
The Rapid City Daily Journal
Saskatchewan Herald (Battleford)
Scientific Monthly
The Sower in the West and Church Monthly
Square Butte Tribune (Montana)
Toronto Daily Mail
Western Standard Illustrated Weekly
Winnipeg Free Press

JURISPRUDENCE

Connolly v. Woolrich and Johnson et al. (1867) University of Saskatchewan Library
   website. *http://library.usask.ca/native/cnlc/vol101/070.html*
   Accessed 12/13/2004
Regina v. Nan-E-Quis-A-Ka (1889). University of Saskatchewan Library website.
   http://library2.usask.ca/native/cnlc/vol02/368.html. Accessed 04/14/2003.
"Regina v. Labrie." *The Montreal Law Reports: Court of Queen's Bench.* Vol. 7 Montreal:
   Gazette Printing Co., 1891.
Re Sheran (1899). University of Saskatchewan Library website.
   http://library.usask.ca/native/cnlc/vol03/636.html. Accessed 10/21/2003.
Regina v. Bear's Shin Bone. University of Saskatchewan Library website.
   http://library.usask.ca/native/cnlc/vol03/313.html. Accessed 07/10/2001

GOVERNMENT PUBLICATIONS

Canada. *Debate in the Senate on the Bill Relating to Marriage with Deceased Wife's Sister.*
   Ottawa: A. and Geo. C. Holland, Senate Reporters, 1879.
Canada. Parliament. *House of Commons Debates.*
Canada. Parliament. *Senate Debates.*
Canada. *Report of the Royal Commission on Chinese Immigration: Report and Evidence.*
   Ottawa: Printed by Order of the Commission, 1885.
Canada. *Sessional Papers.*
Canada. *Special Joint Committee, Minutes of Proceedings and Evidence.* No. 3, Friday, 14
   March 1947.
Canada. *Special Joint Committee of the Senate and the House of Commons Appointed to
   Examine and Consider the Indian Act.* Ottawa: Edmond Cloutier, 1946.
"Customary Marriages." Indian and Northern Affairs Canada,
   http://ainc-inac.gc.ca/pr/pub/matr/cm_e.html, 16 June 2004.
An Ordinance Respecting Marriage, North-West Territories Ordinance. No. 9 of 1878.
   Canadian Inventory of Historic Microreproductions, no. 52120.

PUBLISHED PRIMARY SOURCES

Abbott, Frederick H. *The Administration of Indian Affairs in Canada.* Washington,
   D.C.: s.n., 1915.
Ahenakew, Freda, and H.C. Wolfart, eds. and trans. *Kôhkominawak Otâcimowiniwâwa:
   Our Grandmothers' Lives as Told in Their Own Words.* Saskatoon: Fifth House,
   1992.

Anglican Diocese of Calgary. *Diocese of Calgary: Report on Indian Missions, 1895–6.* Toronto: Oxford Press, 1896.

Anonymous. *How to Be Happy Though Being Married: Being a Handbook to Marriage by a Graduate in the University of Matrimony.* London: T. Fisher Unwin, 1896.

Anonymous. *The Ladies Book of Useful Information: Compiled From Many Sources.* London, ON.: s.n.,1896.

Anonymous. *Marriage and Home, or Proposal and Espousal: A Christian Treatise on the Most Sacred Relations to Mortals Known: Love, Marriage, Home etc.* Brantford, ON, Port Adelaide and Melbourne, Australia: Bradley, Garretson, 1888.

Anonymous. "A Quaker District." *Saskatchewan History* 16, no. 1 (Winter 1963): 36.

Austen, B. F. *Woman: Her Character, Culture and Calling.* Brantford, ON: Book and Bible House, 1890.

Baker, William M., ed. *Pioneer Policing in Southern Alberta: Deane of the Mounties, 1888–1914.* Calgary: Historical Society of Alberta, 1993.

Binnie-Clark, Georgina. *Wheat and Woman.* 1914. Reprint, Toronto: University of Toronto Press, 1979.

Blewett, Jean. "The Doukhobor Woman." In *Canada's West and Farther West,* edited by Frank Carrel, 223–24. Quebec: The Telegraph Printing Co., 1911. Previously published in *Collier's Weekly* 9, n.d.

Bradley, James H. *Lieut. James H. Bradley Manuscript.* Vol. 9. *Contributions to the Historical Society of Montana.* Boston: J. S. Canner and Co., 1966.

Brass, Eleanor. "Recollections and Reminiscences: The File Hills Ex-Pupil Colony." *Saskatchewan History* 6, no. 2 (1953): 67–70.

Brooks, Edward J. "The Edward J. Brooks Letters: Part I." *Saskatchewan History* 10, no. 3 (Autumn 1957): 109–10.

Carnegie, James, Earl of Southesk. *Saskatchewan and Rocky Mountains: A Diary and Narrative of Travel, Sport, and Adventure During a Journey Through the Hudson's Bay Company's Territories in 1859 and 1860.* Toronto: J. Campbell, 1875.

Cohen, Felix S. *Handbook of Federal Indian Law.* Washington: United States Government Printing Office, 1945.

Colenso, J.W. *Remarks on the Proper Treatment of Polygamy as Found Already Existing in Converts From Heathenism.* Pietermaritzburg: May and Davis, 1855.

Crankshaw, John E., and Alexandre Chevalier. *Crankshaw's Criminal Code of Canada.* 5th ed. Toronto: The Carswell Co., 1924.

Denig, Edwin Thompson. *The Assiniboine.* Edited by J. N. B. Hewitt. Regina: Canadian Plains Research Centre, 1998.

Durham, Mabel. *Canada's Welcome to Women.* London: Canadian Pacific Railway, n.d.

Forget, Henriette. "The Indian Women of the Western Provinces." In *Women of Canada: Their Life and Work.* Ottawa: National Council of Women of Canada, 1900.

Frederiksen, Ditlew M. *The Land Laws of Canada and the Land Experience of the United States*. s.l.:s.n, 1907. Peel Collection, microform, no. 1932.

Frog Lake Community Club. *Land of Red and White, 1875–1975*. Heinsburg: s.n., 1977.

Goldfrank, Esther S. *Changing Configurations in the Social Organization of a Blackfoot Tribe During the Reserve Period*, Monographs of the American Ethnological Society. Edited by A. Irving Hallowell. Seattle and London: University of Washington Press, 1944.

Grinnell, George Bird. *Blackfoot Lodge Tales: The Story of a Prairie People*. Lincoln and London: University of Nebraska Press, 1962.

Hawkes, John. *The Story of Saskatchewan and Its People*. Regina: S.J. Clarke Publishing Co., 1924.

Higginbotham, John D. *When the West Was Young: Historical Reminiscences of the Early Canadian West*. Toronto: The Ryerson Press, 1933.

Hines, John. *The Red Indians of the Plains: Thirty Years' Missionary Experience in the Saskatchewan*. Toronto: McClelland, Goodchild and Stewart, 1916.

Houghton, Rev. Ross C. *Women of the Orient: An Account of the Religious, Intellectual and Social Condition of Women in Japan, China, Indian, Egypt, Syria and Turkey*. Cincinnati: Hitchcock and Walden, 1877.

Jameson, Anna Brownell. *Winter Studies and Summer Rambles in Canada*. 1837. Reprint, Toronto: Thomas Nelson and Sons, 1943.

Jefferis, B.G., and J.L. Nichols. *The Household Guide or Domestic Cyclopedia*. Toronto: J.L. Nichols, 1897.

Johnson, E. Pauline. "A Red Girl's Reasoning." In *E. Pauline Johnson (Tekahionwake): Collected Poems and Selected Prose*. Edited by Carole Gerson and Veronica Strong-Boag, 188–202. Toronto: University of Toronto Press, 2002.

Jones, Peter. *History of the Ojibwa Indians*. London: Q.W. Bennett, 1861.

Mackie, John. *The Heart of the Prairie*. London: James Nisbet, 1899.

Maclean, John. *Canadian Savage Folk: The Native Tribes of Canada*. Toronto: William Briggs, 1896.

———. *The Warden of the Plains: And Other Stories of Life in the Canadian North-West*. Toronto: William Briggs: 1896.

Macoun, John. *Manitoba and the Great North-West*. Guelph: The World Publishing Co., 1882.

Maude, Aylmer. *A Peculiar People: The Doukhobors*. London: Grant Richards, 1904.

McClintock, Walter. *The Old North Trail: Life, Legends and Religion of the Blackfeet Indians*. 1910. Reprint, Lincoln and London: University of Nebraska Press, 1992.

McDougall, John. "The Red Men of Canada's West Yesterday and Today." In *The 100,000 Manufacturing, Building and Wholesale Book Editions of the Morning Albertan*, n.p. Calgary: The Albertan, 1914.

Meikle, Lyndel, ed. *Very Close to Trouble: The Johnny Grant Memoir*. Pullman:
   Washington State University Press, 1996.

Missions de la Congrégation des missionaries Oblats de Marie Immaculée. Paris:
   Typographie A. Hennuyer, 1897.

Muir Edwards, Henrietta. *Legal Status of Women of Alberta*. Edmonton: University of
   Alberta Extension, 1917.

Muir Edwards, Henrietta. *Legal Status of Women of Alberta*. Edmonton: Office of the
   Alberta Attorney-General, 1921.

Murphy, Emily. *Janey Canuck in the West*. 4th ed. Toronto: Cassell, 1910.

Murray, Alexander Hunter. *Journal of the Yukon, 1847–48*. Edited by L. J. Burpee.
   Ottawa: Government Printing Bureau, 1910.

Napheys, George H. *The Physical Life of Woman: Advice to the Maiden, Wife and Mother*.
   Toronto: Maclear and Co., 1871.

Nute, Grace Lee, ed. *Documents Relating to Northwest Missions*. Saint Paul: Minnesota
   Historical Society, 1942.

Paget, Amelia M. *People of the Plains*. 1909. Reprint, Regina: Canadian Plains
   Research Center, 2004.

*Picturesque Cardston and Environments: A Story of Colonization and Progress in Southern
   Alberta*. Cardston: N.W. Macleod, 1900.

Raney, W. E. "Bigamy and Divorces." *The Canadian Law Journal* 34 (January–
   December 1898): 546–53.

Reid, A. P. "The Mixed or 'Halfbreed' Races of North-Western Canada." *Journal of
   the Anthropological Institute of Great Britain and Ireland* 4 (1875): 45–52.

Roper, Edward. *By Track and Trail: A Journey Through Canada*. London: Whalen and
   Co., 1891.

Semmens, John. *The Field and the Work: Sketches of Missionary Work in the Far North*.
   Toronto: Methodist Mission Rooms, 1884.

Sinclair, Robert V. *Canadian Indians*. Ottawa: Thorburn and Abbott, n.d., ca. 1911.
———. *The Rules and Practice Before the Parliament of Canada Upon Bills of Divorce*.
   Toronto: Carswell, 1915.

Slattery, Brian, ed. *Canadian Native Law Cases*. Vol. 2. 1870–1890. Saskatoon:
   University of Saskatchewan Native Law Centre, 1981.

Spry, Irene, ed. "The 'Memories' of George William Sanderson, 1846–1936."
   Canadian Ethnic Studies 17, no. 2 (1985): 115–34.

Steele, S. B. *Forty Years in Canada: Reminiscences of the Great North-West*. Winnipeg:
   Russell Lang; London: Herbert Jenkins, 1915.

Stock, Eugene. *The History of the Church Missionary Society: Its Environment, its Men
   and its Work*. Vol. 2. London: Church Missionary Society, 1899.

Stocken, H.W. Gibbon. *Among the Blackfoot and Sarcee*. Calgary: Glenbow Alberta
   Institute, 1976.

Tanner, John. *A Narrative of the Captivity and Adventures of John Tanner During Thirty Years Residence Among the Indians in the Interior of North America*. Prepared for the press by Edwin James. 1830. Reprint, Minneapolis: Ross and Haines, 1956.

Tanner, Annie Clark. *A Mormon Mother*. Utah: University of Utah Library Tanner Trust Fund, 1983.

Tyrrell, J. B., ed. *David Thompson's Narrative of the Explorations in North America, 1784–1812*. Toronto: The Champlain Society, 1916.

Uhlenbeck, C. C. *A New Series of Blackfoot Texts From the Southern Peigan Blackfoot Reservation, Teton County, Montana*. Amsterdam: Johannes Muller, 1912.

Venne, Sharon Helen, ed. *Indian Acts and Amendments 1868–1975: An Indexed Collection*. Saskatoon: University of Saskatchewan Native Law Centre, 1981.

Watt, Robert D. "Introduction." *Woodward's Catalogue 1898–1953: The Shopping Guide of the West*. Vancouver: J. J. Douglas, 1977.

Woodsworth, James S. *Strangers Within Our Gates: Coming Canadians*. Toronto: F.C. Stephenson, Methodist Mission Rooms, 1909.

Yeigh, Frank. *Through the Heart of Canada*. Toronto: Henry Frowde, 1910.

SECONDARY SOURCES

Abu-Laban, Baha. *An Olive Branch on the Family Tree: The Arabs in Canada*. Toronto: McClelland and Stewart, 1980.

Allman, Jean, and Victoria Tashjian. *"I Will Not Eat Stone": A Women's History of Colonial Asante*. Westport: Greenwood Publishing Group, 2000.

Arima, Eugene Y. *Blackfeet and Palefaces: The Piikani and Rocky Mountain House*. Ottawa: The Golden Dog Press, 1995.

Backhouse, Constance. *Petticoats and Prejudice: Women and Law in Nineteenth-Century Canada*. Toronto: The Osgoode Society, 1991.

Bannerji, Himani. "Age of Consent and Hegemonic Social Reform." In *Gender and Imperialism*, edited by Claire Midgley, 21–44. Manchester and New York: Manchester University Press, 1998.

Barber, Marilyn. *Immigrant Domestic Servants in Canada*. Ottawa: Canadian Historical Association, 1991.

Barman, Jean. "Taming Aboriginal Sexuality: Gender, Power, and Race in British Columbia, 1850–1900." *B.C. Studies* 115/116 (Autumn/Winter 1997/98): 237–66.

Blackstock, Michael D. "Trust Us: A Case Study in Colonial Social Relations Based on Documents Prepared by the Aborigines Protection Society, 1836–1912." In *With Good Intentions: Euro-Canadian and Aboriginal Relations in Colonial Canada*, edited by Celia Haig-Brown and David A. Nock, 51–71. Vancouver: University of British Columbia Press, 2006.

Bland, Lucy. *Banishing the Beast: Feminism, Sex and Morality*. 1995. Reprint, London and New York: Tauris Parke Paperbacks, 2002.

Boag, Peter. "Sexuality, Gender, and Identity in Great Plains History and Myth." *Great Plains Quarterly* 18, no. 4 (Fall 1998): 327–40.

———. "Thinking Like Mount Rushmore: Sexuality and Gender in the Republican Landscape." In *Seeing Nature Through Gender*, edited by Virginia J. Scharff, 40–59. Kansas City: University of Kansas Press, 2003.

Bradbury, Bettina. "Colonial Comparisons: Rethinking Marriage, Civilization, and Nation in the Nineteenth-Century White Settler Societies." In *Rediscovering the British* World, edited by Philip Buckner and R. Douglas Francis, 135–58. Calgary: University of Calgary Press, 2005.

Bredbenner, Candice Lewis. *A Nationality of Her Own: Women, Marriage, and the Law of Citizenship*. Berkeley: University of California Press, 1998.

Brown, Jennifer S. H. "Partial Truths: A Closer Look at Fur Trade Marriage." In *From Rupert's Land to Canada*, edited by Theodore Binnema, Gerhard Ens, and R.C. McLeod, 59–80. Edmonton: The University of Alberta Press, 2002.

———. *Strangers in Blood: Fur Trade Company Families in Indian Country*. Vancouver: University of British Columbia Press, 1980.

Brownlie, Robin Jarvis. "Intimate Surveillance, Colonization and the Regulation of Aboriginal Women's Sexuality." In *Contact Zones: Aboriginal and Settler Women in Canada's Colonial Past*, edited by Katie Pickles and Myra Rutherdale, 160–78. Vancouver: UBC Press, 2005.

Burton, Antoinette. *Gender, Sexuality and Colonial Modernities*. London and New York: Routledge, 1999.

Byrne, M.B. Venini, *From the Buffalo to the Cross: A History of the Roman Catholic Diocese of Calgary*. Calgary: Calgary Archives Historical Publishers, 1973.

Cannon, Brian Q. "Mormonism in Montana." *Montana: The Magazine of Western History* 6, no. 1 (Spring 2006): 2–19.

Carter, David J. *Samuel Trivett: Missionary with the Blood Indians*. Calgary: Kyle Printing and Stationery, 1974.

Carter, Sarah. *Aboriginal People and Colonizers of Western Canada to 1900*. Toronto: University of Toronto Press, 1999.

———. "Britishness, 'Foreignness,' Women, and Land in Western Canada, 1890s to 1920s." In "Britishness and Whiteness: Locating Marginal White Identities in the Empire." Special issue, *Humanities Research* 13, no. 1 (2006): 43–60.

———. *Capturing Women: The Manipulation of Cultural Imagery in Canada's Prairie West*. Montreal: McGill-Queen's University Press, 1997.

———. "Categories and Terrains of Exclusion: Constructing the 'Indian Woman' in the Early Settlement Era in Western Canada." *Great Plains Quarterly* 13, no. 3 (Summer 1993): 147–61.

———. "Demonstrating Success: The File Hills Farm Colony." *Prairie Forum* 16, no. 2 (1991): 157–83.

———. *Lost Harvests: Prairie Indian Reserve Farmers and Government Policy.* Montreal: McGill-Queen's Press, 1990.

———. "'We Must Farm to Enable Us to Live': The Plains Cree and Agriculture to 1900." In *Native Peoples: The Canadian Experience*, 3rd ed., edited by R. Bruce Morrison and C. Roderick Wilson, 320–40. Don Mills: Oxford University Press, 2004.

Cavanaugh, Catherine. "The Limitations of the Pioneering Partnership: The Alberta Campaign for Homestead Dower, 1909–1925. " In *Making Western Canada: Essays on European Colonization and Settlement*, edited by Catherine Cavanaugh and Jeremy Mouat, 186–213. Toronto: Garamond Press, 1996.

———. "'No Place For A Woman': Engendering Western Canadian Settlement." *Western Historical Quarterly* 28 (Winter 1997): 493–518.

Champion, Brian. "Mormon Polygamy: Parliamentary Concerns, 1889–90." *Alberta History* 35, no. 1 (Spring 1987): 10–17.

Chanock, Martin. *Law, Custom and Social Order: The Colonial Experience in Malawi and Zambia.* Cambridge: Cambridge University Press, 1985.

Chapman, Terry L. "Women, Sex, and Marriage in Western Canada, 1890–1920," *Alberta History* 33 (Autumn 1985): 1–12.

Clancy-Smith, Julia. "Islam, Gender, and Identities in the Making of French Algeria, 1830–1962." In *Domesticating the Empire: Race, Gender, and Family Life in French and Dutch Colonialism*, edited by Julia Clancy-Smith and Frances Gouda, 154–74. Charlottesville and London: University Press of Virginia, 1998.

Comacchio, Cynthia R. *The Infinite Bonds of Family: Domesticity in Canada, 1850–1940.* Toronto: University of Toronto Press, 1999.

Comaroff, Jean, and John Comaroff. *Of Revelation and Revolution: Christianity, Colonialism and Consciousness in South Africa.* Vol. 1. Chicago and London: The University of Chicago Press, 1991.

Coontz, Stephanie. *Marriage, a History: From Obedience to Intimacy, or How Love Conquered Marriage.* New York: Viking, 2005.

Cooper, Barbara M. *Marriage in Maradi: Gender and Culture in a Hausa Society in Niger, 1900–1989.* Portsmouth, NH: Heinemann, 1997.

Cott, Nancy. *Public Vows: A History of Marriage and Nation.* Cambridge: Harvard University Press, 2000.

Danysk, Cecilia. "'A Bachelor's Paradise': Homesteaders, Hired Hands and the Construction of Masculinity, 1880–1930." In *Making Western Canada: Essays on European Colonization and Settlement*, edited by Catherine Cavanaugh and Jeremy Mouat, 154–85. Toronto: Garamond Press, 1996.

Davin, Anna. "Imperialism and Motherhood." In *Tensions of Empire: Colonial Cultures in a Bourgeois World*, edited by Frederick Cooper and Ann Laura Stoler, 87–151. Berkeley and Los Angeles: University of California Press, 1997.

Daynes, Kathryn M. *More Wives Than One: Transformation of the Mormon Marriage System, 1840–1910*. Urbana and Chicago: University of Illinois Press, 2001.

Delday, Eva. *Brooks Beautiful–Bountiful*. Calgary: D.W. Friesen and Sons, 1975.

DeMallie, Raymond J. "Kinship: The Foundation for Native American Society." In *Studying Native America: Problems and Prospects*, edited by Russell Thornton, 306–56. Madison: The University of Wisconsin Press, 1998.

Dempsey, Hugh. *Charcoal's World*. Saskatoon: Western Producer Prairie Books: 1978.

———. *Red Crow, Warrior Chief*. Saskatoon: Fifth House, 1995.

Devereux, Cicely. "'And Let Them Wash Me From This Clanging World': Hugh and Ion, the 'Last Best West,' and Purity Discourse in 1885." *Journal of Canadian Studies* 32, no. 2 (Summer 1997): 100–15.

Erickson, Dan. "Alberta Polygamists? The Canadian Climate and Response to the Introduction of Mormonism's 'Peculiar Institution.'" *Pacific Northwest Quarterly* 86, no. 4 (Fall 1995): 155–74.

Erickson, Lesley. "Constructed and Contested Truths: Aboriginal Suicide, Law and Colonialism in the Canadian West(s), 1823–1927." *Canadian Historical Review* 86, no. 4 (December 2005): 595–618.

Etherington, Norman. "Natal's Black Rape Scares of the 1870s." *Journal of Southern African Studies* 15, no. 1 (1988): 36–53.

Ewers, John. *The Blackfeet: Raiders on the Northwestern Plains*. Norman: University of Oklahoma Press, 1958.

Finlay, Henry. "Victorian Sexual Morality: A Case of Double Standards." *Australian Journal of Law and Society* 14 (1998/99): 43–64.

Foster, Henry H. "Indian and Common Law Marriages." *American Indian Law Review* 3 (1975): 83–102.

Freeman, Victoria. "Attitudes Toward 'Miscegenation' in Canada, the United States, New Zealand, and Australia, 1860–1914." *Native Studies Review* 16, no. 1 (2005): 41–69.

Gibson, Dwight L., and others. *All About the Law: Exploring the Canadian Legal System*. 4th ed. Toronto: Nelson Canada, 1996.

Godfrey, Donald G. "Zina Presendia Young Williams Card: Brigham's Daughter, Cardston's First Lady." *Journal of Mormon History* 23, no. 2 (1997): 107–27.

Gölz, Annalee. "Family Matters: The Canadian Family and the State in the Postwar Period," *Left History* 1, no. 2 (Fall 1993): 9–50.

Goodwill, Jean, and Norma Sluman. *John Tootoosis*. Ottawa: Golden Dog Press, 1982.

Gordon, Sarah Barringer. "'The Liberty of Self-Degradation': Polygamy, Woman Suffrage, and Consent in Nineteenth-Century America." *Journal of American History* 83, no. 3 (December 1996): 815–47.

Grant, John Webster. *Moon of Wintertime: Missionaries and the Indians of Canada.* Toronto: University of Toronto Press, 1984.

Grewal, Inderpal. *Home and Harem: Nation, Gender, Empire and the Cultures of Travel.* Durham and London: Duke University Press, 1996.

Hämäläinen, Pekka. "The Rise and Fall of Plains Indian Horse Cultures." *The Journal of American History* (December 2003): 833–62.

Handley, William R. *Marriage, Violence, and the Nation in the American Literary West.* Cambridge: Cambridge University Press, 2002.

Hanson, Jeffery R. Introduction to *Buffalo Bird Woman's Garden: Agriculture of the Hidatsa Indians,* by Gilbert L. Wilson. St. Paul: Minnesota Historical Society Press, 1987.

Harring, Sidney L. "Indian Law, Sovereignty and State Law." In *A Companion to American Indian History,* edited by Philip J. Deloria and Neal Salisbury, 441–59. Malden and Oxford: Blackwell Publishers Inc., 2002.

———. *White Man's Law: Native People in Nineteenth-Century Jurisprudence.* Toronto: Osgoode Society for Canadian Legal History and University of Toronto Press, 1998.

Hawkins, R. E. "Lillian Beynon Thomas, Woman's Suffrage, and the Return of Dower to Manitoba." *Manitoba Law Journal* 27, no. 1 (1999): 45–113.

Hawkins, Sean. "'The Woman in Question': Marriage and Identity in the Colonial Courts of Northern Ghana, 1907–1954." In *Women in African Colonial Histories,* edited by Jean Allman and others, 116–43. Bloomington and Indianapolis: Indiana University Press, 2002.

Henderson, James [Sákéj]. "First Nations' Legal Inheritances in Canada: The Mikmaq Model." *Manitoba Law Journal* 23 (1996): 1–31.

Hopwood, Victor G., ed. *David Thompson: Travels in Western North America, 1784–1812.* Toronto: Macmillan of Canada, 1971.

Howell, Colin D. "Arthur Alexander Reid." *Dictionary of Canadian Biography.* Vol. 14, 1911–1920. Toronto: University of Toronto Press, 1998.

Hungry Wolf, Adolf. *Pikunni Biographies.* The Blackfoot Papers. Vol. 4. Skookumchuck: The Good Medicine Cultural Foundation, 2006.

Hungry Wolf, Beverly. *The Ways of My Grandmothers.* New York: Quill, 1982.

Isichei, Elizabeth. "Does Christianity Empower Women? The Case of the Anaguta of Central Nigeria." In *Women and Missions: Past and Present,* edited by Fiona Bowie, and others, 209–26. Oxford: Berg Publishers, 1993.

Jeater, Diane. *Marriage, Perversion and Power: The Construction of Moral Discourse in Southern Rhodesia, 1894–1930.* Oxford: Clarendon Press, 1993.

Johnston, Alex, "Nicholas and Marcella Sheran: Lethbridge's First Citizens." *Alberta History* 31, no. 4 (Autumn 1983): 1–10.

Katz, Yosse, and John C. Lehr. *The Last Best West: Essays on the Historical Geography of the Canadian Prairies*. Jerusalem: The Magnes Press, The Hebrew University, 1999.

Kehoe, Alice. "The Plains: Blackfoot Persons." In *Women and Power in Native North America*, edited by Laura F. Klein and L.A. Ackerman, 113–25. Norman: University of Oklahoma Press, 1995.

Kerber, Linda K. *No Constitutional Right to Be Ladies: Women and the Obligations of Citizenship*. New York: Hill and Wang, 1998.

Klein, Alan. "The Political Economy of Gender: A 19th-Century Plains Indian Case Study." In *The Hidden Half: Studies of Plains Indian Woman*, edited by P. Albers and G. Medicine, 143–73. Lanham, MD: University Press of America, 1983.

Kline, Benjamin. *Genesis of Apartheid: British African Policy in the Colony of Natal, 1845–1893*. Lanham, MD: University Press of America, 1988.

Lang, Sabine. *Men as Women, Women as Men: Changing Gender in Native American Cultures*. Austin: University of Texas Press, 1998.

Lewis, Oscar. "Manly-Hearted Women among the Northern Piegan." *American Anthropologist* 43 (1941): 173–187.

Lindgren, H. Elaine. *Land in Her Own Name: Women as Homesteaders in North Dakota*. Norman and London: University of Oklahoma Press, 1996.

Litz, Joyce. *The Montana Frontier: One Woman's West*. Albuquerque: University of New Mexico Press, 2004.

MacDonald, Alex. *Practical Utopians: The Lives and Writings of Saskatchewan Cooperative Pioneers, Ed and Will Paynter*. Regina: Canadian Plains Research Center, 2004.

MacEwan, Grant. *Mighty Women: Stories of Western Canadian Pioneers*. 1975. Reprint, Vancouver: Douglas and McIntyre, 1995.

Macleod, R.C., and Heather Rollason. "'Restrain the Lawless Savages': Native Defendants in the Criminal Courts of the North West Territories, 1878–1885." *Journal of Historical Sociology* 10, no. 2 (June 1997): 157–83.

Mandelbaum, David G. *The Plains Cree: An Ethnographic, Historical and Comparative Study*. Regina: Canadian Plains Research Center, 1979.

Martens, Jeremy. "Polygamy, Sexual Danger, and the Creation of Vagrancy Legislation in Colonial Natal." *The Journal of Imperial and Commonwealth History* 31, no. 3 (September 2003): 25–45.

Mawani, Renisa. "In Between and Out of Place: Racial Hybridity, Liquor, and the Law in Late 19th- and Early 20th Century British Columbia." *Canadian Journal of Law and Society* 15, no. 2 (2000): 9–38.

McCue, Robert J. "Anthony Maitland Stenhouse, Bachelor 'Polygamist.'" *American History and Life* 23, no. 1 (1990): 108–25.

McDonald, Donna. *Lord Strathcona: A Biography of Donald Alexander Smith*. Toronto: Dundurn Press, 1996.

McDonald, Robert A. J. *Making Vancouver: Class, Status and Social Boundaries, 1863–1913*. Vancouver: University of British Columbia Press, 1996.

McGrath, Ann. "Consent, Marriage and Colonialism: Indigenous Australian Women and Colonizer Marriages." *Journal of Colonialism and Colonial History* 6, no. 3 (2005): 1–51.

McKay, Eva (Dakota Sioux, Dakota Tipi, Manitoba). *In the Words of Elders: Aboriginal Cultures in Transition*. Toronto: University of Toronto Press, 1999.

McLaren, John. "The Failed Experiments: The Demise of Doukhobor Systems of Communal Property Landholding in Saskatchewan and British Columbia, 1899–1925." In *Despotic Dominion: Property Rights in British Settler Colonies*, edited by John McLaren and others, 222–47. Vancouver: University of British Columbia Press, 2005.

Miller, J. R. *Shingwauk's Vision: A History of Native Residential Schools*. Toronto: University of Toronto Press, 1996.

Moore, John H. "The Developmental Cycle of Cheyenne Polygyny." *American Indian Quarterly* (Summer 1991): 311–28.

Morse, Bradford W. "Indian and Inuit Family Law and the Canadian Legal System." *American Indian Law Review* 8 (1980): 199–247.

Morton, W. L. *Manitoba: A History*. 2nd ed. Toronto: University of Toronto Press, 1967.

Muhn, James. "Women and the Homestead Act: Land Department Administration of a Legal Imbroglio, 1863–1934." *Western Legal History* 7, no. 2 (Summer/Fall 1994): 283–307.

Nichols, Jeffrey. *Prostitution, Polygamy, and Power: Salt Lake City, 1847–1918*. Urbana and Chicago: University of Illinois Press, 2002.

Nicola, Patricia Hackett. "Rebecca Lena Graham's Fight For Her Inheritance." *Pacific Northwest Quarterly* 97, no. 3 (Summer 2006): 139–47.

Nietzsche, Friedrich. *The Genealogy of Morals*. Mineola, N.Y.: Dover Publications, 2003.

Nugent, David. "Property Relations, Production Relations, and Inequality: Anthropology, Political Economy and the Blackfeet." *American Anthropologist* 20, no. 2 (May 1993): 336–62.

O'Hanlon, Rosalind. "Gender in the British Empire." In *The Oxford History of the British Empire*. Vol. IV, *The Twentieth Century*, edited by Judith M. Brown and William. R. Louis, 379–97. Oxford and New York: Oxford University Press, 1999.

Osburn, Katherine M. B. *Southern Ute Women: Autonomy and Assimilation on the Reservation, 1887–1934*. Albuquerque: University of New Mexico Press, 1998.

Paul, Mandy, and Robert Foster. "Married to the Land: Land Grants to Aboriginal Women in South Australia, 1848–1911." *Australian Historical Studies* 34, no. 121 (April 2003): 48–68.

Perry, Adele. "Metropolitan Knowledge, Colonial Practice, and Indigenous Womanhood: Missions in Nineteenth-Century British Columbia." In *Contact Zones: Aboriginal and Settler Women in Canada's Colonial Past*, edited by Katie Pickles and Myra Rutherdale, 109–30. Vancouver: University of British Columbia Press, 2005.

———. *On the Edge of Empire: Gender, Race, and the Making of British Columbia, 1849–1871*. Toronto: University of Toronto Press, 2001.

Petrik, Paula. "If She Be Content: The Development of Montana Divorce Law, 1865–1907." *The Western Historical Quarterly* 18, no. 3 (July 1987): 261–91.

Pickles, Katie. "Empire Settlement and Single British Women as New Zealand Domestic Servants During the 1920s." *New Zealand Journal of History* 35, no. 1 (2001): 22–44.

Posel, Deborah. "State, Power and Gender: Conflict over the Registration of African Customary Marriage in South Africa, ca. 1910–1970." *Journal of Historical Sociology* 8, no. 3 (September 1995): 223–56.

Prentice, Alison, and others. *Canadian Women: A History*. Toronto: Harcourt, Brace, Jovanovich, 1988.

Rasporich, Anthony. "Utopia, Sect, and Millennium in Western Canada, 1870–1940," *Prairie Forum* 12, no. 2 (Fall 1987): 217–43.

Rees, Ronald. *New and Naked Land: Making the Prairies Home*. Saskatoon: Western Producer Prairie Books, 1988.

Rural Municipality of Rosser Centennial History Book Committee. *The First Hundred Years, 1893–1993: Rural Municipality of Rosser*. Winnipeg: Herff Jones Canada Inc., 1993.

Sanders, Douglas. "Indian Women: A Brief History of Their Roles and Rights." *McGill Law Journal* 21, no. 4 (1975): 656–72.

Sangster, Joan. *Regulating Girls and Women: Sexuality, Family, and the Law in Ontario, 1920–1960*. Don Mills: Oxford University Press, 2001.

Satzewich, Vic, and Linda Mahood. "Indian Affairs and Band Governance: Deposing Indian Chiefs in Western Canada, 1896–1911." *Canadian Ethnic Studies* 26, no 1 (1994): 40–58.

Schwartz, Mary Ann, and B. M. Scott, eds. *Marriage and Families: Diversity and Change*. 3rd ed. Toronto: Prentice-Hall Canada Ltd., 2000.

Sinha, Mrinalini. "Gender and Imperialism: Colonial Policy and the Ideology of Moral Imperialism in Late Nineteenth-Century Bengal." In *Changing*

Men: New Directions in Research on Men and Masculinity, edited by Michael S. Kimmel, 217–31. Newbury Park: Sage Publications, 1987.

Snell, James G. "The 'White Life' For Two: The Defense of Marriage and Sexual Morality in Canada, 1890–1914." In *Canadian Family History: Selected Readings*, edited by Bettina Bradbury, 381–400. Toronto: Copp Clark Pitman, 1992.

Snell, James G., and Cynthia Comacchio Abeele. "Regulating Nuptiality: Restricting Access to Marriage in Early Twentieth-Century English-Speaking Canada." *Canadian Historical Review* 69, no. 4 (1988): 466–89.

Stoler, Ann Laura. "Sexual Affronts and Racial Frontiers: European Identities and the Cultural Politics of Exclusion in Colonial Southeast Asia." In *Tensions of Empire: Colonial Cultures in a Bourgeois World*, edited by Frederick Cooper and Ann Laura Stoler, 198–237. Berkley and Los Angeles: University of California Press, 1997.

———. "Cultivating Bourgeois Bodies and Racial Selves." In *Cultures of Empire: Colonizers in Britain and the Empire in the Nineteenth and Twentieth Centuries*, edited by Catherine Hall, 87–119. New York: Routledge, 2000

———. "Tense and Tender Ties: The Politics of North American History and (Post) Colonial Studies." *The Journal of American History* 88, no. 3 (December 2001): 829–65.

Strong-Boag, Veronica. *The New Day Recalled: Lives of Girls and Women in English Canada, 1919–1939*. Markham: Penguin Books, 1988.

Stout, C. H. *From Frontier Days in Leduc and District: Sixty-Five Years of Progress, 1891—1956*. Leduc: Representative Publishers, 1956.

Swyripa, Frances. *Wedded to the Cause: Ukrainian-Canadian Women and Ethnic Identity, 1891–1991*. Toronto: University of Toronto Press, 1993.

Tarasoff, Koozma J. *Traditional Doukhobor Folkways: An Ethnographic and Biographic Record of Prescribed Behaviour*. Ottawa: National Museum of Canada, Canadian Centre for Folk Culture Studies, Paper No. 20, 1977.

Thompson, E. P. *Customs in Common: Studies in Traditional Popular Culture*. New York: The New Press, 1993.

Utley, Robert M. *The Indian Frontier of the American West, 1846–1890*. Albuquerque: University of New Mexico Press, 1984.

Valverde, Mariana. *The Age of Light, Soap and Water: Moral Reform in English Canada, 1885–1925*. Toronto: McClelland and Stewart, 1991.

Van Kirk, Sylvia. "From 'Marrying-In' to 'Marrying-Out': Changing Patterns of Aboriginal/non-Aboriginal Marriage in Colonial Canada." In *Rethinking Canada: The Promise of Women's History*, 5th ed., edited by Mona Gleason and Adele Perry, 115–23. Don Mills: Oxford University Press, 2006.

Van Kirk, Sylvia. *"Many Tender Ties": Women and Fur Trade Society, 1670–1870*. Winnipeg: Watson and Dwyer Press, 1980.

Walkowitz, Judith. *City of Dreadful Delights: Narratives of Sexual Danger in Late-Victorian London*. Chicago: The University of Chicago Press, 1992.

White, Richard. *"Its Your Misfortune and None of My Own:" A New History of the American West*. Norman: University of Oklahoma Press, 1991.

Wilkins, David E. *American Indian Sovereignty and the United States Supreme Court*. Austin: University of Texas Press, 1997.

Wilson, James Q. *The Marriage Problem: How Our Culture Has Weakened Families*. New York: HarperCollins, 2002.

Wilson, Kathleen. "Empire, Gender and Modernity in the Eighteenth Century." In *Gender and Empire*. Ed. Philippa Levine, 14–45. Oxford: Oxford University Press, 2004.

Wissler, Clark, and D.C. Duvall, *Mythology of the Blackfoot Indians*. Lincoln and London: University of Nebraska Press, 1995.

Woodcock, George, and Ivan Avakumovic. *The Doukhobors*. Ottawa: McClelland and Stewart, Carleton Library no. 108, 1977.

Zlotkin, Norman. "Judicial Recognition of Aboriginal Customary Law in Canada: Selected Marriage and Adoption Cases." *Canadian Native Law Reporter* 4 (1984): 1–17.

UNPUBLISHED PAPERS, THESES, AND DISSERTATIONS

Dick, Lyle. "Male Homosexuality in Saskatchewan's Settlement Era: The 1895 Case of Regina's 'Oscar Wilde.'" Paper presented to the eighty-fifth meeting of the Canadian Historical Association, York University, 30 May 2006.

Goulet, Keith. "The Cumberland Cree Nehinuw Concept of Land." Paper presented at Indigenous Knowledge Systems: International Symposium, University of Saskatchewan, 10–13 May 2004.

Hicken, John R. "Events Leading to the Settlement of the Communities of Cardston, Magrath, Stirling and Raymond, Alberta." Master's thesis, Utah State University, 1968.

Kidd, Kenneth E. "Blackfoot Ethnography: Being a Synthesis of the Data of Ethnological Science with the Information Concerning the Blackfoot Indians Contained in the Writing of Explorers, Travellers and Traders From the Time of First Contact to the Year 1821." Master's thesis, University of Toronto, 1937.

Pascoe, Peggy. "The Architecture of White Supremacy in the Multiracial West: The Case of Miscegenation Law." Paper presented at "Dancing on the Rim: Nations, Borderlands and Identities," 2005 Pacific Coast Branch of the American Historical Association, Corvallis, Oregon, 6 August 2005.

Pulsipher, John David. "The Americanization of Monogamy: Mormons, Native Americans, and the Nineteenth-Century Perception that Polygamy was a Threat to Democracy." PhD diss., University of Minnesota, 1999.

Smith, Keith. "'An Indian is almost as Free as Any Other Person': Exclusionary Liberalism, Surveillance and Indigenous Resistance in Southern Alberta and the British Columbia Interior, 1877–1927." Ph.D. diss, University of Calgary, 2007.

Index

Numbers in italics indicate photographs.
Where provinces or states have been
added to locations, the current ones are
given.

Abbott, Frederick H., *The Administration*
    of Indian Affairs in Canada,
    232–34, 241, 267
Abeele, Cynthia Comacchio, 92, 287
Abikoki, Jim and family, *218*
Aboriginal marriage, 31–37, 174–75.
    See also marriage, by consent;
    kinship in Aboriginal society;
    polygamy
    Aboriginal words related to,
        264–66
    age at, 107, 130, 214, 224–27
    alignment of legality of with
        Christianity, 187
    arranged, 55, 107, 124, 235–42,
        250
    attitude of missionaries toward,
        35–36, 130–32, 156–57,
        238–39, 246–54, 257–58, 290
    comparison of United States and
        Canada, 142

    debate on legal validity of, 104,
        134–43, 160–65, 174–5,
        188–90, 202–3, 213, 225–27,
        247, 266–67
    definitions related to, 10, 104–7,
        126–27
    effect on women's Indian status,
        245
    family involvement in, 107, 119
    fidelity in, 110–11, *111*, 114
    in fur trade society, 6, 21–29,
        35–39, 128, 134–39, 169–70
    government recognition of, 11–16,
        149, 155–68, 171–74, 201–2,
        214, 232–42, 248–53, 256–57,
        260–61, 268–69, 284–85,
        292–95 (*See also* Department of
        Indian Affairs; Indian agents)
    legal decisions concerning, 11,
        134–42
    Métis, 5, 8, 35–39, 68–71, 151–52,
        202–3, 227, 245
    oral traditions concerning, 112–13
    persistence of, 164–66, 216–23,
        228, 259–60
    representations of, 9–11, 27,
        127–30

as a social obligation, 117–18
Aboriginal people, 9, 14, 16, 216, 268.
    See also Aboriginal women
    attitude of missionaries toward,
        130–32, 150–61, 180–81,
        195–200, 223–24 (*See also*
        polygamy; attitude of
        missionaries toward)
    flexibility of gendered roles,
        122–25
    intermarriage as central to
        relations with Euro-Canadians,
        31
    Latter Day Saints (Mormon)
        prophesies concerning, 205
    nationhood, 136, 183
    representations of, 11–12, 20–21,
        70, 123, 126, 134–5, 159
    representations of society, 30–31,
        108, 113, 120, 180–82, 234–35
Aboriginal women
    ability to testify against husbands
        in court, 212–13, 219, 222
    as chiefs, 124
    determination of Indian status of,
        12–13, 168–70, 245–46, 294–95
    employment of, 118–19, 132–34,
        180, 197, 198
    flexibility of gendered roles,
        123–25
    legislation concerning First
        Nations, 143, 163, 168–70,
        189, 243, 248, 285–86, 294
        (*See also* Criminal Code; Indian
        Act; Ordinance Respecting
        Marriage)
    legislation concerning Métis, 169,
        201–2 (*See also* scrip, Métis)
    relations with Euro-Canadian
        men, 38, 70–73, 87, 99, 149–60,
        150, 153–57, 180–82, 289

    representations of, 11–12, 15–16,
        53, 68, 127–29, 133, 149–55,
        260–61, 282
    restrictions on freedom of
        movement of, 152–53, 180–82
    sexuality of, 10–11, 16
    social roles and status of, 111,
        115–17, 128–29, 133, 253–54
    unmarried, 118, 123–24
    as widows, 14, 115, 117–19, 189,
        234, 238, 243, 260
Aborigines Protection Society (APS)
    (England), 11, 149, 156, 161
abuse (spousal), 133–34, 156, 181,
    250–52
    Aboriginal beliefs concerning, 106,
        111–13
    in plural marriages, 49
Acres, Lizzie, *236*
adoption, 37, 76
adultery, 258
    in Aboriginal society, 110–11, 114,
        121
    attitude of church toward, 97
    DIA efforts to combat (*See* bigamy,
        DIA efforts to combat)
    as grounds for divorce, 25–26
    legal decisions concerning, 183,
        217
advertisements, *81*, 82, 88
Afghanistan, 11
African-Americans, 37
African-Canadians, 39
Africans, Africa, 27, 40, 175, 195,
    203–04. *See also Bethell v.
    Hildyard*
    colonial intervention in marriage
        laws, 176–80
    missionaries, 199

age of consent, 224–25. *See also*
Aboriginal marriage, age at;
marriage, age at
agriculture, 39, 83. *See also* farm
instructors; homesteading
Aboriginal people's involvement
in, 111, 152, 206
family farms, 6, 74–75, 78
gendering of, 283
women's involvement in, 39–40,
52
Alberta Star, 89
alcohol, alcoholism, 39, 49, 77, 78
Alert Bay, BC, 262
alimony, 71
alternative marriages, 38–40, 68
American Horse, 211–12
Ancient Pipe, 109
Anglicans, Anglican Church, 26,
247–48. *See also* Bourne, H.T.;
Canadian Churchman; Church
Missionary Society; Colenso,
J.W.; Hines, John; Stocken,
Canon H.W. Gibbon; Taylor,
Rev. I. J.; Tim, J.W.; Trivett,
Samuel
debate over polygamy, 194–98
first marriages of Aboriginal
people, 165
organizations, 149, 156, 201, 204,
272
relations with other churches,
253–54
Anglo-Saxons, 65
Anishinabe, 128. *See also* Ojibway
annuities, 123
commutation of, 246, 276
deserted wives' entitlement to,
234
eligibility for, 169–71, 173,
200–201, 204, 239, 245, 266
redirection of, 243, 260
withholding of, 221, 222–23
annulment of marriages, 66–67,
95–96, 247, 257
anthropology, 10, 28, 68–70, 132
Anti-Polygamy Standard, 49
apartheid, 176, 177
Apiteheiskouis (Chatelaine), 202
APS. *See* Aborigines Protection Society
Arcand, Abraham, 203
Arcand, Julia and Angelique, 202
Asians, 27, 53–54, 84, 273
Asokoa (fictional character), 130
Aspdin, Thomas, 250–53
Assiniboia district, 38, 247
Assiniboine (Nakoda), 119, 249–50
Athabasca district, 121
Australia, 70, 185–86
Awatoyakew (Mary Brown), 140–42

bachelor balls, 81–82
bachelor tax, 83
Backhouse, Constance, 22, 24
Bacon, N'Pastchuk, 202
banns, 67–68, 172
baptism, 138, 195–98, 219–20, 253
Barman, Jean, 180
Battleford (SK), 51, 73, 292. *See also*
Saskatchewan Herald
Baussard, Jeanne Josephine Ida, 95–96
beads, 122
Bear, Glecia, 171, 288
Bear Chief, Chief, 107
Beardy, Christy Bell, 202–3
Bear's Shin Bone, 13–14, 86, 222–23
Beaulieu, François, 121
Begg, Magnus, 214–17, 237
Begin, J.V., 207
Bennett, R.B., 90
Benton River Press, 21

Bethell v. Hildyard (S. Africa), 186–88, 226, 249, 275
betrothal, 107, 201, 213–16
Bible, 41
bigamy, 256–57. *See also* polygamy
    definition of, 16, 52, 85, 209, 262–67, 271–72, 274–76
    DIA efforts to combat, 15, 92, 185, 235, 243, 254–55, 290–91
    as grounds for divorce, 269–70
    legal decisions concerning, 15–16, 91, 96–97, 137
    legislation concerning, 8–9
Big Swan, 111
Big Wolf (daughter of), 109
Binnie-Clark, Georgina, 39, 78–79
bison. *See* buffalo
Blackfeet, MT, 205, 261
Blackfoot, 87, 105–9, 111, 159, 199, 208–9, 224. *See also* Elk-Hollering-in-the-Water; Kainai (Bloods); Middle Woman No Coat; Piikani (Peigan); Siksika
    first Christian marriage, 165
    lack of word for "polygamy," 115
    marriages, 109, 113–15
    population, 132
    representations of society, 108, 120, 124
    response to Latter Day Saints (Mormon) missionaries, 205
Blake, Edward, 44
blankets, 272
Bloods. *See* Kainai
Boag, Peter, 74
boarding houses, 38, 39
Board of Indian Commissioners (U.S.), 232
Bohen, Sister (nun), 240
Book of Mormon, 48, 49, 205
Borden, Robert L., 77

Borden (SK), 54
Borne, Henry. *See* Dutch Henry
Bourne, Rev. H.T., 149, 153, 156, 214
Bowell, Sir Mackenzie, 160
Boyer River Band (AB), 295
Bradbury, Bettina, 5–6
Brass, Eleanor, 240–41
Breland, Marie Ann, 37
bride purchase, 27. *See also* gifts
    English custom, 65–67
    representations of, 149, 154, 157, 248
bridewealth, 176
British Columbia, 45, 72, 180–82, 289
    legal decisions, 15–16
    marriage legislation, 54, 90, 174
British Empire. *See also* Africans, Africa; East Indies; India
    colonial policies on Indigenous marriage, 174–77
    colonial policies on polygamy, 13, 195–97, 227
    principle of indirect rule, 175
    status and rights of subjects, 24, 99, 276, 291
British North America Act, 290
Broken Head Reserve (MB), 173
Brooks (AB), 80
Brooks, Edward J., 123
broomstick marriage, 22, 67
Brown, Jennifer S. H., 31, 137–38
Brown, Mary. *See* Awatoyakew
Browning, MT, 261
Brunette, Lottie, 92
Budge, William, 128
buffalo, 132–33
Buffalo Bill. *See* Cody, Buffalo Bill
Buffalo Bird Woman. *See* Maxidiwiac
Burbridge, George W., 156–57, 159, 161
Burgess, A.M., 84

Burton, Antoinette, 277
Bush, George W., 2
Byfield, Ted, 2, 3

Caldwell, A. E., 293
Calgary (AB), 73, 79, 95, 280–81
Calgary Herald, 57, 59, 87
Calgary Sunday Sun, 2
Calgary Women's Press Club, 280
Callendar, Trooper, 40–41
Cameron, Malcolm, 150, 155
Canada, 30
    colonization of Western Canada,
        4–6, 8, 40, 59–60
    government of, 28, 155, 261 (*See
        also* Department of Indian
        Affairs; legislation)
    House of Commons, 87, 93, 94
    role of marriage in nation
        building, 2–9, 14, 16–17,
        20–22, 28–31, 44–45, 56–60,
        74–75, 152, 175, 280–86
    same-sex marriage debate in, 2
    three legal traditions of, 10
Canada Gazette, 25
Canada Lancet, 84
Canadian Churchman, 27, 29, 56, 57
Canadian Pacific Railway (CPR), 38,
    51–52, 82
Card, Charles Ora, 42–43, 48, 84, 205
Card, Zina Young, 42, 46–49, 89
Cardston (AB), 45, 48, 84–85, 87–88,
    89, 205, 293. *See also* Card,
    Charles Ora
Cardston Record, 88
Carrot, The, 120
Carry the Kettle, Chief, 251
Catholics, Catholicism. *See also*
    Grandin, Bishop Vital;
    Hugonnard, Fr. Joseph; Riou,
    Fr. J.

    attitude toward divorce and
        remarriage, 97, 159, 246
    inter-faith marriages of, 92, 95–96
    marriages of Aboriginal people,
        165, 219
    relations with other churches, 248,
        253–54
Cavanaugh, Catherine, 40, 282, 283
censuses and enumerations
    1891 census, 38
    Aboriginal population, 121–22,
        129, 199–200, 207
Charcoal, 217–18
Charnock, Martin, 178
chastity, 111, 151
Chatelaine, Jacob, Marie, and Pierre,
    202
Chesson, F.W., 156
Cheyenne, 121
childbearing, 134
childlessness. *See* infertility
child marriages, 14, 53, 91–92, 226,
    259–60. *See also* marriage, age
    at
children, 11, 15, 197–98, 224. *See also*
    illegitimacy
    care of, 40, 51–52, 71
    consequences of divorce on, 26,
        112, 250, 294–95
    eligibility for rations and
        annuities, 223
    legal rights of, 199–200
    Métis, 201–2
    paternity of, 176
    in polygamous families, 42, 83–84,
        119
    separation from parents, 15, 260
        (*See also* schools)
    support of, 171, 254, 264, 270
    value of in Blackfoot society,
        109–10

Chisholm, Mrs., 57

Chown, Rev. Samuel D., 257

Christian conjugality. *See* marriage, ideal type

Christians, Christianity (mainline), 4, 27, 31, 91–92, 149. *See also* Anglicans, Anglican Church; Catholics, Catholicism; Congregationalists, Congregationalism; Methodists, Methodism; United Church of Canada

in Africa, 178–79

attitude toward cohabitation, 38, 71–72, 154–55

attitude toward polygamy, 13, 130, 194, 198–99, 204–5, 227, 246–48

clergy role in marriage ceremonies, 35–37, 67–68, 172

conflict over government policy, 246–48

conversion to (*See* baptism)

debate on divorce, 257–58

efforts to combat Aboriginal marriage, 165, 180, 238–39, 251–52, 272–74

inter-church relations, 248, 250, 253–54

missionary work among Ukrainians, 53

model of marriage, 22, 143–44 (*See also* monogamy, lifelong)

Church Missionary Society (CMS), 149, 156, 195, 198. *See also* Anglicans, Anglican Church

Church of England. *See* Anglicans, Anglican Church

citizenship, 24, 52, 96. *See also* British Empire; enfranchisement

clans (Aboriginal), 110

Clink, D. L., 201

CMS. *See* Church Missionary Society

Cochrane, Senator Matthew H., 48

Cocking, Matthew (daughters of), 32

Cody, Buffalo Bill, 212

cohabitation, 86, 154–55, 171, 256, 273 (*See also* Aboriginal marriage)

definition of, 104, 266, 274–75

interracial, 38, 71–72, 184

co-husbands (*nita-yim*), 114

Colenso, Bishop John William, 195–96

Collier's Weekly, 51

colonialism, 30–31, 64, 132, 174–76, 196, 224. *See also* British Empire

Colonist, The (Winnipeg), 55

Comacchio, Cynthia. *See* Abeele, Cynthia Comacchio

Comaroff, Jean and John, 178

common law, 22, 24, 136–40, 275

communal and co-operative living, 50, 52, 55–56. *See also* Hutterites

concubinage. *See* cohabitation

Congregationalists, Congregational Church, 272

Connolly, Suzanne, 31

Connolly, William, 31, 134–38

Connolly v. Woolrich and Johnson et al., 11, 134–38, 186–88, 275–76

consent divorce. *See* divorce by consent

consent marriage. *See* Aboriginal marriage; marriage, by consent

Conservative Party. *See* Macdonald, John A.

Conybeare, C. F., 220, 222

Cook, W. H., 32

Cooke, Hazel, 94

Cory, Thomas, 260–61, 272

Cory, W. (DIA solicitor), 293

Costigan, J. R., 141, 219

cost of living, 246

Cotler, Irwin, 10

Cott, Nancy, 3, 28, 67, 90

country marriages. *See* marriage, by consent

Court (SK), 98

Court of Indian Offences (U.S.), 203, 211

courtship, 73, 82. *See also* spouses, selection of

co-wives, 119, 198. *See also* polygamy relations between, 115, 120–22, 133–34

representations of of, 131

Crane Woman, 111

Crankshaw's Criminal Code of Canada, 96–97

Cranworth, Lord (Robert Monsey Rolfe), 25–26

Cree, Mable, 216

Cree, Plains Cree, 165. *See also* Bear, Glecia; Brass Eleanor; Fine Day; Poundmaker; Star Blanket, Chief; Suzanne "Pas-de-Nom"

marriage among, 113–115, 268–69

polygamy among, 122, 197–98

and word for "family," 127

and word for "polygamy," 115

crime, 159–60, 289

arson, 149

horse killing, 120

murder, 29, 128, 217–19, 290

treason, 46

Criminal Code of Canada, 16, 289

treatment of polygamy in, 84–86, 209–11, 222, 224, 227, 276

treatment of spousal desertion in, 290

Crooked Arm, Headman, 251

Crooked Lake (SK), 208, 248, 260, 268

Cross, Alexander, 104, 135, 138–39

cross-dressing, 31, 123–25

curfews, 68

custom of the country (*mariage à la façon du pays*). *See* Aboriginal marriage; marriage, by consent

Dakota nation, 113, 119–20. *See also* McKay, Eva

dancing, 82, 87

Darwinism. *See* natural selection

Davis, D. W., 70, 86–87

Dawes Severalty Act, 1887 (U.S.), 206, 211

Deane, Richard B., 87–88

Deerfoot, 159

Delorme, Marie Rose, 69

deMallie, Raymond, 105

Dempsey, Hugh, 216, 219–20

Denig, Edwin Thompson, *Five Indian Tribes of the Upper Missouri*, 124, 198

Department of Indian Affairs (DIA), 9–11, 14–15, 234–35, 268, 270–71

efforts to end interracial marriage, 155 (*See also* reserves, confinement to)

efforts to eradicate polygamy, 13–16, 127, 206–7, 210, 213–14, 219–24, 227–29, 240, 288–91

failure to eradicate polygamy, 166, 199–201, 266–67, 275

policies on Aboriginal marriage and divorce laws, 232–35, 269–70, 275, 290–91

requirement of employees to
marry, 155
Department of the Interior, 74
desertion (spousal), 8, 40–41, 50,
92–97, 130. *See also* separation
Criminal Code treatment of, 290
effect on wives of, 77, 220, 224,
269
Indian Act treatment of, 170–71
DIA. *See* Department of Indian Affairs
Dick, Lyle, 83
digging sticks, 111
diseases. *See* smallpox; tuberculosis;
venereal diseases
divorce (legal), 3. *See also* remarriage;
separation
Christian attitude toward, 6,
26–27, 29–31, 97, 157–59
cost of, 25, 95–96
diversity of beliefs on, 41–42, 50,
55–58, 66, 90–91
effect on women's homesteading
rights, 76
grounds for, 25–26, 41, 58, 93–96,
250–53, 270
legal decisions concerning, 159
legality of in United States, 56–58,
159
legislation concerning, 8
procedure, 25–26, 58
divorce by consent, 5, 9–16, 111–12,
137–38, 173–74, 227, 267. *See
also* remarriage; separation
government policy on, 161–63,
242–43, 255–58, 269–70,
294–95
prevalence of, 171
divorce ceremonies, 67. *See also* gifts,
return of following separation
or divorce
domestic labour, 8, 38, 79, 80

Dominion Lands Act (DLA), 74–75,
96, 206
Doukhobors, 8, 75, 89–91, 276
dower rights, 24, 98
dowries, 53. *See also* bridewealth; gifts
Drumheller (AB), 94
Duck Lake Agency (SK), 208. *See also*
McKenzie, R. S.
Dunbow (AB), 235–36
Dungloe (SK), 77
Dutch Henry (Henry Borne), 41
Duwamish, 142–43

East Indians, East Indies, 27
economy, 30. *See also* buffalo
effect of horse on, 133
effect on polygamy of, 132–33
following collapse of HBC
monopoly, 282
women-owned businesses, 38–39,
281
Edmonton Bulletin, 46, 54, 56–57, 74.
See also Fort Edmonton
Edmunds Act (1882, U.S.), 42, 210,
212–13
Edmunds-Tucker Act (1887, U.S.), 86
education, 53. *See also* schools
Edwards, Henrietta Muir, 25
Eglington, T., 41
Elk-Hollering-in-the-Water, 107
Elk-Yells-in-the-Water, 124
elopement, 110
Elton, David H., 89
Empty Coulee, 123–24
enfranchisement, 42, 169, 200, 281,
289
England. *See* Anglo-Saxons; British
Empire; United Kingdom
Erickson, Dan, 88
Erickson, Lesley, 288
ethnology, 132

eugenic legislation, 287
Euro-Canadian men. *See also*
    Aboriginal women, relations
    with Euro-Canadian men;
    Indian agents
  conversion to Mormonism, 45
  pressure to marry, 149–50, 181
  unmarried, 6, 22, 38, 54, 80–81, 83
Euro-Canadian women, 30,
    79, 118–19, 138. *See also*
    Doukhobors
  as heads of families, 75–76
  employment of, 38–40, 128, 251
  legal status and rights of, 24, 42, 46
  married, 27–28, 45–46, 54–55, 98
  rights under common law, 22–23
  social status of, 8, 11, 79, 132, 197,
    280–81
  unmarried, 5–6, 8–10, 38–40,
    79–80, 82, 197
  widowed, 75–76, 96
Evangelical Churchman, The, 156
Ewers, John, 107, 132
excommunication, 195

Faithful, George and Philomena, 259
family, 12, 75–78, 119, 179. *See
    also* Aboriginal marriage;
    agriculture, family farms;
    kinship in Aboriginal society;
    nuclear family
farm instructors (reserve), 72–73, 150,
    155
farms. *See* agriculture; homesteading
femininity (social definition of),
    52–53, 79–80
feminism, 280
fiction, 6, 20–21
File Hills Colony (SK), 220, 240–41,
    294
Fine Day, Chief, 114, 115–17

Finnish people, 56
First Nations. *See* Aboriginal people
Fleming, Mrs. (Alberta rancher), 80
Forget, Amédée E., 127, 207–14,
    220–21
Forget, Henriette, "Indian Women of
    the Western Provinces," 127
Fort Belknap Agency, MT, 261
Fort Chipewyan (AB), 121
Fort Edmonton (AB), 37, 199. *See also
    Edmonton Bulletin*
Fort Ellice (MB), 122
Fort Macleod (AB), 38–39, 70–71, 73,
    95, 129–30, 140, 222, 256. *See
    also* Fort Whoop-Up; *Macleod
    Gazette*
Fort Pelly (SK), 122
Fort Resolution (NWT), 121
Fort Whoop-Up (AB), 21. *See also* Fort
    Macleod
Fort Yukon (AK), 122
Foster, George Eulas, 57, 160
Fraser, Alexander, 138
Fraser, Florence, 95
Fraser v. Pouliot, 104, 138–39, 188
Free Cutter Woman, 222
free love. *See* sexual relations,
    extramarital
Frog Lake (AB), 259
Fulham, Caroline, 39, 79
fur trade society, 5, 31–32, 35, 198. *See
    also* Hudson's Bay Company;
    North West Company

Gagnon, Capt., 74
Galbreath, John Jackson "Jack," 205
gender (demographic imbalances in),
    5, 122
gender roles, 30, 39, 224, 283–84, 288
  in Aboriginal society, 104–06,
    122–25, 128–29

imposition of, 3, 28, 74–75, 168,
241
in relation to marriage, 3, 24–27,
93–94, 112, 167, 252–53
representations of, 8, 21, 24–25,
27, 78–80, 84, 251, 282–83
gifts, 107–9, 126, 155, 160, 262
return of following separation or
divorce, 112, 262–64
social purposes of, 113–14
at time of marriage, 271–72
Gleichen (AB), 158
Glendining, Mary, 39
Glenn, Mrs. John, 282
Globe, The (Toronto), 151, 154–55
Globe and Mail, 16–17, 200–201
Godkin, Catherine, 75
Goldfrank, Esther, 108–9, 122–24,
259–60
Gölz, Annalee, 30
Gooderham, J. H., 72
Good Hunter, 111
Goulet, Keith, 127
Goulet, Roger, 202–3
Graham, H.V., 240
Graham, J. F., 200
Graham, Rebecca Lena, 142–43
Graham, William M., 238–39, 241,
261
Grandin, Bishop Vital, 204–5
Grant, John F. and Quarra, 37
Grewal, Interpal, 132
Grier, D. J., 70–71
Grier, Lily, 70
Griswold Agency (MB), 288–89
Gros Ventre, 124
Gwynne, Justice, 56

Hämäläinen, Pekka, "The Rise and
Fall of Plains Indian Horse
Cultures," 133–34

Hamona Colony (SK), 55
Hanks, Jane and Lucien, 109, 112–13,
118, 120, 124
Hardy, Thomas, *The Mayor of
Casterbridge*, 65–66
Harmony Experiment. *See* Sojntula
Colony
Harper, James, 32
Harper, Magnus, 33
Harper, Stephen, 2
Harring, Sidney L., 135, 137
Harriott, John Edward, 135
Haynes. W. R., 290
head tax, 53, 54
health certificates, 291
Heath, Maria, 76–77
Henry, Alexander, the Younger, 122
Herchmer, Lawrence, 73–74
heterosexuality (perceived threats to),
83. *See also* gender roles
Hidatsa. *See* Maxidiwiac
Higginbotham, John, 22, 48–49
High River (AB), 159
Hines, John, 197–98
historical records (reliability of), 134
Hobbema Agency (AB), 201
homesteading, 8, 24–25, 55
men's access to, 38, 77, 83
role in western Canadian
settlement, 60, 74
women's access to, 39–40, 58–59,
75–79, 96, 99
Horns society, 112–13
horses, 52, 108–9, 111, 127, 133–34.
See also gifts
Houghton, Rev. R.C., *Women of the
Orient*, 131
Howe, Inspector J., 259
Hudson, Susan, 205
Hudson's Bay Company (HBC), 32–33,
136, 197, 199, 282. *See also*

Connolly, William; Harriott, John Edward; Murray, Alexander Hunter; Thompson, David

Hugonnard, Fr. Joseph, 128, 238–40, 246–47

human development, 28

Hungry Wolf, Beverly, 111, 118–19, 121

Hunter, Justice, 265, 266

Hutterites, 75

Hyde v. Hyde and Woodmansee, 67, 86, 135

Île à la Crosse (SK), 122

illegitimacy, 10, 14, 26, 110, 114, 174

immigrants, immigration
    British, 51, 80
    citizenship status of, 24
    European, 5, 6, 11–12
    female, 22, 79–80
    imposition of Christian-monogamy model on, 284 (*See also* Latter Day Saints, Church of Jesus Christ of; Doukhobors
    non-British, 99 (*See also* Asians; Ukrainians)
    representations of, 44–45, 54, 90

Imperial Colonist, The, 40

incest, 29, 174

India, 132, 175

Indian Act, 12, 140, 163, 259
    changes to, 71, 273–74, 290, 95, 201, 210, 237, 294–95
    compulsory education provisions of, 213
    definition of "Indian" under, 168–70
    determination of place of residence under, 261
    interaction with Criminal Code, 276
    interaction with provincial legislation, 291
    prosecution of bigamy under, 276
    provisions affecting women, 14, 140, 168, 170–71, 242–43, 292

Indian agents, 122–23, 172–73, 181–82, 269. *See also* Begg, Magnus; Markle, J.A.; Wilson, James; Wilson, R.N.
    authority over Indian marriages, 148, 207–8, 238–39, 247–48, 260–61
    marriage requirement of, 72–73, 155
    relations with Aboriginal women, 38, 72, 150, 155
    role in governance of reserves, 14, 38, 214–16, 206, 252, 258–59, 261

Indian Girls' Home (Kainai Reserve, AB), 39

Indian Head (SK), 82

Indian Register, 295

Indian status, 12–13, 292, 293. *See also* Indian Act

industrialization, 30

infertility, 70, 83, 120

informal marriage. *See* marriage, by consent

Ingram, Harry Miller and Hope Jessie Hall, 97

inheritance, 44, 134–38, 219–20, 243–45

interpreters, 251, 262

Iraq, 11

Ireland, 40

Isbister, A.K., 37, 281

Islam. *See* Muslims, Islam

ius gentium (law of the people), 137–38

Jack Head Reserve (MB), 254
Jameson, Anna Brownell, *Winter Studies and Summer Rambles in Canada*, 128–29
Jamison, Mary and Robert, 7
Jeater, Diana, 179
Jefferson, Thomas, 74
Jenkins, Fred (A. S. Fraser), 95
Jesus Christ, 45, 205
Jews, Judaism, 199
Johnson, Mrs. Anton, 40–41
Johnson, E. Pauline, "A Red Girl's Reasoning," 164–65
Johnston, Alex, 141
Journal of the Anthropological Institute of Great Britain and Ireland, 68–70
journals, 6, 253
Jubilee Marriage Scheme, 82
jumping the broom. *See* broomstick marriage
Justices of the Peace, 33, 67–68, 172–73, 269
Kainai (Bloods), 13–16, 70, 150, 156, 204, 243. *See also* Blackfoot; Charcoal; Hungry Wolf, Beverly; Red Crow, Chief
first Christian marriages, 165
gender roles, 123–25
marriage laws, 108, 142, 208–9, 220–21
reserve, 39, 43, 197, 205, 223, 261, 271
"Kanaka" (Pacific Islanders), 184
Kaulbach, Senator Henry, 93–94
Keewasens, 140
Kekanus case. *See Rex v. Kekanus*
Kenlis (SK), 54
Key to the Science of Theology, A, 49
Killed Herself, 222
Kingston, ON, 159
kinship. *See* family

kinship in Aboriginal society, 31, 104–10, 118–19, 127
effect of government policies on, 234, 288
heads of household, 120
relation to marriage, 113–15
terminology surrounding, 119–20
Kirby, Frances, *218*
Klein, Alan, 132
Kobogum v. Jackson Iron Co. (U.S.), 182–83, 212

Labrie case. *See Regina v. Labrie*
Lac La Biche (AB), 55
Lacombe, Fr. Albert, 40
Ladies' Book of Useful Information, 28
Laird, David, 223–24, 249–50, 254–57, 261, 267, 271
Lake St. Martin Reserve (MB), 254
Lakota, 105, 183, 211, 245
Lambeth Conference (1888), 195
land and/or property. *See also* Dominion Lands Act; gifts; homesteading; reserves; scrip
communal ownership of, 50
inheritance of, 219–20 (*See also Connolly v. Woolrich and Johnson et al.*)
ownership of, 24–28, 65, 74–75, 185
payment for surrender of, 248
women's access to, 74–75, 112
La Pierre, Peggy, 33
Laroque, Joseph, 135
"last best west," 280
Latter Day Saints, Church of Jesus Christ of (LDS, Mormons), 5, 13, 41–50, 83–89
cessation of plural marriages, 42, 87

immigration to Canada, 43–44,
204–6
polygamy rates, 49
Lawford, Rev. C. H., 92
law of the people. *See ius gentium*
LDS. *See* Latter Day Saints, Church of
Jesus Christ of
Leader, The. See Regina Leader
leap year, 82
Lebanese. *See* Syrians
Lebret, Fr, 141
Leduc (AB), 76–77
Legal, Fr. Emile, 219
legislation, 2, 8, 33. *See also* British
North America Act; Dominion
Lands Act; Indian Act;
Naturalization Act
marriage related, 54, 56, 67–68, 71,
83–87, 287, 288
provincial/territorial, 54, 67,
89–90, 142, 172, 174, 275–76,
287–88, 291
United States, 42, 86, 206, 210,
212–213
leisure and recreation, 82, 83
Lethbridge (AB), 21, 38–40, 140, 220
Lethbridge News, 22
Lewis, C. F., 82
Lewis, Oscar, 133
lex loci, 86
Liberal Party, 44. *See also* Blake,
Edward; Cotler, Irwin
Lillooet, BC, 181
literature. *See* fiction
Little Bow River, 105
Livingstone, Stanley, 199
Loggie and Manley (Wetaskiwin law
firm), 290–91
Lone Bull, 224
Lorne, Marquis of, 282
Lougheed, Isabella Hardisty, 281–82

Lougheed, James A., 79, 93, 281
love (romantic), 26, 27, 40, 50, 51.
See also courtship; spouses,
selection of
Lower Fort Garry (MB), 122
Lowie, Robert, 107

Ma'toki. *See* Women's Society
Macdonald, John A., 87
divorce policy, 94
meetings with LDS leaders, 43–44,
84
as superintendent of Indian
Affairs, 153, 156, 160, 166,
199–200
MacInnes, T. R. L., 292–93
MacKenzie, A. F., 290–91
Mackie, John, 20
Maclean, H. A., 263, 265–66
Maclean, John, *The Wardens of the
Plain*, 130
Macleod. *See* Fort Macleod; Fort
Whoop-Up
Macleod, James F., 129–30
Macleod, R. C, 166
Macleod Gazette, 70, 93, 151, 152–54,
159, 217–18
Macoun, John, *Manitoba and the Great
North-West*, 127–28
Maggie (wife of Nan-e-quis-a-ka), 139
Mail, The, 156
Mandelbaum, David, 114
Manderfield, Matilda and Peter, 96
Manitoba, 37, 172
Manitoba Act, 1870, 201
Manitoba Free Press, 159–60
Manton, Susan Ash, 159
Many Wives. *See* Card, Charles Ora
Maple Creek (SK), 73

mariage à la façon du pays. See
    Aboriginal marriage; marriage
    by consent
marital unity, doctrine of, 24
Markle, J.A., 224–27
Marlatt, S.R., 254
marriage, 6, 22, 50, 67, 172. *See also*
    Aboriginal marriage; Canada,
    role of marriage in nation
    building; marriage ceremonies;
    polygamy; spouses; United
    States, role of marriage in
    nation building
    advice on, 70, 79, 83–84, 132, 249,
        252–53, 287
    age at, 91
    alternatives to, 38–42 (*See also*
        women, single)
    in Australia, 185
    by consent, 31–37, 65–67, 70 (*See*
        also Aboriginal marriage)
    definition of in Euro-Canadian
        society, 2–5, 16–17, 125–26,
        143–44, 155
    encouragement of women toward,
        79
    under English common law, 22, 24
    European customs, 31, 65–67 (*See*
        also United Kingdom)
    ideal type, 8, 22, 280, 283 (*See also*
        monogamy, lifelong)
    indissolubility of, 25 (*See also*
        divorce)
    inter-faith, 92, 95–96, 248–49
    medical requirements for, 287–88
    intra-racial, 21–22, 31, 68–71, 80,
        82
    variety in customs concerning, 55
marriage, interracial, 6–8, 31, 54,
        68–71, 281, 288. *See also*
        miscegenation

    in Africa, 185–88
    in Australia, 184–85
    effect on Indian and Métis status,
        169–70, 245
    government policy on, 71–73,
        184–85, 245, (*See also* schools,
        arranged marriages at)
Marriage Act (NWT), 275–76
Marriage Act (SK), 287–88
marriage ceremonies, 32–35, 50,
        66–68, 90, *218. See also* bride
        purchase; wife exchange
    Aboriginal, 5, 107–9, 115–17, 126,
        140, 155, 160–61, 268–69,
        272–73 (*See also* gifts)
    African, 186
    changes in wording of services, 27
    clergy role in, 33, 35, 259
    cost of, 68, 172
    Doukhobor, 50–51, 89–90
    Métis, 35–37
    Quaker, 54–55, 89–90
    in second marriages, 109
    witnesses, 32–33, 68, 90
marriage contracts, 32–33, 35, 66–67
"marriage fever," 22
marriage licenses and certificates,
        54–55, 67–68, 82, 165, 291. *See*
        also health certificates
    African, 179
    cost of, 172, 292
marriage records, 267
Marsden, Chief Samuel, 254
Marshall, John, 136
Masseuas (husband of Christy Bell
    Beardy), 203
matchmaking, 234 (*See also* spouses)
Matheson, Rev. E., 165
Matthias, Franklin, 142
Maxidiwiac, 119
McCarty, Charles, 87–88

McCarty, Maude (Mrs. Mercer), 88

McClung, Nellie, 53

McColl, Ebenezer, 172, 235

McDonald, Allan, 208

McDougall, John, "The Red Men of Canada's West Yesterday and Today," 130–31

McFarland, Joseph, 21, 141

McFarland, Marcella Sheran, 21, 141

McGrath, Ann, 185–86

McHarg, Mr. (lawyer), 263

McKay, Eva, 125

McKay, Rev. Hugh, 248

McKenna, J., 225–26, 247, 249, 268–69

McKenzie, E. (missionary), 250–51

McKenzie, M., 222

McKenzie, R. S., 245–46

McLean, J. D., 171, 184–85, 220, 257–58, 270

McLeay, Misses, 39

McNeil, Mrs. Thomas, 77–78

Meadows, Angelique, 138

medical books, 83

Medicine Hat (AB), 95–96

Medicine Pipe Stem, 217

Mellam, John, 128

Mennonites, 75

Methodists, Methodism, 27, 53, 72, 91, 257–58, 290. *See also* Maclean, John; Semmens, John; Woodsworth, James S.; Young, E. R.

Métis, 5–6, 8, 202–3. *See also* Beaulieu, François; Galbreath, John Jackson "Jack"; Grant, John F. and Quarra; North-West resistance; Paget, Amelia McLean
   allocation of scrip to, 201–3
   population, 37

representations of, 50, 68–70, 152

scientific "classification" of, 68–69

social segregation of, 11

Métis status, 169–70

Mexico, 88

Michaud, Pauline, 138

Middle Woman No Coat, 118–119

midwives, 39

Milk River (AB), 41

Millar, M., 248–49, 268–69

minipokas, 108

miscegenation, 6, 50, 70, 152, 157 (*See also* marriage, interracial)

missionaries. *See* Christians, Christianity; Latter Day Saints, Church of Jesus Christ of

Monk, Samuel C., 135–37, 161

monogamy (lifelong), 12–16, 26–31, 33, 35, 59, 90, 115, 137–38, 161–62, 223
   and Canadian identity (*See* Canada, role of marriage in nation building)
   challenges to, 8–9, 29–37, 53–56, 59, 98–100, 176, 287
   colonial discourse on, 5–6, 28
   historical development of, 3
   and homesteading policy, 78
   imposition of in Western Canada, 28, 83, 92, 170–71, 148, 161–67, 235–42, 260–61, 284, 287–92

monogamy (serial), 115, 235. *See also* bigamy

Montana, 37, 40–41, 58, 120, 149

Moore, John H., 121, 129

Moore, Rev. T. Albert, 184

Moose Jaw Times, 40

Moose Mountain (AB), 242, 246, 260, 272

Moosomin (SK), 73, 259

morality, moral reform, 3, 9, 16, 184, 272–73
Morgan, Henry Lewis, 28
Morley (AB), 255, 260
Mormon Bible. *See Book of Mormon*
Mormons. *See* Latter Day Saints, Church of Jesus Christ of
Mountain Chief, 205
Mountain Horse, Joe, 237
Murphy, Emily, *Janey Canuck in the West*, 52
Murray, Alexander Hunter, 122
Muscowpetung Reserve (SK), 239
Muslims, Islam, 44, 55

Nakoda. *See* Assiniboine
names (Aboriginal), 259
Nan-e-quis-a-ka, 139
Napi. *See* Old Man
National Council of Women of Canada, 272–73
National Women's Suffrage (U.S.), 48
Naturalization Act (1919), 96
natural selection, 45
Nevada, 184, 205–6
Newcombe, E. L., 76, 95, 209, 220, 244–45, 270
Newell, Thomas, 262–63, 265
Newfoundland, 33
news media, 49, 54, 87, 89, 93
    anti-polygamy, 46, 49, 84, 120, 150–54, 200–201, 212, 217–19
    debate on married NWMP officers in, 73–74
    farm journals, 80–81
    Métis ownership of, 37
    promotion of intra-racial marriage in, 21, 22, 70, 82, 280–82, 149
    promotion of lifelong monogamy model of marriage in, 2, 6, 16–17, 26, 56–57, 59

representations of Aboriginal people in, 68, 126, 149, 152–56, 159–60
    representations of Doukhobors in, 51
    representations of Quakers in, 55
    response to CPR Jubilee Marriage Scheme, 82
    sensationalism in, 150–51, 159, 272–73
    use as evidence of polygamy, 88
    women's publications, 40, 46
Nicolls, Rev. W., 245
nita-yim. See co-husbands
North West Company (NWC), 122. *See also* Laroque, Joseph
North-West Mounted Police (NWMP), 21, 31, 38, 41, 95, 149. *See also* Begin, J.V.; Grier, D.J.; Herchmer, Lawrence; Steele, Col. S. B.; Wilde, Sergeant W. B.
    Aboriginal resistance to, 216
    fictional accounts of, 20
    intervention in Aboriginal marriages, 207, 238–39, 259
    marriage of members, 40–41, 73–74
    polygamy-related surveillance, 87–88, 90–91
    role in enforcement of Indian Act, 237
    service as Justices of the Peace, 68, 172
North-West Rebellion Script Commissions, 152
North-West resistance, 11, 12, 151, 188, 200
North-West Territories (NWT), 21, 139, 141. *See also* Marriage Act; Ordinance Respecting Marriage

Norton, Moses, 32

Norway House (MB), 271

nostalgia, 3, 22

novels. *See* fiction

nuclear family, 2, 29–30, 75, 105

nudity, 52, 83

Nugent, David, 132–33

O'Hanlon, Rosalind, 175, 178

oaths of allegiance, 52

Oblates (Missionary Oblates of Mary
    Immaculate), 95, 180–81

Office of Indian Affairs (U.S.), 184

Ojibway, 32, 122

Old Man (Napi), 106

Old Man River, 140

Oliver, Frank, 78, 80, 163, 257, 273–74

Onion Lake (SK), 165

oral traditions, 105–6, 111, 113–14

orders-in-council

    1887 Canadian, 12, 16, 155, 160,
        188, 257, 272, 293

    African, 179

Ordinance Respecting Marriage
    (1878, NWT), 67, 71, 89–90,
    142, 172

Oregon, 184

orphanages, 141

Ostrander, J. P. B., 292

Oxford House (MB), 207

Pacific Islanders ("Kanaka"), 184

pacifism, 52

Paget, Amelia McLean, *The People of
    the Plains*, 129

Pall Mall Gazette, 150–51

Parliament (acts of), 25

Parts His Hair, 109

Pedley, Frank, 243, 244, 271

Penzance, Lord. *See* Wilde, Sir James
    O.

Perkin, Joan, 65

Perry, Adele, 4

personhood (legal definition), 168

petitions, 50, 72, 91, 173, 180–81, 182

Petrik, Paula, 58

*Physical Life of Woman: Advice to the
    Maiden, Wife and Mother, The*,
    70, 83

Piapot, Chief, 165

Piapot Reserve (SK), 261

Picturesque Cardston and Environments,
    88

Pigeon Woman, 124–25

Piikani (Peigan), 126, 133, 256–57. *See
    also* Awatoyakew; Blackfoot;
    Tailfeathers, Molly; Three Calf

    oral traditions, 105

    polygamy among, 117, 208

    reserve, 149, 214, 290

Pincher Creek (AB), 39, 40, 69

Pine Creek (AB), 7

Pine Ridge Agency, SD, 212

Plains Cree. *See* Cree

Plaited Hair, 210–11, 229

plural marriage. *See* polygamy

polyandry, 176. *See also* co-husbands

polygamy

    in Aboriginal society, 5, 10, 28,
        42, 115–22, 129–31, 199–203,
        216–17 (*See also* Aboriginal
        marriage)

    in African society, 178, 187, 204

    attitude of missionaries toward,
        129–34, 194–99, 201, 214–16,
        219, 227

    division of labour in, 118–20

    government efforts to combat, 8,
        83–89, 138–39, 203–8, 223–24,
        227–29

    family size in, 115–17

government's failure to combat, 13–16, 88, 166, 254–57, 262–67, 276–77

legal decisions concerning, 13–14, 42, 135–37, 210–13, 214–29

in Métis society, 202–3, 227

no word for in Aboriginal languages, 115

penalty for, 86

persistence of, 166, 199–201, 266–67, 275

positive representations of, 48–50, 89, 129, 199

prevalence of, 32, 37, 121–22, 129–32, 198, 201, 207–8, 223

social benefits of, 117–18, 121, 132–133, 204

polygyny. *See* polygamy

population. *See* censuses and enumerations

pornography. *See* nudity

Poundmaker, 119–20

poverty, 8, 65, 77, 275

Power, Augustus, 162

prairie turnips, 111

pregnancy (extramarital). *See* illegitimacy

Presbyterian Record, 27

Presbyterians. *See* McKay, Hugh; McKenzie, E.; Shearer, Rev. John G.

Pretty Wolverine, 217–18

Primrose, P.C.H., 256–57

Prince Albert (SK), 202, 292

Privy Council, 149, 156–57, 160–62, 167

promiscuity, 28, 282

prostitutes, prostitution, 38–39, 49, 68, 180, 273

in England, 150–51

social definition of, 9, 10, 53–54, 153

Protestants, Protestantism, 92, 95–96. *See also* Christians, Christianity

provinces (jurisdiction), 290, 293–94

Pruden, Isabella, 246

Pruden, John (daughter of), 135

Pulsipher, John D., 28, 203

Qu'Appelle Industrial School, 240. *See also* Hugonnard, Fr. Joseph

Qu'Appelle (SK), 55, 123

Quakers (Society of Friends), 8, 54–55, 89–90, 276

Quebec, 37, 104, 134, 138, 174, 210–11, 275

rape. *See* sexual assault

rape (statutory). *See* age of consent

Rapid City Daily Journal, The, 212

rations, 223, 226

Rat River. *See* Rivière-aux-Rats

Reader, Joseph, 173

reconciliation (marital), 113

Red Crow, Chief, 70, 107–8, 110–12, 115, 219, 221

Red Crow, Frank, 220

Red River Settlement (MB), 36–37, 68, 198, 282

Reed, Hayter, 71–72, 173, 206–11, 237, 238

Regina (SK), 73–74, 74, 97, 128

Regina Industrial School, 239, 249–50, 252

Regina Leader, 49, 73, 74, 82

Regina Leader Post, 68

Regina v. Labrie, 210–11

Regina v. Nan-e-quis-a-ka, 139–40, 163, 213, 222, 265

registrar of deeds, 68

Reid, Alexander, 68–70

religion, 138–39. *See also* Christians,
　　Christianity; Jews, Judaism;
　　Latter Day Saints, Church of
　　Jesus Christ of; Muslims, Islam;
　　oral traditions; Quakers; Sun
　　Dances
remarriage, 5, 33, 40, 198
　　in Aboriginal society, 112
　　Doukhobor beliefs concerning, 50
　　effect on annuity eligibility, 173
　　in England, 66
　　of Euro-Canadian men, 70–71, 87
　　government policy on, 162–63,
　　　242–43, 257–58, 292
　　intra-familial, 118
　　Mormon beliefs concerning,
　　　41–42
　　legislation concerning, 85–86
　　relation to polygamy, 29, 85,
　　　96–97, 119
　　representations of, 29, 57, 254
　　status of second wives, 222
　　United States policy on, 56
Renton, Jane, 32
repudiation (law of). *See* divorce by
　　consent
reserves, First Nations, 261. *See also*
　　Blackfoot; Cree, Plains Cree;
　　File Hills Colony; Kainai;
　　Piikani; Siksika)
　　confinement to, 159–60, 180–81,
　　　238
　　DIA authority over, 14, 151,
　　　165–66, 201, 214–16, 235,
　　　239–40, 254–55, 261, 290–91
　　　(*See also* Department of Indian
　　　Affairs, Indian agents)
　　pass system, 68, 152–53, 181–82
　　relocation to the north, 11, 152
　　self-management of, 165
Revenge Walker, 70

Rex v. Kekanus, 262–63, 267
Ridley, Bishop William, 226
Riel, Louis, 157. *See also* North-West
　　resistance
Rimmer, Reginald, 224–27
Riou, Fr. J., 225
Rivière-aux-Rats, 134, 136
Rolfe, Robert Monsey. *See*
　　Cranworth, Lord
Rollason, Heather, 166
Roman Catholic Church. *See*
　　Catholics, Catholicism
Roper, Edward, 123
Rosser (MB), 81
Rouleau, Judge C., 222
Rowland, W.P., 92
Royal, Emma Blanche, 73–74
Royal Commissions, 53
Royal Proclamation (1763), 136
Running Deer, 130
Running Eagle, 124
Rupert's Land Industrial School, 235
Russian Orthodox Church, 50
Russians. *See* Doukhobors
Ruthenians, 52–53

Sadie Hawkins Day, 82
St. Albert (AB). *See* Grandin, Bishop
　　Vital
St. Cyprian's mission (Piikani
　　Reserve, AB), 214
St. John's mission (Siksika Reserve,
　　AB), 201, 216
St. Joseph's Industrial School, 235–37
St. Paul des Métis (AB), 95
St. Paul's School, Blood Reserve (AB),
　　242
St. Peter's Reserve (MB), 235
St. Victor (SK), 96
Salt Lake Herald, 88

same-sex marriage, 2, 5, 31, 122, 124–25

Sanderson, George W., 35–36

Sarcee. *See* Tsuu T'ina

Saskatchewan, 8, 39, 198, 287, 291–92

Saskatchewan Herald, 51, 120

Saskatoon (SK), 55, *81*

Saulteaux, 125, 268. *See also* Ojibway

Saunders, Anne, 39

Saunders, Douglas, 138

Saxby, Jessie, 80, 81

Schlosser, Carl, 95–96

schools, 201, 204, 252
    arranged marriages at, 235–42, 247, 250
    boarding schools, 213–14, 237
    classification of students, 240
    compulsory attendance at, 216–17, 237
    day schools, 214
    deaths of students at, 213–14, 216
    evasion of, 259–60
    forced committal to, 210
    industrial, 214, 235, 237
    residential, 13, 15, 210–16
    use to enforce monogamy policy, 213–14, 241, 260

Scollen, Fr. Constantine, 21, 141

Scott, Justice, 141, 217

Scott, Duncan Campbell, 240, 257

Scottish people, Scotland, 37

Scraping Hide, 216

scrip (Métis), 142, 152, 169–170, 202–3

seduction, laws related to, 181, 290

segregation, 11–12, 68, 167, 281–82. *See also* reserves, First Nations, confinement to

self-government (doctrine), 182–84

self-marriage. *See* marriage, by consent

semi-widows. *See* separation, surrender of plural wives

Semmens, John, 130, 198

Senate, Canadian, 25, 29, 93–94

separation (marital), 76–77, 294
    government policy toward, 43–44, 196, 211–12, 235, 238–39, 260–61, 270
    surrender of plural wives, 195–99, 201, 209–11, 219, 223–27, 254–55

sexual assault ("outrage"), 159, 177

sexual relations
    age of commencement of, 260
    extramarital, 28, 38, 55–56, 114, 121
    men's freedom in, 110
    interracial, 181, 289 (*See also* marriage, interracial; miscegenation)
    women's sexuality, 9, 25, 124

sexually transmitted disease. *See* venereal disease

sex work. *See* prostitutes, prostitution

Shearer, Rev. John G., 273

Shepstone, Theophilus, 175–77

Sheran, Marcella. *See* McFarland, Marcella Sheran

Sheran, Nicholas (lawsuit involving family), 140–42, 249

Short, James, 14, 225, 226, 227

Shoshoni, 205–6

Siberians, Siberia, 27

Siksika, 109, 118, 120. *See also* Blackfoot
    first Christian marriage, 165
    prevalence of polygamy among, 208, 223–24
    representations of, 224, 225
    reserve, 165, 201, 208, 214–17

Simpson, George, 33

Sinclair, R.V., 291
Singing Before, 219
Sioux, 20–21, 183
Sioux, Annie, 113, 119
Skynner, Francis, 216
slave wives, 133–34
Sleeping Woman, 217
smallpox, 119
Smart, James, 220
Smith, Charles, 69
Smith, Donald (Lord Strathcona), 33, 35, 282
Smith, Isabella (Bella) Hardisty (Lady Strathcona), 33–35, 282
Smith, Joseph, 45
Smith, Margaret Charlotte, 33
Smith, Mary Anne, 69
Snell, James G., 29–30, 287
socialism, 52
social reform, 16
society (Aboriginal). See Aboriginal marriage; kinship in Aboriginal society
society (Euro-Canadian). See Euro-Canadian men; Euro-Canadian women; Canada, role of marriage in nation building
Society of Friends. See Quakers
Sojntula Colony ("Harmony Experiment"), BC, 56
Sons of Freedom (Doukhobors), 52
South Dakota, 183, 211
Southesk, Earl of, 199
space (gendering of), 282–84
spouses (selection of), 32
    in Aboriginal society, 113–15, 119–20, 124–27, 268–69
    in Euro-Canadian society, 29, 82, 110
    at residential and industrial schools, 235–42, 247, 250

"squaw" (term), 35, 128
Star Blanket, Chief, 220
Stead, W.T., 150–51
Steele, S.B., 48, 87
Stenhouse, Anthony Maitland, 45–46, 85
Stirling, Justice, 187
Stocken, Canon H.W. Gibbon, 198
Stoler, Ann Laura, 31, 64
Stony Mountain Penitentiary (MB), 41
Strathcona, Lord. See Smith, Donald
Strzelewski, Count, 70
suicide, 92, 197, 288
Sun Dances, 109, 110, 111
Suzanne "Pas-de-Nom," 134–38
Swainson, Rev. F., 165
Sweden, 96
Swift Current (SK), 55
Switzer, B., 98
Swyripa, Frances, 52–53
Syrians, 55

Tailfeathers, Molly, 70–71
Tanner, John, 125
taxes. See bachelor tax; head tax
Taylor, Rev. I.J., 253
Teepoo, 186–88
Telegraph (St. John, NB), 82
The Pas Band, 173
Therien, Fr. J.A., 95
Thompson, David, 107, 112, 117–18, 122, 128
Thompson, E.P., 65–66
Thompson, John, 12, 86, 94, 157–59
Three Calf, 113, 118
Thunder Hill Colony (Doukhobor), 51
Tims, Rev. J.W., 201, 204, 216–17, 218
Tims, Violet Wood, 218
Toronto Mail, The, 126, 149

Toronto World, 89
treaties, 13, 165, 208–9, 246, 292–93
Treaty 4 area, 220. *See also* Piapot,
    Chief
Treaty 7 area, 13, 14, 205, 206, 223.
    See also Blackfoot
Trim Woman, 123–24
Trivett, Samuel, 150–51, 153–54, 197
Tsuu T'ina, 198, 227. *See also*
    Blackfoot
tuberculosis, 214, 216, 245, 288
Tucker, Rev. Canon, 273–74
Tupper, Charles, 156
Turner, Charlet, 32
Turtle Mountain (ND), 272
Two Spirits, 122, 125

Ukrainians, 52–53
United Church of Canada, 241, 259
United Farmers of Alberta (UFA), 40
United States, 6, 56–58, 166–167, 212
    Canadian representations of, 4,
        56–57, 86, 284
    efforts to eradicate polygamy,
        40–42, 201, 205–6, 211–12
    extradition from, 40
    government policies regarding
        Aboriginal people, 28, 161,
        182–83, 233
    homesteading policy, 78
    immigrants from, 5, 56–59
    interracial marriage in, 184
    legal decisions related to marriage,
        142–43, 149, 183–84, 211–12
    marriage by consent in, 65, 90
    representations of Canada in, 232
    role of marriage in nation
        building, 3–4
    women's rights in, 48, 78, 184
United States Constitution, 183
United States v. Quiver, 183–84

Utah, 42, 49. *See also* Latter Day
    Saints, Church of Jesus Christ
    of
Utley, Robert, 211–12

vagrancy, 181, 252
Van Kirk, Sylvia, 6, 32
Vancouver, BC, 182
Vancouver Island, BC, 272–73
Vankoughnet, Lawrence, 153, 155–56
Varcoe, F. P., 294
vegetarianism, 52
venereal disease, 38, 167, 288
Venn, Henry, 195
Veregin, Peter, 52
veterans' benefits, 294
Victoria, BC, 181, 182
Vincent, Thomas, 32
virginity, 110
vital statistics, registration of, 90, 267
voting. *See* enfranchisement

Wabamun (AB), 257
Wabasca (AB), 172
Waite, P. B., 157
Wakes at Night, 108–9
Wales, 67
Walker, Alfred Percy and Emily
    Herald, 93
Walkowitz, Judith R., 150, 151
wardship under Indian Act, 16, 150,
    275
warfare, 165
warriors (female), 123, 124
Wat Shee, 54
Western Standard Illustrated Weekly,
    280, 281–82
Wetaskiwin (AB), 290–91
Wetmore, Justice Edward L., 139–40,
    163, 168
White Buffalo Robe, 108

White Buffalo Woman, 105–6
Whitehorse, YK, 290
White Pup, 214–16
White-Tailed Deer Woman. *See* Awatoyakew
wife exchange, 114. *See also* bride purchase
Wilde, Sergeant W. B., 217–18
Wilde, Sir James O. (Lord Penzance), 4–5, 67
Williams, A. S., 289
Williams, Thomas, 48
Williams, Zina Young. *See* Card, Zina Young
Wilson, James, 209, 219, 222–23
Wilson, Kathleen, 59
Wilson, R. N., 142, 219, 243–45, 271
Wing Sang Company (Vancouver, BC), 54
Wolfart, H. C., 114
Woman Who Married the Morning Star, 111
Woman's Exponent, 46
Woman, Her Character, Culture and Calling, 132
women. *See* Aboriginal women; Euro-Canadian women

women's associations, 40, 91–92, 112–13, 272–73, 280–81
Women's Christian Temperance Union, 91
Women's Society (Ma'toki, Kainai), 112–13
Wong Wai, 54
Wood, C. E. D., 96
Woodsworth, James S., 44–45
Woolrich, Julia, 31, 134–35
Worcester v. Georgia (U.S.), 136
World War I, 98
World War II, 294
Worm Pipe, 105–6
Wright, Corporal T. B., 74

Yarwood, Miss, 92
Yellow Wolf, son of, 108–9
Yip Sang, 54
York Factory. *See* Budge, William
Yorkton (SK), 91
Young, Brigham, 41, 46–48. *See also* Card, Zina Young
Young, E. R.
Yukon, 122